CreateSuccess

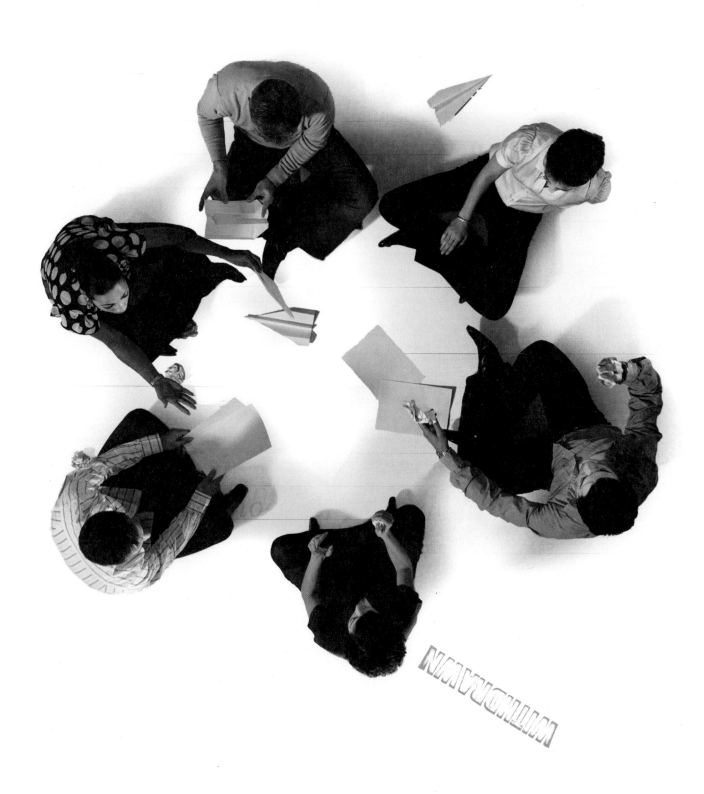

CreateSuccess
agile social learning

JON DOYLE
Curriculum Technology

Mc Graw Hill

Connect
Learn
Succeed

CREATE SUCCESS

Published by McGraw-Hill, a business unit of The McGraw-Hill Companies, Inc., 1221 Avenue of the Americas, New York, NY, 10020. Copyright © 2013 by The McGraw-Hill Companies, Inc. All rights reserved. Printed in the United States of America. No part of this publication may be reproduced or distributed in any form or by any means, or stored in a database or retrieval system, without the prior written consent of The McGraw-Hill Companies, Inc., including, but not limited to, in any network or other electronic storage or transmission, or broadcast for distance learning.

Some ancillaries, including electronic and print components, may not be available to customers outside the United States.

This book is printed on acid-free paper.

1 2 3 4 5 6 7 8 9 0 QDB/QDB 1 0 9 8 7 6 5 4 3 2

ISBN   978-0-07-337513-7
MHID   0-07-337513-6
ISBN   978-0-07-757940-1 (Comp Edition)
MHID   0-07-757940-2 (Comp Edition)

Publisher: *Scott Davidson*
Development editor II: *Alaina G. Tucker*
Executive marketing manager: *Keari Green*
Digital development editor: *Kevin White*
Director, Editing/Design/Production: *Jess Ann Kosic*
Lead project manager: *Susan Trentacosti*
Senior buyer: *Carol A. Bielski*
Senior designer: *Srdjan Savanovic*
Senior photo research coordinator: *Keri Johnson*
Photo researcher: *Michelle Buhr*
Manager, digital production: *Janean A. Utley*
Media project manager: *Brent dela Cruz*
Media project manager: *Cathy L. Tepper*
Cover design: *Srdjan Savanovic*
Interior design: *Srdjan Savanovic and Laurie Entringer*
Typeface: *11/13 Helvetica Neue LTStd Roman*
Compositor: *Laserwords Private Limited*
Printer: *Quad/Graphics*
Cover credit: *©Adie Bush/cultura/Corbis*
Comp Edition additional cover credits: *paper planes: © The McGraw-Hill Companies, Inc/Ken Karp photographer. Active Classroom Guide panel: (top): © Stockbyte/Punchstock, (bottom): © Goodshoot/Punchstock. Portfolio Activities panel: (bottom): © Comstock Images/Alamy*
Additional frontmatter photo credits: *p. xxvi (top): Stockbyte/Punchstock, (bottom): Purestock/SuperStock; p. xvii (top): PhotoAlto/Alix Minde/Getty Images, (bottom): © Goodshoot/Punchstock; p. xxvii: Purestock/Getty Images; p. xxx: Ingram Publishing; p. xxxi (top): © ONOKY - Photononstop/Alamy, (bottom): McGraw-Hill Companies, Inc. Mark Dierker, photographer*
Credits: The credits for this book are at the end of each chapter and are considered an extension of the copyright page.

Library of Congress Cataloging-in-Publication Data

Doyle, Jon.
    Create success/Jon Doyle.
        p. cm.
    ISBN 978-0-07-337513-7 (alk. paper)—ISBN 0-07-337513-6 (alk. paper)
    1. College student orientation—United States. 2. College students—United States—Life skills guides. 3. Study skills—United States. 4. Vocational guidance—United States. 5. Education, Higher—Curricula—United States. I. Title.
    LB2343.32.D69 2013
    378.1'98—dc23

                                    2012014732

The Internet addresses listed in the text were accurate at the time of publication. The inclusion of a Web site does not indicate an endorsement by the authors or McGraw-Hill, and McGraw-Hill does not guarantee the accuracy of the information presented at these sites.

www.mhhe.com

Series Editor—Jon Doyle

Jon Doyle has led a varied 20-year career in post-secondary education, splitting time between instruction, curriculum development, and program management. His work in student success began as coordinator of a large-scale development project seeking methods to improve student retention. These efforts included extensive analysis of student attrition data, conducting focus groups with students new to college as well as those nearing graduation, and interviews with students who had already dropped out of college. These experiences demonstrated to Jon that student success coursework is most effective when the instructor is able to deliver an active, engaging learning environment utilizing a highly integrated text, lesson plan, and related supporting course materials.

Jon is President of Curriculum Technology, a company focused on developing highly interactive curriculum and training content. His success in the classroom and with curriculum design flows from his passion for students and providing instructors with the best tools possible to enable them to deliver engaging course experiences.

Jon earned his BA from the University of California, Santa Barbara, and later went on to earn an MBA. He is married with one child and is very happy to be living in San Diego, California.

Activities Editor—Heather Fullerton

Heather Fullerton was the pilot instructor for the Student Success curriculum at Heald College, San Francisco campus. In this role, she developed innovative and active lesson plans and in-class activities. Her success in facilitating an active instructional style, with an emphasis on collaborative exercises, led her to become the faculty mentor for new Student Success instructors, as well as a contributor to the materials they implemented in their own classes. In addition, her passion and commitment to empower students with the skills and strategies necessary to be successful academically, professionally, and personally positioned her as the lead Student Success instructor.

Heather has been teaching between three to five Student Success classes every quarter, which provides her with a unique opportunity to consistently be informed of the emerging and changing needs of incoming college students. This insight propels her to continually re-imagine and create current lesson plans and activities to ensure that any new population of students will receive the most pertinent and beneficial material for their success.

Heather earned her BA in English with an emphasis in Teaching from the University of California, Davis, and went on to obtain a MA in English Literature from Mills College.

ACKNOWLEDGMENTS

Contributors

Create Success could not have existed without the generous input of time, energy, and expertise from our primary contributors for each module. The following people were fundamentally involved in authoring and developing the material in their respective modules.

Bob Busha, *The Art Institute of Ohio*—Writing with Clarity; Taking Notes

Steven Campbell, *Empire College*—Learning Strategies

Karen Durand, *Miller-Motte College*—Setting Goals

Sharon Occhipinti, *Corinthian College*—Studying for Quizzes and Exams

Komi Shah, *Colorado Technical University*—Managing Time

James Siebert, *Heald College*—Building Positive Relationships; Focusing on Health

Participants

Over the years of development for the *Create Success* program, we have had the great good fortune to work with literally hundreds of people involved in student success curriculums from across the country. This includes instructors, deans, administrators, and students. For every name you see in this list, there are at least five more who have touched this project and guided it to its current incarnation. These are the names of the people who have participated in a review, focus group, survey, or *Create Success* specific conference.

Sandy Aguilar, *Florida State College—Jacksonville*

Mary Alexander, *Ashford University*

Leiauanna R. Allen, *Virginia Western Community College*

Emily Battaglia, *IEC, UEI College*

Lori Blewett, *Austin Community College*

James Arthur Bond, *California Luthor University*

Teresa Bridger, *Prince George's Community College*

David Brigham, *Walden University*

Charyn Lynn Brown, *Long Beach City College*

Garamis Campusano, *Brown Mackie College—Miami*

Fabian Cone, *AIU—Weston*

Mary Elizabeth Cooke, *Surrey Community College*

Gary M. Corona, *Florida State College—Jacksonville*

Micah Cox, *Kaplan Higher Education*

Jim Dalton, *Sanford-Brown College—Fenton*

Billy R. Davis, *Florida State College—Jacksonville*

Tina Diggs, *Carrington College*

Teri Dillon, *MTI College*

Dr. Tim Dosemagen, *Blue Cliff College*

John Drezek, *Richland College*

William Dudeck, *Carrington College*

Al Ebert, *Brown Mackie College*

Michele Ernst, *Globe University/Minnesota School of Business*

Mominka Filev, *Davenport University*

John Flanders, *Central Methodist University*

Bruce Fleming, *College of Charleston*

Agnes Flores, *Del Mar College*

Meg Foster, *J. Sargeant Reynolds Community College*

Abby Freeman, *City College*

Christine Gaiser, *Bryant & Stratton College*

Janell Gibson, *Keiser University—eCampus*

Jacqueline Goffe-McNish, *Dutchess Community College*

Andrea Goldstein, *South University Online*

Nichole Gotschall, *Columbia Southern University*

Carlond Gray, *Florida State College—Jacksonville*

Dr. Toni Greif, *Colorado Technical University*

Tim Gregory, *Full Sail University*

Laura Ristrom Goodman, *Pima Medical Institute*

Monica Hamlin, *Palm Beach State College*

Marilyn Harper, *Pellissippi State Community College*

Christina Havlin, *ECPI College of Technology*

Gretchen Hendricks, *Westwood College*

Marsha Hinnen, *Columbia Southern University*

Richard Holbeck, *Grand Canyon University*

Jennifer Holmes, *Concorde Career Colleges*

Valencia W. Huggins, *Centura College—Peninsula*

DeLandra Hunter, *Clayton State University*

Brian James, *Globe University/Minnesota School of Business*

JoAnn Jenkins, *Moraine Valley Community College*

Melanie Jenkins, *Snow College*

Jim Jeremiah, *Ashford University*

Deborah Jones, *High Tech Institute*

Nichole Karpel, *Strayer University*

Stacy K. Kirsch, *Orange Coast College*

Frank Ko, *Heald College Concord*

Leigh Kolb, *East Central College—Missouri*

Joe LaMontagne, *Davenport University*

Kathy Lazenby, *College of the Ouachitas*

David Levy, *Housatonic Community College*

Forrest Marston, *Sanford-Brown*

Mindy Miley, *College of Charleston*

Michael Montalbano, *Bentley University*

Melissa Munoz, *Dorsey Schools*

John Olson, *ECPI University*

Connie Park, *Austin Community College*

Richard Piper, *Anthem Education Group*

LeAnne Sue Prenovost, *Ken Blanchard College of Business*

Colleen Quinn, *Heald College—Rancho Cordova*

Kristen Rasmussen, *Heald College*

Richard A. Reid, *South Dakota State University*

Dawn Rhea, *Grand Canyon University*

Adrian Rios, *Newbridge College*

Reymundo Robledo, *Santa Ana College*

Nadine Rosenthal, *City College of San Francisco*

Tracy Rusco, *East Central College–Missouri*

Jean Rydahl, *Milan Institute*

Rebecca Samberg, *Housatonic Community College*

Lisa Schaffer, *Newbridge College*

Bonnie Scott, *Santa Ana College*

Thomas Sepe, *Community College of Rhode Island*

David Shaw, *American University of Afghanistan*

Brenda Siragusa, *Corinthian Colleges, Inc.*

Sean C. Smith, *Ivy Tech Community College*

Patricia Stewart, *Albany Technical College*

Marsha Stowe, *Ivy Tech Community College*

Elizabeth Tice, *Ashford University*

Tonya Troka, *Colorado Technical University*

Lynda Villanueva, *Brazosport College*

Ann Voorheis-Sargent, *Baker College Online*

Colleen Wagner, *Florida State College—Jacksonville*

Franklin Wells, *Dyersburg State Community College*

Meg Whiston, PhD, *National American University*

Toni Woolfork-Barnes, *Western Michigan University*

Edgar Wulf, *IBMC*

CONTENTS

Building a **Career** Foundation **1**

Create Success represents a paradigm shift in its approach to student success in that it prioritizes active student interactions over passive learning. The included training and development package provides instructors with a broad understanding of today's students and the unique challenges they face. The curriculum support materials provide a wealth of resources that can be utilized by instructors to better connect with each of their students through the delivery of an active, engaged classroom learning environment—even in purely online settings.

Additional features and benefits of *Create Success* include:

- Get Ready activities are at the start of every lesson; get started connecting right away!

- Modular format enables a school to readily select a customized set of topics for their student success course, or incorporate individual topics in those courses that include a student success component.

- Activities are built into the fabric of every lesson.

- Additional activities are in the Active Classroom Guide, and online versions of the activities make it easy to adapt the *Create Success* program to your course.

- The content continually relates academic content to real-world applications and builds students' connection with the school community.

- Portfolio Activities provide trackable, tangible proof of learning, ready for export.

- Rich content and tools result in improved instructional effectiveness.

Create Success provides instructors and students with an interactive text and extensive supplementary materials. Students will experience thought-provoking and challenging activities that will help prepare them to successfully meet the requirements of school while managing the ongoing demands of their personal lives. The net result is students who are more confident and have greater motivation to stay in school and complete their education.

Our Mission

Our mission is to provide Instructor Materials that easily support a social learning environment.

- Traditionally, publishers provide materials that support a lecture.

- We have created a new design, specifically developed to help you:
  - Break away from the front of the classroom.
  - Encourage discussion.
  - Work away from the text, while still having full support.
  - Get your students working together effectively.

- 95% of the active instructors we surveyed agreed that instructor materials need to be easily implemented and should be available immediately, especially if an instructor has minimal prep time.

- Jon Doyle and Heather Fullerton worked together to bring this new approach to you and your students.

How Do the Active Classroom Guides Do All That?

Lesson Plans

At-a-glance overview of the module, with time estimates built in. You can plan and adjust ahead of time, or use the Guide to always be prepared in an instant!

Click-Back Links

If you're viewing the Instructor Materials online, it is hyperlinked throughout so you can navigate without endless scrolling.

Taking Charge, Section 1

In this section, students will discuss approaches to college—the hard way versus the easy way. They will also begin to build connections with peers, learn about academic accountability, and utilize your school's college catalogue.

LESSON OVERVIEW

SECTION 1: GETTING INVOLVED, OVERCOMING BARRIERS		
Learning Outcomes		1. Develop a proactive mindset to increase academic success 2. Learn how connecting with others can help students make it to graduation

Lesson Flow Overview	60 minutes	• Lecture and Discussion
		  • Get Ready! Exercise—Warm-Up
		  • LO 1: The Hard Way versus the Easy Way
		    ♦ Lecture/Activity
		    ♦ Discussion
		  • Transition—Common Ground Activity
		  • LO 2: Connecting at College
		    ♦ Lecture/Activity
		    ♦ Discussion
		  • Student Activity: College Catalogue Resources
		  • Lesson Review, Wrap-Up, and Discussion

Lecture and Discussion	30 minutes	• Get Ready! Exercise • Refer to the Instructor Guide on pages 4–10 for lecture/discussion notes • Common Ground Exercise • PowerPoint slides
Student Activity	25 minutes	• Students work individually or in groups for the exercise presented on page 12 in the textbook – College Catalog Scavenger Hunt

TAKING CHARGE   2

TAKING CHARGE Module Overview

This module focuses on assisting new students with recognizing and accessing available resources, as well as teaching them how to create and modify plans for utilizing these resources to the fullest. The goals of this module are for students to:

1. Develop a proactive student mindset to increase academic success
2. Learn how connecting with others can help students make it to graduation
3. Explore the variety of personal and community resources available to support your academic efforts
4. Identify the critical school departments and personnel who can provide the guidance and answers you need to be successful
5. Improve your ability to prioritize, plan, and adjust to changing situations as you progress through college

First Section: Students explore how get involved with various on campus resources for support, as well as how to overcome barriers through accountability, which concludes with an activity that asks students to list important information from their college catalog.

Second Section: Students examine their available support services at home, at school, and in the community, as well as how to take advantage of them, which includes an activity that asks students to list all of their resources on campus.

Third Section: Students develop smart planning habits, learn the importance of flexibility, and how to make positive choices, which are supported in an activity designed to have students identify support services and indicate how they will utilize those services.

Lesson Outlines: Before each section's lesson plan, you will find an overview of that lesson, indicating learning outcomes, time on task, and resources.

TAKING CHARGE   1

Printable

Get away from your computer screen! Print out the pieces you need for reference.

Active Classroom Guides

You won't find a more comprehensive walk-through of material anywhere. Use it as you see it, or use it as a jumping-off point for your own material, but you'll never be lost for words.

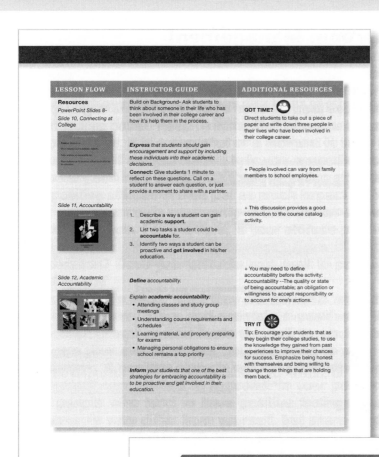

Activity Guides

There's more to the activities than what's in the text. Guide the students through the activities more effectively with the Activity Guides. See page xxii for more detail!

Section 1: Detailed Activity Notes

COLLEGE CATALOG SCAVENGER HUNT

This activity educates students on the importance of understanding their college catalog, as well as identifying crucial information contained within it.

Preparation: This activity requires copies of the college catalog for each student if completed individually or one per each group if completed in teams.

Classroom Management: This activity can be completed individually or in assigned teams. Once everyone is finished, you will reconvene as a class for the wrap-up discussion.

LESSON FLOW	INSTRUCTOR GUIDE
Instructor Guide	**Student Actions**
Explain to your class that they will be looking up specific information in their college catalog, which will be important for them to be educated on in order to become a more self-sufficient, confident, and better student.	
• To begin, have each student or group take a college catalog.	• All students or groups should be in possession of a college catalog.
• **Ask** your class to turn to page 16 in their textbooks.	• Students should be following along to directions on page 16 of their textbooks.
• **Explain** to your students that they will research the information noted in this activity in their book, as well as record their answers in the space provided in the textbook.	• Students should start looking up the information requested in the activity and recording their answers in their textbooks.
If any students struggle with a particular section, feel free to offer them some assistance.	
• Once a student or group completes this activity, you should review their answers to ensure accurate responses.	• Students should have completed this activity.
• **Refer** to the discussion questions on page 6 of the lesson notes in the: Lesson Review and Wrap-Up Discussion 1	• Students should reconvene as a class to begin the discussion
Ask you students the following discussion questions (from page 6 of the lesson notes):	
Did you and your team find everything?	
Did you find some things you didn't know before?	

TAKING CHARGE 4

Lesson Guides for Easier Classroom Management

LESSON FLOW

Resources

PowerPoint Slides 8-
Slide 10, Connecting at College

Slide 11, Accountability

Slide 12, Academic Accountability

Lesson Flow: *Where Should We Be?*

This column gives you time estimates, links to the book, and is tracked to an accompanying PowerPoint presentation.

LESSON FLOW	INSTRUCTOR GUIDE	ADDITIONAL RESOURCES
Resources *PowerPoint Slides 8-* *Slide 10, Connecting at College* *Slide 11, Accountability* *Slide 12, Academic Accountability*	Build on Background- Ask students to think about someone in their life who has been involved in their college career and how it's help them in the process. ***Express*** *that students should gain encouragement and support by including these individuals into their academic decisions.* **Connect:** Give students 1 minute to reflect on these questions. Call on a student to answer each question, or just provide a moment to share with a partner. 1. Describe a way a student can gain academic **support**. 2. List two tasks a student could be **accountable** for. 3. Identify two ways a student can be proactive and **get involved** in his/her education. ***Define*** *accountability.* *Explain* **academic accountability**: • Attending classes and study group meetings • Understanding course requirements and schedules • Learning material, and properly preparing for exams • Managing personal obligations to ensure school remains a top priority ***Inform*** *your students that one of the best strategies for embracing accountability is to be proactive and get involved in their education.*	**GOT TIME?** Direct students to take out a piece of paper and write down three people in their lives who have been involved in their college career. + People involved can vary from family members to school employees. + This discussion provides a good connection to the course catalog activity. + You may need to define accountability before the activity: Accountability --The quality or state of being accountable; an obligation or willingness to accept responsibility or to account for one's actions. **TRY IT** Tip: Encourage your students that as they begin their college studies, to use the knowledge they gained from past experiences to improve their chances for success. Emphasize being honest with themselves and being willing to change those things that are holding them back.

INSTRUCTOR GUIDE

Build on Background- Ask students to think about someone in their life who has been involved in their college career and how it's help them in the process.

Express that students should gain encouragement and support by including these individuals into their academic decisions.

Connect: Give students 1 minute to reflect on these questions. Call on a student to answer each question, or just provide a moment to share with a partner.

1. Describe a way a student can gain academic **support**.
2. List two tasks a student could be **accountable** for.
3. Identify two ways a student can be proactive and **get involved** in his/her education.

Define accountability.

Explain **academic accountability:**
- Attending classes and study group meetings
- Understanding course requirements and schedules
- Learning material, and properly preparing for exams
- Managing personal obligations to ensure school remains a top priority

Inform your students that one of the best strategies for embracing accountability is to be proactive and get involved in their education.

Instructor Guide: *What Should I Say?*

For an instructor new to this course, this section provides suggestions for what to say and do. For a more experienced instructor, this column can act more as a jumping-off point for his or her own class notes.

ADDITIONAL RESOURCES

GOT TIME?

Direct students to take out a piece of paper and write down three people in their lives who have been involved in their college career.

+ People involved can vary from family members to school employees.

+ This discussion provides a good connection to the course catalog activity.

+ You may need to define accountability before the activity: Accountability --The quality or state of being accountable; an obligation or willingness to accept responsibility or to account for one's actions.

TRY IT

Tip: Encourage your students that as they begin their college studies, to use the knowledge they gained from past experiences to improve their chances for success. Emphasize being honest with themselves and being willing to change those things that are holding them back.

Additional Resources: *Is There More?*

This column contains anything else that may help you in your class including links to activities, recommendations for class preparation, links to outside information, online options, or other resources.

Activity Guides

Choose Your Activities

- Three activities per module in the text.
- 3–5 *additional* activities in the Instructor's Materials.
- Expand the number of activities your class does, or choose activities that better fit your educational focus.

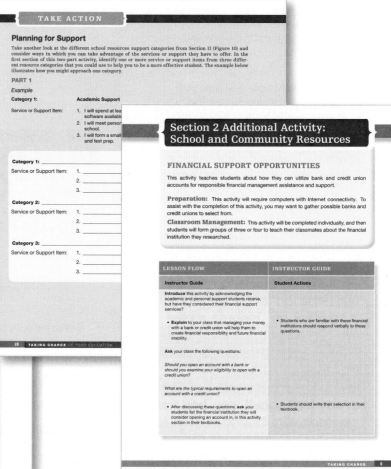

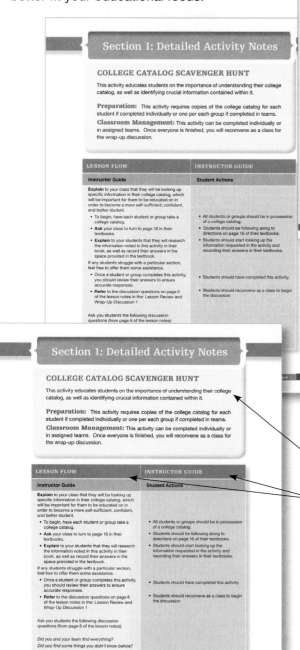

Structured for Ease of Use

- An introductory paragraph describing the purpose and output of the activity.
- A two-column guide to follow both sides of an activity.
  - What should student be doing?
  - What should I be encouraging?
- As a Word document, it is easily printed for use as a worksheet.

PowerPoint Presentations

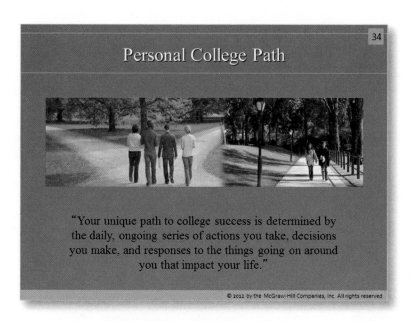

Strategically Designed

Our presentations are designed to feature only images and keywords.

- Our intention is to facilitate discussion rather than lecture.
- Encourage student interaction.
- Take the focus off the front of the class, and put it on group activity.

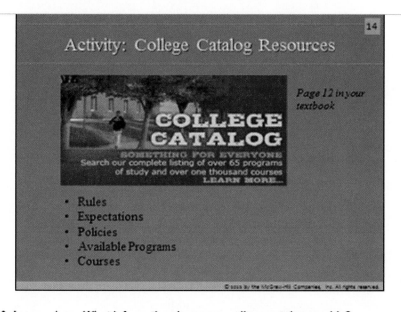

Printable Section

The information from the Active Classroom Guides is embedded in the PowerPoint's notes sections.

Online Accessibility

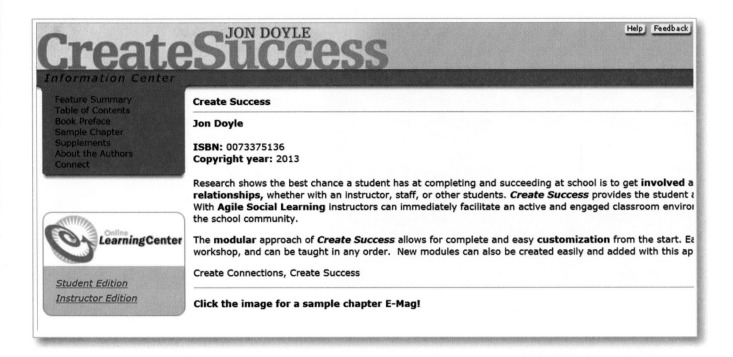

Create Success

Jon Doyle

ISBN: 0073375136
Copyright year: 2013

Research shows the best chance a student has at completing and succeeding at school is to get **involved a** **relationships,** whether with an instructor, staff, or other students. *Create Success* provides the student a With **Agile Social Learning** instructors can immediately facilitate an active and engaged classroom enviror the school community.

The **modular** approach of *Create Success* allows for complete and easy **customization** from the start. Ea workshop, and can be taught in any order. New modules can also be created easily and added with this ap

Create Connections, Create Success

Click the image for a sample chapter E-Mag!

How Do you Prefer to Deliver Your Class?

- Access all the materials for your classroom at the Online Learning Center.
  www.mhhe.com/createsuccess
  - All the Active Classroom Guides.
  - Additional activities with worksheets.
  - Full testbanks for your custom exams.
- Track your students' progress with *Connect Plus*, fully integrated with Blackboard or other learning management systems.
  www.mcgrawhillconnect.com
  - Assign online homework assignments.
  - Conduct a fully online course.

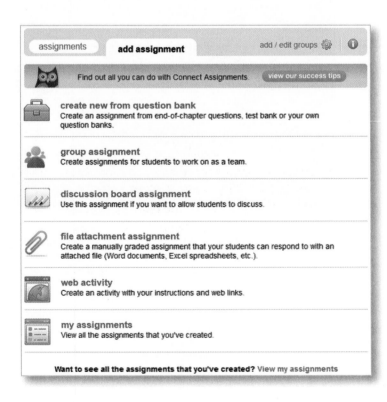

Faculty Development

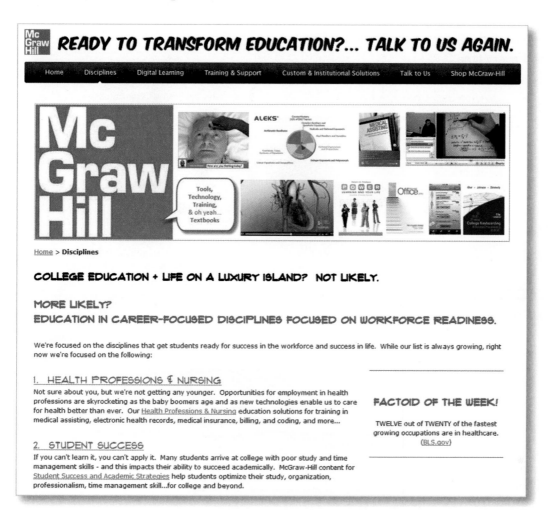

- Are you interested in learning more about **Create Success?**
- Workshops are available on these and many other subjects for anyone conducting or even just considering a first-year experience program.
- Each workshop is tailored to the needs of individual campuses or programs.
- For more information, contact your local representative, email us at **fye@mcgraw-hill.com**, or visit **http://www.talktousagain.com/faculty-development.html**.

Know What to Expect

Self-Contained

- The modules are self-contained, 32-page units about a single topic.
- Modules start on page 1 every time.
- The bold word tells you the main topic.

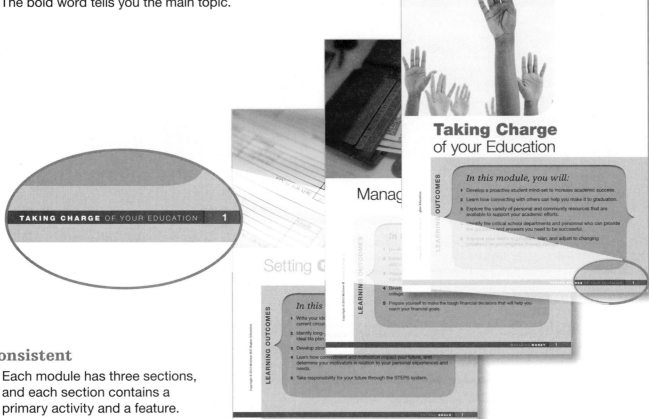

Consistent

- Each module has three sections, and each section contains a primary activity and a feature.

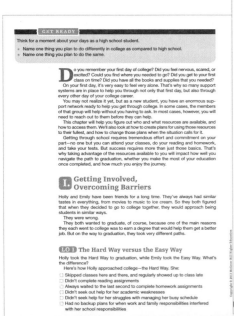

Take Action! to Connect with Your Class

Each of the three sections, contains an activity and a feature. Each activity encourages you to Take Action! to connect with your class.

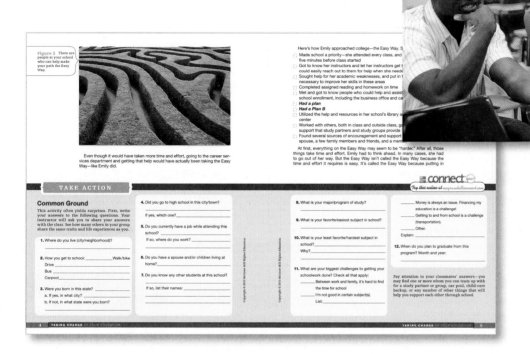

Amplify Your Experience

- **Summary**
  - Time to check your notes and find out if you got what you needed.

- **Discussion Questions**
  - Dive into an issue in more depth.

- **Thinking Critically**
  - Flex your mind and work out new solutions.

- **Key Terms**

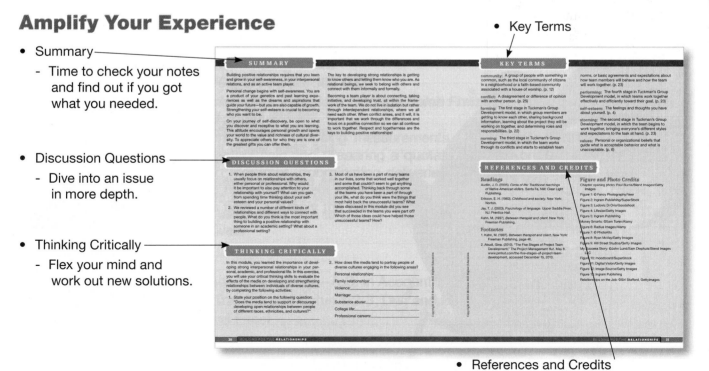

- **References and Credits**
  - Curious? Find out more!

Go Beyond the Classroom

Every module has one of each of the following features:

Money Smarts

The number-one concern for many people is money—how to get it and how to use it. The Money Smarts feature is specifically written to address money-related questions beyond financial aid, with topics like "Credit Unions," "Credit Cards," and "Retirement Plans."

---

and the value of an education is linked to more than just money. One example is the long-term satisfaction that working in a challenging and rewarding career field will bring.

With this in mind, how would you complete the following sentence?

I will be wealthy when . . . .

The way you finish the sentence will help you think about your definition and attitude toward personal wealth. Here's one example:

"I will be wealthy when I'm not living paycheck to paycheck and am capable of purchasing a home of my own."

image. . . . . three . . . . . how you perceive wealth, but they also shape your educational, career, and lifestyle choices. Let's see how this works.

Reflect on your answer and now consider what it will take to achieve each priority you identified to its fullest. You will find that most, if not all of your financial priorities will require some combination of long-term effort, including education, work, and

Figure 5 Home ownership is a common dream, but what's yours?

MONEY SMARTS

Employee Benefits—Saving for Retirement

Enrolling in college is an investment in your future. Compared to the length of your career, your time spent in school is relatively short, but this short-term effort can produce long-term gain.

Planning for retirement is just the opposite: The long-term actions you take over your working years will determine the quality and quantity of your retirement. Have you thought about at what age you'd like to retire? How long you might live beyond retirement age? What kind of retirement lifestyle you want to lead? How much all that will cost, and where the money will come from? These are just a few of the questions that must be considered when planning for retirement. And unlike planning for your education, the earlier you begin planning and saving for retirement, the easier it will be to reach your financial goals.

How do you save for retirement? For most people, the best way is through an employer-sponsored retirement benefit plan. Here are just a few of the various retirement savings programs currently available:

401(k) Plans Many small- to large-sized, for-profit companies offer their employees a 401(k) retirement savings plan. Employees who participate in these programs enjoy several advantages, including employer matching and the ability to save money using pretax dollars, which lowers your current income and employment taxes.

While private, for-profit companies can participate in 401(k) programs, 403(b) programs are the equivalent retirement plan offered by schools, religious, charitable, and some other tax-exempt organizations.[3]

Defined Benefit Pension Plans These retirement plans were common in the past, with few private organizations now offering them. However, they

are still common in government and military jobs. The important advantage of these plans is that "defined benefit" means you know how much you will receive each month in retirement based upon a simple table that includes salary level and number of years worked for the company.[4]

IRA Small employers often offer simple IRA (individual retirement account) savings plans. A simple IRA lets you invest a portion of your pretax income on a tax-deferred basis. Likewise, your employer may elect to make a matching contribution to your account as well.

The simplified employee pension, or SEP, IRA is ideal if you are self-employed. Like the 401(k) and simple IRA, your money is invested using pretax dollars, with income tax paid on the money once you take withdrawals in retirement.[5]

Social Security As long as you work, you pay into Social Security through automatic payroll deductions.

You can receive monthly payments as early as age 62 or wait a few years to receive increased payments. Few people can live comfortably in retirement on Social Security income alone, so most people use the savings plans listed above to provide additional money.

---

expenses is just as important as creating and following a monthly budget. . . . you have a credit card, you may think you can just use it in an emergency. But the risk of relying on your credit card to get you through financial emergencies is that it doesn't take too many financial hits to put you in deep debt, with minimum

cial stability . . . . age and beyond . . . you should create a plan that anticipates and addresses these potential and significant expenses. Your plan can then be

Money ON THE JOB

Budgets at Work

Successful businesses create and follow a strategic plan and then make adjustments as time goes by. Planning for future income and spending is part of this process and an important management task. The heart of this plan is the yearly budget, which plays a big role in determining whether the business will be healthy and prosperous. The typical budget process involves developing plans and projections for several distinct parts of the business, some of which include planning for (or forecasting) sales revenue, or money coming in to the business; planning for business operations and overhead expenses; planning for capital investments (for example, purchasing new equipment) for the purpose of growing the business; and planning cash flow to ensure that money is available during the year to pay for expenses when they arise.

Revenues can come from many different sources, but the largest is usually sales of the business's product or service. Expenses include anything a business plans to spend money on in the coming year, such as the cost of making the product the business sells, employee salaries, rent, marketing costs, and other related expenses. The cash flow forecast is a month-

Principal Budget Components	
Revenue Projection	**Expenses**
Sales projections	Material and production costs
Other revenue sources	Employee expense
	Marketing expense
	Overhead (rent, utilities, etc.)
	Capital improvements
Cash Flow	
Planned monthly money flow into and out of the business over the coming year	

by-month projection of the projected revenues minus the projected expenses.

Following a budget plan is important for a healthy business. If expenses go beyond what has been

planned for, especially for long periods of time, the business may experience serious financial difficulty and may even fail. On the other hand, when sales are strong and expenses are under control, profits will increase and the leaders of the business will have the opportunity to make decisions about whether to reinvest those profits back into the business to help it grow larger, pay off debt the business may have, distribute the money to employees as bonuses, or perhaps all three!

Businesses adjust their budgets throughout the year. If in the middle of the year the business experiences a large, unforeseen expense, spending in other areas may have to be cut back in order to make up the difference. Employee hiring, as well as layoffs, are a direct result of continuous monitoring and managing of the business's budget plan.

Near the end of the year, businesses begin planning for the next year's budget, as well as evaluating their performance on the current year's budget plan. Employee bonuses may be paid based on whether or not the business met its budget goals. These bonuses usually vary depending on how well the business performed beyond the minimum budget plan. And so, the budget cycle starts again, providing the business

with a road map to follow, and a target destination in mind, so it knows when it has reached and possibly exceeded its goals.

On the Job

Every module relates to your future career, and the On the Job feature shows you how! Tie what you're learning now to what you'll be doing on the job!

My Success Story

The best role models aren't always famous or wealthy; they can be someone just like you, who worked their way through difficult times. Find the story of someone you can relate to!

MY SUCCESS STORY

When Diane started college, she was nervous. As a 41-year-old, she was afraid she'd be much older than all her fellow students. And while she had taken one year of college classes after high school, she hadn't finished her degree, so it had been more than 20 years since her last time in a classroom. She worried that being a college student would be so different this time that she wouldn't be able to keep up. But she knew that going back to school and getting her degree would make a big impact on her career, so she tackled the nervousness and became a college student once again.

One thing she did to help calm her nerves was ask for help. A friend of hers who had graduated from the same college a few years earlier told her about all of the great resources available to students who were willing to seek them out. "It's funny," her friend told her, "there are so many great people at the college who will bend over backwards to help you out if you just ask. But so many people struggle because they are afraid to ask, or don't realize that all that help is there just waiting for them."

Diane took her friend's story to heart, and on the very first day of classes, she walked into the Academic Support Center, where she met with an academic advisor. Diane explained her situation, and her advisor, Marcus, said, "Diane, don't worry. I see lots of students in situations just like yours. But not all of them are as good about seeking out help on the first day. You've already got a head start!" As they reviewed her course schedule, Marcus suggested a few resources for her classes that she didn't know about, and told her that, if she had any trouble with any of her classes, she shouldn't hesitate to come back and see him because he could get her set up with a tutor for the class.

Her advisor also suggested she visit Career Services to get a head start on career planning. At the Career Services Center, she met a career advisor, Joan, who talked with her about her interests and career aspirations. Joan made a career file for Diane so she could start keeping track of her experience and opportunities and added her to an email newsletter that would send her updates about job fairs, career workshops, and internships that were related to health information technology, which was the field she wanted to pursue.

Joan also suggested that Diane visit the Student Services Office, where staff could help Diane connect with clubs and organizations that might be interesting to her. As Diane headed toward the Student Services Office, she had a spring in her step—it was her first day back as a college student, but already she felt like she was making connections all over the school and taking charge of her education.

The college catalog is a handbook for everyone at your college. It lays out the rules and expectations you must follow as a student at your college—and it also lays out what you can expect from your college. Understanding those rules and policies as described in your catalog will help you develop a realistic understanding of what to expect as you progress through your classes.

The catalog doesn't only include rules, though. Your college catalog lists all the courses available in all the programs offered at your school. If they read the catalog at all, most students do so when they are trying to decide which classes

Any Activity You See in the Text Is Available in *Connect Plus*

With *Connect Plus*, students can engage with their coursework anytime and anywhere, making the learning process more accessible and efficient.

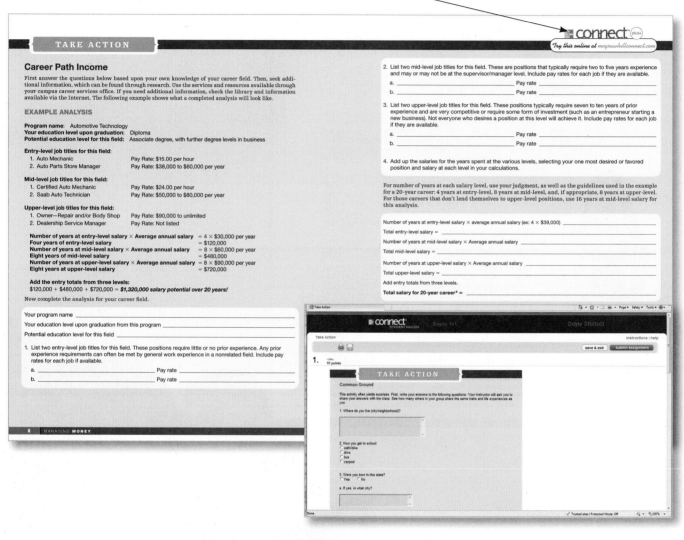

Try the Portfolio Activities

These ongoing projects provide a tangible output, so not only do you learn by doing, but you can prove what you did. You can even print out the output for future reference, or to add to a portfolio.

Get Your Text On-the-Go with the eBook

- *Connect Plus* reinvents the textbook learning experience for the modern student.
- *Connect Plus* eBooks are designed to keep students focused on the concepts key to their success.
- Provide students with a *Connect Plus* eBook, allowing for anytime, anywhere access to the textbook.
- Pinpoint and connect key concepts in a snap using the powerful eBook search engine.
- Manage notes, highlights, and bookmarks in one place for simple, comprehensive review.

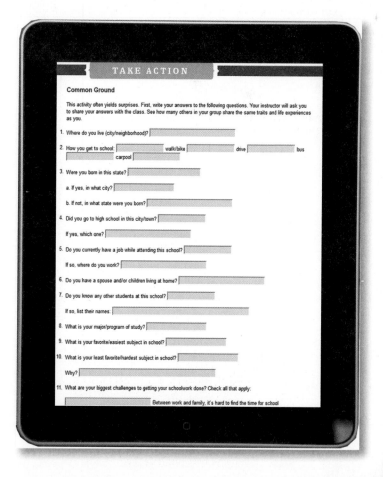

Foundations for Student Success

LEARNING OUTCOMES

In this module, you will:

1 Develop a college mission statement that will form the cornerstone of your personal foundation for college success.

2 Identify the changes in your life—both positive and challenging—that come with the transition to college.

3 Learn how to manage those changes and be better equipped to incorporate your school responsibilities into the rest of your busy life.

4 Review student examples to learn how you can address any weaknesses in your foundation for college success.

5 Understand how knowing your strengths and addressing your weaknesses can impact your school performance and overall college success.

Words can be very powerful. The right words can change your life when they lead to actions.

- What are some powerful phrases? They can be mottos, advertisements, or movie quotes.
- What is it about those phrases that feels powerful to you?

Man-made structures that have stood the test of time all have one thing in common—they are built upon strong, stable **foundations.** The pyramids in Egypt and Mexico, the Great Wall of China, and the Notre Dame cathedral in Paris were built many years ago upon carefully prepared foundations and remain magnificent structures today.

foundation \au̇ n- dā-shən\: A basis upon which something stands or is supported; a body or ground upon which something is built up or overlaid.

The basic premise for a country's system of government is also considered a foundation. The U.S. Constitution provides the foundation for U.S. government and laws. The country's strength flows from this document written more than 200 years ago.

In this module, we consider another type of foundation, one especially important to you right now: your personal foundation for college success. You bring this foundation to your college endeavor. If it's strong enough, it will support you all the way to graduation day.

Your foundation has been built through your school and life experiences. This module introduces ways to develop and strengthen that foundation.

Figure 1 Starting with a strong base is the first step to great works.

We'll look at your commitment to completing your program and graduating, your ability to manage change and additional commitments, your ability to recognize your own strengths and weaknesses, and your willingness to take action when you need help. We'll also explore how you can clarify, develop, and strengthen these abilities and commitments to solidify and strengthen your personal foundation. Just as the great structures of the world needed a strong foundation, you too need a strong foundation to achieve college success and enjoy the resulting benefits, which will last a lifetime.

I. Personal College Mission Statement

This module really starts at the beginning: with your choice to attend college. This choice is at the core of your personal college foundation. It follows that in choosing to *enroll* in college, you also have in your power the choice to *finish* college. You may think that this is a given, that making the choice to enroll is the same as making the choice to finish. But in reality, finishing college requires *another set of choices* in addition to those you made when you enrolled. Those choices will become a big part of your foundation as you work toward completing your program and graduating.

LO 1 Why Are You Here? Your Personal College Mission

That question—"Why are you here?"—might sound odd at first. But your answer to it is important. You see, this book, as well as your instructor and the people who work at your college, are all devoted to helping you succeed in school. Yet for their efforts to achieve the desired effect, they must have a solid foundation to build upon. Your reason for being in college is a critical building block in your personal foundation for college success.

To begin answering the "Why are you here?" question, think back to when you first considered coming to this school. In many cases, this may have involved meeting with a representative in the admissions or enrollment department. While proceeding through the enrollment process, you were probably asked a question like "What are your goals?" or "What are your career aspirations?" or "How will earning a college diploma help you?" For most students, the answers to these questions lead to the same realization—enrolling in college is a big step in anyone's life, and big steps in life usually have the potential for big rewards.

The reason your answer to the "Why are you here?" question is so important is because your answer is a strong indicator of how successfully you will manage this brand-new college experience. The strength of your answer also gives clues to your commitment and focus toward completing your studies and earning that diploma. Those who have a clear vision of *where* they want to go and *why* they want to go there can usually find ways to overcome the obstacles that inevitably come their way. Your answer—your reason for being in college—will help you during the tough times by reminding you of what lies on the other side of those tough times. Revisiting your purpose for becoming a college student, and refocusing your mind on the benefits of earning your diploma, will help you face your challenges and do amazing things, some you probably never thought possible.

One of the many reasons employers hire college graduates is that a college graduate has demonstrated the ability to finish something he or she started—something challenging, full of obstacles, and full of pitfalls. In addition, the process of working through those challenges is in itself a life-changing experience.

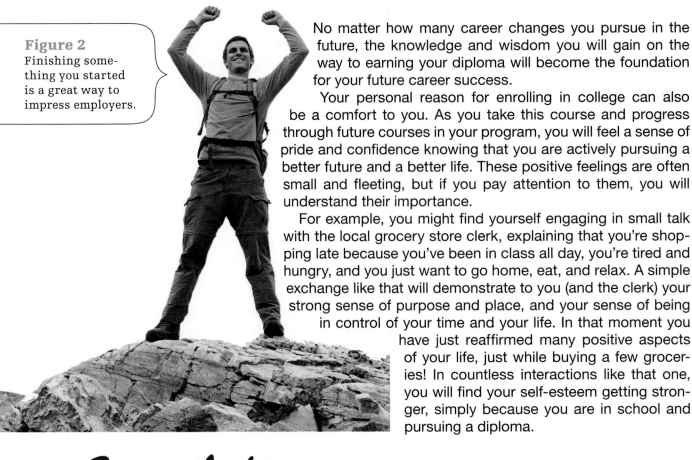

Figure 2
Finishing something you started is a great way to impress employers.

No matter how many career changes you pursue in the future, the knowledge and wisdom you will gain on the way to earning your diploma will become the foundation for your future career success.

Your personal reason for enrolling in college can also be a comfort to you. As you take this course and progress through future courses in your program, you will feel a sense of pride and confidence knowing that you are actively pursuing a better future and a better life. These positive feelings are often small and fleeting, but if you pay attention to them, you will understand their importance.

For example, you might find yourself engaging in small talk with the local grocery store clerk, explaining that you're shopping late because you've been in class all day, you're tired and hungry, and you just want to go home, eat, and relax. A simple exchange like that will demonstrate to you (and the clerk) your strong sense of purpose and place, and your sense of being in control of your time and your life. In that moment you have just reaffirmed many positive aspects of your life, just while buying a few groceries! In countless interactions like that one, you will find your self-esteem getting stronger, simply because you are in school and pursuing a diploma.

Foundations

ON THE JOB

Mission Statements in Business

Successful businesses develop a strong central theme to describe their core purpose and focus. These descriptions are called mission or vision statements and are usually short, sometimes one or two sentences. In some cases, they might be a paragraph or two. Here are a few examples:[1]

We stand today as a global company deeply committed to a single Mission: to discover, develop and deliver innovative medicines that help patients prevail over serious diseases.

—*Bristol-Myers Squibb Co.*

We provide expert care and innovative solutions in pharmacy and health care that are effective and easy for our customers.

—*CVS Corp.*

We will provide branded products and services of superior quality and value that improve the lives of the world's consumers, now and for generations to come. As a result, consumers will reward us

with leadership sales, profit, and value creation, allowing our people, our shareholders, and the communities in which we live and work to prosper.

—*Global Gillette*

To serve our customers, employees, shareholders, and society by providing a broad range of staffing services and products.

—*Kelly Services*

To enable people and businesses throughout the world to realize their full potential.

—*Microsoft*

Our mission is to empower consumers with information and tools to make smart decisions about homes, real estate, and mortgages.

—*Zillow*

Mission statements serve an important purpose for their companies. A mission outlines a company's core values, giving employees a sense of purpose for their work and also a source for guidance. When managers in these companies have to make a difficult or important decision, they can refer to their company's mission

In addition, the discussions you have about your life, with your family, friends, children, your significant other . . . they all become more positive. As someone pursuing an education, you are now speaking from a position of strength: You are taking action, and you are going places. Standing still is no longer an option for you. That is a strong position to be in, and again and again, you will find comfort in that place of strength.

How Is Being a College Student Different?

Enrolling in college brings another opportunity: You are now a positive role model for others. This benefit cannot be emphasized enough. You may not realize it yet, but starting today, your actions can have a positive impact on countless others around you. Think of the many people you come in contact with each day—whether family, friends, or the checkout clerk at the grocery store. When they find out what you are doing, it may just be the inspiration they need to take action on their own personal goals. Though you may never know the extent of it, the positive influence you can have on others is real.

As a college student, you are now on the path to becoming a *professional*, and the skills you acquire through your studies will become a part of who you are. They will instill in you a sense of pride, accomplishment, and capability that you may have never felt before. Being a professional carries both substantial reward and substantial responsibility. The rewards mean greater career opportunity—the opportunity to earn a higher income, and the opportunity to lead a fulfilling and happy life.

While those rewards may still be years away, the responsibility begins now—as a college student, you are now a role model for others. Others will observe

statement before making that decision to confirm that what they decide will support that mission.

The mission statement also provides the basis for the culture of the company. Employees are trained to learn their mission statements, and many companies post their mission statements throughout their offices. Consider a few of the mission statements above: Microsoft supports and enables people's full potential. Gillette seeks superior quality and value. Zillow wants consumers to feel knowledgable and powerful. When meetings are held, decisions are made, and business is conducted in these organizations, you can be sure that these concepts are an important guide to their workers' actions.

At times, companies choose to revise their mission statements. Perhaps the company gets involved in a new line of business, or economic conditions cause it to focus on a new product or customer type. In the same way, when you finish with this program and graduate, it will be time to revise your mission statement. The new statement may then be focused on your career, and it just might include another higher-level educational goal!

your actions and be inspired to act themselves. Throughout your program, your instructors will ask you to be and act like the professional you are training to become. Listen to them and do your best.

At this point, you don't need to worry about getting everything exactly right. College is a time to practice and learn, and making mistakes is a natural part of the learning process. Your instructors are there to help you learn from your mistakes, so regardless of your major, now is the time to try new things, make mistakes, and learn how to get it right.

This is an exciting time! By enrolling in this course and this school, you have taken a large first step toward a brighter future, filled with a better understanding of the world around you, and a greater opportunity for career and financial success.

Turning Your Mission into Action

Now read aloud what you just wrote in the "Personal Mission Statement for College" Take Action activity. How does it make you feel? Pay attention to those feelings! If you feel excitement and anticipation at the prospect of working hard to learn new skills, earning your diploma, and then entering a well-paying career, congratulations! Just by the actions you have already taken—and are taking at this moment—you are well on your way to making that dream a reality.

Yet perhaps you read that answer and feel a sense of anxiety. Sometimes students enroll in college with big dreams for a better life, but when it comes to actually making those dreams a reality, they question whether they can actually do it or whether the road they have chosen is the right one for them. If you're feeling this way, congratulations to you, too! The actions you have taken so far in

> ### TAKE ACTION

Personal Mission Statement for College

Let's go back to the original question: Why are you here? Perhaps you have thought a lot about this already. Just the process of enrolling in school encourages you to think seriously about the commitment of time, money, and energy you face. We are now going to take the next step in that thought process, and put your answer in writing. Take a few minutes to think about the question again, and then write your answer in the space provided below.

Question: Why are you here?

Answer: My number one reason for enrolling in school is . . .

_____

_____

_____

Before we discuss your answer and what it might mean, let's first make it *better*. If you've ever placed a classified ad in the newspaper, you know that most papers charge for these ads by the word. This means that, when writing your ad, you want to choose your words carefully, so you can get your message across most effectively for the least amount of money. We're going to do something similar here: Our goal in this exercise is to get the most bang for our buck.

enrolling in this school, in this program, taking this course, and reading this book are all bold, positive steps toward a brighter future.

Let's try something—read your number one reason for enrolling in school once again. This time, however, imagine that the reason has already been fulfilled. For example, if your number one reason for enrolling in school is to become a professional in the medical field so you can earn more money to support your family and a better lifestyle, visualize that you are *now* a medical professional. You are *now* working in the job (or career) that you have trained for! You are *now* making the kind of money that you deserve! How does

STEP 1:

Write your answer to the question again, but this time include two parts: *what* you want to do with your education, and *why*. Here's an example:

> My number one reason for enrolling in school is to be able to get my degree so I'll be qualified to enter the criminal justice profession. This will provide me with the opportunity to earn a high enough salary to be able to afford to buy a home for my family.

- *What do I want to do?* Obtain a job in the criminal justice field.
- *Why?* To earn a good income so I can buy a home.

Now, you try again:

Question: Why are you here?

Answer: My number one reason for enrolling in school is . . .

_____

_____

_____

(continued)

this make you feel? In all likelihood, you will feel good . . . very good! And any anxiety you may have felt before should be significantly decreased because you are focusing on the outcome and not how to get there.

Feeling anxious about school and all that comes with it is completely normal. In fact, it's rare for new students *not* to feel at least some nervousness about whether they will be able to successfully complete their program and graduate. If you find yourself feeling anxious or stressed about school, remind yourself of your number one reason for going to college. Envision yourself already working in your chosen career field. Keep your dream burning bright in your mind and your heart. The simple act of remembering that goal and keeping it in focus will serve you well as you move through this and the rest of the courses in your program.

The power of your number one reason for going to college should not be underestimated.

Mission statements play a big role in successful businesses. Your **personal college mission statement** can play a big role in your success as well. If you make it the cornerstone of your educational foundation, it can help guide your

TAKE ACTION (concluded)

STEP 2:

Next, let's tighten your answer up—and let's assume your answer must fit into a classified ad space in a newspaper (without the abbreviations), which means two things: You have about two lines of space, and every word costs money! In other words, you want to make each word count. So let's take your answer from step 1 and find a way to eliminate at least three words, while still using proper grammar and complete sentences. Here's the example above, with the wording edited:

My number one reason for enrolling in school is to *complete* be able to get my degree so I'll be qualified to

enter the criminal justice profession. This will provide me with the opportunity to earn a high enough salary

to be able to afford to buy a home for my family.

Now it reads:

My number one reason for enrolling in school is to complete my degree so I'll be qualified to enter the

criminal justice profession. This will provide me with the opportunity to earn a high enough salary to be able

to afford to buy a home.

Now you try:

Question: Why are you here?

Answer: My number one reason for enrolling in school is . . .

_____

_____

_____

mission statement: *A short phrase or paragraph that describes the core purpose and objectives of a business, organization, or individual.*

personal college mission statement: *A mission statement that is focused on an individual's goals and objectives while in college.*

own actions and decisions over the coming months and years while you pursue your diploma.

Before making a decision—small or large—ask yourself if the result will support your mission. If not, then perhaps you are not being true to yourself. Imagine one morning you want to stay in bed and sleep instead of going to class (not hard to imagine, I know). If you are committed to your college mission, and missing a class is in complete opposition to that mission, your decision should be easy: You get up and go to class. (You can plan to take a nap in the afternoon, if you have time.)

STEP 3:

Now, let's do it one more time: Take your response in step 2, and delete at least three more words—more, if you are able. Here's our example:

My number one reason for enrolling in school is to complete my degree so I'll be qualified to enter the criminal justice profession. This will provide me with the opportunity to earn a high enough salary to ~~be able to get afford to~~ buy a home.

Now it reads:

My number one reason for enrolling in school is to complete my degree so I'll be qualified to enter the criminal justice profession. This will provide me with the opportunity to earn a high enough salary to buy a home.

Your turn:

Question: Why are you here?

Answer: My number one reason for enrolling in school is . . .

_____

_____

_____

Compare this response to your first try. Is it better? Not only should your message be better and more focused, but you have also learned an excellent technique for improving your writing. Your response is now easier to read, understand, and, most importantly, remember.

II. Managing the Transition to College— Meeting School, Personal, and Career Expectations

Everyone gets nervous about something, but sometimes nervous energy can help!

- Share an event you prepared for that made you nervous, like a big game, giving a speech, or meeting new people.
- How did you prepare and how did you feel when it was over?

The day you enrolled in this college and stepped foot on this campus (even if it was a virtual footstep as an online student), you chose a new path. This new path brings with it changes, both small and large, short- and long-term. It also brings with it a new set of expectations. These include concrete expectations by your school to attend class, to study, and to perform well on homework and exams. You also have your own personal expectations to do all this while maintaining your obligations and responsibilities. It's easy to see just how challenging the early months of college can be. Fortunately, you have a wealth of support and resources at your disposal to help you along the way.

LO 2 Tools and Resources for Adapting to Change

Schools realize that students transitioning to college life must not only adapt to the rigors of college-level study, but they must also quickly acclimate to an unfamiliar college environment. These challenges can cause stress and are a big reason that new students drop out. That's why colleges and universities expend so much time and effort to assist new students during this time. They offer new-student orientations, first-year-experience programs, courses in college survival skills, and more, all to better prepare new students to successfully navigate these crucial early months of classes. In fact, this course is one such offering.

Figure 4 Going to school is a decision that brings other decisions and changes with it.

Colleges offer these courses and programs because they work. Studies consistently show that students who are given the proper support and resources can better integrate and manage both their requirements in college and their ongoing personal responsibilities. These students also have a higher chance of continuing their education and graduating.

Successfully addressing the challenges and stressors you will have as a new student will not only help reduce them to a more easily manageable level, but also help you succeed academically. More importantly, managing these new stressors will enable you to truly enjoy the college experience. By successfully navigating your own transition to college, you are setting yourself up for a lifetime of great memories!

Planning, Prioritizing, and Focusing: Tools for College Success

This module, as well as others in this program, focuses on giving you the tools you need to successfully transition to the everyday reality of life in college. Three critical tools in the toolkit of every successful college student are *planning*, *prioritizing*, and *focusing*. These tools can help you tackle your day-to-day and term-to-term obligations, both personal and academic.

☐ Successful *planning* involves goal setting, time management, financial planning, and use of available student support resources.

☐ *Prioritizing* involves managing general school requirements such as class schedules, personal needs such as exercise and family time, and perhaps also a work schedule. Prioritizing also includes balancing specific academic requirements such as studying, completing homework, and preparing for exams. For many, prioritizing also means seeking out extra help in a particularly difficult subject.

☐ *Focusing* simply means *doing* those things that your planning and prioritizing tell you need to be done, which includes *applying* the academic skills necessary to get the job done. Those academic skills include your listening, reading, and note-taking skills; proper study techniques used to prepare for tests and quizzes; and writing skills appropriate for the college level. The most effective and productive work occurs when your focus combines the right attitude and commitment with the proper technique.

Figure 5 highlights additional attributes of each of these areas. What else do you notice about the table? The keys to long-term student success shown in the

Do the Planning	Prioritize	Focus on Results
• Goal setting	• School requirements	• *Doing* what needs to be done
• Time management	• Family and work	• Applying academic skills:
• Getting involved, making the most of available resources	• Attention to health and fitness	• Listening and note-taking
• Personal financial planning	• Addressing academic needs; getting help from instructor	• Reading and writing
• Setting realistic expectations		• Preparing for tests
• Managing change and the unexpected		• Applying interpersonal skills with other students, faculty, and administration
		• Attitude and commitment

Figure 5 Keys to long-term student success.

table make up the bulk of the content addressed in this course. Applied correctly, the techniques learned here can and will serve you for the rest of your college and professional career.

LO 3 Addressing School Anxiety

Most students feel at least a little anxiety when entering school . . . and some experience a lot. How much have you felt? Do you know where it comes from? One source may be the realization that college brings multiple changes and challenges for you and your family, some of which are unknown and won't be fully appreciated until you complete one or two terms. One common source of anxiety for adult students is the uncertainty of being able to juggle the requirements of work, family, and school all at the same time.

In addition to the general challenges associated with beginning a new program, anxiety about school can also come from other sources. These include past school experiences (positive and negative), other students ("Am I as smart as they are?"), family and friends, media and the Internet, and especially your own expectations about college.

Anxiety can also come from the goal itself. If you are the first in your family to go to or graduate from college, the anxiety attached to achieving that goal can cause a great deal of stress: "What if I fail?" "What if I let everyone down?" "What if I don't like my new career?" "What if my children see me fail?" The list of reasons and potential sources of anxiety and stressors is long, and as individual as you are.

Figure 6 Stress and anxiety are normal parts of an active, challenging life.

MY SUCCESS STORY

Although Robyn was only 25, she already had eight years' experience in the retail industry, In fact, she had reached a plateau in her career, working for the past two years as a department manager at a major retail store in a busy shopping mall. Now, Robyn wanted more. With her limited education past high school, she was not likely to be promoted further. In addition, after eight years, she was ready for a change to a more normal Monday-to-Friday workweek. In retail, her hours were never really set, her schedule changing from week to week especially during the December busy season. Robyn decided to enroll in a one-night-per-week bachelor's program, setting her goal to achieve her degree in three years.

Robyn was very excited to start school, and on her first night everything went great except for one thing. The instructor asked the class to form groups and then assigned each group to give a 12-minute oral presentation the very next week. Each person in the group was required to speak. For the next week, Robyn could not stop worrying and got little sleep. She was terrified of having to stand up and speak in front of her class. She immediately began to question her decision to return to school. Was she really cut out for this?

On the big night, her group was second to give their presentation, and when it was her turn, she stood up and before she could even say one word, she froze. She literally saw stars and could not read the words on her notes card. Luckily, her group members realized what was happening, and they jumped in to cover her part of the presentation while she sat down to catch her breath. Needless to say, Robyn was extremely embarrassed about the whole thing. Her instructor gave her some encouraging words at the end of class and told her it would be better next time.

Robyn went home and seriously considered dropping out of school right then and there. She was not ready for this! But then she thought of her reason for being there in the first place: She was determined to make a better life for herself. She decided not to give up. It turns out that her instructor continued to assign oral presentations, so it was only two weeks before she had to do it again. The next time, after much practice, Robyn was able to get through the presentation without incident.

Just a little more than three years later, Robyn walked across the stage in her cap and gown and received her diploma. Not long after that she landed a well-paying job (with "regular" work hours) as a regional sales representative for a furniture company servicing the restaurant and hotel industry.

Looking back on her first few weeks of school, Robyn explained, "If I hadn't been very strong in my reasons for returning to school, with a clear purpose for completing my education, I know I would have dropped out soon after I started. Those first few weeks were harder than I ever imagined. I now know that I would have been very foolish to give up so easily. It would have cost me my hopes and dreams."

When Anxiety Leads to Poor Decisions

It's easy to see why having some anxiety is not only to be expected, but completely normal. However, if you don't address anxiety and stress, they can become a negative force in your mind, planting seeds of doubt and giving you second thoughts about what you are doing in school and why you enrolled in the first place. Here's an example:

Tom is a new student and has algebra scheduled in his first term. Tom doesn't like math and has never been very good at it. He therefore feels a lot of anxiety about this course—in fact, he dreads going to class. He knows it's required, but isn't sure he'll be able to understand it well enough to pass the course. He loves his other classes, though, and otherwise really enjoys school.

When Tom wakes up on Monday of the second week of the term, he feels so anxious about algebra (his first course of the day) that he decides to skip class and go out for breakfast. But the service is slow, so breakfast takes longer than he planned, and he hits a lot of traffic on the way to school, so he winds up missing his second and only other class of the day, too. When Wednesday comes, with algebra on the schedule again, Tom feels even more anxious than he did on Monday. Now he's behind on *two* courses—algebra and history, the second course he missed on Monday.

TAKE ACTION

Exploring Life Changes, New Expectations, and School Anxieties

In this activity, list all of the changes that you have experienced as a direct result of your college enrollment. Some may be short-term, such as having to pay for textbooks. In the first section, just list these changes. In the second section, list any sources of anxiety relating to school that you can think of. Some of those sources of anxiety may come from the first list of changes, while others may come from new expectations related to school, tests, and papers, or having to spend time away from your family to attend class.

I. List the recent changes you've made in your life that are directly related to your decision to enroll in college. A few examples include:

Work and/or work schedule changes

Changes to hobbies, sports, or other regular nonschool activities

Having to read or study on a regular basis

Having to learn a new technology (such as a new software program) to successfully complete assignments

1. _____

_____

_____

2. _____

_____

_____

3. _____

_____

_____

4. _____

_____

_____

5. _____

_____

_____

6. _____

_____

_____

7. _____

_____

_____

8. _____

_____

_____

What has Tom done? Obviously, he made the wrong choice to skip algebra on Monday. What *should* Tom have done?

A Better Solution: Asking for Help

A better decision would have been to go to algebra class on Monday, and then make an appointment with the instructor to discuss his concerns about the course. The instructor could then show Tom how to get help and improve his math skills. While Tom, like you, may feel nervous approaching an instructor to ask for help, most instructors have heard Tom's story before—probably a couple of thousand times! But no instructor can read your mind. The only way your instructor can understand that you are struggling and help you get the support you need is for you to reach out, initiate that conversation, and ask for help.

McGraw Hill **connect** (plus+)

Try this online at mcgrawhillconnect.com

9. _____

10. _____

II. List the sources of any anxiety you have felt as a result of your decision to go to college. A few examples include:

Meeting expectations: I don't know if I will be able to handle my family, job, and school expectations all at the same time.

General academic: I don't know if I'm prepared to be successful in college.

Specific academic: I'm not good at math.

Time management: Where will I find the time for all of this?

Social or family pressure: My friends resent me going to class and not hanging out with them.

Financial: Can I really afford this?

1. _____

2. _____

3. _____

4. _____

5. _____

6. _____

7. _____

Figure 7 Don't be afraid to approach instructors for help.

Taking this new course of action and asking for help would diminish Tom's anxiety. The instructor would be able to help him develop an action plan for working on his math skills. He could then prioritize his plan and apply focused effort to improve those skills. Tom would stand an excellent chance of successfully passing the course.

As a new student, you have completed the enrollment process and are in school, taking classes and doing homework and everything else that goes along with the college experience. You have made financial arrangements, work arrangements, and family arrangements to make this all happen. In other words, you have already demonstrated that *you are a person of action. Don't stop now.* Take action to address any stresses and anxiety you feel that have come with the changes, expectations, and additional responsibilities you are faced with as a result of your new life in college.

You can begin the process of taking action by first analyzing the changes that being in school has brought to your life. Change—or the prospect of change—generates a great deal of anxiety. Recognizing and understanding your sources of anxiety will make them less intimidating and enable you to deal with them in a constructive way.

"Knowledge is power."

—FRANCIS BACON

Turning Anxiety into Action

In recognizing the various new expectations and changes you are experiencing as a new student, you now have a starting point to cope with the stresses associated with your transition to college. Take each item you listed in both sections of the previous Take Action activity and give some focused thought on how you might take action on the issue. Some of the items you listed may have already been resolved, such as receiving approval from your employer to adjust your work schedule around school. Others may be easy to manage, and you won't need any help with them. In those cases, just recognizing the changes you are experiencing can help you become a stronger student and a stronger person ("If I can do all this, I can do anything."). With some of your other items, a solution may not be readily apparent. How might you address test anxiety? As you progress through your coursework, you will find that seeking help when needed will usually save a lot of time and avoid a lot of fruitless effort.

Reaching out for help, either with someone at school, a family member, or both, can often provide you with surprisingly simple solutions to your challenges and anxieties. Yet many students transitioning to college can't see the forest for the trees. In other words, they get so focused on the details immediately in front of them that they can't see the big picture that they are a part of. This is understandable—so much is going on in your life as a college student that it's easy to overlook or not even know about simple solutions to the challenges you face. This is why reaching out for help and guidance is so important, especially during the first few months of class. Don't waste this valuable time groping in the dark for answers. By asking for help right away, you will save a lot of time and learn more quickly how to function in your college environment.

As you reach out to the people who have those answers, you will also be developing relationships with them, making it easier for you to reach out to them later and for them to help you when a new challenge arises. The better they know you, the higher quality help you will receive.

III. Being a Proactive Student: Understanding Personal Strengths and Weaknesses

> **GET READY**
>
> It's easier to succeed if you anticipate problems instead of simply react to them.
>
> - Can you share a situation where you anticipated a problem and fixed it?
> - How about a situation where you let a problem get too big to manage alone?

Success in college does not happen by itself. Getting the most out of your college experience takes a combination of desire and commitment, a good ability to manage and balance the demands of school with your other obligations, and finally, the capability to learn and understand a great deal of new material. To complicate matters, weaknesses in one or more of these areas will likely affect your performance in the others. The interrelationships of these "success ingredients" are illustrated in Figure 8.

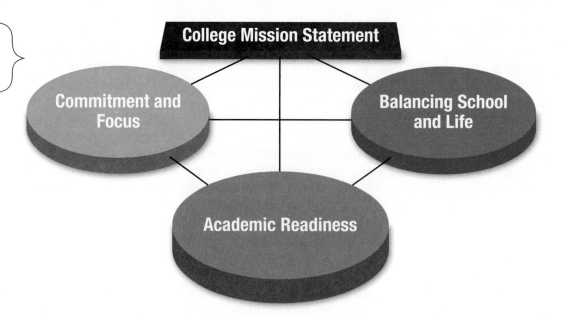

Figure 8
Foundation for
college success.

Figure 9 Sam
isn't sure about his
direction.

LO 4 Your Foundation in Practice: Student Examples

To see how commitment and focus, academic readiness, and successful balance of school and life all play a critical role in the foundation for student success, let's meet a few students.

Commitment Needed

Sam is strong in two of the three areas—he can easily manage school and his personal obligations, and has no problem learning the academic content. His area of weakness is his commitment to the program. He's not really sure about the job he might get when he graduates or if he'll even like the type of work. He started school because he needed to do something with his life, and when his enrollment advisor suggested this program, it sounded good at the time. Now he's not so sure.

One outcome of this scenario might be Sam earning As and Bs, but losing interest and eventually dropping out. To strengthen his foundation and ensure his success, Sam needs to address a weak commitment and focus on the program.

Striking a Balance

Although Lisa did not finish high school, she is bright and able to earn all As and Bs in her medical assisting program. She is also motivated to finish her program, because when she does, she'll be able to make far more money that she does now and won't have to work evenings, weekends, and holidays like she does in her current retail job.

However, Lisa has difficulty integrating her irregular work schedule with her school schedule. She also must use public transportation, and the bus and train schedules don't always fit with her college schedule. Lisa is considering dropping out of school because the logistics are so difficult to manage. Lisa must address weaknesses in her ability to balance school and obligations in her personal life.

Reaching Out for Resources

Tara is excited to be enrolled in a pharmacy technician program and has done a lot of research about the career opportunities that earning a diploma in pharm tech would provide. She has also made scheduling arrangements with her current employer to go to school every day in the mornings. However, Tara is concerned about her math skills. She understands that a good grasp of basic math is necessary for a job filling prescriptions in a pharmacy.

Since Tara is weak in math, she is afraid she might not be able to pass her classes. Tara is therefore considering dropping out and taking occasional classes that don't involve math, although she knows going that route will probably require many more years of school.

Figure 10 Lisa is a wonderful student, but has a lot of obstacles to overcome.

Planning for Financial Success

Earning a college education can put you on the fast track to financial success. But what defines financial success? Is it earning a lot of money? Having a lot of free cash to spend on lavish parties and great vacations? If you have a nice, big house, are you financially successful? How about the couple who can retire at 50, but have to live on a budget to maintain their independence from work?

Any or all of the above might represent financial success. Yet in reality, each of those descriptions is an incomplete picture: The guy who drives nice cars and throws great parties might also have high levels of debt on multiple credit cards that are charging 23.9 percent interest (he made a few late payments). The owners of the nice, big house may be rapidly approaching the point of defaulting on their home loan.

True financial success is defined by the person who is pursuing it, and a complete definition includes income, expenses, belongings, savings, lifestyle, and opportunities.

Take a look at the financial overviews below. Who do you think is in a stronger financial position? Remember, looks can be deceiving!

"Modest-Income" Betty, age 46, divorced, one child

Income and Cash Assets

Monthly take-home income	$2,600
Monthly child support received	$350
Personal savings and investment accounts (not including retirement account)	$27,000

Monthly Expenses

House (mortgage)	$900
Monthly house expense (Includes utilities, insurance, property tax)	$450
Car payment	$0
Credit card payment (Betty only uses a debit card)	$0
Monthly food bill (Includes eating at modest restaurant 1 time per week)	$400
Spending money (Includes gas, entertainment, clothes, car maintenance)	$1,000
Personal savings	$200
Total monthly expenses and savings	$2,950
Total monthly income	$2,950
Difference	**$0**

Copyright © 2013 McGraw-Hill Higher Education

As you can see from this breakdown, Betty is living within her means, including paying herself first by saving at least $200 each month, in addition to her retirement savings that come out of her paycheck.

"Six-Figure" Jim, age 48, married, two children	
Income and Cash Assets	
Monthly take-home income	$8,075
Personal savings and investment accounts (not including retirement account)	$3,100
Monthly Expenses	
House (mortgage)	$3,900
Monthly house expense (Includes utilities, insurance, property tax)	$1,000
Car payment	$630
Credit card payment	$400
Monthly food bill (Includes eating at restaurants 2–3 times per week)	$900
Health club membership	$210
Spending money (Includes gas, entertainment, clothes, swimming and piano lessons for the girls)	$2,000
Personal savings	$0
Total monthly expense and ($0) savings	$9,040
Total monthly take-home income	$8,075
Difference	**–$965**

Though he earns a higher salary, Jim regularly spends more than he earns each month. He is living beyond his means. This is one reason why his credit card balances continue to climb. In addition, he is not saving and has little money available as an emergency fund. At the very least, Jim must significantly decrease his spending. On his current path, he stands a greater and greater chance he'll be forced into bankruptcy.

What does this scenario tell you about the path to financial success? Do you have to earn a six-figure income to *be* wealthy? To *become* wealthy? Does a high salary guarantee wealth?

The weak link in Tara's foundation is her academic readiness. Yet by reaching out and taking advantage of the resources available to her, she can address this weakness without missing a beat of her current program.

Strengthening Your Foundation

Each of these students may be at risk to not complete his or her education. They all have a weakness in their educational foundation that could mean the difference between reaching their goals and dropping out. They all enrolled in school with dreams of making a better life for themselves and their families. However, the daily challenges they face can have an impact on those dreams, causing them to seem less vivid, less important, or further removed from their own reality.

All of these students may face a day when they must decide whether to see it through and stay in school, or take a break. Yet for the majority of students, "taking a break" means dropping out for good. Dropping out might seem to make sense at the moment, but it is a decision that can cause long-term harm: to their finances, to their self-esteem, and to their chances of actually completing their education.

The decision to stay in school or drop out is one that no one wants to face. That's why building a strong educational foundation is so important—because students with strong foundations almost never face that question once they start school. When they encounter challenges, they only consider solutions that allow them to continue with their education. They find ways to solve these challenges, usually with help from others. For them, quitting is not an option.

Having a strong educational foundation has additional benefits. Not only does it help ensure your graduation, it also makes going to school a far more enjoyable and rewarding experience. When your college experience is grounded in a solid educational foundation, school is more enjoyable and easier to look forward to. School provides challenges you won't find at home or in the everyday work world. Whether it's learning a new subject, completing a lab project, or working with a team to produce a class presentation, those learning experiences add value to your life.

The good news is that, if you need to *and want to*, you have the power to strengthen each of the foundational areas. However, in order to improve, you must first know specifically what needs improving.

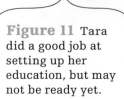

Figure 11 Tara did a good job at setting up her education, but may not be ready yet.

LO 5 Understanding Strengths and Weaknesses: SWOT and SWOO Analyses

The **SWOT analysis** is a technique used in business to analyze a situation before making an important strategic decision. SWOT is an acronym for strengths, weaknesses, opportunities, and threats.

SWOT analysis: *A technique used in business to analyze a situation before making an important strategic decision. SWOT is an acronym for Strengths, Weaknesses, Opportunities, and Threats.*

Imagine you want to open a new coffeehouse and are considering a space that is available in a busy strip mall. Before signing the lease, you want to conduct an analysis to help you make the best decision. A very brief SWOT might look like this:

- ☐ *Strengths:* High-traffic area, good signage, good visibility, easy access. Cars can turn into the parking lot coming from either direction.
- ☐ *Weaknesses:* Too few parking spaces, available space is a little bigger than needed, there's a Starbucks counter in the grocery store in the same center.
- ☐ *Opportunities:* Landlord offering a great deal on the lease, larger space would allow room to grow, especially by adding food items.
- ☐ *Threats:* Another strip mall is under construction across the street; don't know if another coffee house or Starbucks will be moving in. With all the extra space, monthly rent could become very expensive over time.

In this situation, are the weaknesses and threats enough to find another location? Are the strengths and opportunities too compelling to pass up? Only you can make that decision. However, armed with this analysis, you can take action and make the best decision. In this case, by talking to the developer of the new mall across the street, you might find out that only medical and professional businesses will be moving in. By speaking to the landlord about your concerns, you may find she would be willing to subdivide the space later on if it's just too big. She is also willing to post a 10-minute parking zone directly in front of your new shop, allowing customers to more easily find a parking space when they want to quickly drop in and order a drink to go.

As you can see, the SWOT analysis in this scenario gives you, the potential business owner, a clear picture of issues critically important to your new business. It provides you with the areas of concern that warrant additional questions and follow-up before a "go or no-go" decision can be made. Can you think of other business situations where a SWOT analysis would be useful? How about situations in your personal life?

The strengths, weaknesses, opportunities, and threats analysis used in business can also be used to analyze your own college situation. In this case, replace "threats" with "obstacles," which more accurately reflects impacts on personal situations. This personal **SWOO analysis** will provide you with valuable information that you can use to take action to strengthen your personal foundation for college success.

Understanding your weaknesses and potential obstacles enables you to take action to address your needs and overcome the barriers you face. For example, knowing where and how to get help when it's needed are important skills for every new student. While you address your weaknesses and obstacles, you can use your strengths to keep you on track. Don't underestimate the value and power of these strengths. They are what brought you to school in the first place, and you can use them now to help overcome any weaknesses you currently have.

SWOO analysis: *A technique used to analyze a situation before making an important strategic decision. SWOO is an acronym for Strengths, Weaknesses, Opportunities, and Obstacles.*

SWOO Self-Evaluation

This two-part activity begins with a series of questions that indicate your strengths and weaknesses as they relate to your foundation for college success. The second section asks you to consider the opportunities of and obstacles to your college education. In addition, you'll conduct a review of your results that will highlight those areas that you can work on in the coming months.

PART 1: STRENGTHS AND WEAKNESSES SELF-EVALUATION

Answer each question below by placing a check mark indicating whether you agree or disagree with the statement. If the statement does not apply to you, write "N/A."

Commitment and Focus

	Agree	Disagree	
1.			I am excited to be in school—this is exactly what I need to improve my chance for future career success.
2.			I view my college education as a "required" activity—it is my number one personal goal to complete my program.
3.			I am excited about the career opportunities that will become available to me by completing my education.
4.			I am able to sit down and focus on my studies, whether it's reading my textbook, completing homework assignments, or preparing for an exam.
5.			My immediate family (parents, children) is supportive of my decision to go to college.
6.			My spouse/boyfriend/girlfriend supports my commitment to college.
7.			I have friends who currently attend this same school.
8.			It's *not* OK if I don't finish school—I would *not* be happy with my old career and/or job prospects.
9.			I set realistic expectations for myself and others. I am patient when things don't turn out the way I expect.
10.			I am good at planning and prioritizing so that I don't fall behind.

Balancing School and Life

	Agree	Disagree	
1.			I am good at managing my money, and have enough each month to pay my bills and have at least a little left over to either save or spend on things I need or like.
2.			I have a savings account with a balance that can cover at least two months of expenses.
3.			I use credit cards, but carry no balance or only a small balance on them because I pay them off each month.
4.			I have reliable transportation to/from school.
5.			My employer is willing to adjust my work schedule so I can attend class.
6.			I have healthy eating habits.
7.			I exercise regularly.
8.			I usually get enough sleep each night.
9.			I know who to go to (name and office location) if I have questions or concerns about:
a.			• Paying for tuition, textbooks, or anything related to financial aid or how to pay for college, both during and after college.
b.			• My program, including getting help with scheduling, classes, tutoring, computer labs, and other learning resources.

Academic Readiness

	Agree	Disagree	
1.			I am a good reader and usually have no problem comprehending what I read, including difficult material in college textbooks.
2.			I regularly read the news (Internet or newspaper), magazines, or books for enjoyment.
3.			I can use a computer.
4.			I can type by touch.

(continued)

	Agree	Disagree	
5.			I am a confident writer and have completed written assignments of five pages or longer. I have worked successfully in an environment in which I had to write memos, e-mails, or reports to other employees.
6.			I enjoy math and/or I am not fearful of having to complete math courses as part of my program.
7.			I have worked on a team or committee as part of my job or previous schooling and am comfortable participating in group meetings, whether in work or other situations.
8.			I know how to capture important information (i.e., take notes) so that I will be able to review later.
9.			I am good at preparing for quizzes and tests. If I properly prepare, I feel very little anxiety when I have to actually take the test.

ANALYZING YOUR RESULTS—STRENGTHS AND WEAKNESSES

You may have already discovered that each item you checked "agree" can be considered a personal strength. Likewise, any item you checked "disagree" can be considered a potential weakness that could impact your foundation for college success. One way to strengthen your foundation is to set a goal to turn the "disagree" responses into "agrees," one by one.

Many potential weaknesses have simple solutions. Questions 9a and 9b in the *Balancing School and Life* section asks if you know where to find help for a variety of school-related issues. If you don't know the answers right now, you can get those answers quickly by checking your college catalog or college website or asking your instructor. For other topics, such as basic computer skills, the solution may be to take a computer course or spend time in your school's learning resource center, learning and practicing on their computers.

PART 2. OPPORTUNITIES AND OBSTACLES SELF-EVALUATION

For this next section, first make a list of all the opportunities that you believe attending college (*and graduating!*) will provide you. Some that may apply to you include:

A chance to prepare for a rewarding, well-paying career

Learning new skills such as how to use a computer

Meeting new people and making new friends

Opportunities (list as many as you can):

1. _____

2. _____

3. _____

4. _____

5. _____

6. _____

7. _____

Next, list anything you see that could be an obstacle to succeeding in your college education, such as:

My car is old and might break down, leaving me no way to get to class

I'm not good at math and am afraid I might flunk that course

There is no minimum number you should write down. Some students can't think of any. Others may only have one or two. In most cases, students perceive fewer obstacles than opportunities.

Obstacles:

1. _____

2. _____

3. _____

4. _____

5. _____

Compare your new opportunities list with the opportunities that were available to you just before you enrolled in and started school. You don't need to write these down. Just think about or discuss them with your group. Do you find that college provides significant long-term opportunities that you did not have (or had less of) before you started school? How big is the difference? Is it a potentially life-changing difference for the positive?

Finally, let's look at your potential obstacles. Review each obstacle you wrote down, and discuss with your classmates (others are likely to share the same obstacles) possible solutions that will enable you to successfully manage them, should they occur at some point in your future.

Figure 12 People in businesses have to understand strengths and weaknesses too, or they won't have a realistic grasp on their business.

The opportunities you now have as a result of enrolling in college can support your motivation and commitment to succeed. Keep these opportunities in your thoughts, and you'll find that you'll be ever more determined to find effective ways to manage the obstacles you may face along the way toward graduation. Finally, the SWOO analysis (or SWOT for business) is an excellent tool that can be used for many situations and decisions you'll face in the years to come. Keep this tool in your back pocket because you may find yourself going back to it again and again.

SUMMARY

In this module, you began to build your foundation for long-term college success. We started by creating a personal college mission statement. This clear, concise declaration was directed at helping you to reach your college and career goals. Your mission statement serves as the cornerstone for your personal foundation for college success. You should keep it near, and refer to it often. Your mission statement can help ensure that decisions that could affect your school success align with your goals and objectives.

The stresses that naturally come from the changes, expectations, and anxieties related with being a new student can erode your foundation for college success, if you let them. An effective method for addressing these stresses is to identify them, and then create a plan to address each one. Effectively managing your stress and anxiety will enable you to practice the everyday techniques utilized by successful students: planning, prioritizing, and focusing on results.

A proactive student is a strong student. Your SWOO analysis provides the information you need to create a plan to address your weaknesses and overcome obstacles. Through this analysis and your follow-up actions, you can proactively strengthen your educational foundation and improve your chances for long-term college success.

Starting college is a big step for every new student! It changes your life, and it presents a new set of opportunities and challenges that are the hallmark of the student experience. Embrace this exciting time in your life.

DISCUSSION QUESTIONS

1. What are the similarities and differences between your personal college mission statement and one that a business organization develops?

2. Answer the following questions regarding the Money Smarts section found on p. 20. Base your answers upon your current knowledge level about personal finance.

   a. Compare Betty and Jim with regard to their monthly spending in relation to their incomes. Here are some aspects to consider:

      1) Who carries more financial stress? Why?

      2) Who is in a riskier financial position? Why?

      3) What can Jim do to get his monthly expenses under control? Will it be enough if interest rates continue to rise?

      4) What can Betty do to improve her financial situation? What if she needs to buy a new car?

   b. Compare Betty and Jim in terms of net worth. Here are some aspects to consider:

      1) How will this impact their retirement planning?

      2) What risk is Jim taking by not having any savings in a nonretirement account?

      3) Since Jim is four years older than Betty, he is approaching retirement age sooner. How do they compare in their preparation for retirement? If Betty wants to retire young, can she?

   While reading through the scenario, did you identify any financial terms or concepts that you would like to learn more about? Which ones?

foundation: A basis upon which something stands or is supported; a body or ground upon which something is built up or overlaid. (p. 2)

mission (or vision) statement: A short phrase or paragraph that describes the core purpose and objectives of a business, organization, or individual. (p. 8)

personal college mission statement: A mission statement that is focused on an individual's goals and objectives while in college. (p. 8)

SWOO analysis: A technique used to analyze a situation before making an important strategic decision. SWOO is an acronym for *strengths, weaknesses, opportunities,* and *obstacles.* (p. 23)

SWOT analysis: A technique used in business to analyze a situation before making an important strategic decision. SWOT is an acronym for *strengths, weaknesses, opportunities,* and *threats.* (p. 22)

REFERENCES AND CREDITS

Footnotes

1. www.missionstatements.com

Websites

National Resource Center for the First-Year Experience and
Students in Transition: www.sc.edu/fye/

Figure and Photo Credits

Chapter opening photo: © Stockbyte/Getty Images

Figure 1 (left): Brand X Pictures/Getty Images;
Figure 1 (right): © Author's Image/PunchStock

Figure 2: Rubberball Productions/Getty Images

Figure 3: Fuse/Getty Images

Foundations on the Job: ©Siri Stafford, Gettyimages

Figure 4: Ludovic Di Orio/Goodshoot

Figure 6: Asia Images/Getty Images

Figure 7: Ingram Publishing

My Success Story: Ingram Publishing

Figure 9: Rubberball/Getty Images

Figure 10: Image Source/Getty Images

Figure 11: © Rubberball/PunchStock

Figure 12: © Corbis. All rights reserved.

Money Smarts: ©Sam Toren/Alamy

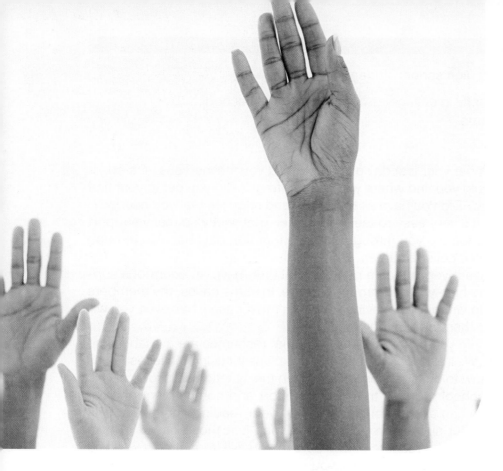

Taking Charge
of your Education

LEARNING OUTCOMES

In this module, you will:

1 Develop a proactive student mind-set to increase academic success.

2 Learn how connecting with others can help you make it to graduation.

3 Explore the variety of personal and community resources that are available to support your academic efforts.

4 Identify the critical school departments and personnel who can provide the guidance and answers you need to be successful.

5 Improve your ability to prioritize, plan, and adjust to changing situations as you progress through college.

Think for a moment about your days as a high school student.

- Name one thing you plan to do differently in college as compared to high school.
- Name one thing you plan to do the same.

Do you remember your first day of college? Did you feel nervous, scared, or excited? Could you find where you needed to go? Did you get to your first class on time? Did you have all the books and supplies that you needed?

On your first day, it's very easy to feel very alone. That's why so many support systems are in place to help you through not only that first day, but also through every other day of your college career.

You may not realize it yet, but as a new student, you have an enormous support network ready to help you get through college. In some cases, the members of that group will help without you having to ask. In most cases, however, you will need to reach out to them before they can help.

This chapter will help you figure out who and what resources are available, and how to access them. We'll also look at how to create plans for using those resources to their fullest, and how to change those plans when the situation calls for it.

Getting through school requires tremendous effort and commitment on your part—no one but you can attend your classes, do your reading and homework, and take your tests. But success requires more than just those basics. That's why taking advantage of the resources available to you will impact how well you navigate the path to graduation, whether you make the most of your education once completed, and how much you enjoy the journey.

I. Getting Involved, Overcoming Barriers

Holly and Emily have been friends for a long time. They've always had similar tastes in everything, from movies to music to ice cream. So they both figured that when they decided to go to college together, they would approach being students in similar ways.

They were wrong.

They both wanted to graduate, of course, because one of the main reasons they each went to college was to earn a degree that would help them get a better job. But on the way to graduation, they took very different paths.

LO 1 The Hard Way versus the Easy Way

Holly took the Hard Way to graduation, while Emily took the Easy Way. What's the difference?

Here's how Holly approached college—the Hard Way. She:

- ☐ Skipped classes here and there, and regularly showed up to class late
- ☐ Didn't complete reading assignments
- ☐ Always waited to the last second to complete homework assignments
- ☐ Didn't seek out help for her academic weaknesses
- ☐ Didn't seek help for her struggles with managing her busy schedule
- ☐ Had no backup plans for when work and family responsibilities interfered with her school responsibilities

☐ Didn't get to know anyone in the school business office (the office that handles tuition payments, financial aid, and all school-related money matters)
☐ Never used the school's learning resource center
☐ Didn't get to know anyone in the career services department
☐ Worked alone, both in class and outside class

Part of the reason Holly did things this way was that, to her, each of those things seemed "easier." They took less time and less effort. Easy, right? After all, taking the time and making the effort to find the career services department, go over there, introduce herself, and establish a relationship with someone there could take days or even weeks. Not worrying about what the career services department was or whether there was anybody there worth talking to took no time or effort at all.

But can you think about the problems taking this approach might have created for Holly? Can you see how what she saw as the "Easy Way" actually made things much harder for her?

For example, she wanted to graduate so she could get a good job in a field that she liked. But by never going to the career services department or taking the time to find out what resources were there or how they could help, she had to make a choice about which career field to pursue without really understanding what working in that field was really like. She eventually did make a choice about which field to pursue, but never had any internships or other experience in that field, which made trying to find a job as she prepared to graduate even harder. Those are both hard things to deal with, but both are things that someone in the career services department could have helped her with.

Figure 2 There are people at your school who can help make your path the Easy Way.

Even though it would have taken more time and effort, going to the career services department and getting that help would have actually been taking the Easy Way—like Emily did.

Common Ground

This activity often yields surprises. First, write your answers to the following questions. Your instructor will ask you to share your answers with the class. See how many others in your group share the same traits and life experiences as you.

1. Where do you live (city/neighborhood)?

_____

2. How you get to school: _____Walk/bike

Drive _____

Bus _____

Carpool_____

3. Were you born in this state? _____

a. If yes, in what city? _____

b. If not, in what state were you born?

_____

4. Did you go to high school in this city/town?

_____

If yes, which one?_____

5. Do you currently have a job while attending this

school? _____

If so, where do you work? _____

_____

6. Do you have a spouse and/or children living at

home?_____

7. Do you know any other students at this school?

_____

If so, list their names: _____

_____

_____

Here's how Emily approached college—the Easy Way. She:

- ☐ Made school a priority—she attended every class, and showed up at least five minutes before class started
- ☐ Got to know her instructors and let her instructors get to know her, so she could easily reach out to them for help when she needed it
- ☐ Sought help for her academic weaknesses, and put in the extra time necessary to improve her skills in these areas
- ☐ Completed assigned reading and homework on time
- ☐ Met and got to know people who could help and assist her throughout her school enrollment, including the business office and career services
- ☐ *Had a plan*
- ☐ *Had a Plan B*
- ☐ Utilized the help and resources in her school's library and learning resource center
- ☐ Worked with others, both in class and outside class, gaining the invaluable support that study partners and study groups provide
- ☐ Found several sources of encouragement and support (including her spouse, a few family members and friends, and a mentor)

At first, everything on the Easy Way may seem to be "harder." After all, those things take time and effort. Emily had to think ahead. In many cases, she had to go out of her way. But the Easy Way isn't called the Easy Way because the time and effort it requires is easy. It's called the Easy Way because putting in

Try this online at mcgrawhillconnect.com

8. What is your major/program of study?

   _____

9. What is your favorite/easiest subject in school?

   _____

10. What is your least favorite/hardest subject in school?_____

    Why?_____

    _____

11. What are your biggest challenges to getting your schoolwork done? Check all that apply:

    _____ Between work and family, it's hard to find the time for school

    _____ I'm not good in certain subject(s).

    List:_____

    _____ Money is always an issue. Financing my education is a challenge!

    _____ Getting to and from school is a challenge (transportation).

    _____ Other.

    Explain: _____

12. When do you plan to graduate from this program? Month and year:

    _____

Pay attention to your classmates' answers—you may find one or more whom you can team up with for a study partner or group, car pool, child-care backup, or any number of other things that will help you support each other through school.

the time and effort it requires makes it much easier to get to graduation and beyond. The Hard Way requires less time and effort—but makes getting to your graduation destination much more difficult.

Career Services, the Easy Way

Let's think about you for a minute, and take a closer look at the role your career services department might take if you choose the Easy Way. Imagine that in the first few weeks of school, you follow the path through the front door of the career services office, and get to know one of the career counselors. You talk with her about what you're studying, your level of work experience, the kind of jobs you think you're interested in after graduation, and the internships or externships you think you'd like to pursue.

During your conversation, the career counselor takes down notes on everything you say, creates a file for you, asks more questions to get a better understanding of your academic and career goals, and says, "This is great—you're really getting a head start by coming in here so early. I'll be able to help you find lots of opportunities, and I'll keep my eye open for things that might be a good fit for you. I've got your contact information, so I'll let you know if something interesting comes along, but you should definitely come back periodically, and keep me up-to-date on how you're doing and how school is going. That will help me help you even more."

How much more motivated would you be to do well in school and graduate if you personally knew someone like that who is going to work hard to help you land a job once you graduate? Would you be motivated enough to keep visiting

Figure 3 Career counselors can help you get a job, but can also guide your educational path.

that career counselor once a month or so, to provide updates on your progress and discuss potential opportunities? Would you be motivated by the possibility that when your career counselor hears about a good internship opportunity or job opening, she might think of you first?

There are two amazing things about the career services office: One, it provides services for free that people who aren't in college often pay thousands of dollars for. And two, most college students fail to fully take advantage of the services it offers. Instead, like Holly, those students take the Hard Way—because it looks to them like the Easy Way.

This discussion about career services is but one small example of the value of being active and involved in school, and taking charge of your education.

Some people might look at the Hard Way and Easy Way lists and think one is a "good student" list while the other is a "poor student" list. Yet it's not that simple: Taking the Hard Way doesn't mean you can't get good grades and graduate, just like taking the Easy Way doesn't mean you can't still struggle academically. Every person brings different skills, experience, and resources to his or her college career. Choosing whether you take the Hard Way or the Easy Way isn't about grades alone—it's about how you experience all that school has to offer.

Even if you find that you've already started down the Hard Way, or you know in your heart that the Hard Way is the way you have approached school in the past, there are lots of links and connections between these two paths to graduation. At any point, you can make the choice to switch and start going the Easy Way.

LO 2 Connecting at College

Earning a college diploma is an individual accomplishment. However, college is conducted in a group environment. You can choose to use that fact to your advantage.

Encouragement and Support

When you think about people by your side as you go through school, who do you think of? Do you think of family, friends, other students? Your employer and co-workers? Who else that you know might support you? Think of anyone who ever asks you, "How's school going?" Don't assume they're just being polite. If someone thinks to ask how school is going instead of just, "How are you?", it's a good bet they care about your success in school and want to help. To get their support, you need to let them know how you're doing and how they can help. Their encouragement and support can be extremely valuable during those times when school and life feel a bit overwhelming.

Do you know anyone who has graduated from your college, or even another college? They may be your best cheerleaders because they've traveled the path you're taking, and truly understand what it takes to stay focused on completing school. They also know firsthand the rewards that a college diploma can bring. They can offer sound advice when you need it, helping you stay on track as you work through any problems you might encounter with changing work schedules, difficult subjects or teachers, or just the stress and tiredness that comes with going to school and being accountable on a daily basis—on top of all of the rest of your personal responsibilities.

You also have great resources available to you in members of the school staff. Remember the discussion in the last section about career services? Your school has many departments similar to career services whose focus is encouraging and supporting students. Take time to learn about these different student services, and get to know the people there. If they don't know who you are, they can't help you. But once you establish a relationship with people in those offices, they can be a great source of encouragement and support.

Figure 4 There are people all around you ready to help, but you have to contact them first.

Sometimes it feels like you're the only one facing the challenges of school that you face. While no one has exactly the same school experience as you, your background may be very similar to some of your fellow students. Getting to know your classmates should be one of your first goals as a college student. Not only does it give you an opportunity to develop lifelong friends, but your fellow students can be some of your best resources for overcoming the challenges of school. And how they solve their challenges may help you work successfully to meet yours. The next activity will help you find some common ground with your fellow students.

Accountability

As a student, you have **accountability** for a lot of things: attending classes, participating in those classes (especially lab classes), learning the material presented to you, and demonstrating that learning through preparing for and successfully completing numerous exams. You also have to pay for your education, have transportation to get to class every day (for online students, transportation means having access to a working computer and Internet connection), and complete homework and reading assignments outside class.

If that sounds like a lot to be accountable for, that's because it is. That's also why graduation ceremonies are such celebrations—the students who walk across the stage and receive their diplomas have been accountable to their instructors, fellow students, academic programs, and school for an extended period of time. They very much deserve the rewards due to them.

As a college student, being held accountable in school can be fun and rewarding. As discussed earlier, your fellow students are going through the same school accountability requirements as you are, and there is nothing like the bonds forged between people when they face a common struggle over an extended period of time. That's why school friendships often become lifelong friendships.

If you ask your instructors why they teach (and you should!), you will probably hear many responses like, "I love to teach! Seeing my students learn the material I'm teaching is one of the most rewarding things I do all day." Your instructors teach because they love it. What does that mean for you? Simply, it means they are there for you, and if you are having difficulty learning the material—if you are having a hard time being accountable to the course—and you ask for help from your instructors, your instructors will typically take the time and invest the effort to help you.

Even if you are not struggling, getting to know your teachers, and letting them get to know you, can help them teach you more effectively. How can this be? Well, teaching requires a great deal of preparation, of customizing the material being presented to the audience who will be receiving it. The more your instructors understand you and your classmates, the better prepared they can be to walk into the classroom and deliver instruction that you are able to understand and learn.

Involvement

Seeking encouragement, by aligning yourself with supportive and understanding people, and embracing accountability to your school responsibilities are the first steps in taking charge of your education. Few students are able to make it to graduation without being accountable and having encouragement.

If you want to get more out of your college education—if you want to really ensure success as a college student—you need to be *proactive* and get involved. This means you don't wait for someone to tell you what you have to do or only do the minimum requirements needed to get through. It means taking the Easy Way—which requires an investment of your time and energy—and reaching out to tap into all the resources your institution has put in place to help you become a strong student.

Being a strong student starts with knowing the expectations, rules, and policies of your school. These are the rules of the road. It also means knowing who is there to help you when you need help, whether the help you seek is school related or not. This may mean taking advantage of the tutoring, learning resource center, and other academic support that is available to help you succeed, or it may mean getting connected to your new career through the school's career center, professional organizations, clubs, student groups, and other outside activities.

Where can you start learning these rules and understanding the resources available to you? Your college catalog.

MY SUCCESS STORY

When Diane started college, she was nervous. As a 41-year-old, she was afraid she'd be much older than all her fellow students. And while she had taken one year of college classes after high school, she hadn't finished her degree, so it had been more than 20 years since her last time in a classroom. She worried that being a college student would be so different this time that she wouldn't be able to keep up. But she knew that going back to school and getting her degree would make a big impact on her career, so she tackled the nervousness and became a college student once again.

One thing she did to help calm her nerves was ask for help. A friend of hers who had graduated from the same college a few years earlier told her about all of the great resources available to students who were willing to seek them out. "It's funny," her friend told her, "there are so many great people at the college who will bend over backwards to help you out if you just ask. But so many people struggle because they are afraid to ask, or don't realize that all that help is there just waiting for them."

Diane took her friend's story to heart, and on the very first day of classes, she walked into the Academic Support Center, where she met with an academic advisor. Diane explained her situation, and her advisor, Marcus, said, "Diane, don't worry. I see lots of students in situations just like yours. But not all of them are as good about seeking out help on the first day. You've already got a head start!" As they reviewed her course schedule, Marcus suggested a few resources for her classes that she didn't know about, and told her that, if she had any trouble with any of her classes, she shouldn't hesitate to come back and see him because he could get her set up with a tutor for the class.

Her advisor also suggested she visit Career Services to get a head start on career planning. At the Career Services Center, she met a career advisor, Joan, who talked with her about her interests and career aspirations. Joan made a career file for Diane so she could start keeping track of her experience and opportunities and added her to an email newsletter that would send her updates about job fairs, career workshops, and internships that were related to health information technology, which was the field she wanted to pursue.

Joan also suggested that Diane visit the Student Services Office, where staff could help Diane connect with clubs and organizations that might be interesting to her. As Diane headed toward the Student Services Office, she had a spring in her step—it was her first day back as a college student, but already she felt like she was making connections all over the school and taking charge of her education.

The college catalog is a handbook for everyone at your college. It lays out the rules and expectations you must follow as a student at your college—and it also lays out what you can expect from your college. Understanding those rules and policies as described in your catalog will help you develop a realistic understanding of what to expect as you progress through your classes.

The catalog doesn't only include rules, though. Your college catalog lists all the courses available in all the programs offered at your school. If they read the catalog at all, most students do so when they are trying to decide which classes to take. But being an involved student means getting to know everything that's in the catalog, not just the small part of it that relates to the classes you plan |to take.

Why read through the parts of the catalog that don't have anything to do with you? Why read the program descriptions and course lists of programs that don't have anything to do with what you're studying?

There are so many interesting subjects being taught, studied, and discussed on your campus, and so many teachers and students with a great passion for each of them. That's why even if you keep your focus and passion on your major or program, it's worthwhile to find out what else is happening at your school—and what all those other people are so excited about.

Plus, outside the walls of your school, whether those walls are physical or virtual, there are no clearly defined lines between majors. You are guaranteed to interact with people who studied all kinds of different subjects, as well as some

Figure 5 Your school may have an online or a printed course catalog. If it has both, they may be different, so double-check your classes.

who never went to college. And to succeed, you must be able to work well with all sorts of people. Reading the other sections of your college catalog will help you discover more about what your fellow students are learning, and help prepare you for interacting with them and collaborating in the world. It can also help you start conversations with other students you meet on campus. Everybody can ask, "What are you studying?" But if you've read the other parts of your college catalog, you can follow up that question with a comment or question that keeps the conversation going and demonstrates an interest in things beyond your expertise.

Reading the other sections of the catalog may also help you stumble across a course description that sounds interesting to you. Many students find some of their favorite classes by skimming through these "other" parts of the catalog.

When you find yourself faced with a challenging issue, the two best places to start your search for a solution are your instructor and your college catalog. Sadly, the catalog—which is free to every student—is one of the most underutilized resources students have at their disposal. Keep your catalog handy, and take the time early in your college career to become familiar with its contents. Simply reading your catalog will make you a much stronger student, one who is more self-sufficient, more confident, and better able to solve problems when the need arises.

TAKE ACTION

College Catalog Scavenger Hunt

In this activity, you (or you and your assigned team) will search for one or more items in your college catalog from the list that follows. After finding each item, provide a brief description of each item in the space provided.

1. School (or program) dress policy

_____

_____

2. Your program's "home page"—course outline, requirements, and course descriptions

Page numbers: _____

3. One other program that seems interesting

Name of program and page numbers:

_____

4. Academic standards (list page numbers)

a. Grading _____

b. Attendance _____

c. Graduation requirements _____

5. Drop and refund policies (list page numbers)

_____

_____

_____

6. Financial aid resources—list four items and their page numbers

_____

_____

_____

_____

In this section, we began to explore the better, "easy" way to go through college. Taking charge of your education is an active, ongoing process. Make the effort to seek out those people in your life who can be encouraging and supportive of your college endeavor.

Understand that as a student, you are now accountable for the requirements of your classes, program, and school. Embrace that accountability and be proud of it. Going to college to gain an education and earn a diploma is a voluntary activity. Not everyone has the desire to become accountable for such a significant endeavor. Just by enrolling, you took a big step toward future success.

Be a strong student—be proactive, involved, and knowledgeable about your school. Take pride in it as much as the people who work and teach there do. Making the extra effort now will provide benefits to you in ways that can't be predicted. Begin your journey by reading your college catalog. Keep it handy and use it often to reference anything and everything about your school and the program you are enrolled in.

If you can't find an answer, reach out to those at your school who can help. Simply understanding the information that is provided in your catalog will improve your communication with the different members of the school staff. They will quickly appreciate the efforts you have taken before coming to them and will be more willing to help.

Try this online at mcgrawhillconnect.com

7. Class schedule and registration procedures (if included)

Page number: _____

8. Your college's accreditation(s)

_____

_____

9. Student services (list two or three services offered)

_____

_____

_____

10. Your school's mission statement and history

_____

_____

Did you and your team find everything? Better yet, did you find some things you didn't know before? Don't hesitate to highlight your catalog for later reference. Dog-ear pages you may want to quickly find again, such as your program's description page, or school schedule. Don't lose your catalog—keep it in a handy and safe place at home.

II. School and Community Resources

Did you attend a New Student Orientation?

- Share the name of one student you met who you didn't know before starting school.
- Can you name one campus staff member you were introduced to at orientation?

It should be clear by this point that success in school goes beyond just attending class, studying and doing homework, and then taking tests. Teaming up with a fellow student to study together, as discussed in the previous section, is an excellent first step in assuring your ongoing college success. But what else can you do? What other resources does your school offer in the way of academic, student, and financial support?

> *"Graduating from college is an individual achievement best pursued as a group effort."*
>
> —JON DOYLE

Experience shows that even if you attended a new student orientation session, it's worth reviewing that information again once you have started school. So many people are introduced to you and so much information is provided to you prior to beginning school that it's easy to lose or forget most of that information by the time your first day of class rolls around.

Not only are there numerous, high-quality resources and support services available at your school, but you have already paid for them—your tuition dollars support these resources. All you need to take advantage of those benefits is a little effort to see what's offered and what applies to your needs.

In this section, we'll explore those resources in detail and encourage you to make the most of them as you progress through your coursework. You may not need or have access to all of these specific support categories or individual items, and that is okay. Taking advantage of just a handful of them can give you all the help and support you need to be successful.

LO 3 Your Personal and Community Resources

The support resources available to most college students can be described using several broad categories, the first of which was touched upon in the previous section on Encouragement and Support: *family, friends, and classmates.*

Family, Friends, and Classmates

Probably the most important support your family, friends, and classmates can provide is encouragement and advice when you need help. Having someone that you trust to talk to when times are tough is a truly important asset to have and one that you should actively seek out if you haven't identified someone already. However, in addition to the emotional support you need to succeed, you also need functional, logistical support that will help make attending school each day a little more manageable. If your car breaks down, you don't need someone to just lift your spirits—you need a way to get to class.

Your personal support network will be much more ready, willing, and able to assist you in these kinds of situations if they understand that you are being proactive and organized in your commitment to school. Asking for help in an emergency situation goes much better when the person you are asking has some idea that such a request might be coming. For example, *before* the day your child is sick and can't go to day care, ask your family member if you can call on her for help in those rare cases when you need it. You will be more likely to receive "yes" for an answer when you have given this person fair warning than if you call out of the blue with a last-minute plea for help.

With this in mind, it's a good idea to think *now* about situations in which you might need help *later*, such as:

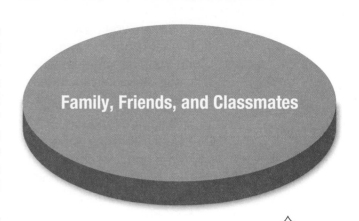

☐ Emergency transportation to or from school and work
☐ Childcare when you need additional assistance
☐ Short-term financial challenges ("I need to buy books but don't get paid until next week!")
☐ Stress relief, whether you need advice or simply someone to listen

Figure 6 Building the big picture of student support resources.

Community

In addition to the support you can get from your personal network of family, friends, and classmates, you may be able to get valuable support from various **community resources.** These may include resources provided by your employer or military branch.

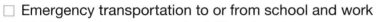

community resources: Resources available to you through community agencies (such as public transportation and public libraries) or your employer or military branch (such as tuition assistance and veterans benefits) that can support your efforts as a student.

Figure 7 You don't have to go it alone. Make a friend and be each other's backup person.

It's likely you have an office or bulletin board on campus that provides details on what is offered locally. If not, it's worth it to find out on your own (or together with your classmates) what resources may be available to you. The list of these resources usually includes:

- ☐ Public transportation
- ☐ Childcare (options for low-cost and emergency care)
- ☐ Public libraries (may include computer access)
- ☐ Free and low-cost health services
- ☐ Free and low-cost food programs
- ☐ Financial counseling
- ☐ Through your employer and/or military, the list may also include:
- ☐ Tuition assistance
- ☐ Coordination of work and school schedules
- ☐ Transfer credit evaluation and assistance (military)
- ☐ Veterans benefits

LO 4 Your School Resources: Academic, Financial, and Career Support

You have access to a number of great resources that are offered by your school as a benefit of your enrollment (meaning, these resources would not be available to you should you decide to stop attending school).

Student Services

There are many resources offered through a typical college's **student services** department, but advising is probably the most important and valuable one

---

MONEY SMART$

Choosing a Bank or Credit Union

With so many options for accessing and managing money, choosing the best one for your needs should start with some analysis of what you want, and what you need, in financial services. Take a look at your current money habits—more specifically, how much do you regularly spend to access your money? This can be from banks, ATMs, payday loan, and check cashing stores.

If you pay more than just a few dollars per month in fees, you can easily save money with better money management choices. If you pay penalty and specialty fees, or regularly pay for cashing a check or getting a few days advance on a paycheck, it's almost like you're throwing money away. No matter how much or how little you have in savings or income, the amount you spend on fees *should be a very small amount.* If it's not, then reducing this amount should be your

highest financial priority, because money spent on these fees and charges is almost entirely optional—there are many who pay $0 each month yet still have sufficient access to the money they keep at the bank.

When choosing a financial institution, pay close attention to the fees they charge for their services. With a little research, you can often find the following features and benefits:

- Free ATMs in network, with minimal or no charges for using ATMs out of network. (Even if your bank does not charge you to use an out-of-network ATM, there is usually a separate fee for using the machine.)
- Checking accounts with free or low fixed monthly charges
- Free debit cards, with free overdraft protection.
- Free online banking. This is a great convenience and makes managing accounts and balances between monthly statements easy and accurate.

Figure 8 The list of resources grows.

Family, Friends, and Classmates

Community Resources

Student Services

Financial Advising

offered to students. This includes academic advising, in which you are able to sit down with an advisor and ensure you are taking the correct courses, plan your future schedule, and discuss possible course scheduling alternatives. Your academic advisor can also direct you to the right people who can provide additional academic help (that is, tutoring) should you need it.

student services: The department or departments at your college that are responsible for providing general support to students, including advice and counseling on class scheduling, getting academic help, housing and transportation, and campus activities.

Credit unions have emerged as an excellent alternative to banks. Typically their fees are lower, they have fewer of them, and they provide all the conveniences of the big banks, including online banking, large ATM networks, and multiple branch locations. Membership is obligatory to join a credit union, with the requirements set by the individual credit union. It can be as simple as being a resident of the city or county, a member or ex-member of the military, or just being a college student.

With a little homework and proper planning, your choice of financial institution can be one that lasts for many years and saves you many hundreds, if not thousands, of dollars. Before opening any new account read the bank's policies for penalty and specialty fees. Choose the account options that are best for you. For example, what happens if you use your debit card and your balance accidently goes below zero? Will the transaction be denied or will you be charged a penalty? With a typical NSF (non-sufficient funds) fee being $35, that $6 lunch could end up costing you $41.

Here is a more complete list of resources you might find in your student services office:

- [ ] Student advising
- [ ] Class scheduling
- [ ] Guidance to receive academic help
- [ ] Information on campus student clubs
- [ ] Listing of campus events
- [ ] Information about local housing, transportation, childcare and food programs

Financial Advisors

A financial advisor (or student accounts representative), who can typically be found in the **financial services** office, works with you to plan how to pay your college expenses. Even those students who have spent many years going to college find it nearly impossible to understand all the changing rules, regulations, and monetary limits for the different kinds of financial aid, so your student financial advisor is truly a valuable person! This advisor may also be able to assist you with other opportunities for financial assistance, such as scholarships and grants that could result in less overall student loan debt to pay back when you graduate.

financial services: Resources available at your college to help with areas related to paying for college, including financial aid information regarding loans and grants, school expense planning, and information about work-study programs.

Your college's business office or financial services office is the place to go if you want to learn more about:

- [ ] Financial aid (loans and grants)
- [ ] Overall school expense planning
- [ ] Scholarships
- [ ] Out-of-pocket expense planning
- [ ] Private loans
- [ ] Work-study programs

Your campus may offer additional student and financial services. Make sure to ask directly about them, as they may not be listed in your college catalog.

Academic Support

The next major resource category is **academic support**, which is likely your school's strongest resource. Beginning with your instructors, there are more staff working at your school who are responsible for providing you with this kind of support than any other. The list of these resources includes:

- [ ] Instructors
- [ ] School tutors
- [ ] Remediation/brushup resources
- [ ] Study partners and teams
- [ ] Computer lab
- [ ] Library or learning resource center
- [ ] Textbook publisher support

academic support: Professional staff at your college, including instructors and tutors, as well as other resources, such as libraries and computer labs, whose purpose is to help you succeed in school.

Figure 9 If you're having trouble, ask your instructor or counselor about tutoring options.

This category is where most schools shine. Dedicated instructors, learning resource centers (such as libraries), computer labs, and student lounges to make a long day on campus more comfortable are all in place to give you the best chance of academic success.

Don't be shy about asking about other services such as tutoring, basic skills development (such as a math refresher, learning to use a computer, or keyboarding practice), or even the office hours for your program's department chair or academic dean. The textbooks you use in school often have a wealth of additional resources, which can usually be found on a specific website identified in the front matter of the book. These resources can really make a difference when trying to learn a difficult concept or study for an exam.

Finally, one of your best academic support resources is a study partner or study team to work with outside of class. Spending time with classmates can not only be enjoyable, but also really help you to better learn, understand, and remember new material. Your campus may even provide facilities (such as the library or student lounge) to make meeting together more convenient and comfortable.

Career Services

The last major category to discuss in this section is **career services.** Some schools include this department under the heading of student services; however, for our purposes, because of the broad range of services they offer and the importance of this resource to you as a student and a graduate, we'll discuss

career services: *The department at your college dedicated to providing career support for students and recent graduates. Assistance includes résumé writing help, interview training, access to job fairs, internship placements, setup of interviews, and access to professional organizations and trade groups.*

career services as a separate group. The list of valuable services that are offered by your school's career services department is long and likely includes:

- ☐ Résumé writing assistance
- ☐ Help with interview skills
- ☐ Assistance locating a part-time job while in school
- ☐ Assistance with work-study programs, if offered by your school
- ☐ Internship or externship placements for those programs that offer them
- ☐ Assistance with job placement upon graduation, including setting up interviews and prescreening services (for the employer)
- ☐ Access to professional organizations and trade groups while in school
- ☐ Access to job fairs

Remember the example used in the first section of this module about getting to know someone in your career services department early (not late) in your college enrollment? The list above clearly underscores the value of following through on

Figure 10 The global view of commonly available student resources.

Family, Friends, and Classmates

Community Resources

Student Services

Financial Advising

Academic Support

Career Services and Externship Placement

TAKE ACTION

Your Campus Resources

Fill in the blanks for each person or department below. To gather all the information for each person, you will need to ask for help. It's also a good idea to make note of the names of those who provide that help—they may also be a great resource for you in the future!

CAMPUS RESOURCES LIST

Instructor #1 Name: _____

Contact Info: _____

Office Hours: _____

Instructor #2 Name:_____

Contact Info: _____

Office Hours: _____

Instructor #3 Name:_____

Contact Info: _____

Office Hours: _____

Program/Department Chair Name: _____

Contact Info: _____

Office Hours: _____

that opportunity, and shows the wealth of support and resources available to you *right now*. Outside school, these services cost thousands of dollars. For you, they are simply a benefit of being a student.

Keep in mind, it's never too early to work on your résumé, and it's never too early to develop your interview skills—you never know when an interesting opportunity may come up and you'll want to have a résumé ready to send. If you've never written a résumé before, the career services department can help you get started.

Many professional associations welcome student involvement, and getting involved in these associations can benefit you when it's time to look for a job. Your career services department can help connect you with the appropriate professional associations. For example, if you are a business student, your career services department may be able to put you in contact with your local chamber of commerce. Students can participate in many of their functions, as attendees, volunteers, and even as interns. These associations can help you begin developing your business network right now.

Knowing about the resources available to you is the first step in taking advantage of these resources. The next step is actually getting to know these people and asking for help with your specific needs. In the following activity, you will create a list of campus personnel whose job it is to help you succeed in school and graduate from your program.

Making the most of the resources offered by your school is one of the most common characteristics of students who take the Easy Way. Hopefully now you see the value and benefit in making the effort—in taking the time to get to know the large number of people whose job it is to provide students with the support and help they need to be successful in school, and to understand how these people can help you on your college path. Quite often, the students who make this effort enjoy the process along the way. After all, they are developing relationships and getting more connected to their school, which makes school more than just a place to take classes and read books, but also a place for making personal connections with great people who are passionate about students and education.

Try this online at mcgrawhillconnect.com

Academic Dean or Education Director Name: _____

Contact Info: _____

Office Hours: _____

Career Center Director Name: _____

Contact Info: _____

Learning Resource Center/Librarian Name: _____

Contact Info: _____

Hours of Operation: _____

Business Office (Financial Services) Name: _____

Contact Info: _____

Student Services Representative: _____

Contact Info: _____

School President / Director Name: _____

Contact Info: _____

School Website: _____

III. Planning, Flexibility, and Choices

What are you doing this weekend? Some people plan their weekends well in advance, even making back-up plans in case their first choices fall through.

- What was the last fun thing you made a plan for?

In the beginning of this module we described two roads students can choose to follow as they navigate school: the Hard Way or the Easy Way. If your goal is to complete your program and graduate, it's not difficult to understand that following the road described as the Easy Way will dramatically improve your chances for success. Here's a recap of the 10 key components of the Easy Way:

1. Make school a priority—attend every class, and show up at least five minutes before class starts
2. Get to know your instructors and let your instructors get to know you, so you can easily reach out to them for help when you need it
3. Seek help for your academic weaknesses, and put in the extra time necessary to improve your skills in these areas
4. Complete assigned reading and homework on time
5. Meet and get to know people who can help and assist you throughout your school enrollment, including the business office and career services
6. Have a plan
7. Have a Plan B
8. Utilize the help and resources in your school's library or learning resource center
9. Work with others, both in class and outside class, gaining the invaluable support that study partners and study groups provide
10. Find at least one source of encouragement and support, such as a spouse, family member, friend, or mentor

Remember, the Easy Way does not mean that school will be easy! It means that you are doing everything in your power to make school an enjoyable and successful experience, and avoiding those things that can make school unnecessarily hard on you. It means giving yourself the best chance to graduate, and doing so while making friends and creating memories that will last a lifetime, while also taking advantage of the networking and career-building resources that will jump-start your postcollege job prospects.

Your unique path to college success is determined by the daily, ongoing series of actions you take, decisions you make, and responses to the things going on around you that impact of your life.

LO 5 The Path to Success

Since the Easy Way is the best road to take toward school success (and the one you should choose to take!), how can you make sure to stay on it through all the events and challenges that will come your way as you progress through college?

Everyone's college experience is different, shaped by their unique personal history and current college and living situation. For example, a student who takes courses entirely online will have a far different experience and set of responsibilities than the student who must physically be in class every day. Both students can choose to take the Easy Way, but their experiences or path along that road will look and feel far different. Think of it as two cars heading down the same freeway, with each having the same destination that is several days away. Each car will travel at its own speed and make its own set of stops along the way. Both use the same road to get to their destination, but each car creates its own best path to get there.

As another example, a student who has been to college before and is confident in her academic abilities will experience a different set of emotions when starting school again compared to the 35-year-old mom who has not attended school since graduating high school. Both students can adopt the Easy Way, but the second student may choose to seek extra help in math so that she can improve her skills and confidence in this area.

What are the important features of your personal college path? Some of them will include:

☐ Your school location and class schedule
☐ Your ability to pay for school plus ongoing personal and family expenses
☐ Fulfillment of your academic program's requirements for graduation
☐ Your academic abilities
☐ Your daily school habits (Easy Way versus Hard Way)
☐ Your attitude and desire for school success

Figure 11 Even when you're doing everything right, school can be tough. Plan your own path so that it isn't harder than it has to be.

Your path to college success may also include your ability to:

- ☐ Work while attending school (for example, getting your employer to cooperate with your class scheduling needs)
- ☐ Manage your family, spouse, and/or childcare responsibilities
- ☐ Manage emergencies or other challenging life situations while attending school
- ☐ Properly prioritize your social life, social influences, and school responsibilities

Developing an accurate and honest understanding of yourself, your habits, your needs, your strengths, and your weaknesses contributes to your ability to stay on the right path. And as you may already be able to see, your path to success is probably not going to be a straight line! It will go through some twists and turns as you navigate your daily responsibilities just to get to school on time each day, and then on to your job after class and then home to your family. For example, let's say normally you drive your car to school. One morning you find the car won't start when it's time to leave home for school—the battery is dead. This event represents a twist in your path to success. Does no car mean no school? Not if you're committed to the Easy Way. Remember that part about having a Plan B?

Having a **Plan B** means being ready for obstacles that may arise (dead battery) when your normal plan (driving your car to school) gets sidetracked. The more prepared you are for these unexpected events, the greater your chances to overcome the obstacles.

Taking Charge

ON THE JOB

Planning in the Workplace

Detailed planning is one of the cornerstones of American business. Plans are made for everything: It's a manager's job to create the plan that will enable the most *effective* and *efficient* use of the company's resources. As an employee in an organization, you are hired to help that company carry out its plan and are given a certain job with a list of tasks and responsibilities to attend to each day. Sometimes, those tasks can remain the same over a long period of time. For example, if you are hired to work the assembly line of a manufacturing company, you may find yourself doing the same task over and over again, literally thousands of times.

For many jobs, however, the job description is a one- or two-page laundry list of everything and anything that needs to be done. For today's worker—for you—this means a great challenge and great opportunity. This means you have to be willing to do different things, be able to keep track of several things at the same time (multi-task), and of course, be ready for plans to change on an almost daily basis.

Here's a common example. One week you are asked to complete a high-priority task, and you do your best to get the job done. But before you can finish, you are asked to stop what you are doing and work on something else. So now you have two projects, but only enough time to complete one. Matters get more complicated when your boss goes on vacation and your temporary supervisor doesn't want you to work on either of the first two projects, but now focus on a new one! No one has told you that you don't have to finish the first two projects; they still need to be completed. So in a matter of a week or two, you have worked on three different projects but finished none of them, and are still responsible for all of them. Frustrating, right?

Experienced workers learn how to deal with these shifting priorities and find ways to follow through—often on all three projects that the inexperienced worker isn't able to finish. The experienced worker understands that only those businesses that can react and adjust to the rapidly shifting and changing demands of today's economy will profit and survive.

Planning and Flexibility

Let's use the example of the car with the dead battery to think about planning skills. Start with your primary mode of transportation to school. Is it the car, bus, train? What about if your first choice is not available? If you drive, how will you get to school if your car breaks down? If you take the bus or a train, what would you do if you were running late and going to miss your ride? Here's a planning example for someone who normally drives to school.

If my car is not available, I will take the bus, which means I need:

☐ To consult a current bus schedule

☐ To identify the location of the relevant bus stops and any transfers

☐ To know the overall time it will take to get to school (and back home)

☐ To make sure I always have bus money available (put away in my bedroom drawer)

If you have all of those things, your car breaking down won't be a disaster. It will only be a bump in the road. But what if you miss the bus? Even your Plan B can have a Plan B. Here's a backup plan to the backup plan for the person described above:

So how can you be like the experienced worker and manage these multiple changing projects?

- **Prioritize.** Determine which project requires immediate attention, and focus on that one first.

- **Take charge.** Though three projects need to be completed, no one person can do all three alone. Find the help and resources to get them done.

- **Communicate.** Present a plan for completing the projects using additional resources. Based upon the conversation with your supervisor, she may decide to drop the second project altogether, apply your idea for new resources to the third project, and ask you to finish the first project yourself.

In this case, you have taken the initiative and not only helped the company move ahead, but also made life better for yourself and your supervisor. When raises and promotion time comes, who do you think your manager is going to choose?

Figure 12
Whether the bus is your Plan A or Plan B, allow time for traffic delays.

If I miss the bus, I will call my "transportation partner," who also drives to school, and ask him to pick me up. He won't be mad because we have both agreed in advance to be each other's backup in case we have an emergency. When I call him, he is happy to help! To find my transportation partner, I asked my classmates at school and found one who lives near me. He was glad to have a backup plan as well!

As you can see, when you have a plan in place, you increase your ability to be flexible in the current situation. If your first try at resolving a problem doesn't work, remain focused on your goal and then try your backup plan. Remain flexible. Solutions to your problems can come in many forms. Nobody plans to have a problem with a course, but if you are having a problem with one of your courses, your first plan should be to talk to your instructor. If the first answer you receive doesn't help (after you have tried to do what he asks), try again, but consider who else may be able to help you. If your approach is flexible and proactive, your next step may be to visit your program's department chair or director. The answers and help you seek may be as close as the short walk down the hallway to her office.

Choices

To achieve college success, many things must go right over an extended period of time. You have the biggest role in making sure this happens. Assuming a sense of accountability to your college responsibilities will play a critical role in your future success. That choice to be accountable as a college student began the day you chose to enroll in school. The next logical choice you have is to use the resources that are available to you to make your college efforts go more smoothly. Proactively planning for how you will deal with obstacles, issues, problems, and emergencies when they arise is another choice you can make right now to help you stay on that path to college success.

Clearly, you have a tremendous amount of control over the quality of your college experience. Choosing to go down the Easy Way instead of the Hard Way will produce a dramatically different college experience and potential for success. Being ready when problems arise will empower you to see situations through to resolution without missing a beat. And making these choices does one other thing that will make your life easier and less stressful: by making these choices now—by deciding now how you will respond if faced with a certain situation—you won't feel the pressure or stress that many people feel when faced with challenging circumstances. After all, you will have already decided what to do.

For example, imagine you are sitting in the coffee shop, hanging out until your next class, and you look at your watch and see that it's time to leave. However, your friend asks you to stay just a little longer so she can finish the "very important story" that she's in the middle of telling you. Since you've already chosen the Easy Way, which includes arriving to your classroom a minimum of 5 minutes before class starts, you politely excuse yourself, letting your friend know that you'll need to pick up the conversation at a later time. There's no need to think about it, and no need to feel guilty that you are leaving your friend. Your choice to be accountable to school is a quality you can live with, and if your friend is truly a friend, she will respect you even more because you have just demonstrated an accountability to your convictions that is worthy of a true friend's admiration. You may even be able to avoid the situation altogether by telling your friend when you sit down together, "I want to let you know, I have to leave for class in 45 minutes."

Planning for Support

Take another look at the different school resources support categories from Section II (Figure 10) and consider ways in which you can take advantage of the services or support they have to offer. In the first section of this two-part activity, identify one or more service or support items from three different resource categories that you could use to help you to be a more effective student. The example below illustrates how you might approach one category.

PART 1

Example

Category 1:   **Academic Support**

Service or Support Item:

1. I will spend at least 30 minutes per week learning to type using typing software available for free in the computer lab.
2. I will meet personally with my instructors during the first two weeks of school.
3. I will form a small study group to meet once per week to work on homework and test prep.

Category 1: _____

Service or Support Item: 1. _____

2. _____

3. _____

Category 2: _____

Service or Support Item: 1. _____

2. _____

3. _____

Category 3: _____

Service or Support Item: 1. _____

2. _____

3. _____

PART 2

In this second part, create a Plan B—a backup plan you can use in case the resource identified is not available—for each service or support item you listed in Part 1. Below is an example of a set of backup plans for the items listed in the example in Part 1.

Example

Plan B for: **Academic Support**

Service or Support Item:

1. *Plan B: If the computer lab or software is not available, I will go to my local library to check on the software's availability.*
2. *Plan B: If I'm not able to meet with each instructor personally, I will write to them using email, asking at least one question that will require a response (to begin a dialogue).*
3. *Plan B: I will set up a regular time each week to spend one hour in the learning resource center and will invite at least one classmate to join me.*

Plan B Category 1: _____

Service or Support Item: Plan B: _____

                                        Plan B: _____

                                        Plan B: _____

Plan B Category 2: _____

Service or Support Item: Plan B: _____

                                          Plan B: _____

                                        Plan B: _____

Plan B Category 3: _____

Service or Support Item: Plan B: _____

                                          Plan B: _____

                                        Plan B: _____

Once completed, share both lists with your classmates—they may have thought of more ways to utilize these services and might help you fine-tune your list. Identifying and thoughtfully considering how you will utiliize the many support services available to you is an important part of being a proactive student. Seek help early and often, before something becomes a problem!

SUMMARY

The central concept for this chapter is that taking a *proactive approach* to your education is the best way to give yourself the greatest chance for college success. Being proactive means choosing how to approach your responsibilities.

We looked at two paths: the Easy Way and the Hard Way. Both lead to the same place, but taking the Hard Way hurts your chances of reaching your final destination, which is college graduation. Taking the Easy Way is more fun and more effective, especially when you seek out the support and encouragement of family and friends. Graduating from college is an individual achievement best pursued as a group effort.

We next explored the many resources available to you as a college student, specifically those offered at your school that can be provide academic, financial, and career support.

Each student's path to college success is unique, and staying on that path requires effort, planning, and flexibility. We explored these ideas and encouraged you to develop a proactive plan—and a Plan B—to deal with issues, obstacles, and opportunities as they arise.

Ultimately, college is about choice. Your first choice was deciding to enroll. The choices you have made and will continue to make will be the biggest factor in determining whether your personal path to college success leads to graduation and a diploma.

DISCUSSION QUESTIONS

1. Students who attend school remotely via computer (online students) can't just walk down the hall between classes and talk with someone in the career services department. Do online students have it easier or more difficult than on-site students when accessing the variety of student resources offered through their school?

2. Why is having a Plan B so important to school success? Give an example of a plan for utilizing school resources, and then an appropriate backup plan in case the first one fails.

3. Why does planning work better when one has a strong sense of accountability?

KEY TERMS

academic support: Professional staff at your college, including instructors and tutors, as well as other resources, such as libraries and computer labs, whose purpose is to help you succeed in school. (p. 18)

accountability: The quality or state of being accountable; an obligation or willingness to accept responsibility or to account for one's actions. (p. 8)

career services: The department at your college dedicated to providing career support for students and recent graduates. Assistance includes résumé writing help, interview training, access to job fairs, internship placements, setup of interviews, and access to professional organizations and trade groups. (p. 19)

community resources: Resources available to you through community agencies (such as public transportation and public libraries) or your employer or military branch (such as tuition assistance and veterans benefits) that can support your efforts as a student. (p. 15)

financial services: Resources available at your college to help with areas related to paying for college, including financial aid information regarding loans and grants, school expense planning, and information about work-study programs. (p. 18)

Plan B: A strategy for dealing with obstacles that may arise when you cannot follow your normal plan. (p. 24)

student services: The department or departments at your college that are responsible for providing general support to students, including advice and counseling on class scheduling, getting academic help, housing and transportation, and campus activities. (p. 16)

Figure and Photo Credits

Setting **Goals**

LEARNING OUTCOMES

In this module, you will:

1 Write your ideal life plan, and understand how past experiences and current circumstances connect to it.

2 Identify long-, mid-, and short-term goals to help you achieve your ideal life plan.

3 Develop strong goals using the SMART method.

4 Learn how commitment and motivation impact your future, and determine your motivators in relation to your personal experiences and needs.

5 Take responsibility for your future through the STEPS system.

Looking back on the things you accomplished over the past five years, which professional athlete, sports team, or performer would best describe your own performance?

- In the next five years, who or what team would you like your accomplishments to mirror?

"All our dreams can come true, if we have the courage to pursue them."

—WALT DISNEY

Think about the last time you went on vacation. How did you prepare? Did you shop online to find the best flight? If you drove, did you map your route online and print directions? Did you check the weather, gather up your toiletries, buy travel-sized toothpaste? Did you research fun things to do? Did you have to request time off from work, or ask a neighbor to check your mail?

Even for a short trip, the better your plan, the more likely you will have fun and make the most of your time.

Your future is a lot like a vacation. It's nice to dream about it, but it takes careful planning and preparation to make those dreams reality. This module is about setting goals to help you plan and prepare to achieve your dreams.

By becoming a college student, you have already taken an important step toward your personal success. But now that you are in college, do you have a plan to get successfully through school? How about a plan for life after college, with concrete steps that will lead to a fulfilling future?

Being at college with no specific goals or plans is like showing up at the airport with no luggage or plane ticket, expecting to go on a nice vacation. Yes, many great vacations begin at the airport, but you wouldn't just show up there without a plan and hope everything will work out. College is the same way.

I. Your Ideal Life Plan

Since you were small, you have probably dreamed about your future. Do you remember what you wanted to be when you were younger? As you grow older, your dreams change as you learn more about your gifts and talents, what you truly love, and what you find less enjoyable. School and life experiences also impact how you think about the future. If a family member gets sick, you may be drawn to the medical field, or if a teacher says you excel in writing, you may consider a career as a journalist.

As an adult, you can still dream. You can consider what makes you happy and what you hope to accomplish. The exciting difference between being a child and an adult is that adults can gain the tools needed to move successfully toward their life plan, turning dreams into reality. The more equipped you are, and the harder you work, the closer to your target you will get. Just as a star athlete must still practice hard and often, and diligently study game footage to be the best, you will need to work hard and stay focused to hit your own personal bull's-eye—your ideal future.

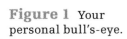

Figure 1 Your personal bull's-eye.

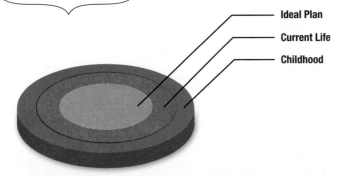

Ideal Plan
Current Life
Childhood

LO 1 Writing Your Ideal Life Plan

Your first step toward hitting that personal bull's-eye will be to consider your **ideal life plan.** Your ideal life plan is a written statement that describes your perfect future. It states clearly what you want for your life. Writing this statement requires reflection and careful thought.

> *ideal life plan: A written statement that describes your perfect future. It states clearly what you want for your life.*

An ideal life plan is not one defined by your parents, friends, or teachers; it is created by you. It includes the people, career, belongings, and activities that you think will bring you fulfillment. To create an effective plan, you must reflect on your past experiences, consider your current situation, and think ahead to your future.

Rather than trying to tackle the entire plan in one shot, it may be helpful to break your plan into pieces first. A good place to start is by answering the following questions that your ideal life plan should answer:

- ☐ Who will share my life with me?
- ☐ What will I be doing?
- ☐ Where will I be living?
- ☐ When will this take place?
- ☐ How do I see myself?

When you think about how to answer these questions, think about your past, and your current life. Analyzing this information will help you make logical, clear choices for the future.

Assessing the Past

Let's take a look at how analyzing your past can help you plan for the future. Think back through your past. What accomplishments are you most proud of? What obstacles have you overcome on your way to those accomplishments? What things have been most challenging to you? What have you struggled with in the past? What have you learned about yourself from past experiences? Take some time to think about your answers to these questions, and consider writing them down. What you uncover about your past can help you shape your future.

For example, when Sara was in high school, her mother become ill with cancer. Because she was very close to her mother, Sara went with her for every doctor's appointment, and cared for her through the various and difficult treatments. Unfortunately, all of the time she spent with her mother affected Sara's attendance in school, and her grades started slipping. Eventually, she fell so far behind that she chose to drop out. She took a job at a gas station at night, but knew she wanted much more for her life.

Let's look at how Sara used her past experiences to help make decisions about her future.

When she thought about time she spent caring for her mother, she realized it never felt like a burden to her—helping someone who needed help made her feel good. She also realized that the time spent with her mother at the doctor's office—learning about complicated treatments, medications, and side effects—sparked an interest in health care. She had always known it was a mistake to drop out of school, but now she realized how much it limited her job options. She wanted a daytime job, because the night schedule at the gas station was wearing her out. But all the jobs that interested her required a high school diploma or GED.

Let's look again at Sara's reflections based upon her past experiences.

Figure 2 Sara's reflections.

Likes to Help People

Interested in Health Field

Doesn't Like Working Late at Night

Wished She Had a Diploma

By taking time to think about her past, and the important connections she can make that may shape her future, Sara has begun the first step toward creating an ideal life plan.

This technique can also be useful when determining what you do or don't want included in your future. If you lived in a big city growing up and hated the fast pace, you may put moving to a small town in your plan. If you hated sitting at a desk all day at school, you may avoid careers where you would sit at a desk. This approach helps you change the direction in which your life moves—closer to things that bring happiness and away from things that cause displeasure.

Examining Your Current Life

Just as you looked at your past, it's also helpful to assess your current situation. What parts of your life do you like? What parts do you wish you could change? If there are areas that make you unhappy, you can make sure that your life plan changes whatever you don't like. You can also keep the things in your life that bring you real happiness. You have the power to keep what makes you happy and to change what doesn't. What an amazing gift!

Now, let's go back to Sara and see how her life is going . . .

After looking back on her past experiences, Sara decided she needed to go back to school to achieve her ideal future. She's now taking classes to earn a GED.

Figure 3 Sara is working through her challenges.

Sara also faces several other challenges. She is in debt because she made some bad choices with a credit card. She knows paying off this debt with her current job will be tough. Working the night shift at the gas station means she can't go out with her friends at night. She also lives at home because, with her credit card debt and small salary, she can't afford her own apartment.

On the positive side, her mom's health has dramatically improved, and it looks like she will have a full recovery. Also, Sara recently heard about a technical college that offers a program in medical assisting, and she has scheduled an appointment to learn more. Before Sara went back to school, going to college wouldn't have been a possibility, but now that she can see her GED in her future, she thinks she might be able to see college in her future, too.

As Sara thinks about her future, she can reflect on her current circumstances to help point her in the right direction. When reviewing her present life, Sara can make a list of positives and negatives:

Negatives	Positives
Credit card debt	Appointment at a local technical college
Still working late hours	Medical program
Still lives at home	Mom is healthy
No social life	Close to getting a GED
No high school diploma	Has a job

Sara is getting closer to creating her ideal life plan. She knows which parts of her current life she wants to change and which give her hope for the future.

Let's meet another person working on developing an ideal life plan. Zack works for a construction company, but some weeks he barely has enough money for groceries. He hurt his back recently but hasn't gone to the doctor because he has no medical benefits. Business has been slow lately, and there has been talk that, unless things pick up, some people might get laid off. Zack isn't worried about only himself. He supports his two children in a small, cramped apartment. As you can imagine, Zack's stress level is high.

Despite these challenges, Zack has a strong sense of pride in his community, and actively participates in a local neighborhood watch program. People have always told him that he communicates well and is very observant. He is also involved in a relationship that he hopes will lead to a serious commitment, and wants to support this relationship by making a career change that will provide financial stability.

By reviewing his current situation, Zack can make decisions about his ideal life plan. Let's take a look with him:

Negatives	Positives
Inconsistent pay	Two children
Back pain	Strong observer
No medical coverage	Interested in law enforcement
Small apartment	Neighborhood watch volunteer
High stress level	Good communicator
Business is slow	Growing relationship

Like Zack, assessing your current situation can provide insight for your future. Taking the time to analyze both your past accomplishments and present situation carefully will lead to a logical design for your life plan.

Creating Your Own Plan

Now comes the exciting part: After carefully reviewing your past and your present, you are now ready to think about your ideal life plan. Take a few moments to consider this opportunity. What will your future look like? Who will share it with you? What will you do?

Let's take a look at Sara's situation again. Sara can now begin to piece together her ideal life plan. Sara starts her planning process by answering the five questions we looked at earlier:

☐ Who will share my life with me? *My mom*
☐ What will I be doing? *Working as a medical assistant in a doctor's office*
☐ Where will I be living? *I will live in my own apartment*
☐ When will this take place? *2 years from now*
☐ How do I see myself? *Debt-free, not working nights, happy*

Having thought carefully about her past and her present life, Sara could easily answer those questions and felt ready to write her very own ideal life plan. Here is what she wrote:

I am a college graduate with an associate's degree in medical assisting! My mom and I spend time together a few days each week, and I live in my own nice apartment close by my job. I work in a pediatrician's office from 9 A.M.–5 P.M. Monday through Friday. I am debt-free and happy with life.

When writing your plan, it helps to write in present tense, like Sara did, to encourage you to make it happen.
Let's look at how Zack answered the questions:

☐ Who will share my life with me? *My children and my new wife*
☐ What will I be doing? *Working as a corrections officer in a prison*
☐ Where will I be living? *In my own house*
☐ When will this take place? *2 years from now*
☐ How do I see myself? *Pain-free; with good medical benefits; earning a salary; enjoying life—low stress*

Now let's see how Zack took those answers and turned them into his ideal life plan:

I am a corrections officer in the state prison. I am a salaried employee with excellent health benefits. My back pain is gone. I live in a three-bedroom house with my two children and my wife. We just celebrated our one-year wedding anniversary. My stress level is under control, and I look forward to earning a retirement through my job!

Just like Sara and Zack, you can develop a future plan that connects with your past and your present. When writing your ideal life plan in the following activity, make sure to:

1. Write in first person *(I, me)*.
2. Use present-tense verbs *(I am, I live, I work, etc.)*.
3. Be specific.
4. Consider who, what, where, when, and how.

MY SUCCESS STORY

Athletes, politicians, and movie stars are frequently considered role models today, and we are drawn to them for many reasons. Unfortunately, people are often disappointed when they hear that their hero uses drugs, commits adultery, or lies and cheats.

Instead of only looking up to the rich and famous for positive examples, you can also find role models from everyday people around you. These people battle the same types of obstacles that you may face and don't have fancy agents and lawyers to solve their dilemmas.

Laura Walker-Jenkins is an excellent example of a real person worthy of inspiring others. As a child, Laura was a good student. She possessed a knack for organization and numbers. She made friends easily, although she tended to remain behind the scenes. Her outlook was always positive. She always dreamed of attending college.

As a young woman in her early twenties, Laura struggled as a divorced mother raising her nine-month-old daughter alone. Before her marriage, she tried college but dropped out when she fell in love. Laura worked a retail job, earning $5.50 an hour. It wasn't long before she realized her wages were not enough to raise her daughter the way she hoped.

Laura's luck began to change when she accidentally wandered into a building in her town that turned out to be Miller-Motte Technical College. She was interested in what she discovered there and, with the support of her mother, enrolled in the Management-International Trade program in August 2004. Laura quickly embraced her new school routine, studying and doing homework while juggling work and motherhood. She maintained an A average every term.

Unfortunately, Laura's world began to fall apart approximately nine months into her program. Her job began to dramatically cut her hours, and her mother suffered a stroke. In desperation, Laura visited the office of the director of education, with plans of dropping out of school. Fortunately, the director of education introduced Laura to the Federal Work Study program, which enabled her to earn money at the school and continue her studies. For her work-study job, Laura worked in the Medical Assisting department. She continued to make high grades, and joined the college's business and accounting club, and later became the club president. Laura graduated from Miller-Motte with a 4.0 GPA, despite the obstacles life threw her way. Laura's mother, now in good health, and daughter clapped loudly as she received her degree. A short time after graduation, the school hired her to work in the financial aid department.

Today, Laura is the financial services manager, a position she was promoted to in 2009. She sometimes flies to other campuses across the country to train new planners and is well respected by her peers. Laura represents the realization of a dream. Her motivation and determination continue as she inspires those around her, including her new husband, Travoi, and her three children.

Once you write your plan, put it somewhere visible where you can see it often. When you find yourself growing in a different direction, adjust your plan—remember, it's your plan, and you can change it when you want. With careful planning and hard work, you can make this plan a reality!

Your Ideal Life Plan

Select two important experiences from your past that you feel have impacted you in a positive or negative way. You can look at the following categories for ideas.

- School
- Interests
- Sports

- Art
- Social time
- Work

- Community
- Religion
- Friends

- Family
- Health
- Relationships

Jot down the key points about each event. You can also share these events with a classmate if you feel comfortable.

Event #1

_____

_____

_____

Event #2

_____

_____

_____

Next, reflect on the experiences. What can you learn about yourself through these events? Use the boxes below to list your ideas. Remember, you will look at these boxes later when writing your ideal life plan.

Next, think about your life now. Fill out the short questionnaire below.

What is your current job? _____

What is your program of study at school? _____

What do you do for fun? _____

Who are the most important people in your life? _____

_____

What is the most interesting thing you have learned at school so far?

_____

_____

If you had to describe yourself in three sentences, what would you say?

_____

_____

_____

How do your current circumstances play into your future? Which parts of your life are you happy with? Which would you like to change? List the positives and negatives in the columns below.

Negatives	Positives

Looking at where you are right now will help you move toward your ideal life plan. Was it difficult to describe yourself?

Now comes the exciting part. It's time to create your ideal life plan. By writing down this plan, you will have a tangible picture of your future. Answer each question below, keeping your past and your current situation in mind.

Who will share my life with me? _____

What will I be doing? _____

Where will I be living? _____

When will this take place? _____

How do I see myself? _____

_____

Now, using the answers you have written above, write a clear description of your ideal life plan. Write it in first person (use *I* and *me)* and use the present tense (*am, have, own,* etc.). Be specific and include names if possible.

_____

_____

_____

_____

_____

Can you see your future? It is now something physical that you can hold in your hands! Your vision of your ideal life is a gift you have created for yourself. Bring it home and put it in a place of honor. Moving yourself toward a successful future obviously requires a great deal of effort. But by thinking about past events and honestly reflecting on your current life, you now have a clear plan to reach that future. Now it's time to make it happen!

II. Setting Short-, Mid-, and Long-Term Goals

GET READY

On a scale of one to ten, with "Very Spontaneous" being one and "Always Plans" being ten, where do you rate yourself?

- How can someone who is very spontaneous benefit from making plans and setting goals?

Congratulations! You are on your way to fulfilling your ideal life plan, but you're not there yet. You still have a lot of work to do to make it happen. The next step is to create goals for yourself that will help you reach your ideal life.

LO 2 Making Long-, Mid-, and Short-Term Goals Work for You

Creating effective goals requires thoughtful consideration. As you think about possible goals, keep the ideal life plan you've created for yourself close by. This will help you make sure your goals line up with the future you're trying to achieve.

To understand how goals work with your ideal life plan, let's take a look at Shauna.

Shauna is a new runner. Her runner friends often talk excitedly about how great it feels to train for and finish a marathon. A marathon sounds like an amazing accomplishment, so Shauna has decided she wants to run one, too. Think of running a marathon as Shauna's ideal running plan—kind of like an ideal life plan.

Of course, Shauna is a new runner, so when she goes out for her first run with her new running shoes, she can't stop thinking how hard it is to get through even the first mile. She quickly gets discouraged because she knows a marathon is 26.2 miles. If the first mile hurts like this, she thinks, how am I going to get through 25 more?

Figure 4 Don't try to accomplish a big goal all at once.

After her first run, she calls a friend who has finished several marathons and tells her how hard the first mile was and that she isn't sure about a marathon anymore. Her friend says running will get easier the more she does it, and encourages her to set smaller goals to help her get from being a new runner to a marathoner. Working with her friend, Shauna sets the following goals:

☐ Long-term goal: I will complete a half marathon (13.1 miles) in 8 months.
☐ Mid-term goal: I will complete a 7-mile run in 4 months.
☐ Short-term goal: I will complete a 3-mile run in 2 months

Setting these goals helps her stay focused because the short-term goal of completing a 3-mile run doesn't seem nearly as scary as the full marathon. But she can see clearly how her short-term goal is a step toward completing a marathon. If reaching these goals is harder or easier than expected, Shauna can make new goals or adjust her goals as needed. She will also get a feeling of accomplishment with each completed goal, without feeling overwhelmed about the marathon.

As you set your own goals, think of them as directions that lead to your ideal life plan, using the shortest route possible. If you don't have any directions, you are likely to get lost—and may not ever reach your final destination, your ideal life plan. Turning your plan into smaller pieces by creating goals will keep you focused and encouraged. Now, let's set some goals!

> *"A goal is a dream with a deadline."*
>
> —NAPOLEON HILL

Long-Term Goals

Because you have already begun to change your life dramatically by attending college, and because you now have a written ideal life plan, you are ready to create **long-term goals.** Long-term goals generally take a year or more to accomplish.

long-term goals: Goals that generally take a year or more to accomplish.

Figure 5 Smaller goals should lead up to a big win!

Focus on three to five long-term goals to get started. You should review your long-term goals often. If you find that one is no longer relevant to your life, you can remove it from your list and replace it with a new goal. You can also adjust your long-term goals without eliminating them completely.

The first column in the chart below includes examples of long-term goals. Some may be similar to goals that you have for yourself.

Long-Term (1 year or more)	Mid-Term (over 6 months to 1 year)	Short-Term (1 day to 6 months)
Graduate with a college diploma or degree		
Join the professional organization for my field		
Use my professional portfolio on job interviews		
Get a job in my field		

Mid-Term Goals

Creating long-term goals helps you create smaller goals: mid-term and short-term goals. By breaking long-term goals into manageable chunks, these smaller goals make the long-term goal process less overwhelming. A **mid-term goal** can take from six months to a year to complete. Each mid-term goal you achieve should move you closer to achieving a long-term goal.

mid-term goals: Goals that can take from six months to a year to complete.

The chart below shows the connection between long-term goals and mid-term goals. You should not set a mid-term goal unless it directly supports a long-term goal.

Long-Term (1 year or more)	Mid-Term (over 6 months to 1 year)	Short-Term (1 day to 6 months)
Graduate with a college diploma or degree	Pass all classes	
Join the professional organization for my field	Become an officer in a school club	
Use my professional portfolio on job interviews	Add accomplishments and projects to my professional portfolio	
Get a job in my field	Research companies in my area and check newspapers and the Internet for job postings	

Short-Term Goals

The last type of goals you will set is short-term goals. **Short-term goals** take less than six months to complete. Because you will accomplish them often, short-term goals will be more likely to help you stay focused as you work toward your mid-term and long-term goals.

short-term goals: *Goals that take less than six months to complete.*

Long-Term (1 year or more)	Mid-Term (over 6 months to 1 year)	Short-Term (1 day to 6 months)
Graduate with a college diploma or degree	Pass all classes	Study for tests and complete homework
Join the professional organization for my field	Become an officer in a school club	Join a school club
Use my professional portfolio on job interviews	Add accomplishments and projects to my professional portfolio	Start my professional portfolio
Get a job in my field	Research companies in my area and check newspapers and the Internet for job postings	Introduce myself to the career service coordinator at my college

LO 3 Setting SMART Goals

When setting goals, the more clear and exact you are, the more likely you are to accomplish them. The **SMART method** helps you remember the areas to consider when creating your goals. It is a goal-setting formula that ensures each goal you set is specific, measurable, attainable, results-driven, and time-focused. Following this method will move you one step closer to success in achieving your goals.

SMART method: *A goal-setting formula that ensures each goal you set is specific, measurable, attainable, results-driven, and time-focused.*

Specific

The first step in the SMART method of goal setting is making sure your goals are specific. The more detail you can provide in describing your goal, the better. A few things that can help make your goal more specific would be to include a specific action, a set time frame, and a reason for achieving the goal.

For example, "I want to finish school" might sound like a good goal, but it is a broad statement that doesn't provide much specific focus or direction. How long will you take to finish school? What is your reason for finishing school? What are your academic expectations? If your goals are too general, you won't feel the same urgency to reach them as if they are clear and specific.

If you wrote that same goal using the SMART method, you might write the following:

In order to become a paralegal, I will finish college in two years with a 3.5 grade point average.

That version of the goal has a specific purpose (in order to become a paralegal), time frame (in two years), and expectations (with a 3.5 grade point average). These details provide a clear challenge—hopefully one that will motivate you to work hard and succeed.

Figure 6 More specific goals make it easier to outline the steps to reach that goal.

Measurable

Once you've created a specific goal, you will also need to make sure that it is *measurable*. This means that you must be able to review your goal periodically to determine if you are closer to achieving it. It's admirable to have a goal that says, "I want to be the best student I can be." But how would you measure that? The sample education goal above provides specific targets that you can measure, such as grade point average and time to graduation. You can check your progress toward the goal each term. With each class you pass, you move closer to success.

Attainable

The goals you set should challenge you—they should require hard work and dedication—but they should also be goals that you have the power to accomplish. *Attainable* goals are goals that you can reach. But because you select your goals sincerely, you will find yourself developing new skills and working beyond your current level of achievement. So an attainable goal is not an easy goal, and you may also have to attain new skills or experiences to reach it.

In order to graduate from college in two years with all passing grades, I will study my class notes daily for at least 30 minutes.

Look at the goal above. Following through on this commitment to daily study will not be easy, but if you remain dedicated, you can do it. As you study every day, your academic performance will improve, your skill level will increase, and your professionalism will grow. Attainable goals make you aspire to a better you.

Results-Driven

Another key factor in effective goals is that they are results-driven, meaning that, once you reach the goal, you will have something to show for your accomplishment. For example, if your goal is to lose weight, the result may be a slimmer middle. If you work for a college education, your result is a degree or a diploma. Results-driven goals resemble an addition problem.

Exercise + Better eating habits = Weight loss

Studying + Attending class   = Passing grades

Results-driven goals provide motivation because you have something concrete to work toward. You will also be ready to conquer the next goal once you accomplish the first!

Time-Focused

With SMART goal setting, time becomes a critical factor. Setting a specific time frame ensures that you won't put off your goals for tomorrow. You will need to work hard and remain focused in order to finish as you planned. Imagine setting your education goal, but instead of 2 years, giving yourself 10 years to finish your college education. What changes would occur? Would you be as likely to remain focused? Would it be easier to be distracted by outside forces?

Final Goal Preparation

Now it's time to determine what areas of your life require goal setting. You are familiar with the three types of goals—long-, mid-, and short-term—and

Figure 7
Limiting your time frame will focus you.

Setting Goals

In the chart below, choose a few topics for which you would like to set long-term goals (if you need help, review the list of topics in the Final Goal Preparation section).

Long-Term Topics
Example: Physical health

Next, consider mid-term goal topics that would support the long-term goal topics. These are not specific goals, but areas that you might address sooner than the long-term topic.

Long-Term Topics	Mid-Term Topics
Physical health	*Fitness level*

Now, add short-term goal topics in the final column to create support for the mid- and long-term topics.

Long-Term Topics	Mid-Term Topics	Short-Term Topics
Physical health	*Fitness level*	*Exercise routine*

Review the information you created in the charts above and focus on one set of goal topics that is the most important to you. Next, create one long-term goal, one mid-term goal, and one short-term goal that correspond with the goal topics. Remember, the mid-term and short-term goals should lead you closer to your long-term goal. After writing each one, use the SMART method checklist to make sure you have clear SMART goals.

Long-Term Goal

_____

_____

_____

SMART Method Checklist

Strategy	Yes	No
Specific		
Measurable		
Attainable		
Results-driven		
Time-focused		

Mid-Term Goal

_____

_____

SMART Method Checklist

Strategy	Yes	No
Specific		
Measurable		
Attainable		
Results-driven		
Time-focused		

Short-Term Goal

_____

_____

SMART Method Checklist

Strategy	Yes	No
Specific		
Measurable		
Attainable		
Results-driven		
Time-focused		

How did it feel to use this method to set goals? How are these goals different from goals you have set in the past? How might this method change the way you pursue your goals? Remember, you can use this approach and these checklists to help you develop strong goals in all the topics you would like to set goals in.

you also know how to use the SMART method to make your goals specific, measurable, attainable, results-driven, and time-focused. You are ready to narrow down the areas in which you want to create your goals.

Look at the following topics:

☐ Education   ☐ Professional skills   ☐ Personal time
☐ Relationships   ☐ Transportation   ☐ Physical health
☐ Employment   ☐ Finances
☐ Home life   ☐ Spiritual life

These are just a few of the areas in your life that may require goals. How should you determine which areas to focus on? The best starting place is to review your ideal life plan, and consider your past accomplishments and current situation. Currently, you are a student. You have made the decision to increase your education in order to prepare for a new career. What goals can you set that will support this important life decision? Do you need to work on your grades or study skills? Are you working on your professional portfolio? Setting education goals will help you maintain focus throughout the education process. You may also discuss your goals with advisors and family members for extra support.

When setting goals, keep the following tips in mind:

1. Write down your goals
2. Put them in a place where you can see them clearly
3. Create mid-term and short-term goals to support your long-term goals

MONEY SMART$

Paying Debts over Time—the "Gift" of Credit

Every day, Americans are bombarded by credit card offers—on commercials, at department stores, and through the mail. Many of them appear to offer "amazing" deals:

- *No Annual Fees*
- *10% off purchases*
- *Free airline miles*
- *0% interest for 6 months*

Unfortunately, credit cards can lead to years of debt and damage to credit scores. Credit cards may seem like a perfect solution when money is tight, but make sure you understand the future implications to your budget. When you use a credit card, you are not solving financial problems—you are creating debt. The more credit cards you use, the more you will owe each month and the harder it will get to pay off your balances. Late or missed payments can ruin your credit score, which makes it difficult to get a bank loan to buy a car or home.

The goal of the credit card company is to make money. They aren't looking out for you. Fortunately,

the federal government passed the Credit CARD Act of 2009 to help protect you, the consumer. Below are a few key points to be aware of:

1. A credit card company cannot charge you a higher interest rate based on a bad payment record with a different company. However, they can increase your interest rate over time if you don't pay your bills.
2. If you try to spend more than the credit you have on your card, your card will be declined. You will no longer be charged overdraft fees for over-spending unless you give written consent.
3. The credit card company has to clearly explain the consequences of only paying the minimum balance of the loan each month.

Credit cards can be useful in certain situations. For example, having a credit card and paying your balance monthly in full will help you build a strong personal credit rating. If you are considering getting a credit card or you currently have one or more, there are a number of important things to consider before making purchases on the card. One of these is the *interest rate* you will be charged. This rate is a percentage of the

4. Review your goals often to make sure they are still appropriate
5. Reward yourself when a goal is accomplished
6. Share your goals with supportive friends and family members
7. Always use the SMART method of goal setting

III. Motivation and Commitment

Think back to the day you started college. What caused you to go? Were you looking for a career change? Were you inspired by a friend or family member? Did curiosity bring you to the door? Whatever the reason, you are now on the way to creating a new life for yourself. You have taken a significant first step.

amount you borrow, and it is calculated as an annual rate. A *fixed rate* means that your interest rate will not change unless you make late payments.

A *variable rate* fluctuates, which means it may change based upon the financial market. This change in rate can cause dramatic increases in your monthly payments. Some credit cards may have low introductory rates, but once this period ends, your interest rate can double or even triple. A fixed-rate card can provide more stability when making a budget.

The chart below highlights how much interest you will pay with different interest rates.

Just remember, no money is free. Credit cards are useful if you need to pay for something important right away. The goal is to never borrow more than you can pay back at the end of the month.

Loan Amount	Interest Rate	Minimum Monthly Payment	Interest Paid	Time It Will Take to Pay Off Loan
$1,000	10%	$25	$ 221	49 months
$1,000	15%	$25	$ 395	56 months
$1,000	20%	$25	$ 662	67 months
$1,000	25%	$25	$1,172	87 months

LO 4 The Formula for Success

The next step in your process will involve two things that you already have inside of you but may not realize you have. Each of these gifts is like your own personal protection. Think of a knight in armor. When he enters battle, he doesn't charge in empty-handed. He is ready with his trusty sword and shield. Commitment and motivation can serve as your sword and shield, to protect you and help you defeat obstacles on your road to success. Understanding these tools and how to use them can help move you more quickly through your goals and onto your ideal life.

Figure 8 The formula for success.

Commitment: Refusing to Give Up

Let's look more closely at your weapon called commitment. **Commitment** means that you are willing to work hard and do whatever it takes to accomplish a specific task. When you are truly committed, you refuse to give up, even when challenges arise. Commitment won't make your life easier, but it will better equip you for tackling obstacles.

commitment: A willingness to work hard and do whatever it takes to accomplish a specific task.

Sam provides a good example of commitment. Sam's car died last week, and he now must make a choice. Because he knows his car will be expensive to fix, dropping out of school enters his mind. Fortunately, Sam is committed to his future. He quickly goes to a group of classmates who live in his area to see if he can get a ride. He checks the local bus route as a backup plan. He also decides to get an estimate at a local garage to see exactly how much he will need to pay. Sam wants to graduate, and he won't let car issues stand in his way. His commitment helps him battle the transportation obstacle.

Understanding What Motivates You

Now let's look at the second tool you carry with you. What got you out of bed this morning? Was it school? Your family? Did you need to get to work, or were you just hungry for breakfast? Something motivated you to get up and start your day. **Motivation** is a driving force that leads you to take action. It is another tool that will lead you to obtaining success.

motivation: A driving force that leads you to take action.

There are two types of motivators, internal and external. **Internal motivators** are the motivators you have within yourself. These are often driven by feelings and personal beliefs. If something makes you feel good, you are usually motivated to try it again. For example, if you get excited when you read about owning your own business, you may be motivated to pursue a degree in management. On the other hand, if something makes you feel pain or displeasure, you are not motivated to do it. We each have our own unique qualities that push us to take or avoid action. Your value system may be a motivator. For example,

Figure 9 Car trouble can interfere with your commitment to your goals.

if you go to the store and the cashier overpays you, your values may motivate you to return to the store and give the money back. If you possess a desire to succeed, you have an internal motivator. Internal motivation is a critical part of your journey.

internal motivors: *Motivators you have within yourself. They are often driven by feelings and personal beliefs.*

External motivators are motivators that come from outside sources. For example, if Mark sees a sports car that he really wants, he may use the image of the car as an external motivator. He knows that finishing school will lead to

the type of job he will need to pay for the car, so he is motivated to get to school every day. You may be motivated by a beautiful home or a terrific job as well. What external motivators are visible in your school environment? Do you see a diploma hanging on a wall? How about pictures of graduates or caps and gowns? Make a special point to pass these areas if they inspire you. Placing your ideal life plan and goals on your refrigerator or on the front of a school notebook may be external motivators too.

external motivators: *Motivators that come from outside sources. This motivation can come in the form of people or things.*

External motivators can also be people. Allison is a student who looks up to her older sister, Katie. Katie graduated from college and has a great job working as a paralegal for a law firm. She provides an external motivator for Allison, who studies hard and never misses classes because she wants a career like her big sister. Allison is also internally motivated by her excitement to work in the legal field and her desire to help those who can't afford expensive lawyers. You may be motivated by a positive person or even a negative person. If someone close to you leads a life that you don't approve of, you may be motivated to do the opposite to prevent that life for yourself.

External motivators can help you push forward, but the most important motivators come from within. It's wonderful to feel inspired by people and things, but ultimately, the desire to take action must come from deep inside.

The Power of Motivation and Commitment in Action

In the movie *The Pursuit of Happyness,* Will Smith plays Chris Gardner, a single father who is searching desperately for a job. The movie is based upon the real life of a man who truly understood the need for motivation and commitment. Gardner finds himself without a job and left alone to raise his young son.

He interviews at a financial brokerage firm and finds out the position begins as an internship—which means no pay. Gardner truly wants the job and makes a commitment to get it. Fortunately, Gardner has motivation as well, and as he faces each obstacle—from homelessness to being robbed to sleeping in a public restroom—he is able to push through and keep working toward his goal. This true story epitomizes commitment and motivation. Gardner knew what he wanted and refused to give up despite unbelievable obstacles. You can achieve your goals just as Gardner did.

Can you think of any other people who show true commitment? What ways have you shown your own commitment to your education?

LO 5 The STEPS System

As you develop your ability to use those two powerful tools, commitment and motivation, you can use the STEPS system to help you fight some of the obstacles that may loom ahead. The **STEPS system** is like a staircase that includes five different steps: *self-discipline, taking responsibility, envisioning success, positive self-talk, and sharing goals.* Just like a staircase, you can travel up and down the STEPS to get where you need to go on your journey.

STEPS system: *A system to overcome obstacles that includes five different steps: self-discipline, taking responsibility, envisioning success, positive self-talk, and sharing goals.*

Self-Discipline

You've created an ideal life plan and now have short- and long-term goals. But without self-discipline, those are just nice words on a piece of paper. As a college student, you will be faced with plenty of temptations that may distract you from your goals. Self-discipline is the focus and control you need to make choices that support your ideal future.

Every action you take has an impact. For example, if you have a big test tomorrow and your friends want you to go out late even though you need to study, you will be faced with a tough decision. If you choose to go out, you may fail the test

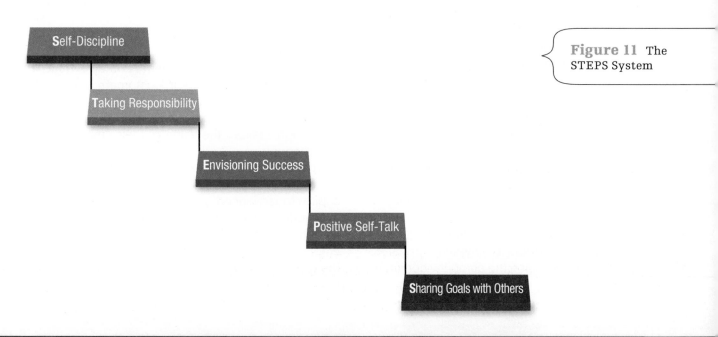

Figure 11 The STEPS System

and even fail the class. Your graduation date can even be impacted! If you have the tool of self-discipline, you will ask your friends for a rain check and will hit the books. For your commitment to your education to be more than just talk, self-discipline must follow. As a mature adult, you can decide that your future happiness is more important than a few hours of short-term fun. You can also think about the negative consequences of making a bad choice. Remember, you have tools within you to battle anything that stands in the way of your future!

Taking Responsibility

Have you ever heard a classmate say, "That teacher failed me"? While the teacher may have assigned the failing grade, the student is the one who failed the course. In this case, the student is not taking responsibility for a poor performance and is instead blaming the teacher. A student who takes responsibility but still fails a class would reflect on his class performance. He might rethink his study strategies and make sure not to miss classes. This individual won't allow others to steer his future and won't give away the power of responsibility.

Take a moment right now and look at the ideal life plan that you created earlier. Read it to yourself, or even say it out loud. This plan belongs to *you*. If you are personally committed to achieving this plan, you must be responsible for what happens next.

Each day, consider how you can make responsible choices. Don't sit back passively waiting for others to determine your future. Taking responsibility means admitting when you make mistakes and also finding solutions when problems occur. This step is in your control.

ON THE JOB

The Power of Employee Motivation

"The magic formula that successful businesses have discovered is to treat customers like guests and employees like people."

—*Thomas J. Peters*

Just as your internal and external motivation will push you through the challenges you face as you work to achieve your goals, many reputable businesses understand the importance of motivation with their employees. Google, for example, creates a motivating environment by providing many perks for their workers, from free lunches to on-site doctor's care. Google wants employees to have fun, which inspires creativity. Productivity doesn't appear to be impacted negatively since the company continues to grow.

Another company that understands the importance of motivation is Marriott. J. W. Marriott, Jr., chairman and chief executive officer of the company, has been quoted as saying:

"Motivate them, train them, care about them, and make winners of them . . . they'll treat the customers right. And if customers are treated right, they'll come back."

Marriott realizes the value of their employees and was recognized in 2009 by several groups.

The awards listed in the table can be found on the Marriott website. By encouraging employees to aspire to advanced positions and providing positive work environments, Google and Marriott are just two companies that realize the value of motivation. If employees possess internal motivation paired with the external factors provided by the company, a perfect union has been created.

Envisioning Success

Visualization is a strategy that involves creating a clear picture of something in your mind. Seeing this image in your head can help you make it a reality. For example, instead of thinking about situations where you have failed, as many of us tend to do, picture yourself experiencing success. How does it look? What does it feel like? Your ideal life plan and goals can help you create the image. You can visualize small accomplishments like passing a test, or significant feats like receiving a huge promotion.

visualization: A strategy that involves creating a clear picture of something in your mind.

Visualization can help you address an area you want to improve. For example, if you fear public speaking, you might imagine yourself giving an amazing speech in a room filled with supportive people. If your brain is filled with positive images, it will be more likely to support the actualization of those images.

Margaret is a student with a strong academic record but a fear of interviews. As she got close to graduation, she got an interview for a job she really wanted, but she got so nervous about messing up the interview that she actually considered not going. Fortunately, Margaret remembered what she learned about visualization and took a few moments to relax and picture herself answering questions in the interview calmly and confidently. The more time she spent visualizing the interview, the clearer her picture got, and the less the interview seemed like a scary, unknown situation. The more she visualized success, the

Magazine	Award
Working Mother	*Working Mother* 100 Best Companies
BusinessWeek	Best Places to Launch a Career
LatinaStyle	50 Best Companies for Latinas to Work for in the U.S.
Black Enterprise	40 Best Companies for Diversity

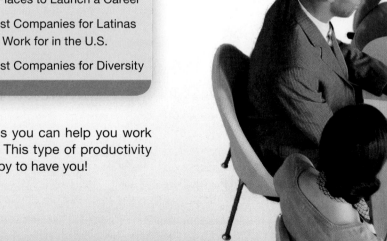

Identifying what motivates you can help you work harder and more efficiently. This type of productivity will make any employer happy to have you!

more her motivation to go to the interview and make a good impression grew. For Margaret, visualization was a big STEP in the right direction—she aced the interview and got the job!

Positive Self-Talk

Just as picturing yourself succeeding can help you succeed, using positive self-talk can be another effective success strategy. Imagine you have a big exam tomorrow in your hardest class. You may be tempted to think negative thoughts, like, "What if I fail this test?" or "What if my alarm doesn't go off and I miss class?" Unfortunately, the more you fill your head with negativity, the more likely you are to focus on the worst, and the less likely you are to do your best.

Positive self-talk retrains your brain by replacing the negative thoughts with positive ones. For instance, you might say to yourself, "I will pass this exam because I studied and prepared for it," or " I will take my time, stay calm, and make sure I complete all sections of the test," or "I will arrive early for the exam and give myself enough time to review my notes." Saying things like this to yourself not only helps you focus on the positive, but it can help you relax and keep your cool. Being calm, relaxed, and positive is always a better state of mind for taking a test than being nervous and negative.

Consider Anise's story. Her mother constantly discourages her. She did not support Anise's decision to go to college and often tells her, "You know, I don't know why you bother with school. You'll never graduate." Anise is truly committed to her future, but the more she hears this negative talk, the more she doubts herself and begins to worry that maybe she won't finish. But Anise is motivated and pulls out her positive self-talk shield to deflect all that negativity. She tells herself, "I will graduate. I can and will do this despite what anyone says. I know I am a good person and deserve personal success." By hearing positive words, Anise can help with her own motivation.

Figure 12
STEPS can help you prepare for many stressful events.

The positive self-talk technique can completely change your outlook, rebuilding your confidence in yourself. Your words are your commitment to your future.

Sharing Your Goals with Others

You are working hard to reach an amazing future. Don't keep the good news to yourself. Share your plans with others. Supportive family and friends will encourage you during the challenging times and will cheer you on during the victories. Connect with classmates with similar goals and discuss your future dreams.

Friends can be wonderful external motivators. When you are feeling down or overwhelmed, go to people who believe in you, the people who know of your future plans. Just the act of sharing can help you regain your focus.

You can also share your dreams with your instructors or advisors. As educators, they understand how challenging school can be, but also know how

Figure 13
Sharing your goals puts you in touch with people who can help or cheer you on.

worthwhile your efforts will be. Surrounding yourself with people who believe in you can be extremely motivating. Remember, negative people can drain your motivation as well, so try to steer clear of these types of individuals.

Motivation and commitment are your tools, but you must use them regularly to improve your skill level with them. Finding out what your motivators are can be instrumental as you battle obstacles that appear on your path to success. By

TAKE ACTION

The STEPS System

In this activity, identify an area of academic weakness that could prevent you from achieving your educational goals.

For example: procrastinating on assignments, partying and hanging out with friends instead of studying, wasting time, not studying for exams, not completing homework, not asking questions when confused, etc.

My academic weakness is: _____, which I will improve by implementing the STEPS system.

Use the table and instructions below to list ways that you will use the STEPS system to remain motivated and committed in order to overcome your academic weakness.

Self-Discipline	Taking Responsibility	Envisioning Success	Positive Self-Talk	Sharing Goals
How will I stay on track? **List 3** ways you will improve your self-discipline to overcome the personal weakness.	*I am responsible for . . .* **List 3** things that will help you to take personal responsibility over your weakness.	*How do I see myself in the future?* **List 3** different ways you can see yourself in the future if you overcome your weakness.	*What do I need to say to myself to stay positive?* **List 3** different motivating affirmations to improve your self-esteem and keep you on track.	*Who do I tell about my goals and dreams?* **Identify 3** people who you will share your goals with in order to motivate you to overcome your weakness.

Self-discipline

_____

_____

Taking responsibility

_____

_____

Envisioning success

_____

_____

using the STEPS technique as support for your motivation and commitment, you truly will be able to overcome many types of challenges.

Once you verbalize your dreams, you have made a stronger commitment to make them become a reality. Your commitment and motivation are two critical tools that can be used to achieve your goals. Now, pick up your weapons—and go conquer your future!

Try this online at mcgrawhillconnect.com

Positive self-talk

_____

_____

Sharing goals

_____

_____

From the STEPS table you completed above, choose two STEPS that you feel will be the most crucial to your academic success:

1. _____

2. _____

Why do you feel that these are the two most important STEPS for you in overcoming your academic weakness?

_____

_____

_____

_____

How will implementing the STEPS system in your life contribute to your academic and professional success?

_____

_____

_____

_____

Consider how you can use the STEPS system to help you reach your short-term and mid-term goals. Do you now have a better understanding that strong motivation and commitment are essential ingredients for achieving success?

This module focuses on the importance of connecting past experiences and current circumstances to create an ideal life plan. Considering what you have learned from your past and the positives and negatives of your current situation are the first steps in determining your future. Once you know who you are and what you would like to become, you can answer the who, what, where, when, why, and how questions for your ideal life plan.

We discussed the need for long-, mid-, and short-term goals with the SMART method of goal setting. The SMART method ensures that goals are specific, measurable, attainable, results-driven, and time-focused. Goals written using this strategy are clear and easy to follow. With the completion of a goal, new goals can be created. Goals can also be adjusted based on life changes. Having goals that take varying lengths of time to complete encourages you to stay focused on your ideal life plan. Long-term goals require long-term dedication, while short-term goals help you achieve small wins on a regular basis.

We also discussed the need for commitment and explained two types of motivation. Internal motivators come from inside you, while external motivators are triggered by outside sources. Both commitment and motivation are useful when obstacles stand in the way of your success.

The STEPS system can be used at any time to help reinforce your motivation and commitment. Self-discipline, taking responsibility, envisioning success, positive self-talk, and sharing your dreams are all ways to move closer to your ideal life plan.

DISCUSSION QUESTIONS

Consider this statistic: According to the Bureau of Labor and Statistics of the U.S. Department of Labor, "the average person born in the later years of the baby boom held 10.8 jobs from age 18 to age 42."

1. How can creating an ideal life plan and setting goals help a person decrease the number of jobs held in a lifetime?

2. How can having a high number of jobs help in creating an ideal life plan?

KEY TERMS

commitment: A willingness to work hard and do whatever it takes to accomplish a specific task. (p. 20)

external motivators: Motivators that come from outside sources. This motivation can come in the form of people or things. (p. 21)

ideal life plan: A written statement that describes your perfect future. It states clearly what you want for your life. (p. 3)

internal motivors: Motivators you have within yourself. They are often driven by feelings and personal beliefs. (p. 20)

long-term goals: Goals that generally take a year or more to accomplish. (p. 11)

mid-term goals: Goals that can take from six months to a year to complete. (p. 12)

motivation: A driving force that leads you to take action. (p. 20)

short-term goals: Goals that take less than six months to complete. (p. 12)

SMART method: A goal-setting formula that ensures each goal you set is specific, measurable, attainable, results-driven, and time-focused. (p. 13)

STEPS system: A system to overcome obstacles that includes five different steps: *self-discipline, taking responsibility, envisioning success, positive self-talk, and sharing goals.* (p. 23)

visualization: A strategy that involves creating a clear picture of something in your mind. (p. 25)

REFERENCES AND CREDITS

Websites

http://articles.moneycentral.msn.com/Banking/CreditCardSmarts/What-the-new-credit-card-law-means-for-you.aspx

www.creditcardfinder.com.au/credit-card-calculator

www.marriott.com/corporateinfo/culture/coreValuesCulture.mi

Figure and Photo Credits

Chapter opening photo: © Stockbyte/Getty Images

Figure 3: Robert Nicholas/OJO Images/Getty Images

Figure 4: © Stockbyte/Getty Images

Figure 5: John Lund/Drew Kelly/Blend Images LLC

Figure 6: Corbis/PictureQuest

Figure 7: © Ingram Publishing/Alamy

Money Smarts: ©Sam Toren/Alamy

Figure 9: George Doyle/Getty Images

Figure 10: Eric Audras/Photoalto/PictureQuest

Goals on the Job: ©Siri Stafford, Gettyimages

Figure 12: Nich White and Fiona Jackson-Downes/Cultura/Getty Images

Figure 13: © Punchstock/Digital Vision

Building Positive
Relationships

LEARNING OUTCOMES

In this module, you will:

1 Examine the role self-awareness plays in relationships.

2 Learn strategies to develop and strengthen your self-esteem.

3 Identify the role and impact of your values in your day-to-day life.

4 Learn about being a part of a community, and finding your place in one.

5 Understand how to start and strengthen different types of relationships.

6 Examine different types of relationships, including formal, informal, and electronic.

7 Learn the value of a team concept, and how teams work.

8 Discover strategies for establishing positive relationships within a team.

If a person who just met you 15 minutes ago had to use three words to describe you, what would they be?

- What three words do you think your closest friend would use?

Each of us by nature is unique. There has never been nor will there ever be anyone exactly like you. You express yourself and your uniqueness in a variety of ways. You reveal your thoughts and emotions to others through verbal and nonverbal communication, and you behave in ways that reflect your personal beliefs, values, needs, goals, hopes, and dreams. As you express who you are and who you want to be, you connect with and create relationships with others who are doing the same. The effectiveness of those relationships has an impact on your personal, academic, and professional lives.

In this module, you will first look at your relationship with yourself, and examine the roles of self-esteem, personal values, needs, and levels of motivation relative to your college experience. We will then explore the development of personal, academic, and professional connections, as well as the skills that foster interpersonal communication and productive team membership.

I. Start with Yourself

> "Know thyself."
>
> —ORACLE OF APOLLO AT DELPHI (9TH CENTURY BC)

The discovery of self can be one of the most valuable ventures you ever undertake. This process of self-awareness begins with the image you hold of who you are and how you identify yourself. In this section, we'll look at the concept of self-esteem and the perceptions you have of yourself, which includes your personal thoughts, feelings, and behaviors and their impact on building positive relationships. We'll also look at values, and how they affect your relationships and your choices as a student and beyond. First, though, we need to ask a more basic question: How is your relationship with yourself?

LO 1 What Is a Relationship with Yourself?

Who are you? Are you the person that others see when they meet you, the person who tries to make a good first impression? Are you the person your close friends and family know, the person you are when you're with someone you know well and have known for a long time? Are you the person you see when you look in the mirror, the person who every day makes the small and the big decisions that impact your life?

The short answer to all of those questions: yes. You are all of those people, and more. Of course, who you are depends on many things—the situation you are in, who you are interacting with, what kind of day you're having. Some days, when things are going great, you are your best self. You feel confident, happy, generous, and strong. Other days, when things aren't going so great, you feel

frustrated, cranky, filled with self-doubt, and unhappy to see your worst self show its face. Sometimes you experience both highs and lows in the same day.

No matter the circumstances, who you are interacting with, or how you are feeling or behaving, you are still you. Having a relationship with yourself means understanding and accepting that you have all of these different sides to you, getting to know yourself so that you understand what brings out your best and worst selves, and working to be the self you want to be as much as you can.

Getting to Know Yourself

In the sections that follow, we'll take a look at how you develop relationships with others, and things you can do to make those relationships work. Establishing a positive relationship with yourself can sometimes be more challenging than establishing positive relationships with others, because you are so close to your relationship with yourself that it can be hard to have perspective on it and see yourself clearly.

That's why getting to know yourself requires taking a mental step back to think about who you are in all of these different situations, and think about why you think, feel, and behave the way you do. For example, think about the last great day you had, a day that you felt really positive and happy. What made you feel that way? Was it a great conversation with a close friend? A fun trip to the beach or to the movies? A tough workout that made you feel strong? On that great day, how did your interactions with others go? What about your last terrible day? What made you feel that way? How did your interactions with others go on that day?

Asking these kinds of questions, and taking time to think about the answers, can help you learn more about what works for you and what doesn't. When you know yourself well, you can work to create situations that will lead to more great days, and avoid things that will lead to bad days. Of course, there will always be things beyond your control. But the better you know yourself, the stronger your relationship with yourself will be, and the more control you will have over your happiness and success.

LO 2 The Power of Self-Esteem

The concept of **self-esteem** has received a lot of attention in the field of psychology and in the media in recent years. It has been defined in many ways, though for our purposes, let's consider self-esteem as the feelings and thoughts you have about yourself. If you think highly of yourself, you have positive self-esteem. If you think poorly of yourself, or have negative feelings about yourself, you have low or negative self-esteem.

self-esteem: *The feelings and thoughts you have about yourself.*

Your self-esteem is partially shaped by what others have told you about who you are. People who played significant roles in your childhood can often have the most influence on your self-esteem. Your family, teachers, classmates, and friends provided information to you and about you that influenced the different perceptions and feelings that affect how you see yourself today.

How others see you does influence how you see yourself, but ultimately, self-esteem is something you are responsible for. If you were told as a child that you weren't good enough, but you know as an adult that you are, your own positive self-esteem will have more impact on your success than anything others may have told you. At the same time, if you are always doubting your abilities, compliments and praise from others may have no impact on your self-esteem at all.

What's important to remember is that self-esteem is not permanent—it is a perception you have of yourself, your worth, and your capabilities that develops

Figure 2
Self-esteem is built when you're young, but continues to develop and change throughout your life.

and changes throughout your life. Things that you may have "learned" about yourself in childhood can be unlearned and modified.

Strategies to Developing Positive Self-Esteem

Understanding that change is possible can help you shift negative self-esteem into positive self-esteem. You have the potential and capacity to change and improve your life. This is not to say that making such a change is easy—after all, some of your thoughts and feelings about yourself may have been around for many years. However, with effort and patience, this is a change anyone can make.

Let's take a look at a few ways you can develop positive self-esteem:

☐ *Choose your focus.* What do you do when you get a disappointing grade on a paper or test? If you focus on the low grade, it's easy to beat yourself up for not doing better, feel sorry for yourself, and bring down your self-esteem. If you focus on figuring out what you can learn from the disappointment, such as how you might have prepared better, or what you need to learn more effectively, you're showing yourself that you believe you're capable of more, and you boost your self-esteem. The grade may still be low, but your focus is on the opportunity that it reveals, not on the disappointment.

☐ *Take responsibility.* When we blame others for our problems and situations, we also shift the responsibility for change to others. By being honest about your role in both your successes and struggles, you take responsibility and increase personal control over your life.

☐ *Identify strengths.* Most of us spend a lot of time worrying over weaknesses or how we might have done better. Instead, ask yourself questions that focus on the positive, such as, "What personal traits am I most proud of?", "In what areas have I improved through the years?", and "How have I contributed to my own happiness and that of others?" Identify the gifts you bring to your relationships, your workplace, and the classroom.

☐ *Give yourself credit.* Focus on what you have accomplished, rather than what you have not. What have been your greatest accomplishments and achievements so far in life? How do you view your accomplishment of starting your college career? By recognizing your own achievements and accomplishments, you give yourself a realistic picture based on what you see in yourself, and not on what others might have told you.

☐ *Forgive yourself.* Reflect on your past behaviors, acknowledge those ways that you might have hurt yourself or others, and make the decision not to repeat those behaviors. Then forgive yourself and let it go. This letting go is a way of being kind and compassionate to yourself, freeing you to be more at peace with who you are.

☐ *Be humble.* Being humble means acknowledging your shortcomings, yet not in a way that is demeaning or negative. It is an ongoing process of recognizing that you have more to learn and allowing yourself to respect what you have accomplished so far in your life.

☐ *Be grateful.* Too often, we fail to appreciate what we have and what others have given us. Think about what you are grateful for in your life. Many people keep a gratitude journal, to help them focus on what they have, rather than what they don't, which is often where many of us focus our mental energy. When something you are grateful for involves others, consider taking the next step and thanking them to show you are grateful for their role in your life or something they have done. This kind of appreciation fosters humility and a positive attitude.

☐ *Utilize positive imagery.* Use your imagination and picture yourself being successful. In this picture, how do you look? What are you doing? What impact are you having on others? Picture yourself one year from now, five years from now, and ten years from now. How does your self-image grow and change in that time?

Remember that the development of positive self-esteem is not an immediate process. Rather, it takes time and continual effort. In other words, it is a step-by-step process that requires loving yourself and believing in your capacity to change and accept yourself more fully. While this growth process can be challenging and even frustrating at times, it is necessary for realizing your full potential.

LO 3 Values

As you interact with others, and make choices and decisions every day, those interactions and choices are rooted in an internal framework, which, like self-esteem, is something that you learn from the moment of birth, and that grows and evolves throughout your life.

This framework is made up of your **values**. Values guide what is acceptable behavior and what is unacceptable. We learn values from family, friends, community, society, culture, and religion. Many of the choices you make each day are based on your personal values and the strongly held principles that underlie your beliefs.

values: Personal or organizational beliefs that guide what is acceptable behavior and what is unacceptable.

Figure 3 Your values are what guide your decisions.

How Your Values Impact Relationships

Your values have an impact on every relationship that you have. For example, let's say that one of your values is respecting your elders. This could be a value that was emphasized in your religious upbringing or your culture, and that was reinforced by your parents, who insisted that you treat adults with respect, even if you disagreed with something they were doing.

If this is one of the values that is part of your internal framework, how might it impact your relationships? It is likely to affect how you interact with your instructors and any future bosses that might be older than you. It also might mean that you would expect to be treated with respect by younger co-workers because of your age and experience.

However, consider the opposite—if you were not taught this value growing up. What alternate values might you have learned that would impact your relationship with people older than you? How might those values affect those relationships?

Personal Values

The personal values we believe in are often abstract concepts, like goodness, kindness, respect, and honesty. Your beliefs about specific situations are usually rooted in your general values. For example, if you place a high value on all people's right to live, you may believe that the death penalty should be outlawed.

The more clearly you can identify and be aware of your values, the more successful and effective you will be in communicating who you are both personally and professionally. To help you better understand some of the most important personal values that guide your behavior, complete the Personal Values Inventory in the activity titled "Your Self-Esteem and Personal Values." It provides a list of personal values that can help you identify some of the things that are most important to you.

Organizational Values

Just like people have values, organizations—colleges, companies, sports teams, campus clubs—have values too. Sometimes these values are stated in a mission statement or a values statement, but the best way to understand an organization's values is to look at its choices and behavior. You can learn a lot about an organization's values by noticing how it treats its people and goes about its daily activities.

Figure 4
Organizations have values too, and you can find out what they are by asking questions and observing.

Your Self-Esteem and Personal Values

In this two-part activity, you will reflect on your own level of self-esteem and personal values.

PART I

As you work to develop more positive self-esteem, it helps to know the current state of your self-esteem. A first step is to become aware of some of the qualities, traits, and characteristics you see yourself possessing that impact how you think, feel, and behave. This Self-Appraisal Inventory provides a list of adjectives that may describe those characteristics.

Self-Appraisal Inventory

Instructions: Circle the five words below that most reflect who you feel you are in most situations.

Sensitive	Good-Natured	Shy
Compulsive	Ambitious	Cautious
Mature	Generous	Pessimistic
Angry	Relaxed	Friendly
Humorous	Obsessive	Honest
Sociable	Faithful	Talented
Warm	Compassionate	Depressed
Optimistic	Boring	Religious
Orderly	Jealous	Loyal
Spiritual	Considerate	Loving
Boring	Comforting	Organized

After choosing the five characteristics that you feel most describe you, share them with a classmate by saying, "I am . . ." before completing the phrase with each word you circled.

Questions for Discussion:

- How did it feel to say to your classmate that you were those five things?

- How do you feel about the five words you circled?

- Were there any words you circled that you were proud of? Which ones?

- Were there any words you circled that were accurate, but that you wish you hadn't circled? Which ones?

- Were there any words you did not circle that you wish you could circle honestly? Which ones?

- As you work to develop more positive self-esteem, what can you do to feel better about the words you wish you hadn't circled? What can you to do develop or emphasize more of the traits you wish you had circled?

PART II

Personal Values Inventory

Review the following list of personal values and check the 10 values that are most important to you.

Loyalty	Adequate sleep	Kindness
Open communication	Healthy family relationships	Consistency
Self-knowledge	Intimacy	Sense of humor
Reliability	Honesty	Fairness
Exercise	Trustworthiness	Alone time
Self-discipline	Pursuit of college education	Respect
Positive attitude	Relaxation	Patience
Religious/spiritual values	Intelligence	Achievement
Financial stability	Compassion	Competition
Perseverance	Integrity	Success
Good nutrition	Love	Efficiency

Of the 10 values you have chosen, write the top 5 in rank order in the spaces below.

1. _____

2. _____

3. _____

4. _____

5. _____

What impact do these top 5 values have on your personal, academic, and professional choices and behavior? Write your answers below, and then share them with at least one other classmate.

Personal: _____

_____

_____

Academic: _____

_____

_____

Professional: _____

_____

_____

By identifying and clarifying your own personal values, you will be better able to examine organizational or corporate values. This can help you make decisions about whether you want to be involved with a certain campus organization, or whether to accept a job or position with a certain company. Remember, values guide behavior. Just as your values influence how you treat others and how you would like to be treated, an organization's values work the same way.

Some organizational values that are important to consider when making an employment decision are:

☐ *Ethics.* Ethics are the most basic values to any organization. They are the guiding principles that direct decisions and the impact of those decisions on employees and the welfare of the organization. Ethics deal with issues like fairness, privacy, safety, diversity, and general codes of behavior.

☐ *Honesty and Integrity.* Does the organization promote a sense of trustworthiness? Is the organization sincere and honest in its relationship and communication with its employees? Integrity, in its simplest form, is doing what you say you will do—practicing what you preach. Organizational integrity is the company's ability to live up to its stated mission and principles, and to take responsibility for its actions regardless of the outcome.

☐ *Respect.* Respect has significant impact on the morale of employees. It forms the cornerstone of relationships between management and staff, and among co-workers. It is the key to team building and positive organizational outcomes.

Figure 5
Excellent social connections can greatly improve your life and career.

☐ *Fairness.* Is the organization fair and equitable in its decisions? Are all employees, regardless of their position, treated consistently? One type of fairness relates to salary. Does the job you are considering pay enough to match the level of work required and expected of you? Is the compensation competitive with other organizations for the same or similar position?

☐ *Diversity.* Is the organization committed to diversity? Does it understand the value of the balance between similarities and differences among people? An organization that embraces diversity and is open to understanding its complexities and challenges is an organization that understands the value of you as an employee based on the skills, talents, and energies you bring to the position, no matter your cultural or ethnic background.

The ethics, honesty and integrity, respect, fairness, and appreciation for diversity of any company you choose to work for are all organizational values that will impact your professional experience. You may notice that these organizational values reflect some of your own personal values. Understand that when your values and the organization's values align, the potential for your professional success and personal satisfaction is significantly greater.

Which values do you believe are important for an organization or place of employment to uphold and practice?

II. Investing in Connections—Personal, Academic, and Professional

GET READY

There's an old saying: "It's not what you know, it's who you know that matters.

- Share an example of this that you've seen from your life, the news, or a fictional story.

> *"Communication leads to community, that is, to understanding, intimacy, and mutual valuing."*
>
> **—ROLLO MAY (1909–1994),**
> *American existential psychotherapist*

Have you ever heard the saying, "It's not what you know, it's who you know"? People often take this as a negative statement, as though it means you have to know the "right" people to succeed, no matter how smart or talented you are. But another way of seeing it is that, while what you know is definitely important, particularly in an academic or professional setting, the quality of your life is significantly impacted by the quality of your relationships with others.

In other words, what you know can only take you so far. Who you know can open doors to opportunities, friendships, mentoring, wisdom, and support.

That's why this section focuses on investing in connections—putting time and energy into building positive relationships in your personal, academic, and professional lives, so that you too can reap the benefits of "who you know."

LO 4 Connections and Community

As a student, you are part of a college **community**. A community is a group of people with something in common. Most of us are part of many communities, such as the local community of citizens in our neighborhood or perhaps a faith-based community associated with a house of worship.

> **community:** *A group of people with something in common, such as the local community of citizens in a neighborhood or a faith-based community associated with a house of worship.*

Being a part of a community makes it easier to connect to other people. Even though many people at your college may be strangers to you right now, you have something in common with them all—you're part of the same college community. This means you have a built-in reason to reach out to and connect with them.

Being Part of a Community

Of course, you can't only look at your community to see what you can get from it. If everyone just looked out for themselves and what they could gain from the community, nobody in the community would benefit. A community works when people find ways to contribute and to benefit—when they give as much and as often as they get.

MONEY SMART$

Understanding and Maximizing Your Credit Rating

Along with their academic responsibilities, most college students face the additional challenges of financing their education, learning to be responsible for expenses, and managing their personal credit. Do these responsibilities apply to you? How well you manage those responsibilities can impact your ability to become financially secure for years to come—well beyond graduation from college. One big reason is because developing and maintaining a good personal credit rating can and will impact your life in so many ways. Good credit can determine your ability to rent or buy a house, buy a car, get a credit card, and borrow money for any other need that may arise.

Credit bureaus are agencies that analyze your past loans and track whether you repaid them promptly. They evaluate your creditworthiness by providing a *credit rating* that predicts whether you are a high- or low-risk borrower, meaning whether

there is a good or bad chance you will repay the loan you are requesting.

Your credit rating is primarily determined by these factors:

- *Payment history*—how often you pay your debts or loans on time.
- *Outstanding debts or balances*—the amount you currently owe. The less you owe, the higher your credit score.
- *Frequency of use*—how often you use available credit.
- *Income level*—the amount of income you earn monthly or yearly.

Your age, job, time at present employment, whether you own or rent your home, time at present address, years you've maintained positive credit, times your credit history has been requested by you or credit institutions, and whether or not you have been involved in bankruptcy decisions or mortgage

You might feel that, as a new member of your college community, you don't have very much to give right now. But you can give your positive energy, your interest in others, your caring, and your time. Every community needs those things, from its newest members as well as from its most experienced ones.

As you spend more time in your community, you will get to know more people and make more and stronger connections. You will eventually become a resource for new people in the community, whether that means pointing a lost student in the right direction, helping a new student find a club that fits her interests, or connecting two people with something in common. You will also learn the many different roles that are played in your community, and how the people who fill all of those roles contribute to the community's success. What roles can you think of in your college community?

Your Place in the Community

Many people find that being a part of a college community gives them a chance not only to learn new things and prepare themselves for the professional world, but also to find a place where they can fit in, be comfortable, and have the confidence to try new things. The more connections you make with others in the community, the more you will experience these positive benefits.

How can you best enjoy these benefits of community? Begin by making an investment in starting and strengthening relationships.

foreclosures or with collection agencies all impact your credit rating.

To improve your credit rating, follow these strategies:

- *Be cautious of credit-card offers.* Before applying for a card, ask: "Do I really need it? Will I be able to pay off the balance in full, or only make partial payments by the due date? What interest, annual, service, and late fees are involved?"

- *Pay off outstanding balances.* Each month, pay off any balances you owe. If you can't pay off credit card balances, you're spending more than you make. For long-term credit, such as car, home, or student loans, pay what is due each month consistently and on time.

- *Review your credit report and rating.* All credit bureaus are required by law to provide one free credit report per year. This can be ordered online at www.annualcreditreport.com. For a fee, you can obtain a copy of your credit rating by contacting one of the major credit bureaus regulated by the U.S. Federal Trade Commission.

- *Learn to budget.* Learning to budget is critical if you are to stay in control of your finances, achieve short-term educational and financial goals, and be successful in saving for longer-term needs.

LO 5 Starting and Strengthening Relationships

Developing positive relationships in college and in the professional world can be one of the most important steps you take to becoming successful. It can also be one of the most rewarding.

Strong relationships require understanding and adjusting to other people's styles and the way they communicate. Making an effort to get along with others is the most crucial element in developing a positive relationship.

Getting Started: Meeting New People

To have a relationship with somebody, you need a starting point: You need to meet them! Whether you meet somebody randomly (such as sitting next to them in class), are introduced to them by a friend, or go out of your way to introduce yourself, these suggestions will help you start your new relationships right:

- [ ] *Smile.* This is always a good place to start. A smile says, "I'm friendly, and I'm interested in meeting you."
- [ ] *Say your name, and say theirs.* It may seem obvious, but you'd be surprised how many people don't say their own name when meeting someone new. If you've ever walked away from a conversation saying to yourself, "What was her name again?", you can relate. A simple, "Hi, I'm _____" is all you need. And when someone tells you their name, repeat it back. "Hi, _____, it's nice to meet you." Saying names out loud helps you remember them in the future more effectively than just hearing them.
- [ ] *Maintain eye contact.* Make eye contact when introducing yourself. This shows a genuine interest in what the other person is saying. Without eye contact, you may seem disinterested or rude.
- [ ] *Be curious.* Get to know the other person. Ask questions that will help you get to know him a little bit better, and help you identify if you have common interests. If you are meeting a fellow student, striking up a conversation is easy: Ask what she's studying, what classes she's taking this term, or what she's involved with outside the classroom. Of course, be open and share a little about yourself when the other person asks questions of you.

Ways to Start New Relationships

As a college student, you will have many opportunities to start new relationships. Every time you go to class, you can sit down next to, and meet, somebody new. You can meet new people in the cafeteria, or sit down to study across from somebody new at the library.

While you are almost guaranteed to develop new relationships with people you meet randomly, don't leave it all up to chance. Below are a few ways to be intentional about starting new relationships as a college student:

- [ ] *Be involved.* Get involved in activities, school events, fundraising activities, or charitable causes. When you are involved, you know you have a common interest with others, which gives you a great starting point for a new relationship.
- [ ] *Join a club or team.* Being on a team builds unity, creates common goals, and adds a cooperative approach to your interactions. It also will expand your network of connections, as you get to know team members who each have their own networks that they can introduce you to.

☐ *Take risks.* Introduce yourself to leaders of your college community. Make appointments to meet with program directors, instructors, deans, and other staff members to learn more about their roles at the college. Prepare questions ahead of time, show interest, and be prompt for your appointments.

Keeping Relationships Strong

Once you start a relationship, it takes commitment and energy to develop and strengthen it. All relationships, including ones you have with family, friends, classmates, instructors, and co-workers, take ongoing effort in order to grow. Here are some points to consider that can help you keep your relationships strong:

☐ *Stay positive.* Every relationship has its rewards and its struggles. When you're struggling, remember that some struggle is unavoidable, and don't let it get you down. Focusing on the positive gives your relationship the best chance to succeed.

☐ *Be open.* Being open and receptive means not judging or evaluating every interaction in a relationship. It's okay to have opinions, but remember that they are just that—opinions—and that judging people's words and actions may keep you from understanding and appreciating what they're saying and doing.

☐ *Be empathic.* Empathy means being able to understand someone else from his point of view. Showing empathy helps the other person feel understood, which helps strengthen his self-esteem. As American psychologist Michael Kahn noted, "If [the other person] thinks it is worth the time and effort to try to understand my experience, I must be worth the time and effort."[1] Expressing empathy is a powerful way to strengthen relationships, but only when it is genuine and authentic.

☐ *Learn to forgive.* Forgiveness is an act of kindness that brings people closer together. It shows caring and compassion rather than anger or resentment. Forgiving someone else can heal wrongdoings and misunderstandings. Forgiveness also frees your relationship to grow, develop, and strengthen to its full potential.

LO 6 Types of Relationships

As we have discussed, building a positive relationship begins with you. How you think, feel, and behave—how you treat yourself and others—significantly impacts the kinds and quality of relationships you develop.

The way you express your beliefs, values, needs, and goals is often the clearest reflection of your thoughts, feelings, and behavior. The effectiveness of this communication also impacts the quality of your relationships. One of the factors that influences how you communicate in your relationships, whether face-to-face, on the phone, or in writing, is whether the relationship is informal, formal, or electronic.

Informal Relationships: Personal

Your relationships with family, partners, and close friends are informal relationships. In family relationships, you are bonded by common blood and shared experience, while in relationships with close friends, or in romantic relationships, you probably share similar values, opinions, or personality. In all of these relationships, what you have in common serves as the foundation for the relationship, and the relationship is maintained and strengthened through the building of trust, commitment, and respect.

Informal relationships are deeply personal, and we are emotionally invested in them. Most operate on a basic set of ground rules. The list in Table 1 identifies some of these, though your relationships may include others as well. These rules reflect and support our basic human needs of warmth and intimacy, which we may not get in our more formal or professional relationships.

Figure 7 You and your closest friends have an informal relationship.

Table 1 Ground Rules for Informal Relationships

- Show interest
- Be attentive
- Approach interactions with trust
- Listen without judgment
- Be sensitive
- Provide support
- Express encouragement
- Share thoughts and feelings openly
- Convey respect
- Display genuine caring
- Be considerate
- Be flexible in decision making
- Share mutually satisfying experiences
- Be invested in the relationship
- Acknowledge similarities and appreciate differences

Formal Relationships: Academic and Professional

Although there are differences between life at school and life at work, both environments encourage a formal approach to personal interactions. Today, more than ever, career-directed students are being required to understand the standards that influence formal relationships, both in college and professionally. Your chances of developing strong connections in these settings will dramatically increase if you follow the general guidelines presented in Table 2.

Electronic Relationships

Few technological developments changed the world as dramatically as the telephone. Yet more recently, mobile phones and the Internet have changed the world again. We don't think twice about using these communication tools, but these powerful devices have enabled a kind of communication that most people couldn't imagine just 25 years ago.

Table 2 Guidelines for Professional Behavior

- *Be respectful.* Respect means being polite and considerate to others. This includes listening carefully when others are speaking, and not interrupting. Slang can be considered a sign of informality and disrespect, and should generally be avoided in professional settings.

- *Be conservative.* In academic and professional settings, your behavior or demeanor should be conservative. For example, shouting, loud laughing, or small talk may be viewed as rude. Also, be careful when using humor. Things that may be fine to joke about or say with close friends may be taken the wrong way or considered rude by others.

- *Dress appropriately.* How you dress conveys a nonverbal message about you and your respect for others. As a college student, you may be surrounded by fellow students wearing sweatpants and T-shirts. But how would your instructors view you differently if you dressed more nicely? In work situations, find out what attire is acceptable and what is considered professional versus casual. Keep in mind that the definitions of formal and casual vary across cultures.

- *Be aware of status and role differences.* Differences in status and roles exist in every organization and environment. At times, the professional hierarchy may be subtle or difficult to identify, but it does exist. Being aware of someone's credentials, training, and experience and addressing him or her with the appropriate title is respectful.

- *Be sensitive to diversity.* At school and work, you will interact with people from different cultures, who have different backgrounds and different practices when it comes to relationships and communication. Pay attention to and respect these differences, but don't be afraid to talk with others about them to learn more about their culture. Developing your cultural knowledge will help you establish connections with new people and strengthen your relationships.

Figure 8 Workplace relationships are more formal, but they can still be friendly and warm.

In many ways, the tools of electronic communication have strengthened interpersonal and business relations. We can now connect with others more quickly, easily, and frequently than ever before. Yet the speed and ease of these communication tools have also led to many instances of poor or even harmful communication, particularly in academic and professional settings. This poor behavior often happens because people forget that the same guidelines that apply to personal and professional relationships apply whether you're communicating in person or electronically.

SOCIAL NETWORKING The popularity of social networks such as Facebook, Twitter, and LinkedIn has exploded in recent years, and many people now use these online tools to build their personal and professional networks, and for personal and professional communication.

Social networking offers many benefits. These tools make it easy to connect with friends and to make new ones. While you are in college, and as you move on into your career, it can be helpful to take advantage of some of the more professional social-networking tools, such as LinkedIn. These tools let you form and develop professional relationships, and these connections can help you find career mentors, ask for professional advice, and even find a job.

Many employers and recruiters now look at a LinkedIn profile the way they might have looked at a résumé in years past, so it's important to prepare your LinkedIn profile in a way that reflects how you want to be perceived professionally. More informal tools like Facebook and Twitter also allow you to make connections that can help professionally, whether by reconnecting with old friends, or introducing yourself to others in your field that you would like to get to know.

Figure 9 Social networks are open to everyone with access to an Internet connection.

While using social networks is easy and can be a lot of fun, keep in mind the dangers that go along with the benefits. Just as companies may look at a LinkedIn profile like they used to review a résumé, many also review Facebook profiles and Twitter accounts of prospective employees. There have been many cases of people not being hired, or creating problems at work, because of pictures or comments posted on a Facebook or Twitter account. Before posting something to your account, consider: Would you be comfortable if your boss or co-workers saw it?

MY SUCCESS STORY

As a college student, Claudia did well. She maintained good grades and excellent attendance, and when it came time to do an externship as part of her medical billing and coding program, she treated the experience as if it were a real job. Her college externship coordinator at the time was very pleased with the reports she got back from the medical office where Claudia was working. She was happy to share those reports with Claudia, and the two of them got to know each other well during the whole process.

Five years later, Claudia was looking for a change. She had a good job with decent pay, but she knew she could do more and could earn more if given the chance. During her five years of experience as a medical biller for a busy family practice, she had been asked to do many different tasks, especially when other staff members were on vacation, out sick, or on maternity leave. She knew she had the knowledge and skills to be the office manager. The problem was the office manager at her medical practice was very good and wasn't going anywhere anytime soon.

A few years after graduating, Claudia had "friended" her old externship coordinator on Facebook. Through the network's messaging system, she sent a quick note asking how the coordinator was doing and explaining that she had a great job but was bored and ready for more. The coordinator was happy to hear from Claudia, remembering her well from the time she spent on her externship. It happened that, because of the coordinator's knowledge of so many different medical practices in town, she was able to refer Claudia to two different offices that were seeking a new office manager. The coordinator remembered how well Claudia performed on her externship, and was happy to be able to help out her colleagues in private practice. Claudia interviewed with both and was offered a job at one of them!

Claudia moved forward in her career because of her consistently good efforts in all she does, the quality of her work, and her realization that the relationships she was developing while in college were perhaps some of the most valuable she'd ever make. To this day, Claudia stays in contact with many of the students, faculty, and administration from her school days. Their shared experiences have led to lifelong friendships that Claudia now cherishes.

Similarly, be careful who you connect with on these social networks. Before you agree to connect with someone, be sure that you know who they really are and ask yourself if you will be comfortable with this person having access to your personal information.

DISTINGUISHING BETWEEN THE PERSONAL AND PROFESSIONAL ONLINE
Knowing how to make connections using these electronic networks can help you succeed academically and professionally. Knowing a few guidelines for communicating effectively online can help you turn those connections into strong professional relationships.

When e-mailing, texting, or sending other online messages to friends and family, it's okay to be informal. But in academic and professional correspondence, whether communicating with an instructor or other member of your college community, or communicating in a professional environment with a co-worker, boss, vendor, or client, keep in mind the following guidelines for good professional communication:

- ☐ Be polite and respectful
- ☐ Avoid words that may be offensive in regard to race, gender, ethnicity, or sexual orientation
- ☐ Avoid slang, and use jargon or technical terminology sparingly, when you know the recipient will understand it
- ☐ Use proper grammar
- ☐ Be aware of business communication practices of other cultures
- ☐ Keep e-mail messages brief and to the point
- ☐ Address the recipient with a polite introduction ("Dear Professor Smith" instead of "Hey Prof")

Note that most of these guidelines are quite similar to the ones we discussed earlier regarding face-to-face communication. Though online relationships may feel different because you can't see the other person, the same rules of respect and consideration apply, and following them will help you keep your relationships strong.

TAKE ACTION

Think and Reflect

A. Reflect for a moment on some of the *informal relationships* you have in your life. In the space below, write some things that make them special. What makes them work? What steps have you taken to make them satisfying or enjoyable?

_____

_____

_____

Considering Table 1, "Ground Rules for Informal Relationships," found earlier in this module, list at least three things you will do in the future to enable your informal relationships to be even better.

1. _____

2. _____

3. _____

B. Reflect for a moment on some of the *formal relationships* you have in your life. In the space below, write some things that make them rewarding. What features of those relationships make them work? What steps have you taken to make them satisfying or enjoyable?

_____

_____

_____

Considering the information in Table 2, "Guidelines for Professional Behavior" found earlier in this module, list three things you will do in the future to enable your formal relationships to be more effective and rewarding.

III. Working in Teams

Imagine you have one week to write a 10-page report and prepare a 15-minute class presentation.

● Would you prefer to work alone, or share the workload with a group of fellow students? Why?

In its most basic definition, a *team* is a group of two or more individuals working together toward a shared *goal* or intended outcome. You have probably been part of many teams throughout your life, whether a sports team, school club, or project team at work. In just about any career you pursue, you will continue to be a part of teams of people working together to accomplish things that no one person could accomplish alone.

Try this online at mcgrawhillconnect.com

1. _____

2. _____

3. _____

C. Reflect for a moment on some of the purely *electronic relationships* you have in your life. In the space below, write some things that make them special (if applicable). What makes them work? What makes them different from your other relationships? What steps have you taken to make them satisfying or enjoyable?

_____

_____

_____

Considering the "Electronic Relationships" section found earlier in this module, can you list at least three things you will do in the future to improve these relationships?

1. _____

2. _____

3. _____

Share your responses with your group or classmates. As you probably found in this activity, your best ideas for improving your future relationships came from incidents that occurred in the past that you now understand could have been handled differently. In order to share more ideas on how you and others plan to improve your relationships, be very brief in describing those situations you've encountered in the past, instead focusing upon the specific actions you plan to take in the future, and how those actions will positively impact your relationships.

"Coming together is a beginning. Keeping together is progress. Working together is success."

—HENRY FORD (1863–1947),
founder of Ford Motor Company

LO 7 Understanding Team Dynamics

Earlier, we looked at keys to successful relationships with yourself and with others. As you might expect, the same things that are important in making those relationships work are also important in making team relationships work. However, because teams can include many sets of interconnected relationships, succeeding as a member of a team and helping your team be successful requires additional understanding and effort from all team members.

Figure 10 Sports teams make it easy to identify who is responsible for what actions.

Roles and Responsibilities

In sports, most people understand the different roles and responsibilities of everybody on the team. Each player has a different position that calls for different activities that contribute to what the team is doing as a whole. Coaches have clearly defined roles in which they teach important skills and develop the strategy for how the team will approach each competition.

In the working world, or in an academic setting, team member roles are usually not so clearly defined. This means that part of what it takes to make a team work is figuring out the different roles needed to help the team succeed, the responsibilities that go with each role, and who will fill each role and handle its responsibilities.

The roles and responsibilities of team members are determined by many factors, including the number of people on the team, the experience of the individual team members, the amount of time the team has worked together, the goals the team is working toward, and any time constraints the team may have. One of the most valuable things you can do as a team member is consider the roles your team needs and, whether you step up to take on a certain role or are assigned a role by a team leader, contribute your best effort and focus to performing your role to the best of your abilities.

Stages of Group Development

Just like relationships go through different stages, so do teams. In 1965, psychologist Bruce Tuckman developed a Group Development model to help people understand these stages and what to expect in each stage.[2]

The first stage of group development in the model is **forming**. In this stage, group members are getting to know each other, sharing background information, learning about the project they will be working on together, and determining roles and responsibilities.

forming: The first stage in Tuckman's Group Development model, in which group members are getting to know each other, sharing background information, learning about the project they will be working on together, and determining roles and responsibilities.

The second stage is known as **storming**. In this stage, the team begins to work together, bringing everyone's different styles and expectations to the task at hand. This stage is where conflict usually bubbles to the surface—which is why it's called the "storming" stage.

storming: *The second stage in Tuckman's Group Development model, in which the team begins to work together, bringing everyone's different styles and expectations to the task at hand.*

Next, in the **norming** stage, the team works through its conflicts and starts to establish team norms. Norms are basic agreements and expectations about how team members will behave and how the team will work together—they're what the team defines as its normal behavior.

norming: *The third stage in Tuckman's Group Development model, in which the team works through its conflicts and starts to establish team norms, or basic agreements and expectations about how team members will behave and how the team will work together.*

Once the team works through those early conflicts and starts to establish group norms, it's ready to do what it was brought together to do: perform. In the **performing** stage, teams work together effectively and efficiently toward their goal. Getting to the performing stage doesn't preclude more Storming or Norming, but it does mean the team has learned how to function as a team, even if it doesn't do it all the time.

performing: *The fourth stage in Tuckman's Group Development model, in which teams work together effectively and efficiently toward their goal.*

Think about teams you have been a part of in the past. Do you recognize your experience with those teams in the descriptions of the group development stages? Knowing about this model can help you, as a team member, have realistic expectations of yourself and the group based on what stage you are in. It can also help you know what is needed to help the group move forward toward its goal.

Figure 11
Featuring your team members' strengths will make your team more successful.

LO 8 Establishing Positive Relationships within a Team

No matter what stage your group is in, developing positive relationships among team members is crucial to the development and progress of the team as a whole.

Each team member brings their own experiences, knowledge, beliefs, values, and personality to the team. This means that the collective group has more potential strengths than any one member of the team. However, for the team to work effectively as a unit, all team members must appreciate that the experiences, knowledge, beliefs, values, and personality that their fellow team members bring may be different from their own—and that those differences make

the team stronger, not weaker. Think of a sports team: Each position on the team requires slightly different skills. If everybody on the team had the same skills, the team might excel in one aspect of the game, but would not be a very strong team on the whole.

Though all teams benefit from this diversity, differences often lead to tension and conflicts between team members. As you work to make your team stronger, be aware of potential conflicts that may arise and make an effort to connect with and develop trust with others. That way, when you do have a conflict, you can work through it from a foundation of trust.

Taking Initiative and Developing Trust

Learning to be an effective team player is important to your success as a student and a professional. These steps will help you take initiative to build trusting relationships and become a more effective team member.

1. *Get acquainted.* It's important to get to know your fellow team members. Take the initiative to share who you are, and to listen to learn who others are, what they bring to the team, and what is important to them. By listening considerately and treating other team members with respect and dignity, you can help create a positive environment for yourself and others on the team.

2. *Cooperate and collaborate.* If your team is cooperative and collaborative, rather than negative and judgmental, the team will be more successful. Each team member contributes to the team mind-set, which means you can't wait for others to be cooperative and collaborative. You need to take the initiative to do so and, through your actions, challenge others to do the same.

3. *Build trust.* Teams grow and develop when the members feel relaxed and comfortable sharing their honest thoughts and opinions. For this to be possible, each member must trust in the other team members. When trust is established, group members are more likely to take risks, be open to new ideas, and communicate more openly. Teams grow best when members feel free to ask questions, express ideas and opinions, and take initiative in generating new and creative ideas. To build trust, start by being open to other perspectives. Listen attentively, and don't criticize or judge. To help the team achieve its goals, commit to being supportive and positive and, most importantly, be respectful.

Becoming a Team Player

The keys to becoming an effective team player are communication and participation. Communication establishes a bond between team members, and participation invites group involvement in discussing issues and solving problems. In college and professionally, your development as a team member will depend on how well you learn to work well with others, develop trust, and approach each group interaction with respect.

Being a team player lets you experiment with different roles. If you tend to be quiet, consider finding opportunities to speak up. If you are comfortable speaking, but struggle to concentrate on what others have to say, think about how you can sharpen your listening skills. A solid team-based approach allows for creativity and open communication. These guidelines can help you become a responsible and effective team player:

1. *Understand your role.* A good team player knows when to lead and when to follow, when to speak up and when to keep quiet. In other words, your role may not be the same in every situation. So you need to pay attention to each situation and determine how you can best contribute to your team's

success in that situation. A good team player can guide others and help the team achieve its goals. Depending on the situation, you may need to help make decisions, step in to smooth over conflicts between team members, or help remind the team of the overall goal. How you handle your role as a team player may determine the success of the team.

Figure 12 With a team backing you up, it's easier to try a new role.

2. *Contribute to the team's energy.* Every team feeds off of positive energy and is drained by negative energy. You know what leads to negative energy—complaining, pointing fingers, making excuses, expecting the worst. You also know what leads to positive energy—encouraging each other, taking responsibility, looking on the bright side, seeing opportunities even in difficulty. Everyone on every team makes choices every day about what kind of energy to contribute. Good team players work to contribute positive energy, which can help others get motivated and work cooperatively. When your team has high energy, team members are more likely to give their best, which leads to team success.

3. *Be a role model.* Think about a time when you were the new person on a team. How did you know how to behave? Probably by watching others and taking your cues from them. In any team, people determine their behavior by observing the behavior of others on the team. This is especially true of new team members. So, by giving your best effort, and behaving in ways that will benefit the team, you send a clear signal to others that it's okay for them to give their best effort too. No matter your role on the team, you can be a role model and lead by example.

4. *Be flexible.* In most teams, things can change quickly from one day to the next. That's why your being flexible is essential to being a good team player. Be prepared for circumstances to change, sometimes without notice. Be open and receptive to others' suggestions and recommendations. Listen carefully to the opinions and viewpoints of others. When you do not know something, admit it. Earn the respect of the team by being flexible and receptive, and treating each member as an equal.

Managing Team Conflict

Even if everybody on your team is a good team player, your team will still experience **conflict**. People will have different opinions about a decision, people will want the team to invest more time or energy into one activity over another, there will be miscommunications and misunderstandings . . . the list of things that might cause conflict is endless. That may sound bad, but it's not. Conflict isn't a problem—it's a natural part of team dynamics. Problems arise when teams cannot manage conflict and let conflict distract them from working toward their goals or, even worse, tear them apart.

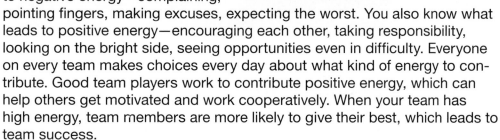

conflict: A disagreement or difference of opinion with another person.

STRATEGIES FOR MANAGING TEAM CONFLICT

The more you work in teams, the more likely you will experience conflict. What's important is that, when it comes up, you deal with it in a mature, professional

Relationships

ON THE JOB

Diversity in the Workplace

To be successful in the workplace involves learning to get along with others. It involves exploring both similarities and differences among co-workers, and opening ourselves to new possibilities of understanding and acceptance. In order to relate to the experiences of others, we must first begin by coming to an understanding of our own identity. When we become self-aware, we acquire a perspective that opens us to an appreciation to those values, customs, and beliefs that are different.

By identifying yourself, you are highlighting you own beliefs, ways of thinking, family history, and cultural heritage as they relate to your past, impact your present values, and guide your future interactions with others. With this awareness, you can foster a more positive intercultural exchange, social connection, and an accepting attitude toward diversity. Take a moment to consider the following questions and review your own background and sense of personal diversity.

- What ethnic group(s) do you consider yourself to be part of?
- As a child, what were you taught about other racial or ethnic groups?
- What religious traditions were practiced in your family? Which one(s) do you currently practice?
- What spiritual beliefs did your family hold when you were growing up?
- What spiritual beliefs do you hold now?
- What languages were spoken in your home as a child? Now as an adult?
- What cultural values were you taught regarding the roles of men and women?
- What beliefs do you and your family have about marriage, separation, and divorce?
- What do you know about your cultural heritage from before your family ancestors moved to another country?
- What were your family's expectations about the value and importance of education?

way that keeps the goals of the team in mind. Below are a few strategies that can help you manage team conflict before it escalates:

☐ *Stay calm.* Admittedly, this is often easier said than done. But that doesn't make it any less important. By remaining calm, you don't add to the conflict. Your body language, tone of voice, and the way you present your thoughts all indicate your reaction to the conflict. If you stay relaxed and calm, you show that you aren't overreacting to the conflict, and you will be more able to help defuse it.

☐ *Listen and let go.* In conflict, we often want to get our point across and be heard. This is understandable, but in the midst of conflict, it may be better to wait and listen. Focus on listening, and allow the other person to completely finish speaking before offering your thoughts. Let go of your need to be right, and concentrate on fully understanding what is being said. Too often in a conflict, we think about counterarguments, how to defend our position, and what we'll say when this other person finally lets us talk. If you step back, you can see this is no way to resolve a conflict—resolution requires both people to really listen to each other, so they can understand both sides of the story.

☐ *Speak directly.* When you have listened, and you fully understand the other person's point of view, you're ready to calmly respond. When you do, be clear, direct, and respectful. Avoid criticizing, accusing, or making any statements that carry the message that you are judging the other person's behavior.

- What were your family's primary beliefs about success? What made a person successful in the world?

Hopefully, these questions have helped you see your own experience from a new perspective. Now ask yourself: "How could I use these questions to cultivate a stronger working relationship with those who are different from me? How would hearing their answers allow for better interpersonal communication and facilitate a more respectful work environment?"

☐ *Be empathetic.* Try to understand the other person's experience and their point of view. Conflict often arises from how we interpret a given event. Everyone has a different way of perceiving and interpreting any situation based on our life experiences, personality, and ability to cope in times of stress or crisis. When expressed genuinely, empathy can lead to compassion, and a solution.

☐ *Ask respectful questions.* When in conflict, there is a tendency to ask the question "Why?", such as, "Why are you acting like this?" or "Why are you so upset?" These questions may be a genuine attempt to understand, but often, because of the timing of your question or the way you ask it, they may put the other person on the defensive, which can escalate the conflict. Before you ask a question, think about how it may be received. "Why are you acting like this?" can sound judgmental—just think how that question might sound to you in a conflict situation. Consider ways to ask the question more calmly and respectfully, with understanding as your goal. So, another way to ask that question might be, "Can you help me understand your side of the story?" If you show respect and work to understand what happened and where the other person is coming from, you increase the chance that he will show you the same respect.

☐ *Don't take it personally.* Many conflicts escalate when someone is hurt by another person's words or actions, and assumes that person hurt her or him

---

TAKE ACTION

Planning as a Team

Your class will break into small groups. Each group has an assignment: to develop a plan to host a panel discussion on a critical thinking topic (such as media stereotypes).

What team roles will be needed to execute the plan?

_____

_____

How will your team decide on the topic and the guests for the panel discussion?

_____

_____

As your team works on the plan, identify as many details as possible to ensure a successful event.

1. _____

2. _____

3. _____

4. _____

on purpose. Most people want to do the right thing and treat others well. If you take things personally, you're almost asking for a fight. But if you take a step back and realize that, while you may be hurt, this person wasn't trying to hurt you, you're one step closer to figuring out what the problem is and resolving it.

☐ *Apologize.* An apology can facilitate acceptance and forgiveness. If you do something that may be insensitive or may disrespect someone's values or beliefs, be mature about it and apologize. It takes humility to admit when our words or actions have been offensive, and courage to say, "I am sorry." In any situation, an apology goes a long way toward resolving conflict.

☐ *Negotiate.* A good team learns how to negotiate. Not everybody will get everything they want in every situation. Negotiating is about figuring out what is best for the team and finding a solution that everyone can agree to, even if everyone has to give a little in the process. Learning to negotiate is the key to cooperation, team building, and conflict management. It begins with the realization that your fellow team members are not rivals, but are partners who are just as committed as you are to reaching the same, common goal efficiently and harmoniously.

As a team member, it's important to stay focused on the team's goals and objectives. A strong and fully functional team is one where everyone feels like they're contributing to the team's success, and everyone feels like a winner.

5. _____

6. _____

7. _____

8. _____

9. _____

10. _____

Once you have developed your plan, your team will present and explain its plan to the rest of the class.

Questions for Discussion:

- What role did you end up playing on this team?

- How did you come to play this role? Were you comfortable with the way your role was defined?

- Was the role you played (or were assigned to play) a good fit for your skills and experience?

- What abilities do you usually contribute to a team?

SUMMARY

Building positive relationships requires that you learn and grow in your self-awareness, in your interpersonal relations, and as an active team player.

Personal change begins with self-awareness. You are a product of your genetics and past learning experiences as well as the dreams and aspirations that guide your future—but you are also capable of growth. Strengthening your self-esteem is crucial to becoming who you want to be.

On your journey of self-discovery, be open to what you discover and receptive to what you are learning. This attitude encourages personal growth and opens your world to the value and richness of cultural diversity. To appreciate others for who they are is one of the greatest gifts you can offer them.

The key to developing strong relationships is getting to know others and letting them know who you are. As relational beings, we seek to belong with others and connect with them informally and formally.

Becoming a team player is about connecting, taking initiative, and developing trust, all within the framework of the team. We do not live in isolation but rather through interdependent relationships, where we all need each other. When conflict arises, and it will, it is important that we work through the differences and focus on a positive connection so we can all continue to work together. Respect and togetherness are the keys to building positive relationships!

DISCUSSION QUESTIONS

1. When people think about relationships, they usually focus on relationships with others, either personal or professional. Why would it be important to also pay attention to your relationship with yourself? What can you gain from spending time thinking about your self-esteem and your personal values?

2. We reviewed a number of different kinds of relationships and different ways to connect with people. What do you think is the most important thing to building a positive relationship with someone in an academic setting? What about a professional setting?

3. Most of us have been a part of many teams in our lives, some that worked well together and some that couldn't seem to get anything accomplished. Thinking back through some of the teams you have been a part of through your life, what do you think were the things that most held back the unsuccessful teams? What ideas discussed in this module did you see that succeeded in the teams you were part of? Which of those ideas could have helped those unsuccessful teams? How?

In this module, you learned the importance of developing strong interpersonal relationships in your personal, academic, and professional life. In this exercise, you will use your critical thinking skills to evaluate the effects of the media on developing and strengthening relationships between individuals of diverse cultures, by completing the following activities:

1. State your position on the following question: "Does the media tend to support or discourage developing open relationships between people of different races, ethnicities, and cultures?"

   _____

2. How does the media tend to portray people of diverse cultures engaging in the following areas?

   Personal relationships:_____

   Family relationships:_____

   Violence:_____

   Marriage:_____

   Substance abuse:_____

   College life:_____

   Professional careers:_____

3. Identify various examples you have seen in the movies or on television, or read in newspapers and magazines, that support your positions above, and explain how.

   _____

   Movies:_____

   Television:_____

   _____

   Newspapers:_____

   _____

   Magazines:_____

   _____

4. Go online to find at least two authoritative sources (written by professional journalists or academic researchers) that address the media portrayal of relationships. Write the names of those sources here:

   _____

   _____

5. Review and summarize what you discovered from reviewing these sources.

   _____

   _____

   _____

6. Evaluate your original position and state whether it has remained the same or changed after reviewing this new information, and why.

   _____

   _____

   _____

community: A group of people with something in common, such as the local community of citizens in a neighborhood or a faith-based community associated with a house of worship. (p. 12)

conflict: A disagreement or difference of opinion with another person. (p. 25)

forming: The first stage in Tuckman's Group Development model, in which group members are getting to know each other, sharing background information, learning about the project they will be working on together, and determining roles and responsibilities. (p. 22)

norming: The third stage in Tuckman's Group Development model, in which the team works through its conflicts and starts to establish team norms, or basic agreements and expectations about how team members will behave and how the team will work together. (p. 23)

performing: The fourth stage in Tuckman's Group Development model, in which teams work together effectively and efficiently toward their goal. (p. 23)

self-esteem: The feelings and thoughts you have about yourself. (p. 4)

storming: The second stage in Tuckman's Group Development model, in which the team begins to work together, bringing everyone's different styles and expectations to the task at hand. (p. 23)

values: Personal or organizational beliefs that guide what is acceptable behavior and what is unacceptable. (p. 6)

REFERENCES AND CREDITS

Readings

Audlin, J. D. (2005). *Circle of life: Traditional teachings of Native American elders.* Santa Fe, NM: Clear Light Publishing.

Erikson, E. H. (1963). *Childhood and society.* New York: Norton.

Jay, T. J. (2003). *Psychology of language.* Upper Saddle River, NJ: Prentice Hall.

Kahn, M. (1997). *Between therapist and client.* New York: Freeman Publishing.

Footnotes

1. Kahn, M. (1997). *Between therapist and client.* New York: Freeman Publishing, page 46.

2. Abudi, Gina. (2010). "The Five Stages of Project Team Development," The Project Management Hut. May 8. www.pmhut.com/the-five-stages-of-project-team-development, accessed December 15, 2010.

Figure and Photo Credits

Chapter opening photo: Paul Burns/Blend Images/Getty Images

Figure 1: © Fancy Photography/Veer

Figure 2: Ingram Publishing/SuperStock

Figure 3: Ludovic Di Orio/Goodshoot

Figure 4: Lifesize/Getty Images

Figure 5: Ingram Publishing

Money Smarts: ©Sam Toren/Alamy

Figure 6: Radius Images/Alamy

Figure 7: © PhotoAlto

Figure 8: Ryan McVay/Getty Images

Figure 9: Hill Street Studios/Getty Images

My Success Story: ©John Lund/Sam Diephuis/Blend Images LLC

Figure 10: moodboard/SuperStock

Figure 11: Digital Vision/Getty Images

Figure 12: Image Source/Getty Images

Figure 13: Ingram Publishing

Relationships on the Job: ©Siri Stafford, Gettyimages

Learning Strategies

LEARNING OUTCOMES

In this module, you will:

1 Learn how pattern development and detection affects the way your brain learns.

2 Discover the four principles of learning, and how they can help you study more effectively.

3 Understand the different learning styles and how we can use those styles to become more effective students.

4 Discover the benefits and challenges of learning in group settings.

5 Identify your academic strengths and build upon them.

6 Acknowledge your academic limitations and keep them from holding you back.

7 Find ways to balance your strengths and weaknesses.

Think back on the classes you've taken in school. Was there a subject that was particularly hard for you to learn? One that you found easy?

● Can you identify one or two reasons why those classes were easy or hard?

The advice, "Know thyself," is especially applicable to college students. This is because knowing your own personal learning styles, your abilities and capabilities, and your academic strengths and limitations is absolutely necessary to ensure your success in college. This module is about getting to know yourself so that you can make the most of your college experience.

We will start by looking at how we learn, and come to understand how two key questions impact your time as a college student: "Why?" and "What's in it for me?"

We will also take a look at learning styles and help you determine your own. Understanding your learning style may help explain why you have difficulty learning from one instructor, while another seems to explain the material in just the right way. Learning about the different ways people learn new information will also help you understand why the course your friend said was "so easy" turned out to be such a personal struggle for you—and even why you and your friend have such different opinions about whether or not the radio should be on while you're studying!

The third section will focus on assessing your own academic strengths and limitations. The better you know your strengths, the better you will be able to make the most of them, and amplify your success in college and beyond.

I. How We Know What We Know

When John walked into his 40-year high school reunion, he immediately recognized his old friend Mickey across the gym. When he yelled out, "Mickey!", Mickey turned and recognized John too!

They hadn't seen each other in 40 years. Mickey had gained 40 pounds, and John's hair had left him decades ago. But John's brain instantly picked Mickey out of the crowd, and they recognized each other . . . from 50 feet away.

You've probably had a similar experience—seeing and recognizing someone you haven't seen for years, even if they look very different from the last time you saw them. How does this work? When John saw Mickey, he didn't have to think about it—his brain simply *knew* him, because he was in John's long-term memory.[1]

So how did John's brain make Mickey a part of his memory so effectively that despite 40 years of time and changes to his appearance, and 40 years of not seeing his friend, he could still recognize Mickey instantly? And more importantly for our purposes here, can *you* use that capacity for recall to help you learn the material you are studying in class?

LO 1 The Brain as a Pattern-Detecting Device

When we see something, our eyes don't recognize it. That's not their job—their job is to perceive light bouncing off objects. The perception of that light is then sent to the brain, which does the rest. But what does the brain do, exactly?

If you saw a picture of a coffeepot—even if it was one you'd never seen before—you would recognize it instantly. But you weren't *born* knowing what a coffee pot looks like. Your brain *learned* that sometime between your birth and now. *All* learning has taken place the same way.[2]

It Starts with an Image

When you were very young, you had no clear concept of what is meant by the word "city." You started with a blank slate.

Imagine you lived in a small town and visited San Francisco. You would probably be impressed by the traffic noise, tall buildings, and all the people. However, a trip to the shopping center in your little town, with crowded sidewalks and many shops, might also impress you.

To clarify your concept of *city,* imagine your parents read you a book about life in the city. Your brain records this reading as an "image." If you watch *Sesame Street*, your brain records another image. Your brain will hold on to these city images for a while, but over time, they will become fuzzier, and though they will never disappear from your memory completely, they will not be *learned*. As a result, if asked to explain a *city* a couple days after reading the book and watching *Sesame Street*, you probably will be able to explain very little.

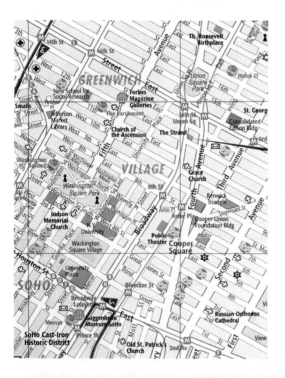

Figure 1 Any one of these images may be what you think of when you think "city," because they follow a pattern.

From an Image to a Pattern

Now add other city-related experiences. You notice the "City Limits" sign for the first time. You see a firehouse in San Francisco. You watch a show on skyscrapers. You visit a Chinese restaurant in San Francisco's Chinatown, and see that a city has smells, along with streetlights and a lot of noise.

All these images you associate with cities are recorded in your brain, which in time begins to see relationships among the images. When your brain realizes there were images of tall buildings in the book, just like on *Sesame Street*, it creates a physical connection, or pathway, between these images in your mind. When it remembers seeing a firehouse on *Sesame Street* and a firehouse in San Francisco, it creates another connection. Each time your brain sees another thing it associates with the idea of *city,* it makes another connection. These connections run into the trillions!

Over time, these connections form a **pattern.** The longer you live, the more connections your brain makes, and the more this pattern for *city* will sharpen and deepen. This pattern is now in your long-term memory and will be there for as long as you live.

pattern: *A physical connection, or pathway, between images in your mind that is built up over time.*

How Pattern Detecting Helps You Study

Your brain uses this same process when you study. Imagine that you're in a medical assistant program, taking a medical terminology class. When the course begins, you know nothing about medical terminology.

After a few classes, you begin to lay down images for each of the anatomical systems you have learned, but the images are just floating around your brain (figuratively, not literally), because your brain hasn't yet perceived any relationships among the images.

Over time, the brain *does* begin to lay down additional connections between these images as it discerns relationships. It begins to extract patterns for each of the systems you learn: digestive, nervous, respiratory, and so on. Just as the concept of a city sharpened in your brain over time as you added more information and developed more patterns, new patterns related to medical terminology also sharpen over time because of the connections your brain creates from these images.

Here's an example of pattern recognition. Can you read the following paragraph?

I cdnuolt blveiee taht I cluod aulaclty uesdnatnrd waht I was rdanieg.

Aoccdrnig to rscheearch at Cmabrigde Uinervtisy, it deosn't mttaer in waht oredr the ltteers in a wrod are, the olny iprmoatnt tihng is taht the frist and lsat ltteer be in the rghit pclae. The rset can be a taotl mses and you can sitll raed it wouthit a porbelm.

Tihs is bcuseae the huamn mnid deos not raed ervey lteter by istlef, but the wrod as a wlohe. Amzanig huh? Yaeh and I awlyas tghuhot slpeling was ipmorantt!

You can read it because your brain has extracted a pattern for every word you have learned, and now instantly recognizes that pattern—even if the letters in the word are out of order. Imagine how many patterns you must be carrying around in your head!

Your Attention, Please

Another critical element to understanding learning is understanding the role that attention plays in processing information.

Imagine you're downtown during the height of the holiday shopping season, trying to find a parking spot. You drive slowly, looking for people walking with

shopping bags, parking lights coming on, or open trunks. None of these is an empty parking space, but your brain knows they soon will be—it's created a pattern that associates them with parking spaces—so it pays close attention to them. In fact, you're so locked in on finding a parking space, there could be a juggler on the sidewalk or a monkey walking a three-legged dog, and you might not even notice. That's how focused your attention is on finding a parking spot.

What's happening here? The value you have placed on a parking spot has focused your attention on all of the cues that might lead to one, heightening your awareness and the amount of information related to a parking spot that your brain processes. You won't always be so attentive to parking-spot cues—if you drive through the same part of town six months later, on your way somewhere else, you might not notice the parking lights or people with bags at all . . . or even an open parking space because right then, they're not important to you. (But you might notice the monkey with the dog.)

THE "WHY?" AND "WHAT'S IN IT FOR ME?" QUESTIONS This principle is important because consciously or unconsciously, most students approach every course they take with two questions in mind: **Why** am I studying this material? and **What's in it for me?** The answers to these two questions play a significant part in how successfully you study and learn in every course you take.

Why?: A question to ask yourself to determine the purpose of pursuing an activity, such as studying certain material.

What's in it for me?: A question to ask yourself to determine what value you might gain from paying attention to certain information.

If you *don't* know why you're taking a course, or understand what you can gain from it, you can apply every study technique, but *nothing will get through.* It's not a matter of intelligence or difficulty of the material: if you don't see the material as important, you won't pay attention to it.

However, if you *do* know why you are taking a course, you also know what you're looking for when you study, and just like the shoppers carrying bags, that information will trigger your attention. That's how our brains work! There is simply too much information vying for our attention for us to process everything around us, so our brains are built to block out information that's not important.

Who decides what is important? You do! The goal you set raises your awareness to information that helps you meet that goal. This means that, to tune your brain in, the *goal* must come first.

This is why you must ask yourself the following questions for every course that you take, and every book that you read, and even every chapter in those books.

About a Course

1. Why am I taking this course?
2. How will this course help me in meeting my ultimate career goals?
3. How might I use the skills and knowledge that I gain from this course?

About a Book

1. How will this material help me to complete this course and my degree?
2. How should I approach each module of the book to most effectively study it?
3. How might I use the skills and knowledge that I gain from this book?

About a Section/Chapter in a Book

1. What part of the class does this section try to present?
2. How will this section contribute to an overall understanding of the content of the module?

Figure 3 Learning with a goal in mind can really help your focus.

LO 2 The Four Principles of Learning

Why does this information about learning matter to you? No matter your goals in life or as a student, the ability to learn new ideas, remember them, and make connections between them will help you achieve your goals. The better you understand how your brain learns, the better you can guide it to learn what is important to you—and the greater your advantage as a student. Let's take a closer look at four principles of how we learn.

Principle One: We All Learn Differently

Although all of us learn through this process, the way we learn is unique to each of us. There are two reasons: our disposition and our experience. Our disposition is what we were born with: our natural personality, temperament, preferences, and character. This is established by the time you are three to five years old.

Our experience—everything we've seen, done, and learned throughout our life, and are learning now—is layered on top of that and impacts how we learn. Learning new information is a continuous process, and we learn from our parents, friends, siblings, reading . . . from just about anyone and anything, if we're paying attention.

The combination of disposition and experience makes you who you are.

Principle Two: We Build On What We Already Know

New learning is heavily based upon past experience—on what we have already learned. What we know serves as the foundation for what we learn.[3]

Think about how a house is built: Construction begins with a foundation, then a framework. Walls, wiring, plumbing, wallpaper, and paint are all built into or onto that framework. When construction is complete, furniture can then go into each room.

Learning new course material is similar. When you begin, you have no foundation or framework. Throughout the class, you are given materials you need to build your knowledge—the mental equivalents of wood, concrete, and nails. These "cerebral building supplies" include the your professor's lectures and demonstrations, and materials from your books and papers.

Over time your brain begins to see how these new materials that you're working with fit together. Metaphorically speaking, wood gets nailed together to form walls, plasterboard goes over the walls, and electricity goes inside the walls. Later, as the rooms appear, your brain can put the couch in the living room, and a sink in the kitchen.

Just as having the foundation and framework of a house in place makes it easy to figure out where furniture fits in each room, having the foundation and framework of a course makes it easy to figure out where the detailed course information fits within that framework. The foundation and framework are the patterns that your brain establishes, and when you learn new information, it doesn't have to float around—your brain has created a place for it. You're giving new information a place to go in your memory.

Figure 4 Focus, memory, and drive are just a few of the tools you need to learn.

Principle Three: Nothing You Learn Is Wasted

The brain is by nature a pattern-detecting device, but the more complex the topic or information you are learning, the longer this pattern detection takes. As you are exposed to more and more images, clues, readings, and other materials, your brain continues to detect more and more patterns among the information, and you continue to learn.

Since the brain learns this way, nothing you learn is wasted. It all adds to the patterns in your brain. So, even that course that may seem meaningless is contributing to your learning, though perhaps indirectly.

Principle Four: Learning Takes Time

Have you ever taken a course where the subject is almost completely new to you? By the end of the first week, the excitement has worn off, and you start to feel overwhelmed by all of the new terms and ideas being presented. Fear sets in—*can I ever learn all this?*

If that sounds familiar, you're not alone. In situations like this, your brain hasn't had the time to assimilate the new images that you have learned. You also haven't had the time to develop connections between these images, which in turn create *patterns* in your brain—which you will never forget. Without these connections, the images are floating around in your mind (figuratively, again) without any real understanding of what they are or how they relate to the other images. This creates the frustration and fear that students feel at times like these.

Often, frustrated students say they feel "dumb," "slow," or "old" when they struggle to make sense of so much new information. However, they are none of these things. Their brains are simply trying to make sense out of what they have been given. These connections are not created overnight. It takes time, but

---

{ **TAKE ACTION** }

Why? and What's In It for Me?

There's no better way to prepare your brain to capture the important information included in this class than to ask yourself the two critical questions we've discussed—about this very class. Ask yourself the following questions about this course, and discuss your answers with a classmate.

1. Why are you taking this course?

_____

2. If the course is required, why do you think the school required you to take it?

_____

_____

3. What skills and concepts taught in this course do you think can have immediate impact on you as a student?

_____

_____

_____

because it takes time, we sometimes become very impatient, which leads to nervousness. We then begin feeling "slow" or "dim" or "thick."

What can we do with these feelings? Realize that the brain doesn't have to be taught or motivated to learn any more than our heart needs to be taught or motivated to pump blood. Most of your fear comes from simply wanting to learn

Try this online at *mcgrawhillconnect.com*

4. What skills and concepts taught in this course do you think can have long-term impact on you in your career?

_____

_____

_____

5. How can what you learn in this class help you meet your academic goals?

_____

_____

6. How can what you learn in this class help you meet your career goals?

_____

_____

MY SUCCESS STORY

When Mario took his first accounting class, he was excited. He had always enjoyed working with numbers and had done well in math classes, so his career counselor suggested accounting might be a good fit for his skills.

From his student success course the previous term, he had learned about how the brain learns, and wanted to put his best learning effort toward his accounting class. There had been times in the past when he had crammed for exams, and while he sometimes did OK on those exams, he didn't remember much a week or two later. If he was going to be an accountant, he knew he would need to remember the material not just a week after the exam, but for years and years—and that the material he learned in his first accounting class would serve as a foundation for his future accounting knowledge.

At the beginning of the course, he decided to think about learning accounting like building a house that he could live in for a long time. He knew the foundation had to be solid, so from the very first day of class, he spent a lot of time laying that foundation. He reviewed the syllabus and did a quick scan of the textbook, to understand the themes and basic concepts in the class. He read the assigned readings before class, so he could ask good questions in class and so the information the instructor covered in class wasn't completely new to him.

After each class session, he took his notes and rewrote them, to help him remember them and to think about the ideas further. He then reviewed his notes each week and scanned back through the chapters to get clear on any concepts that were still confusing.

He had never prepared for a class this way before, but he knew that he was building and strengthening mental pathways with his effort, and with each passing week, he could see how the new material built upon the old material. He could almost picture his accounting "house" taking shape!

Preparing for each test was easier than it had ever been. He had created good study materials and built up the right patterns and pathways in his mind, so he could review for a few hours the day before each exam and not worry about cramming. Thanks to his hard work and preparation, the results were better than Mario expected. He got an A in his first accounting class and knew that it was the first of many accounting classes he would take on the way to a fulfilling career.

faster. Yet if we try to rush the learning process, the connections we make won't be clear and may not "stick" in our minds.

Some Thoughts on Cramming

This is why "cramming" before a test may help you feel somewhat prepared for the test on the test day, but make you more likely to forget what you studied shortly afterward. Because you "crammed" the information into your brain, those connections weren't made and reinforced—and so after a while, the information is figuratively floating again and inaccessible.

In other words, true learning cannot happen overnight. The brain requires *time* for the patterns-from-images extraction process to take place, and cramming the night before an exam does not give it that kind of time.

Cramming is like saying to your brain, "I must know this material by tomorrow morning, so you have only 12 hours to create the patterns I need to pass!" But this is a physiological impossibility.

(BUT IF YOU MUST CRAM . . .) However, there are only so many hours in a day, and all college students are busy. Sometimes, because you've run out of time to do it right, your options are either to cram or not study at all. It's a bad choice, but cramming beats not studying.

If you find yourself stuck in this situation, consider these tips:

☐ *Be realistic about what you can accomplish.* Cramming *may* enable you to pass the test, but no patterns will be extracted, and most of what you learn will be lost as soon as you put the pencil down. Acknowledging this up front can help decrease your stress.

☐ *Skim first.* Skim the chapter or material you are studying. Place an emphasis on the headings, important words, indented and boxed material, tables and figures, and, if you have time, the first and last sentence of each paragraph. These are usually the high-level concepts you most need to know.

☐ *Know the kind of test you are cramming for.* Preparing for a multiple-choice test is quite different from studying for an essay test; a closed-book test is different from an open-book test. Knowing what to expect from the test can help you make better use of your limited study time.

☐ *Study selectively.* Cramming means you cannot learn it all so be choosy about what you study. Emphasize what your professor emphasizes, what past quizzes cover, or information that is repeated in your notes.

II. What Kind of Learner Are You?

{ GET READY }

"I learn best by listening." "I learn best by reading."

"I learn best by watching." "I learn best by doing."

● Which one of these best describes you?

Vicki, Kevin, Ronald, and Alicia were all excited for the first day of their medical terminology class. They'd heard great things about the instructor, and they all saw this class as an important step in their path toward a career in the health care field.

After a week, though, the four of them feel very differently about the class.

Vicki is frustrated. When she's trying to learn new material, she likes to see new concepts visualized in a drawing, but for the first few classes, all the instructor has done is stand in front of the class, name the various medical terms, write them on the board, and describe what they do. Vicki has sat in the front row and taken diligent notes, but without a diagram to help explain each new physiological process, she's having a hard time understanding the relationships between the various anatomical systems.

Kevin is frustrated too, but for a different reason. He also has sat near the front, paid close attention, and taken lots of notes, but he is struggling to grasp the new material as well. Drawings and diagrams would help, but what would really make the information make sense for him would be to experience a hands-on demonstration in a laboratory setting.

Copyright © 2013 McGraw-Hill Higher Education

Ronald, on the other hand, likes the course so far. He's found the textbook very helpful and has read all of the assigned chapters before class. When the instructor writes the terms on the board and talks about them, it helps reinforce what he's learned from the reading.

Alicia has been thrilled with the class. The instructor's style is just right for her, because she's never had a problem listening and remembering most of what she hears in a class. She's taken many pages of excellent notes, and even though they've only had a week of classes, she feels that she has a strong understanding of the material.

Figure 6 This instructor writes keywords on the board and lectures, which may be perfect for you to learn, or make it harder.

LO 3 What Are Learning Styles?

What's the difference between Vicki, Kevin, Ronald, and Alicia? Are Alicia and Ronald smarter than the other two? Are they working harder?

No. The difference is that Vicki, Kevin, Ronald, and Alicia all have different **learning styles.**

Learning styles are the ways we take in, process, and understand new information. Most of us can learn things in multiple ways, but we usually prefer to learn one way over others.

learning styles: *The ways we take in, process, and understand new information.*

Types of Learning Styles

While we all learn differently, and there are many ways to learn new things, researchers have identified four major learning styles: **visual** (seeing), **auditory** (hearing), **read/write** (words), and **kinesthetic** (hands-on).

VISUAL LEARNERS **Visual** learners like Vicki benefit from diagrams, charts, pictures, films, and written directions. Their motto is "Show me and I'll understand."

visual: *A type of learning characterized by a preference for information presented as images or symbols.*

Visual learners usually have a good sense of direction and can easily visualize objects. Visual learning is a style in which ideas, concepts, data, and other information are associated with images and symbols. If you are visual learner, these suggestions might help you make the most of your learning style to learn new material more effectively:

☐ Ask your instructors if they can present information in visual forms like diagrams, charts, pictures, graphics, or films, or create your own visual tools from the material presented to help you study.

☐ When taking notes and studying, use visual aids like idea maps, or other tools that organize information visually.

AUDITORY LEARNERS **Auditory** learners like Alicia learn best when they can hear what is being taught, which explains why in a class where a traditional, lecture-style teaching approach was being used, she picked up the material more easily than Vicki and Kevin did.

auditory: *A type of learning characterized by a preference for hearing new information.*

Auditory learners succeed when directions are read aloud, speeches are required, or information is presented and requested verbally. This also means that auditory learners may struggle to understand the information in a chapter they've read, but will then be able to make sense of the material as they listen to the class lecture about it.

To help them remember a name or phone number, an auditory learner may say it out loud and then remember how it sounded to recall it. They tend to solve problems by talking them through. Auditory learners may also be more tuned in to audible signals that a speaker may give, such as changes in tone or voice inflection. This awareness can help them understand a speaker's true meaning.

When grasping new information, auditory learners will often say sound- or voice-oriented things like, "I hear you," "That clicks," or, "It's ringing a bell." Sometimes these learners will move their lips or talk to themselves to help them accomplish tasks.

If you prefer the auditory learning style, consider these suggestions when studying:

☐ After you have listened to a lecture and taken notes, write down your own thoughts about the material.

☐ Many experts believe that background noise helps improve comprehension for auditory learners when they read. So, when you are reading, it may help you to have music (at a low volume) or white noise (such as people talking, TV, etc.) in the background.

Figure 7 Some auditory learners grasp material better if there's music in the background.

READ/WRITE LEARNERS **Read/write** learners like Ronald have a preference for information displayed as words.[4] Students with this preference like taking in information as text, and also prefer written tests.

read/write: *A type of learning characterized by a preference for information displayed as words.*

Read/write learners succeed when information is presented to them in lists, headings, dictionaries, glossaries, essays, and manuals. Even if the professor delivers an informative lecture, they would usually like a handout to go with it, and reading the textbook is highly valuable to them. The library is usually their preferred study spot.[5]

If you are a read/write learner, the following techniques may help you when studying:

☐ After class, take your notes and rewrite them, reducing and editing them into a page of notes that you can use as a study guide. Having this reduced version of your notes to study from and the process of rewriting your notes will both be valuable to you.

☐ If you are working with material presented in charts, diagrams, or graphs, write out a paragraph or a few bullet points that explain the material.

☐ When working on planning and time management, use to-do lists, assignment logs, and written notes that help you see the information you need to manage.

KINESTHETIC LEARNERS **Kinesthetic** learners like Kevin are most successful when they can be physically involved in the learning activity. People often say kinesthetic learners "learn by doing." They pick things up most quickly and effectively when they participate in hands-on experiences like a science lab, skit or role-play activity, field trip, educational game, or other physical demonstration. Kinesthetic learners might say things like, "I can see myself doing that," or, "It's starting to come alive for me."

kinesthetic: *A type of learning characterized by a preference for being physically involved in the learning activity.*

If you are kinesthetic learner, consider the suggestions below:

☐ Ask your instructors if any of the information can be presented through participatory activities, like experiments, role-playing, or field trips. If not, find other students who might be interested in making the material more interactive, to help you learn and remember it better.

☐ You may benefit from listening to music while learning or studying. It is common for kinesthetic learners to focus on two different things at the same time.

☐ As a kinesthetic learner, you will learn most successfully when you can be fully engaged with the learning activity. Don't sit back and watch, get up and get involved!

Determining Your Learning Style

You probably recognized your own learning style while reading the descriptions above. While you likely felt a strong connection to one of the learning styles over the others, you probably could also think of situations where you learned well using one or both of the other styles. Though most of us prefer one style above the others, we all use each style in particular learning situations.

Once you identify your preferred style, you can learn to maximize it and enhance your ability to study. Below are some websites that can help you determine your preferred learning style:

www.vark-learn.com/english/index.asp

www.chaminade.org/INSPIRE/learnstl.htm

www.usd.edu/trio/tut/ts/style.html

http://homeworktips.about.com/od/homeworkhelp/a/learningstyle.htm

LO 4 Learning with Others

When we visualize someone learning, we usually picture students in a lecture hall, listening to an instructor, or a solitary student bent over a book in the library.

While a lot of student learning takes place one of those two ways, a third way is becoming more and more an essential part of college life: learning with others in a group setting.

Studying alone may be best for memorizing facts or if you need quiet time to read and process new information from a book. Yet for many learning situations, such as understanding complicated ideas or applying facts that you've learned to solve problems, group studying can help you learn and master new material better than studying alone.

The Benefits of Study Groups

Studying with other students in a group offers many benefits.

THE ADDED PERSPECTIVE OF MULTIPLE LEARNING STYLES When you study in a group, you can learn and benefit from people who have different learning styles than you. Think back to Vicki, Alicia, Ronald, and Kevin, who were taking the same medical terminology class. Alicia was having the easiest time grasping the information, while Vicki and Kevin struggled because the material was not presented in a way that fit their learning styles well.

However, if the four of them studied together, all four would benefit from their differences in learning styles.

In this situation, Alicia might be able to help explain the more difficult concepts to the others—but she would also benefit. Have you ever noticed that when you explain an idea to someone else, you begin to understand it better yourself? One of the most effective ways of mastering new ideas and information is to teach them to someone else. When you explain or teach an idea, you need to think it through more thoroughly and actively than you did when you were just learning it for yourself, because now you need to make sure the other person understands it too.

On the other hand, if you don't understand something very well, trying to teach it to someone else will probably be difficult. This struggle will help you realize the gaps in your understanding of the material.

Another benefit of participating in a study group comes from interacting

Figure 8 Other students have different strengths than you, and studying together can help you all learn more effectively.

different learning styles. Whether you teach a concept or learn it from someone else, you will gain a deeper understanding of the material by looking at it through the different angles of multiple learning styles.

For example, if Alicia takes the lead in the study group, as Vicki, Ronald, and Kevin start to understand the information better, they may be able to use their learning styles to help think about the information in a new way that will help everyone. Maybe Vicki will get excited and draw a chart or graph that will help all of them understand more clearly, Ronald will make a useful checklist, or Kevin will come up with an idea for them to practice something in a hands-on way that will reinforce their learning.

Working together in a small group, everyone can be a part of the conversation and contribute the perspective they bring from their learning style. This way, everyone can understand the material more thoroughly and add new depth to their knowledge.

MANY HANDS MAKE LIGHT WORK Another key benefit of group study is thinking out loud. Most people studying by themselves will read, write, and think about the material quietly. Yet hearing and speaking information can help us learn. If you've only heard something once, from the instructor, your understanding or

ON THE JOB

Exploring How Learning Styles Affect the Workplace

Long after you've taken your last class, your learning style will continue to affect your life. It will impact how you process information at work, while out with friends, and when you watch the news on TV or read about it online. It will also influence your interactions with your supervisor.

For instance, if you are an *auditory learner* and you get verbal instructions on a new process, it will be easy for you to remember and successfully apply them. However, if you are primarily a *read/write learner,* you may not fully absorb those instructions, so it would help to ask for written instructions, to make sure you understand the process. If you're primarily a *visual learner,* you might ask for a diagram, or draw a diagram of the process yourself and check with your boss to make sure you understood it right. If you are a *kinesthetic learner,* the most effective way to ensure you learn the process correctly is to have someone show you how to do it rather than just tell you how.

Because different learning styles can have such a big impact on how you work and interact with others, it can help to share your learning style with your manager and co-workers, and to ask others about their preferred learning styles. Talking openly about and appreciating different learning styles can prevent

mistakes and misunderstandings, speed up productivity, and reinforce your confidence.

Let's see how each learning style might play out in the workplace.

The Visual Learner: "Let me show you something." Visual learners learn best by seeing things represented graphically or symbolically, so think about ways to communicate with them other than just speaking. For some visual learners, if they can't see what you are trying to communicate, they won't connect with the information.

Visual learners often like graphic organizers, take detailed notes, and benefit from lists and flashcards. Their language often relates to their visual style, such as, "Do you see what I mean?" and "Let me show you something."

The Auditory Learner: "Can I talk to you a second?" Listening is key for auditory learners. They do well with verbal instructions, sounds, and music. However, they may also be distracted by nonbackground noises, so avoid high-traffic areas for a meeting or important conversation with auditory learners.

Auditory learners use language that relates to their auditory style, such as, "Do you hear what I'm saying?" and "Can I talk to you for a second?" If you are an auditory learner, you might benefit from making

memory of it may be limited. Hearing others talk about it, and talking about it yourself, can improve your understanding and reinforce your memory.

The shared aspect of group study offers many other advantages as well, including:[6]

☐ *Note-taking reinforcement.* Did you struggle to take good notes in class? See if a member of your study group took better notes, and share.

☐ *Sharing talents.* Each person brings different strengths to a study group, such as organizational skills, the ability to stick to a task, a talent for memorization, and so on. What is your contribution to the group?

☐ *Covering more ground.* Simply by having more heads thinking about the problem, three study group members may be able to solve a complicated homework problem that none would have solved alone.

☐ *Support system.* Your fellow study group members probably have similar goals: to get good grades, graduate, and get a good job. Not only can you provide academic support to each other, but you can also provide encouragement and moral support.

☐ *Socializing.* Studying with others is more fun than studying alone, which makes it easier to spend more time studying. (Just don't spend too much time socializing.)

audio recordings of presentations, meetings, and reports, so you can listen to them again later.

The Read/Write Learner: "Send me the memo." Read/write learners, not surprisingly, prefer to learn by reading and writing, so the best way for them to learn is through e-mails, charts, PowerPoint presentations—anything visual that includes words. They also tend to be good proofreaders, so they can help edit documents.

For some read/write learners, if what you are trying to communicate is not written down, or you don't have anything to "show for it," it will not be real to them. Even if you discuss a project thoroughly, they will still want a memo or an e-mail capturing the essential ideas so they can read it again later.

The Kinesthetic Learner: "Let's come to grips with the situation." If you are a kinesthetic learner, you will probably want to simply jump in and get things done! For the same reason, you may also find it difficult to sit still in meetings. You may want to stop talking about the problem or project and just start doing something about it.

Kinesthetic learners are likely to use language that relates to their hands-on style, such as, "I'm trying to get a handle on all of my projects" and "Let's come to grips with the situation."

If you manage kinesthetic learners, let them periodically stand or walk around in meetings, and invite them to participate in simulations, demonstrations, or role-playing. Avoid static situations where they have to just sit and listen.

Looking through the Lens of Learning Styles

For this activity, you will need to partner with a classmate. The pair of you will complete three tasks. Each task will challenge your visual, kinesthetic, and auditory learning styles.

In the first activity, you will fulfill two roles: the speaker and the listener. One of you will be the speaker and the other will be the listener. The speaker can only use verbal descriptions/instructions to direct the listener on how to best draw a picture of an object of the speaker's choosing. The speaker is not allowed to say what the object is. The speaker can choose any object he or she wishes, but it should be something fairly simple that can be readily described. Here are a few suggestions:

Pencil	Rocket	Golf club
Three-ring binder	Chair or table	Football
Book	Ear of corn	Watch

The listener may not view the object, but will be able to ask questions to clarify any instructions. The speaker is not allowed to tell the listener what the object does or how it is used! For example, if the speaker chooses to describe a pencil, he may not tell the listener that the object is "something you write with." The speaker has three minutes to describe the object.

Once the listener has completed the picture, you will switch roles with your partner. In your new roles, the speaker will provide a verbal description of a second picture, while the listener attempts to re-create it on paper.

After you and your partner have completed your pictures, you will view the originals and then respond to the following questions:

1. When you were the one attempting to draw the picture as it was described, what learning style did you use in this activity?

   _____

2. How accurate was your drawing of the original version?

   _____

3. What was the most challenging aspect of this exercise?

   _____

   _____

4. What additional strategies do you wish you could have used in order to produce a more successful result?

   _____

   _____

   _____

5. How would you rate your auditory learning abilities? (1 = greatest area for improvement; 5 = greatest learning style strength.) Please circle the best corresponding number:

   1   2   3   4   5

For the second activity, you will remain in your pair. You each will fulfill two roles: One of you will be the drawer and the other, the respondent. The drawer will select one concept to depict through a drawing. The drawer can choose any concept he or she wishes. Use the list below for some possible ideas:

Graduation from college	First day on the job
An interview for a career	Stuck in traffic, late for work or school
Scoring an A on an exam	Achieving a goal
Typing an essay on the computer	Overcoming an obstacle

The drawer may use symbols and a myriad of images, but *no* actual words—verbal or written—to create a visual representation of the concept he/she selected. As the drawer is creating the illustration, the respondent will attempt to identify the concept. The respondent has only three minutes to determine the concept from the drawer's images.

Once the three minutes have elapsed, you both will switch roles. The new drawer will select a concept and the new respondent will have three minutes to identify the correct concept based on the visual representation.

After you have completed both roles, respond to the following questions:

1. As the respondent, what learning style did you use in this activity?

   _____

2. Did you correctly identify the concept based on the visual representation before the three-minute limit?

   _____

3. What additional strategies do you wish you could have used in order to produce a more successful result?

   _____
   _____
   _____

4. How would you rate your visual learning abilities? (1 = greatest area for improvement; 5 = greatest learning style strength.) Please circle the best corresponding number:

   1   2   3   4   5

For the final activity, you and your partner will each create your own five-step dance/motion routine. Initially, you will work by yourself to develop your routine using the following steps:

1. Identify the first movement (*Example:* Nod head once):

   _____

2. Identify the second movement (*Example:* Shrug shoulders):

   _____

(continued)

Guidelines for Getting a Group Together

Simply studying with others in a group is not an automatic formula for a successful study group. For a group to succeed, it must use its study time productively, and all members must benefit from working with others in the group. Here are a few things to consider when putting a study group together or joining an existing study group:

☐ *Who should be in the group?* Pick classmates who share your interest in doing well in class. Look for people who stay alert in class, take notes, ask questions, and respond to the teacher's questions. John Mitchell, who has researched group work at Central Michigan University, suggests your study group include "someone who understands the material better than you and someone who understands less."[7]

☐ *How many should be in the group?* The ideal group size is four or five. In a larger group, people can get left out of the conversation, and a smaller group can have too few perspectives.

☐ *Where should we study together?* Hold your study group sessions somewhere you can focus, where your conversation will not distract others who are trying to study quietly, and where you will have plenty of room to spread out books and notes.

☐ *When should we study together?* Find a day and time that works for everybody in the group, every week. This is much easier to remember than if you change the day and time each week. Mark your study session in your calendar, and treat it as an appointment.

TAKE ACTION (*concluded*)

3. Identify the third movement (*Example:* Clap hands together):

_____

4. Identify the fourth movement (*Example:* Stomp the right foot):

_____

5. Identify the fifth movement (*Example:* Stomp the left foot):

_____

Once you complete your five-step dance/motion routine, you will demonstrate it to your partner. You may only demonstrate your five steps a maximum of three times. After the third demonstration, your partner will attempt to successfully complete all five movements. Once your partner attempts your routine, he/she will teach you his/her five steps. Again, you will only be able to watch the entire routine three times. Now you will attempt to complete each step.

After you and your partner have attempted each other's routines, you will respond to the following questions:

1. What learning style did you use in this activity?

_____

2. Did you correctly follow your partner's five-step routine?

_____

Figure 9 Have a definite time and location for your study group, such as right after class in an empty classroom.

☐ *How long should we study together?* Study groups should meet for no more than three hours at a time. Having a time limit will help the group focus. If you know you only have an hour, you're more likely to stay on task.

Try this online at *mcgrawhillconnect.com*

3. What additional strategies do you wish you could have used in order to produce a more successful result?

_____

_____

_____

4. How would you rate your kinesthetic learning abilities? (1 = greatest area for improvement; 5 = greatest learning style strength.) Please circle the best corresponding number.

1   2   3   4   5

In summary, what have you learned about your own learning style?

_____

_____

_____

How can you apply what you have learned about your learning style to help you succeed in future classes?

_____

_____

_____

While studying together in person is easiest, new technologies like the video-chatting service Skype and other online chat programs now make it possible to study in a group without all being in the same room.

Getting the Most Out of a Study Group Session

Once you have a group together, here are some tips to help your group get the most out of each study session:

☐ *State your purpose or goals for each session.* Begin by stating what you want to accomplish. It may seem obvious, especially if you're meeting right before a big test. But clearly stating what you are there to do will help you all stay focused and make good use of your time.

☐ *Take turns teaching.* Even if one person has a stronger understanding of the material, don't let that person do all the teaching. When you instruct the group, you not only help other group members, you also reinforce your own knowledge. The group leader can make sure everyone is teaching as well as learning.

☐ *Stay focused.* Scheduling short breaks after every half hour or so can help everyone stay focused. This lets people get off-topic chatting out of their systems and be focused when it is time to work.

☐ *Be prepared.* Before a session, finish the assigned reading, review your notes, list topics you want to review, and write out any questions you want to address. When everyone comes prepared, your time together will be productive.

Effective study groups involve everyone working through the class material together—explaining difficult concepts, arguing about them, answering confusing questions, and figuring out why one person's answer is different from another's. Tackling the material together this way, you learn more than you ever would have studying by yourself.

Studying on your own is still a crucial part of student success. But by supplementing the studying you do by yourself with studying in a group, you can reinforce what you've learned, deepen your understanding of complex concepts, and maybe even make a few new friends along the way.

III. Leveraging Your Strengths

Copyright © 2013 McGraw-Hill Higher Education

GET READY

Team sports are a great example of "leveraging strength." How successful would a pro football team be if the quarterback and the center switched positions for a whole game?

● Could you apply this team concept to your college studies?

Of all the periods in your life, your college years will be some of the most valuable. Being a college student exposes you to many opportunities that are difficult to find after graduation, including the chance to take classes and learn from talented instructors. You will also have the opportunity to make many discoveries about yourself.

College can help you to see who you are, who you want to be, and what steps you must take to get there. It is a time when the real seeds of self-discovery will be planted, followed by nourishment and growth for the rest of your life.

In this section, we'll start by discovering your *natural strengths and talents.* Though this process can be challenging, college provides a great environment to make the most of your strengths and to learn to address your weaknesses. With a little effort and self-reflection, you can arrive at a realistic understanding of your skills that can help you thrive in school and beyond, and that can motivate you along the way.[8]

LO 5 What Are My Key Strengths?

Most of us think we know our academic strengths and weaknesses. Unfortunately, many factors lead to an incomplete or inaccurate self-assessment. These include limited exposure to different subjects, a subject taught using a learning style that didn't match yours, or a prior school experience that corresponded with a difficult time in your life. On the other hand, someone who performed slightly better in one subject than another (say computers over biology) might believe she is bound for success in computers, but destined to struggle with biology. While it's possible that both are true, it's also possible neither is true.

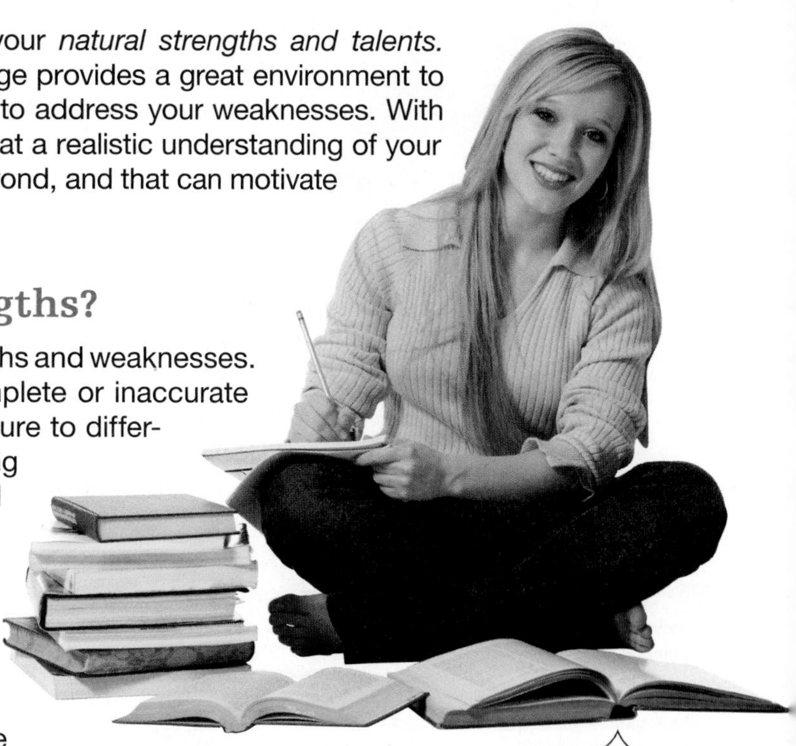

Yet these inaccurate beliefs can become a self-fulfilling prophecy, something that you make come true because you believe it is supposed to. In that last example, if you believe biology is not a strong subject for you, but computers are, you may work less in biology while putting more energy into computers. As a result, you may do better in your computer class and worse in biology, but your results may be due more to effort than ability. Soon, what you believed (even though it may not have been true) starts to look like the truth, which "confirms" what you've believed.

In this section, we're going to learn ways to get a clear look at your strengths and how to make the most of them. We'll also learn how to identify your weaknesses and work with them. Along the way, you may need to let go of some of your beliefs about your strengths and weaknesses. This isn't easy, but doing so can make your college career one of the most rewarding experiences of your life.

So how do you determine your greatest strengths? Below are some things to consider.

Figure 10
Uncover your natural strengths and play to them as much as you can, in school and in life.

What Comes Easily for Me But Is Difficult for Others?

While most of us know our strengths, because they seem so natural and logical to us, we frequently take them for granted and don't realize that we can achieve greater success than others might, with less effort.[9] One way to identify your strengths is to look at your own past and present behavior for a pattern of successful performance. What comes easily to you that might be more difficult for others? Is there a subject in school or a task at work where other people come to you for help or advice? Those things that come naturally or easy to you are probably your greatest strengths.

What Classes Am I Excited to Take?

By the time you started college, you probably had a solid idea of your strengths and may have chosen a career to pursue based on them.[10] Yet many students find that, when they go to sign up for classes, the ones they are most interested in and excited to take aren't always the ones in the field they thought they

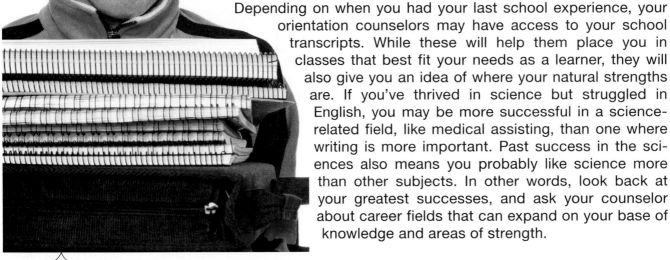

wanted to pursue. Not every class has to be exciting to you every day—by midterms, most students feel a lag in their enthusiasm for just about all their classes. But if you find yourself scheduling classes you can't get excited about, even on the first day, you may have some internal conflicts to work out before choosing a career path.

Many students drop out because they failed at something they really didn't like in the first place. Orientation is designed to help you align your interests with your capabilities. Use it to find classes that hold your interest and nurture your love of the subject.

Prior School Grades and Experiences

Depending on when you had your last school experience, your orientation counselors may have access to your school transcripts. While these will help them place you in classes that best fit your needs as a learner, they will also give you an idea of where your natural strengths are. If you've thrived in science but struggled in English, you may be more successful in a science-related field, like medical assisting, than one where writing is more important. Past success in the sciences also means you probably like science more than other subjects. In other words, look back at your greatest successes, and ask your counselor about career fields that can expand on your base of knowledge and areas of strength.

Figure 11 If you're feeling overwhelmed or bored, check in with yourself and find the things that get you excited.

Honesty

Be honest with yourself about how determined and committed you are to succeed in your education, and what you must do to succeed. If you feel your determination and commitment are low, talk to an advisor or counselor who can help you decide whether college is right for you. If your motivation is high, but you know your study skills need help, orientation is the right time to find a peer mentor or someone in student support services who can help you develop those skills.

Understand the "Average"

At any college, you will find a wide range of students: different ages, from different cultures, with different educational and financial backgrounds. Though it's tempting to compare yourself to your fellow students, don't assume that the students you spend the most time with or the students you sit next to are "average." In reality, underachievers and overachievers tend to form cliques; your friends could be the best or worst students on campus, and you might never realize it. In either case, comparing your friends' performance and work habits to your own can create false self-assessments.

So don't worry about how you compare to others. Focus on your own goals. Keep track of how well you meet or exceed them. There's no shame in failing to meet your goals, as long as you learn from the experience. Do your goals need to be more realistic? Do you need to give yourself more time to study? Do you need help studying? Use your goals as a measuring stick to help you make decisions about your strengths and weaknesses.

Figure 12 These two athletes have very different goals and strengths, so comparing their achievements doesn't make sense. He can't run as fast as she can, she can't lift as much as him, but they are both successful.

LO 6 Acknowledging Your Weaknesses

Before you can truly leverage the strengths you have identified, you must first acknowledge your weaknesses, determine if they have the ability to limit your success, and if so, decide how you will address them.

Keep in mind that your weaknesses are not permanent. They are simply areas that don't come as easily to you right now. This may be due to less natural ability, but they could also be due to less training or time invested in that area, not finding the right teacher, or simply not having as many opportunities in that subject.

How do you identify your weaknesses? The following are some things to consider.

What Do I Have the Most Trouble with at School?

Determining and acknowledging your greatest challenges in school is essential to overcoming them. If you want to be a medical assistant, but struggle in math and science, your college counselors will probably tell you that you should reconsider your goals based on your natural aptitudes. In fact, if you are uncertain about your ability in a particular program or class, it is safest to assume that it is an area of weakness.

Prior School Grades and Experiences

Just as the grades on your transcript can help you and your college counselor identify your strengths, they can also identify your weaknesses. How well you've done in the past doesn't determine how well you'll do in life—after all, you're constantly growing and improving—but if you struggled with a subject before, acknowledge that, and try to understand why. How were your study habits for that class? Were you interested in the subject? Did the teacher's style not fit your

learning style? You can do poorly in high school math but still become a successful accountant—if you figure out why you struggled and are willing to work to overcome those weaknesses.

Challenge Yourself

You'll never fully understand the extent of your strengths and weaknesses if you always stick to safe ground. College is a great opportunity to challenge yourself and go beyond your comfort zone. You'll have to decide whether this means taking a few difficult classes, participating in a new student group, or just getting out there and going to a few parties. You might experience some difficulty and discomfort, but you're almost guaranteed to discover talents you didn't know you had and to find that some things you thought were weaknesses just needed more time and effort.

MONEY SMART$

Home Loans

Owning your own house has long been a part of the American Dream. As houses are often the biggest purchase people make in their lives, most people must borrow money to buy a home. Home loans, also called mortgages, are based on the borrowing principles described here.[11]

- *Down payment.* A down payment is what you pay up front toward the purchase price of your home. The down payment plus the amount of money you borrow in your home loan make up the sale price of the home you are buying.
- *Principal.* The principal is the amount you owe to the lending institution after you have made your down payment. Each month, when you make a mortgage payment, some of the money goes toward paying off the principal, and some of the money goes toward paying off the interest.
- *Interest.* Interest is the fee your lender charges you to borrow money. The interest rate is expressed as an annual percentage rate (APR), and this number explains how much you are charged each year.

- *Monthly payments.* A monthly payment is the amount you pay monthly to your financial institution for principal and interest. However, when considering the total monthly "house" payment you can afford, keep in mind other potential monthly costs such as property taxes, homeowner's insurance, utility costs, and homeowner or condominium association fees.
- *Term of the loan.* The length of time you have to repay what you have borrowed. Most home loans have 15- or 30-year terms.
- *Points.* A point equals 1 percent of the amount you borrow. Points are usually charged at the beginning of the loan and are part of the cost of borrowing money. Points are also referred to as the loan origination fee.
- *Closing.* In a sale, the buyer and seller each pay for costs that are necessary to complete, or "close," the transaction. Who pays for which costs depends on local customs and on negotiations between buyer and seller. Closing costs include fees you pay for the services of the lender and other costs involved with the sale of the home,

LO 7 Balancing Your Strengths and Weaknesses

This section is called "Leveraging Your Strengths." But what exactly does that mean?

Imagine that you are clearing a path, but you come across a very heavy rock. You push and pull, but it won't budge. Luckily, you have a long-handled shovel, so you shove the shovel head under the rock and push down to see if you can lift the rock. But the rock is so heavy, this doesn't help. You push up to see if that works. No luck.

A few feet away, you see a smaller rock. You pick it up and put it a few feet from the big rock. Then you take your shovel, put the blade back under the big rock, and put the middle of the handle on your smaller rock. Now you push down on the far end. You have to push hard, but slowly, the rock comes up, and you are able to dislodge it from the path.

What happened? If you know your physics, you know that the smaller rock served as a fulcrum, or pivot, that transformed your shovel into a lever. The force you applied to the lever was multiplied, which enabled you to move the rock. In other words, the **leverage** that you created multiplied your strength.

> **leverage:** *Something you can use to multiply or make the most of a strength.*

You will surely come across many challenges on your path, in school and in life. Just like with the rock, brute force often won't be enough for you to clear the obstacle. You need to create leverage. You can create the most leverage by concentrating on your strengths.

---

which may include title search, hazard insurance, structural pest control report, credit reports, title insurance, charges for appraisal, and loan document preparation.

- *Disclosures from lenders.* Federal law requires lenders to give you specific information when you get a home loan. You should get a written summary of important terms and costs of the loan, including the finance charge, annual percentage rate, and payment terms.

    If you choose an adjustable rate mortgage (ARM), the lender must provide specific information about the kind of adjustable rate home loan you have applied for. This should include the circumstances under which the rate could increase (for example, a rise in the index rate), the effects of an increase (for example, an increase in your payments or the length of the loan), and any limitations on the increase (such as any caps on the interest rate).

Choosing a home loan is an important financial decision, and you are entitled to all the information you need to make the right decision. Don't hesitate to ask questions when you talk to lenders, real estate brokers, sellers, and your attorney, and keep asking until you get clear and complete answers, and fully understand the impact and responsibility of the decision you are about to make.

Even though most college counselors will say that the way to most effectively develop a student is to tap into their strengths, most people still focus the majority of their personal development efforts on shoring up their weaknesses.

This isn't surprising. From childhood on, most of us have been taught that our greatest potential for growth is in our areas of greatest weakness. If you got an A in English and a C in math, which grade got the most attention from your teachers and parents?

Certainly, everyone needs a certain competency in math, and it would not be helpful to just say, "Well, looks like you're not good at math. Let's give up on it." But often, this approach focuses on weakness, while failing to leverage your strengths.

However, in recent years, social psychologists have learned that focusing on your strengths leads to higher performance, greater productivity, and increased satisfaction. In fact, developing your abilities to their greatest potential can decrease how much your weaknesses will hold you back. This is the reason that as you progress through your college experience, you should concentrate on leveraging your strengths rather than trying to fix every weakness.

Match Your Strengths to Your College Program and Classes

Once you know your strengths, you need to determine how they can be used the best. Years ago, large corporations managed and directed the careers of their

---

TAKE ACTION

Using Your Strengths and Weaknesses to Plan a Project

Your instructor will divide members of the class into small teams of three to five people. Your team has an assignment: to plan a simple project. This could be a class presentation or something outside of class, such as a community-service project. However, the objective with this activity is that everyone in the group makes the most of their strengths to ensure the most successful project. Your task will be to assign the necessary roles and responsibilities to ensure each member contributes to the project's success.

1. In your group, first have members each talk about their strengths and what they can contribute to the team. Also, members should each talk about their weaknesses, and roles or tasks that they would not be well suited for. List your team's strengths and weaknesses here.

Team Strengths: _____

_____

_____

_____

Team Weaknesses: _____

_____

_____

_____

employees for decades. In today's marketplace, that responsibility belongs to you. You now have the opportunity to not only discover yourself, but also determine where and how you will perform best.

With your knowledge of your strengths and weaknesses, you can consider your choice of college program and specific classes in a new light. When you review the course catalog, keep your strengths in mind, and when you talk to your college counselor, explain what you see as your strengths. Based on these, your counselor can recommend programs or courses that would be a good fit and caution you about programs and classes that might not be.

Addressing Your Weaknesses

The whole reason for attending college is to find the help you need to get better: help increasing what you know, developing your academic skills, developing your social skills, and more. Every college is set up to help its students succeed.

One of the most exciting things about college is how it can help you take your strengths and improve on them. But it can also help you address your weaknesses. As we've discussed, just because something isn't a strength doesn't mean you can ignore it. Fortunately, your college has many resources that can help you both leverage your strengths and address your weaknesses.

Try this online at mcgrawhillconnect.com

2. Once everyone has talked about their strengths and weaknesses, the group must brainstorm a project that would be a good fit for the entire group.

   Project Name: _____

3. After you have chosen a project, identify the tasks that must be finished to complete the project, and assign those tasks to people in the group based on their strengths and weaknesses. Everyone in the group must be comfortable with the tasks assigned to them.

   Assignment 1: _____
   Assignment 2: _____
   Assignment 3: _____
   Assignment 4: _____
   Assignment 5: _____

4. Once you have identified your project and the roles assigned to your team members, share these with the rest of the class.

YOUR INSTRUCTORS: A VALUABLE RESOURCE If you're working to improve on a weakness, your instructor should be your first source of help. In fact, very few students make it through college or graduate school without seeking help from an instructor. It is important to seek help before you get into a bad situation, rather than let problems in your courses or programs fester and intensify.

What are common reasons you might seek out your instructor for assistance?

- ☐ You've fallen behind in class
- ☐ You've failed an exam or an assignment
- ☐ You do not understand the course material
- ☐ You have questions about an assignment that has been given
- ☐ You need advice on the subject of your program
- ☐ You need clarification on how the course is being taught

If you find yourself dealing with any of these situations, ask your instructor for help. Your instructors are usually quite busy with teaching and other responsibilities, so approach them politely and be respectful of their time. If you approach an instructor this way, he or she will usually make time to help you.

Finding a Balance

The measure of a successful college education is more than just learning new skills in the classroom. As a student, you want to develop yourself as a complete person, to better prepare yourself for your career, and to contribute as a citizen. A key to this development is adapting your natural strengths to the challenges and demands of your college program, as well as your career.

As you go through college, don't limit yourself to strictly scholastic pursuits—some of your greatest strengths may lie outside of class. Different aspects of college life both require and help you learn different skills. Developing friendships, getting involved in campus activities, and exploring extracurricular interests can be just as important in the long run as taking classes. The choice between taking an extra class and spending time with new friends may be a difficult decision to make. The challenge is to find the right balance that will help you develop into the best person you can be.

Figure 14 Once you're confident of your plans, your school has people to help you.

SUMMARY

We started this chapter by learning how our brains work. This knowledge can help us learn more effectively. Because true learning involves creating patterns and mental pathways in your mind, learning does not happen overnight—it takes time. This is why the more time you spend learning the material for your classes, and building up patterns and pathways in your brain, the better you will know, understand, and remember the information. This is also why cramming is generally ineffective as a learning strategy.

We also looked at two important questions for all college students: *Why?* and *What's in it for me?* Asking these questions about your courses and the material in them can help you understand the value in paying attention to the material—and paying attention can help you learn the material more effectively.

We also learned that everyone has a different learning style. We looked at the four primary learning styles—visual (seeing), auditory (hearing), read/write (words), and kinesthetic (hands-on)—and looked at how each type approaches learning differently.

Finally, we discussed the need to leverage your strengths, rather than trying to fix every weakness. We all have strengths and weaknesses, and the better you understand your own, the more you can apply your effort to using your strengths to support your success.

DISCUSSION QUESTIONS

1. The *Why?* and *What's in it for me?* questions are usually asked by students about material they are studying. Why might it be helpful for instructors to encourage their students to ask these questions about the material they are teaching? How would you feel if your instructor started the term by addressing these questions?

2. Why is it important to know your own learning style, and to appreciate the learning styles of other people in your study group or where you work? Can you give an example of a time when your particular learning style helped you learn something more easily than others, or a time when you think your learning style might have limited your learning?

3. What are the benefits of focusing on your strengths rather than your weaknesses? Give an example of how focusing on your strengths has paid off for you.

KEY TERMS

auditory: A type of learning characterized by a preference for hearing new information. (p. 13)

kinesthetic: A type of learning characterized by a preference for being physically involved in the learning activity. (p. 14)

learning styles: The ways we take in, process, and understand new information. (p. 12)

leverage: Something you can use to multiply or make the most of a strength. (p. 27)

pattern: A physical connection, or pathway, between images in your mind that is built up over time. (p. 4)

read/write: A type of learning characterized by a preference for information displayed as words. (p. 14)

visual: A type of learning characterized by a preference for information presented as images or symbols. (p. 12)

What's in it for me?: A question to ask yourself to determine what value you might gain from paying attention to certain information. (p. 5)

Why?: A question to ask yourself to determine the purpose of pursuing an activity, such as studying certain material. (p. 5)

Footnotes

1. Hart, L. (1983). *Human Brain, Human Learning.* Village of Oak Creek, AZ: Books for Educators, p. 61.

2. Ibid., p. 61.

3. Ibid., p. 64.

4. Fleming, N. (2011). "The VARK Categories." VARK—A Guide to Learning Styles, www.vark-learn.com/english/page.asp?p=categories. *Copyright Version 7.1 (2011) is held by Neil D. Fleming, Christchurch, New Zealand.*

5. Fleming, N. (2011). "Read/Write Study Strategies," VARK—A Guide to Learning Styles, www.vark-learn.com/english/page.asp?p=readwrite. *Copyright Version 7.1 (2011) is held by Neil D. Fleming, Christchurch, New Zealand.*

6. College Board. (2011). "The Power of Study Groups." www.collegeboard.com/student/plan/high-school/50432.html.

7. Ibid.

8. Short, T. (2008). "College Orientation: How to Assess Your Strengths and Weaknesses." Helium: Education, June 29. www.helium.com/items/1096127-how-to-assess-your-strengths-and-weaknesses-in-college.

9. Karlsberg, R., and Adler, J. (2005). "Leverage Strengths for Peak Performance." *Home Business Journal,* March 11. www.homebusinessjournal.net/a/leverage-strengths.asp.

10. Doherty, L. (2008). "College Orientation: How to Assess Your Strengths and Weaknesses," Helium: Education, June 27. www.helium.com/items/1094344-interest-inventories-freshman-orientation-college-life-preparing-for-college-career-placement.

11. "How Home Loans Work." Bahl Homes, www.bahl.com/Pages/Mortgage_Brokerage/basics_of_a_home_loan.html.

Websites

www.vark-learn.com/english/index.asp

www.chaminade.org/INSPIRE/learnstl.htm

www.usd.edu/trio/tut/ts/style.html

http://homeworktips.about.com/od/homeworkhelp/a/learningstyle.htm

Figure and Photo Credits

Taking **Notes**

LEARNING OUTCOMES

In this module, you will:

1 Capture spoken information more effectively.

2 Recognize the barriers to capturing spoken information.

3 Capture written information more successfully.

4 Develop an approach to scheduling your reading.

5 Learn a specific system for reading and taking notes.

6 Apply this note-taking system in class and while reading.

It's hard to listen and understand when people talk about things you don't know anything about.

- Name a subject you're an expert in, like a sport, a book series, cooking, etc.
- What are three basics someone new to the subject needs to know?

You enrolled in college for many reasons: To become a more well-rounded person. To discover new ideas. To learn to think critically. To make yourself a stronger candidate for good jobs. To earn a degree, and the credibility and respect that comes with it. Yet no matter which reasons motivate you most, learning to capture important information is a fundamental skill that can help you achieve that goal.

In college, new and important information will come at you from so many places—from your professors in class and in individual conversations, from textbooks and other assigned readings, from your fellow students in study groups and casual discussions, from speakers in lectures and events on campus, and from countless other experiences and opportunities now open to you as a college student.

But being a college student doesn't mean you automatically capture important information. Many students leave college having learned very little and a few years later have forgotten most of it. Yet others continually capture important information as they go through college, and after they graduate they not only remember it, they also know how to apply it to their lives and careers to make themselves more happy and successful.

I. Capturing Spoken Information

Have you ever seen a cash-grab booth? You step into a small glass booth, and when the door closes, an air blower sends dollar bills swirling into the air. You try to grab and hold on to as much cash as you can before time runs out. Whatever you've got when time is up, you get to keep.

Figure 1 Reading is only one way to hold onto information.

Believe it or not, going to class is a little like stepping into a cash-grab booth.

As in the cash-grab booth, when you're in class, there's something truly valuable in the air. Instead of cash, of course, it's information—spoken information shared by your instructor and classmates.

Like your time in the cash-grab booth, your time in class is limited. That valuable information isn't in the air forever, and it's not there whenever you want it. Each class is a unique, limited-time opportunity for you to capture as much information as you can.

Most important, just as stepping into the cash-grab booth doesn't mean you automatically step out wealthy, stepping into the classroom doesn't mean you automatically step out with a wealth of captured information. Many people enter the cash-grab booth, get flustered and overwhelmed, and walk out with very little cash—the same way some people get flustered and overwhelmed in class, and walk out with very little captured information.

This section is about how to succeed in the information-capture booth known as class, and how to learn listening and observation skills that will help you effectively capture information in any setting. (Sorry, no tips on how to succeed in the cash-grab booth.)

LO 1 Becoming an Active Listener

Most speakers, whether they speak professionally, like a preacher or a news anchor, or whether they just speak casually, like you and your friends, speak between 100–125 words a minute. That may seem like a lot. But studies show most people can hear and understand between 500–650 words a minute.

If we can hear and understand between 500–650 words per minute, and most people only speak 100–125 words per minute, why do we still misunderstand people so often?

The key to understanding the gap between speaking and hearing is also the key to effectively capturing spoken information.

Hearing versus Listening

When we listen to someone speak, we often hear a word or phrase that triggers a thought in our minds: a memory, an idea, a task we forgot, or any of a number of reactions. Sometimes this thought distracts us completely, as we focus on developing the idea or dwelling in the memory. When we are distracted like this, we can still hear the speaker—our ears are aware that noise is still being made—but we're not actually listening.

Other times, we aren't distracted by a wandering thought as much as thinking about what to say next. We form our own response, argument, or personal story before the speaker is finished, and wait impatiently to say it. When we focus on what we want to say next, we're not listening very well either—except to find an opening to speak.

In both these situations, we are still hearing: We still *perceive sounds, noises, and tones as stimuli through our ears* and into our brains. But are we listening? Are we *hearing with thoughtful attention*? Not really. And if we're not listening, we're not likely to capture any important information that is spoken.

Hearing is easy, but true listening takes work. In the next section, we'll look at how to listen and pay attention so you can capture all of this information, using a concept known as **active listening.**

active listening: *Listening in a way that involves you in the communication process, including interacting with the speaker verbally and/or nonverbally. Being an active listener helps you capture spoken information.*

How to Be an Active Listener

Being a passive listener means you are there and you are awake, but nothing more. You are simply hearing spoken words. Information comes at you, but you take no active part in communicating.

Being an active listener means you are deliberately involved in the communication process. You are interested and interacting with the speaker, even if just with eye contact and the nod of your head. Being an active listener helps you capture spoken information, which helps you make use of that information and succeed in class. Being an active listener requires three tasks: you must *focus, engage,* and *respond.*

FOCUS Several states have banned drivers from using hand-held cell phones. But research shows these bans aren't reducing collisions and that the real cause of phone-related crashes isn't holding the phone, but the distraction of the conversation. In other words, having both hands on the wheel is important, but having your full focus on the road is more important. Similarly, if you want to capture spoken information, your full focus must be on the speaker.

Pay Attention Focus begins with the decision to pay attention. This means looking directly at the speaker, and not also focusing on a phone or other device at the same time. (If you are taking notes, it's okay to look down at your notebook. Since your notes are directly related to what the speaker is saying, you are still paying attention.) Pay attention with your eyes as well as your ears. Watch the

Figure 2 Active listeners get more out of a conversation.

speaker's eyes so you don't miss anything that he is communicating with facial expressions or body language, in addition to his words.

When you tune in to what the speaker is saying, you will be alert for main points, primary ideas, and key concepts she is trying to share with you.

Block Out Distractions In any setting, you are surrounded by potential distractions—a cough, a sneeze, singing birds, wailing sirens, whispers behind you . . . the list is endless.

Your brain usually filters out these sounds because, when you tell it to focus, you're telling it to both pay attention to what you have decided is important and also disregard anything that's not important. As a result, you won't notice that conversation in the hallway unless it gets especially loud. Until then, it's just meaningless background hum, so your brain lets it go.

This is where the decision to focus impacts learning. If you walk into class thinking, "I wonder what we'll learn today," you will focus on the instructor, and your brain will filter out distractions. If you walk into class thinking, "Ugh, I don't want to be here," you won't focus on the instructor, and you'll let yourself get distracted by just about anything.

Hold Back The temptation to interrupt a speaker is strong. We hear something, we think of a rebuttal, and our instinct is often to say it. Focusing means resisting this temptation.

When you interrupt a speaker, you may cause her to lose her train of thought, meaning you won't fully hear or understand what she is trying to say. Interruptions also tend to frustrate most speakers, which means they will be less likely to give your comments or rebuttals a fair and complete hearing.

Unfortunately, most of us have gotten so used to being interrupted that we speak in anticipation of being interrupted—we rush or cut to the main point without explaining our ideas fully. If you hold back and give your speaker space and time, you will hear what the speaker really wants to say, and your conversation partner will also be more likely to give you a fuller and more complete hearing when it is your turn to speak.

ENGAGE Even if you are not speaking—whether in a lecture or a conversation—you can still actively participate. Being an active listener means engaging with the speaker and engaging your brain in the discussion.

One of the simplest and best ways to engage your brain is to take notes. If writing notes isn't possible or appropriate, you can still take mental notes. These serve as your abbreviated reminder of what the speaker has said. In class, you should always take written notes.

Give Feedback Giving feedback means reciprocating the speaker's efforts to communicate with you, whether you are speaking one-on-one or in an audience of thousands. Gestures and body language, like a nod, smile, or frown, show that you're listening and understanding—or not understanding. All speakers appreciate feedback, so watch for an opportunity to encourage the speaker in a way that will say, "I'm with you. Keep going."

Be Reflective As an active listener, your job is to understand what is being said. Asking reflective questions, such as, "What do you mean when you say . . . ?" can help with any confusion and ensure you understand. Paraphrasing the speaker's remarks, with phrases like, "It sounds like what you're saying is . . ." or "If I heard you right, you mean . . .," show that you understand and are connecting with the speaker. Asking reflective questions lets the speaker know that you are fully and appreciatively connected to his or her attempt to communicate with you.

RESPOND Often, your role in a lecture or conversation is simply as an active listener. This is an important role to play, for you and for the speaker. In most verbal interactions, though, we are also called on to respond. Active listening makes us better responders.

Patience, understanding, and respect are the marks of an active listener. These traits enable you to give the speaker a fair and open hearing, as well as your most informed response. When it is your turn to offer your reply or opinion, your active listening will have helped you gather the information and perspective that represents their state of mind, their needs, or their opinions, and you will be able to respond appropriately. When you respond in a manner that treats the speaker as you want to be treated, you will be freer to be candid, open, and honest, and your conversation partners likely will be more receptive to giving you the same courtesy and respect that you gave them.

Becoming a good active listener takes practice. Why put so much effort into listening? In addition to the many reasons we've discussed, being an active listener also makes you a more effective speaker. Listening actively prepares you to speak to the issues, concerns, and needs of the people you interact with. By showing respect in capturing their words, you encourage their respect in capturing yours. The benefits of this give-and-take apply to you as a student today, and to the customers, clients, and co-workers you will work with after graduation.

Hurdles to Active Listening

Listed below are a few bad habits that will prevent you from being an effective listener.

FAILING TO FOCUS We discussed the importance of focus. When thinking about focusing, beware of these hazards:

☐ *Faking it.* Pretending to listen can have two negative outcomes. First, you may miss something important, and second, your body language may signal your lack of interest and decrease the speaker's willingness to trust and respect you.

Copyright © 2013 McGraw-Hill Higher Education

□ *Avoiding challenging topics.* Poor listeners pay attention when the topic is easy or agreeable, but let their attention and focus drift when faced with a complex or difficult topic. Some topics are truly difficult, and some seem difficult because of an ineffective speaker. But sometimes topics seem difficult because of poor listening. Focused attention can often help you understand what seemed at first like a difficult topic.

□ *Taking emotional detours.* Emotionally loaded issues can be big distractions for poor listeners, who wander off into their own thoughts when a speaker raises an emotional topic, such as politics or religion. Even if you have a firm set of opinions on such a topic, stick with the speaker and hear them out.

□ *Missing the big picture.* If you are listening to a good lecture or presentation, the speaker is probably using an outline or other predetermined structure. This means that individual points fit into a larger structure. When listening, consider the flow of the overall message and how each individual point fits into the larger context. If the speaker has distributed a printed outline, follow along.

Figure 4 Being an effective listener isn't always easy.

BEING JUDGMENTAL Learning requires you to acknowledge that there are things that you don't yet know. Yet often, we judge a speaker or his or her ideas, which keeps us from being open to what we can learn from them. Watch out for these traps that tempt all listeners:

□ *Making assumptions.* When you make up your mind about the speaker or her intentions, you lose your ability to capture and give a fair hearing to her words and ideas. Put your assumptions aside for the moment, and listen openly.

□ *Jumping to conclusions.* If you make up your mind about a speaker's message before it has been fully delivered, or assume you know where an argument is going, you may misjudge the speaker's ideas, or miss the point entirely. Hold back on any evaluation until the speaker explains his ideas completely.

□ *Fixating on fact accuracy.* Remembering every fact with 100 percent accuracy is almost impossible, especially when you are speaking. Yet many listeners latch onto a speaker's small factual error and lose sight of the main point. Actively listen for primary ideas. You can always go back and fact-check later.

☐ *Critiquing nonessential details.* Hypercritical assessments of anything related to speakers—their tone of voice, verbal tics, hair, clothes—block active listening. To learn from a speaker, focus on what is being said, not everything else.

LO 2 Paying Attention to Nonverbal Communication

What we say is only a small part of what we communicate. Earlier, we mentioned gestures and body language. Being an active listener also includes your deliberate observation and perception of what speakers are saying without words.

In a lecture setting, it may seem like you can "listen" without focusing your eyes on the front of the classroom. But if you are gazing out the classroom window or sketching in your notebook, you may miss a significant portion of the instructor's message. Even in a face-to-face conversation, you can miss (or misunderstand) critical information that is being communicated through nonverbal channels if you're not paying attention.

Let's take a closer look how we use **nonverbal communication** to express ourselves.

nonverbal communication: *Ways of communicating without words, including body language, expressions, tone, and inflection.*

Body Language and Expressions

Body language includes anything people do with their bodies to communicate information, such as facial expressions, arm gestures, and posture. Some body

ON THE JOB

Effective Listening

In college, if you consistently fail to follow written or spoken directions, the professor can just give you a failing grade—but you most likely won't have a negative impact on the rest of the class. Yet in your career, if you consistently fail to follow written or spoken directions, you can negatively impact everyone you work with.

If you listen poorly, others may have to spend valuable time repeating directions or correcting mistakes you made because you didn't listen carefully enough. If you fail to listen actively to instructions, you may have to start a task over from the beginning because you misunderstood what you were supposed to do. Worse, poor listening skills may cause you to miss or misinterpret important information, either spoken or unspoken, which can damage the outcome of a project, assignment, or relationship.

No matter your career path, strong listening skills and the ability to capture spoken words effectively can help you be more productive and efficient. Whether listening to get directions, learn new skills, or understand a customer's concerns, listening skills impact job effectiveness and the quality of your relationships, on and off the job. As we've discussed, strong listeners are usually better speakers too and are more effective at influencing, persuading, and negotiating at work and at home. Ultimately, how you communicate and how you receive communication may determine how valuable you are to your employer and the trajectory your career path will take.

The Cost of Not Listening Carefully Not listening carefully enough to understand someone fully may not seem like a big deal—after all, the person can always repeat themselves. But business owners and

language is easy to interpret—you know what it means when a person rolls his eyes or shrugs his shoulders—while other body language is more subtle.

Paying attention to a speaker's body language in addition to her words will help you "read between the lines" to truly understand what she means. For example, if a speaker is saying words that are positive and upbeat, but is slouching and frowning, then she probably isn't truly positive and upbeat.

Tone and Inflection

What would you think if you heard your supervisor say to another employee in a very loud, high-pitched, angry voice, "I told you that report was supposed to be on my desk this morning!" What if you observed him saying the same thing, except this time using a calm voice, his body relaxed, and with a smile on his face?

These situations show how context, tone of voice, and body language can all impact the meaning of spoken words. "I told him the report was supposed to be on my desk this morning," could be a matter of high urgency, or just another task that needed to be completed. The volume and tone of voice in which it was said, the facial expressions and gestures used when saying it, and the context in which it was said all indicate whether the words were said with anger, sarcasm, seriousness, or silliness. That's a lot to notice, but we pick up these subtleties and nuances of spoken communication all the time.

Context and Setting

Much as tone and inflection can change the meaning of spoken words, so can context and setting. Are the words being said in a small group of people who know each other well or before a large audience of strangers? Are they being said privately, in confidence, or publicly, for anyone to hear? Are they being spoken by someone in the position of leading or teaching, or by a peer? Each of these contexts can impact a speaker's meaning.

bosses in all industries tell horror stories that illustrate the real-world cost of not listening carefully.

An owner of a graphic design firm hired a bright and technically capable employee. Yet despite her talents, she messed up a customer's project—not once, but twice—because she did not pay attention to spoken instructions. The mistake wasn't discovered until the project came back from the printer, and the cost of reprinting the project alone came to nearly $7,500. What was the cost of wasted time, lost goodwill, and diminished reputation for the company? That particular *former* employee will never know.

If you owned or ran a company, what would you expect from your employees when it came to listening and capturing spoken words? How much would you value employees who communicated effectively over those who communicated ineffectively? How patient would you be with employees who consistently proved to be ineffective communicators?

There are no set rules about how context or setting might change the meaning of spoken words. The best approach is to use your active listening skills, be aware of the context and setting, and pay attention to any context clues that might help you understand the meaning of what is being spoken.

Cultural Differences

If you nod your head backward at someone in New York City, with your chin slightly in the air, how will she respond? If you made that same motion at someone among the Navajo people in Arizona, would she respond the same way? In

TAKE ACTION

Practicing Active Listening

In this section, you have discovered the three critical tasks for active listening— focus, engagement, and response—as well as received an overview of potential hurdles to becoming a successful active listener. Now, you have the opportunity to assess your own active listening skills by putting into practice what you just learned.

You and a partner will each read a specific selection of this section: "Tone and Inflection" or "Cultural Differences." You may not both read the same passage; therefore, you will need to decide who will read which section. Once you both agree on your specified reading, you will take on a role of the "listener" while your partner becomes the "talker."

As the listener, you will actively listen to your partner read his or her reading selection by following these five steps:

1. Directly look at the talker, make eye contact.
2. Provide nonverbal feedback during the reading, including hand gestures and head nodding.
3. Do not interrupt the talker.
4. Take the following notes:

   a. Identify the main points of the reading:

   _____

   _____

   _____

   _____

   b. Jot down changes in the talker's body language, tone, and inflection:

   _____

   _____

   _____

   _____

   c. Write three potential reflective questions to ask the talker:

      i. _____

      ii. _____

      iii. _____

New York, that chin motion can be a sign of defiance, but among the Navajo, who do not often point with their fingers, it can be a way of directional pointing.

Across the United States and the world, cultural differences like these—in the meaning of gestures, of vocabulary within the same language, and even in the meaning of the same words in the same language from one region to another—impact communication. You may even find differences among people in the same region who work in different industries, with each group having its own vocabulary and professional culture.

d. After the reading concludes, write a brief summary of the material:

_____

_____

_____

_____

_____

_____

5. Ask the talker your three reflective questions.

6. Ask yourself: Did I block out distractions or avoid making assumptions, passing judgment, faking it, or critiquing nonessential details of the reading?

After you finish your role as the listener, you will become the talker, and your partner will practice his or her active listening skills. Once you both have participated in both roles, consider the following questions to evaluate your active listening abilities:

1. How did the active listening tasks you were asked to perform differ from your own listening strategies that you typically employ?

_____

_____

_____

2. Which active listening task was the most difficult to execute? Why?

_____

_____

_____

3. Which active listening task assisted you the best in retaining the information the talker delivered?

_____

4. Which active listening task will you implement from this point forward to improve your overall listening skills?

_____

_____

Figure 5 You wouldn't speak to your teacher the same way you'd talk with your friends.

The more you interact with cultures outside your own, the more differences you will find in how people communicate. If you travel for business or if someone from another region or country visits you, will you be aware of these differences? Will you understand what others are saying, and will you be understood? Understanding is the first step to capturing spoken information effectively.

II. Capturing Written Information

GET READY

Not everyone works best on the same schedule.

- When do you like to read? In the evening? Early morning or during your lunch break? Is it easier to focus on the words you read at certain times of the day?

Reading—and understanding what you read—is an important skill for all college students. The primary place you will find the written information you are expected to read and capture is in textbooks, with information from magazines, journals, and the Internet supporting your textbook reading.

While textbooks are a vital resource for all college students, many students resist reading them. Boredom is often cited as the reason, and textbooks are admittedly less exciting than novels or comic books. Yet the surprising reason many students avoid textbooks is that they never learned *how* to read them. Reading a textbook is different from reading other books, and if you don't know how to read one, you may struggle with the written information it contains. This section will show you how to approach textbooks and other written information so you can capture what you need to succeed.

Figure 6
Reading a textbook
is different from
reading a novel.

LO 3 How to Read a Textbook: The SQ3R Method

When you sit down to read a textbook assignment, do you plow through from the beginning? Pushing straight through a chapter or even a page of a textbook might seem like the simplest way to read it, but it's usually not the most effective way to learn from it. Just as active listening is key to capturing spoken information, **active reading** is key to capturing written information.

active reading: Reading in a way that causes you to engage with the written material, including taking notes and asking yourself questions as you read.

The active reading method outlined below provides five simple steps you can take to learn more effectively from a textbook reading assignment. Known as the **SQ3R Method**, it has been used by thousands of students, and it can have a serious impact on your reading effectiveness.

SQ3R Method: A method for reading a textbook that involves five steps: survey, question, read, recite, and review.

Step 1. Survey

The goal of this step is to preview the material you'll be reading before you actually read it. This prepares you to effectively capture information by alerting you to the major concepts in the reading assignment and letting you know what to look for as you read.

Most textbooks include a number of tools that can help you navigate the information they present. These tools include:

☐ Chapter titles, section headings, and subheadings
☐ Pictures, charts, graphs, maps, and illustrations, and captions describing them

- [ ] Key words or new terms printed in **bold** or *italics*
- [ ] Bulleted or numbered lists (like this one)
- [ ] Boxes that highlight an example, case study, or application of the information
- [ ] An introduction or overview at the beginning of each chapter
- [ ] A summary or review at the end of each chapter
- [ ] A list of learning objectives for the chapter
- [ ] Review questions or study guides

Each textbook has its own format, style, and approach to emphasizing important material. Every textbook, however, uses these tools to alert you to information that the author thinks you need to know.

With this in mind, survey the chapter instead of diving right in. Scan the headings, pictures, and charts. Skim the chapter to find key words. Review the bulleted lists, introduction, and summary. Learn as much about the material as you can before you begin line-by-line reading. This will help you develop a mental outline of what's ahead, making you more prepared to absorb and understand the material as you come across it in your reading. Remember, a textbook is not a mystery novel—you won't ruin it if you know how the story ends.

Step 2. Question

Now that you have surveyed the chapter and have a general sense of what's to come, begin thinking critically about the information you're about to read. Based on your surveying in Step 1, ask yourself questions about the material in the chapter, such as:

- [ ] What do I already know about this subject?
- [ ] What are three key things to pay attention to when reading this chapter?
- [ ] How does the information in this chapter connect to other topics in the book?
- [ ] What did my instructor say about this chapter or material when it was assigned?

Also, come up with specific questions about the subject matter based on what you have learned from surveying the chapter. Another idea is to take headings and subheadings and turn them into questions. For example, the heading for this section is "Capturing Written Information." You could turn that into a question like, "What are the keys to capturing written information?", "Why is capturing written information important?", or "How can capturing written information help me?" Write these questions down, either in a notebook or in the margins of the textbook.

This step has two significant benefits. First, it helps prepare you for processing the information you're about to read. By the time you start reading the chapter, you've already thought actively about the material and engaged with some of the ideas. The material won't be foreign to you, but will instead be familiar.

Second, reading with specific questions in mind changes the way you read. Now when you read, you aren't just looking at words and trying to understand their meaning—you're working to answer specific questions. Looking for answers will focus your reading efforts and engage your brain at a whole new level. This will help you make sense of the information you're reading and remember it as well.

Step 3. Read

Now it's time to read—in the more traditional sense. However, because of the work you did in the *survey* and *question* steps, you're prepared to engage with the material you're about to read, and you're ready to read with a purpose.

When reading, don't force yourself to read an entire chapter in one sitting. If you're struggling to make sense of everything at once, read smaller sections at a time. If a section is confusing, stop and reread any parts that are not clear. Make your way through the chapter in whatever chunks of text work for you. Remember, getting to the end of the chapter is not your goal. Your goal is to identify, understand, and capture the important information contained within it.

As you read, look for answers to your questions from Step 2. Write down the answers to those questions (in your own words, not the author's) or take notes about important ideas in your notebook or in the margins. Reread all of the headers, graphics, captions, lists,

and key phrases that you identified in Step 1, and make sure that you understand them in context. Use a highlighter to emphasize those portions of the chapter that seem most important. All of these strategies will help you learn the information you're reading and be useful to you in the next two steps of this method.

Step 4. Recite

Through surveying and reading the material, you have processed the information visually. In writing down notes and answers to your questions, and highlighting important information, you have reinforced what you've learned. Up until now, all of your interaction with the material has involved your eyes and hands. In this step, you will add another layer of reinforcement to your learning by speaking and hearing the information in a process known as **recitation.**

recitation: *The act of reinforcing learning by speaking the material out loud to yourself.*

The goal of reciting isn't just to read the information aloud. It's to continue the process you began in Step 2 when you came up with and wrote down original questions about the material. When you get to a section break, say a question out loud, such as:

- ☐ What was the main point of what I just read?
- ☐ Why is this information important?
- ☐ How does this information connect to what I read earlier?
- ☐ How does this information connect with what we've discussed in class?
- ☐ How would I explain this section to a classmate struggling to understand it?

Once again, come up with questions specific to the subject matter. After you ask the questions, answer them aloud—without looking at the material. Saying and hearing these questions and answers engages more of your senses in the learning process than just reading and writing, increasing the chances that you will understand and remember the information. This step will also confirm what you understand, help you identify anything you don't, and help you think about the information in a way that is similar to how you may be tested on it.

Step 5. Review

With the first four steps, you've done more than just read the material: You've previewed what you were about to read, to mentally prepare for it. You've asked yourself questions about the material, to help focus your reading. You've read with a purpose, answering the questions you've identified and highlighting important information in the text. And you've asked and answered questions about the material aloud, engaging more of your senses to help reinforce your learning.

Most students report that using these steps significantly increases what they learn, comprehend, and remember from a reading assignment over just reading through the assignment from start to finish. But you're not done yet.

The final step in this method is to review the material that you have covered. Reviewing can include a number of activities:

☐ Surveying the material again, like in the first step
☐ Rereading specific sections that you highlighted
☐ Rereading sections that were challenging or confusing
☐ Rereading the questions and answers you wrote down
☐ Preparing a review sheet with highlights from the reading that you can use for studying
☐ Writing out flash cards with key concepts and terms that you can use for studying
☐ Writing out questions and answers that address information you think might appear on a test or quiz
☐ Creating an outline of the material in the chapter

Don't limit review to immediately after you read, though. Think of the first four steps of the SQ3R Method as a foundation for your learning. Developing solid review materials helps you build on that foundation, making it easy to quickly

MONEY SMART$

Investing in Stocks and Mutual Funds

One way the reading skills you have learned in this section can benefit you is by helping you to read financial documents, such as information about stocks and mutual funds. If you pay attention to news reports, the business news is often full of talk about investments and the stock market. Knowing a little more about stocks and mutual funds can prepare you for when you have savings to invest.

Stocks A stock represents ownership of a company. So, if you own a company's stock, you are one of its owners. Stock is issued in *shares*, or portions of ownership. Most publicly owned companies issue millions of shares, meaning millions of people may own a part of the company.

How to Read and Understand Information about Stocks If you've ever looked at the section of the newspaper that lists stock prices, you've seen tables filled with numbers. Those numbers are called a *stock table*. This provides investors and potential investors with current information about stocks that are traded on

a specific stock exchange. If you own a stock, you can use a stock table to see its price per share, any recent changes in its value, and other important information. If you are considering buying a stock, a stock table can help you decide whether to make a purchase.

Here are a few of the terms that can help you understand the information in a stock table:

- *52-Week High (often abbreviated as "52W High").* The highest price paid for the stock in the past year (52 weeks), not including the previous day's trading.

- *Company Name, Type of Stock, and Ticker Symbol (Stock).* The name of the company, the type of stock (preferred or common stock), and the stock's *ticker* symbol. Every stock has a symbol, or abbreviation, used to identify it.

- *Dividend per Share (Div).* This number tells you, in dollars, the annual payment per share, or the portion of profits a company would pay to you as a shareholder.

- *Price/Earnings Ratio (P/E).* This is the current price of the stock divided by how much the company earned per share over the last year.

reconnect with the information on a regular basis. Reviewing the material periodically reinforces your understanding and strengthens your retention of what you have learned. Effective review is an ongoing process.

Easier Reading

After a few times using the SQ3R Method, you may feel better about your reading assignments and dread reading less. You may discover that procrastinating,

- *Last or Close.* This number indicates the last price paid for the stock in the final trade of the previous day.
- *Net Change (Chg).* This is the change in the stock price from the previous day, shown in dollar amounts, with a plus or minus to indicate whether the stock increased or decreased (such as +1.23 or −0.45).

To learn more about terms not explained here, check out the resources on the U.S. Securities and Exchange Commission (SEC) website at www.sec.gov/.

Mutual Funds A mutual fund is a collection of stocks and/or bonds. Mutual funds let you buy shares in many stocks and bonds through a single purchase, instead of buying them individually. Mutual funds are not sold directly to the public by the owners of the companies, but instead by investment firms that assemble, manage, and sell shares in the fund to individual investors.

How to read and understand information about mutual funds. A *prospectus* is a document that includes information about the mutual fund, including its investment goals and strategies, risks, fees, and past performance.

It also tells you who manages the fund and how to buy and redeem shares. The SEC requires funds to include specific information in this document in a standard format so that all investors can compare different funds. According to the SEC, "When you purchase shares of a mutual fund, the fund must provide you with a prospectus. But you can—and should—request and read a fund's prospectus before you invest."

skipping homework, and even skipping class stop altogether. Ultimately, SQ3R makes reading assignments less scary. And when they're not so scary, you can stop avoiding them and dive right in. Capturing written information the SQ3R way may even change your overall study habits and the way you look at school and life.

The concepts and strategies in the SQ3R Method can also be applied to other written materials, not just textbooks. Whether you are reading articles, information on the Internet, novels, short stories, or nonfiction books, the principles that make SQ3R effective will work with these materials as well.

However, not all reading assignments will have the clear structure and helpful navigation tools that most textbooks do. This means that while the *read, recite,* and *review* steps will work the same for most reading material, you will probably need to adjust your approach to the *survey* and *question* steps.

LO 4 How and When to Schedule Your Reading

Does it matter *when* you read an assignment? Absolutely. The SQ3R Method is designed both to make your reading more productive and to give you the tools to help you review the material after you have read it. If you read an assignment right before the class when it is discussed or right before a test, you don't give yourself much time to review the material effectively—and review is what helps you retain the material and learn from it.

Consider this approach: When you get a reading assignment, check the due date, when you will discuss it in class, and when you will be tested on the material. Then look at your calendar, and schedule not only time to complete the reading assignment using the SQ3R Method well in advance, but also time to review the material and the notes you took on it. Have you ever approached a reading assignment like this? If so, how did this approach work? If not, how do you think it would impact your learning and retention? How about your confidence and stress levels?

The Hazards of Cramming

The practice of *cramming*—waiting and reading an entire assignment in one sitting at the last minute—is a common habit, even among top students. Yet cramming is not nearly as productive or effective as following the SQ3R Method and allowing time for repeated review.

People cram for many reasons: procrastination, busy schedules, unexpected emergencies, homework avoidance, misplaced priorities, and so on. Some people even believe they do better when they cram, that the adrenaline and deadline pressure help them focus and perform at their best. But cramming doesn't allow your brain enough time to learn the way it learns best.

Figure 9
Cramming just makes a stressful time even more stressful.

Your brain needs time to absorb and store new ideas and key concepts in your long-term memory. Cramming is simply dumping information into your short-term memory, which your mind uses for many things. Research has shown that information you learn while cramming is almost entirely lost within 72 hours of acquiring it. So while you may be able to retrieve crammed information for the short term, if you need to retrieve it later, whether for a pop quiz, scheduled test, midterm, or final, you might find you can't recall much of the information at all.

One of the built-in risks of procrastination and last-minute cramming is that you fail to learn the information for the long term—and you might not even remember it in the short term. So while cramming *may* help you pass an exam, true learning—weaving new information into the fabric of your long-term memory—takes effort, reinforcement, and sufficient rest so that your brain can comfortably and normally process all the information you're putting into it.

In other words, it is far wiser and safer, as well as a much better investment of your valuable time and energy, to read your assignments early, following the SQ3R Method.

Remember, when your instructor gives you a reading assignment, the objective is not reading for the sake of reading or just to become familiar with the information in the chapter. Your reading is part of a bigger plan to help you acquire the knowledge and skills revealed in each reading assignment. Reading is an integral part of your learning, as well as developing critical thinking skills that will be valuable to you throughout college and especially in your career.

Read on a Regular Schedule

Beyond reading your assignments well in advance, how should you schedule your reading?

The first step in effective scheduling is to ask yourself a few questions about your reading habits and tendencies:

☐ What time of day is usually best for me to read? When am I most focused, least likely to be distracted, and most likely to have the mental energy and stamina needed to tackle my reading?

☐ What time of day is usually worst for me to read? When am I most likely to be distracted or doze off while reading?

☐ Where do I do my most productive reading? This could be at the library, at a coffee shop, at the kitchen table, on the bus, or in bed.

☐ Where can I not read productively? This could be any of those same places listed above.

Answering these questions should give you an idea of your ideal time and place to read—and times and places to avoid. Of course, we don't live in an ideal world, and you may not be able to read at the ideal time and place all the time, or even very often. However, with this information, and your class, work, and personal schedules, you can make better decisions about when you plan to read.

Doing this kind of thinking and planning at the beginning of the term, and writing down time for reading in your calendar—essentially, making a regular reading appointment with yourself—will help you commit to reading early and often, which will support your learning efforts. Reading in the same places and times each week will also help make reading a habit, which will make it easier to do consistently.

Practicing the SQ3R Method

As a college student, you will find most of your educational material in your textbook, which is why knowing how to capture written information is imperative to your academic and professional success. In this section, you learned how to apply the SQ3R Method to improve your reading abilities, so let's take the opportunity to practice before you start implementing this method on your own.

Refer to the boxed reading in this module, Money Smarts: Investing in Stocks and Mutual Funds, beginning on page 16. For this reading, you will follow the SQ3R steps below as you read. As you go through the process, check off each completed step or answer the according question. Remember to take your time and review each step before you move to the next.

1. Survey

a. Examine the title, headings, and subheadings.

b. Note any words printed in **bold** or *italics.*

c. Mark any questions in the text.

2. Question

a. Ask: What do I already know about this subject?

_____

_____

_____

b. Ask: What are the three key points to pay attention to when reading this document?

1st Key Point: _____

2nd Key Point: _____

3rd Key Point: _____

3. Read

a. Highlight important/key points.

b. Underline unknown terms.

c. Define unfamiliar words:

_____

_____

_____

_____

_____

d. Take marginal notes on any portion that is unclear.

e. Take marginal notes on any portion that is significant.

4. Recite

a. Ask out loud: What was the main point of what I just read?

Record your response:

_____
_____
_____

 b. Ask out loud: Why is this information important?
  Record your response:

_____
_____
_____

5. Review

 a. Survey the material again.

 b. Reread specific sections that you highlighted.

 c. Reread any sections that were especially challenging or confusing.

 d. List the key concepts or terms that you could benefit from remembering:

  i. _____
  ii. _____
  iii. _____
  iv. _____
  v. _____

Once you complete the reading with the SQ3R Method, consider the following questions:

1. How did these steps for active reading vary from your own?

_____
_____
_____

2. Which step did you find the most difficult to complete? Why?

_____
_____
_____

3. Which step was the most beneficial in retaining the information from the text?

_____
_____

4. Which step will you work on improving to assist in your active reading?

_____
_____

5. How will these steps help you be more successful in all of your classes?

_____
_____

III. Taking Notes

Note-taking is an effective method to help you learn and remember new information.

- Do you plan to be an active note-taker during your college studies?
- Do you have a method that works for you?

So far, we have discussed how active listening can help you capture spoken information, and how the active reading technique known as the SQ3R Method can help you capture written information. In this section, we're going to take a closer look at taking notes, either in class or while reading, as a way to process and store the information you've captured for greater understanding and future application.

Taking notes offers many benefits. In addition to providing a written record of what you have learned, note taking also helps you:

☐ Pay attention, stay alert, and listen carefully
☐ Organize and restructure your thoughts, to aid comprehension
☐ Identify the most important material in a lecture or text
☐ Remember important material better than if you just hear or read it
☐ Put material in your own words, to reinforce learning
☐ Study the information for a test, or use it as a reference for a paper

While there is so much to gain from taking notes, and most people have taken notes before, note-taking is not often considered a skill that needs to be learned or practiced. Yet when asked, many students confess that their note-taking skills could be stronger, and that they never formally learned how to take good notes. That's why by the end of this section, you will know a proven way to take good notes, which you can use and practice to strengthen your information-capturing abilities, in college and throughout your life.

LO 5 The Value of a Note-Taking System

Several note-taking systems are commonly used by students, and many students develop their own systems, which use different notebooks, page layouts, types of abbreviations and shorthand, and even different pen colors to capture information. While every system has its own benefits and limitations, simply having a system is important. A system creates consistency, simplicity, and predictability in your note taking. This means that when you sit down in class for a lecture, you don't have to think about how you're going to take notes—you already know, which frees you to concentrate on capturing the information. It also means that, when you are reviewing and studying, you know exactly where and how to find the information you need.

The Cornell Note-Taking System

One of the most effective and popular systems for taking notes is the Cornell Note-Taking System, developed by Walter Pauk at Cornell University to help students better organize their notes.

The Cornell Note-Taking System uses a specific structure for each page of your notes. You can create this structure with a pen, ruler, and standard notebook paper, or you can go online to find preformatted sheets that you can customize, download, and print. (See the end of the module for online resources.)

The structure divides the page into three sections: *Notes*, *Cues*, and *Summary*. Figure 10 shows how the page will look and includes some information about what goes in each column, which will be explained more below.

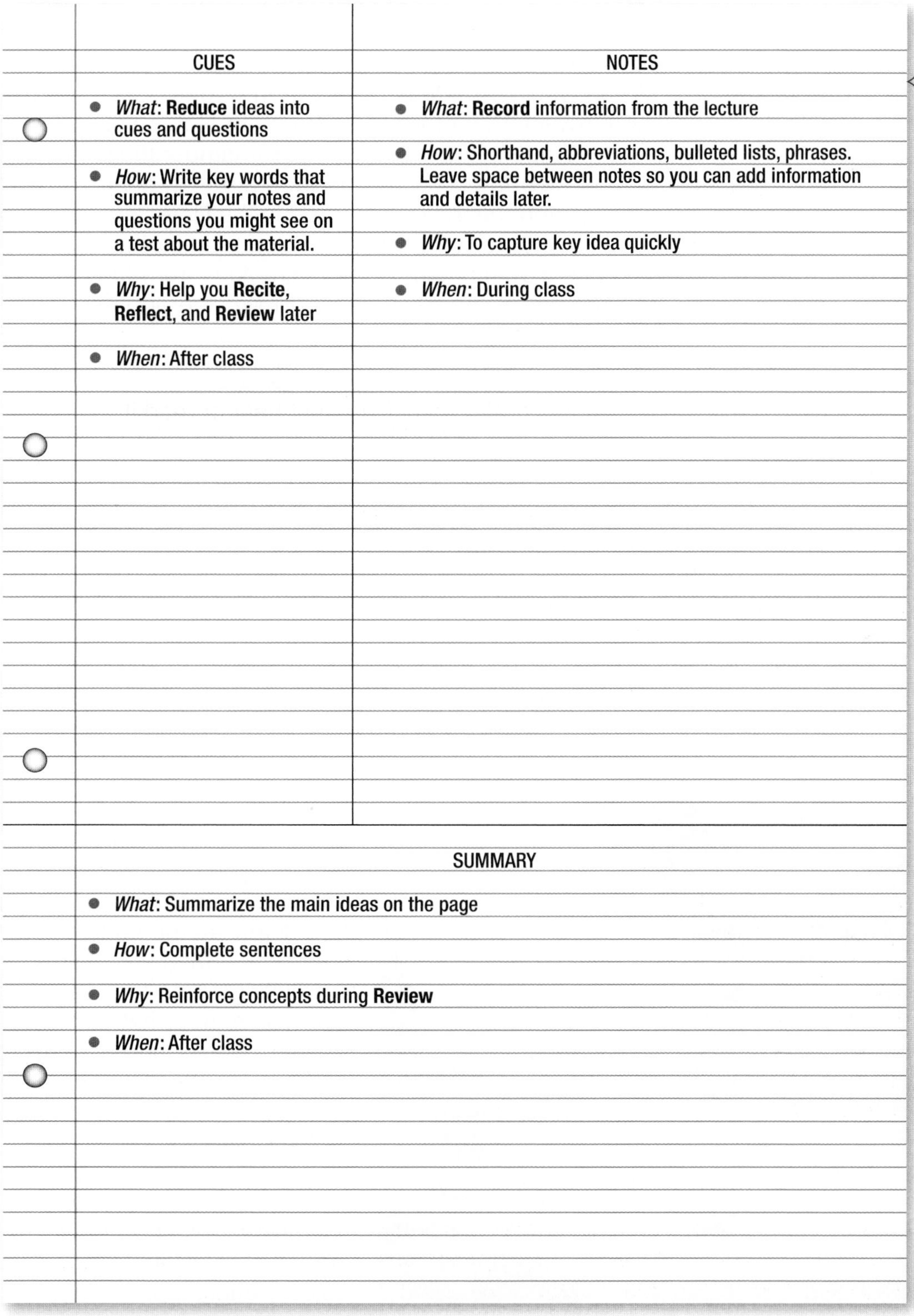

CUES	NOTES
• *What*: **Reduce** ideas into cues and questions	• *What*: **Record** information from the lecture
	• *How*: Shorthand, abbreviations, bulleted lists, phrases. Leave space between notes so you can add information and details later.
• *How*: Write key words that summarize your notes and questions you might see on a test about the material.	
	• *Why*: To capture key idea quickly
• *Why*: Help you **Recite**, **Reflect**, and **Review** later	• *When*: During class
• *When*: After class	

SUMMARY

• *What*: Summarize the main ideas on the page

• *How*: Complete sentences

• *Why*: Reinforce concepts during **Review**

• *When*: After class

Figure 10 The structure of the Cornell Note-Taking System.

This format facilitates the use of the five steps of the Cornell Note-Taking System:

1. RECORD During class, use the Notes column on the right-hand side of the page to record or capture as much meaningful information as you can. Don't try to write down every word the instructor says—focus on major concepts and facts. Also, don't worry about grammar or spelling, but do make sure you write legibly enough to be able to read your own handwriting later. Using shorthand or abbreviations here will make you a more efficient note-taker. In addition to standard abbreviations, such as using "&" or "+" instead of "and," or "Dec." instead of "December," consider developing your own abbreviations, particularly if there are words or phrases that are used frequently in a particular course.

2. REDUCE As soon after class as possible, look back though the information you captured in the Notes column. Clarify or add details to any notes that you didn't capture as well as you would have liked. Then, in the Cues column on the left-hand side of the page, review the information from the Notes column and write down **cues,** or memory triggers, that will help you remember the important points from the lecture. This step is called the Reduce step because you are reducing the large amount of information you captured in the Notes column to a smaller amount of information. In addition to the cues you write in the left-hand column, write a few sentences that summarize the main ideas from the class in the Summary area at the bottom of the page. This will provide another handy reference tool when you are reviewing and studying your notes.

cues: *Memory triggers used to help you remember important points from a lecture or book.*

Another helpful technique is to use the Cues column to write down questions that you think you might be asked on a test or quiz about the material. These questions can be used to clarify meaning, strengthen your memory, make connections between topics, and help you review the material when you are studying later.

3. RECITE Once you have reduced your notes, you are ready to begin reinforcing what you have learned, and begin the process of capturing it in your long-term memory. First, cover the Notes column of your page, ideally with another sheet of paper. Then, using either the cues or questions in the Cues column, speak what you know about the material *out loud*: If you have written a cue, say what the cue reminds you of, and if you have written a question, answer the question aloud. Then uncover your notes to see if you remembered and understood the material correctly. If you did, keep moving down the page. If you did not, take a few moments to reread your notes, then try again.

Reciting the material will help you retain what you learn. Hearing your thoughts spoken out loud is different from just reading them from notes and will help you develop your ideas and understanding of the material. It's a good idea to do your recitation soon after taking your notes and also periodically afterward.

Figure 11 The Cornell system works whether you take notes by hand or type them.

4. REFLECT Now that you have a solid sense of the material, it's time to take a step back to think about it. In this step, you want to ask yourself broader questions, such as:

☐ How does this information fit in with what I already know?
☐ How does it connect to other material in the course? In my life?
☐ Why would it be important to know this information?
☐ How can I apply this information?
☐ Now that I've learned this, what else do I want to know about the topic?

By helping you relate this new information to things you already know, reflection fosters deeper learning, weaving new knowledge in with your existing knowledge. As you take time to think about and make sense of these new concepts that you're learning, you will also be examining, organizing, classifying, and structuring your knowledge, making it easier to apply it and recall it when needed.

5. REVIEW The investment you have made in the Record, Reduce, Recite, and Reflect steps has not only helped you learn and understand the material, it has also built you a great study tool. Your notes are now a resource you can use to review the material so that you can remember it and recall it as needed for a test or quiz.

While your notes will serve as a fantastic study tool right before the test, don't wait until then to review them. If you take 10 minutes or so every week to review your notes, you will be more likely to retain what you've learned, and you'll be better able to integrate the information with other things you learn in the course, whether from other lectures, study group discussions, or reading materials. It's also a good idea to recite from your notes, as you did in the third step of this system, in addition to rereading them.

The Cornell Note-Taking System is especially helpful for taking notes during class, but it can also be adapted to taking notes while reading.

LO 6 Taking Notes in Class

Taking notes in class is not about writing down every word the instructor says. Rather, it is about capturing the important information the instructor is sharing so that you can learn it and apply it. Taking notes is also an investment of effort that helps your brain fully engage in the learning process.

To get the most from your investment, you should break down your note-taking into three stages: before class, during class, and after class. Think of these stages as *preparation*, *attention and investigation*, and *organization and clarification*.

Before Class: Preparation

The note-taking preparation stage—which should happen *before you go to class*—includes three main parts:

1. Complete all assigned readings well before the class begins. This gives you a preview of the information that will be emphasized or explained during the lecture or discussion.

2. Review your notes from the previous class session, as well as your reading notes. This will help your mind be more receptive and attentive to the words and ideas you will see and hear in class.

3. Check your equipment. Being prepared to take effective notes in class means having all the materials you need to do so: notebook, paper, pens, pencils, erasers, and so on. Make sure these are all in your backpack before

you leave home—and consider stashing a few extra pens or pencils in your backpack and pockets just in case. Taking this simple step will keep a supply shortage from being a distraction.

Taking effective notes comes when you combine an effective note-taking process with the right mind-set—which is set *before* you go to class. To get yourself in the right frame of mind, go to class mentally hungry, ready and eager to get all that you can out of it. If you're prepared, you'll already know some of what's to come in class that day, and you can let your mind get excited or curious about what you're about to learn.

Going to class in a passive—or worse, resistant—state of mind can be deadly, to your learning and your motivation. In fact, because it's something you do to yourself, it's like academic suicide, and it often leads to doing the same thing to your career potential. If you bring a passive, resistant, or negative attitude to class, you limit the success of your career before it even begins.

During Class: Attention and Investigation

Class time is watching-and-listening time. In class, you want to be an active listener, as we discussed in the first section, and be especially alert for *signal statements*. These are words or phrases that the instructor says that indicate something important has just been said or is about to be said. Common signal statements include:

- ☐ "Remember . . ."
- ☐ "The most important point is . . ."
- ☐ "Here's something you may see again . . ."
- ☐ "This will be on the test." (This one is the best!)

Figure 12
Taking the most useful notes starts by preparing before class.

When you hear one of these invaluable indicators, it's as though your instructor is using a verbal highlighter or saying, "Pay attention—this is important to know!" This information will usually appear on a test, quiz, or exam, but it is often an essential building block for the course and perhaps for your career as well. If one of these important concepts is not totally clear to you, raise your hand and ask for clarification, or see the instructor after class to ensure you fully understand what was communicated.

The notes you take in class should indicate concepts and ideas more than just facts and figures. The objective is to capture key elements of the presentation, not every word. Write in short sentences and phrases, and use abbreviations and symbols that make sense to you. As you take notes, leave room on the page, in the margins as well as between sections, so you can add notes later if the instructor says more about a topic later in class.

If you have prepared for class as discussed above, then what is presented in class should emphasize and reinforce course materials you're already familiar with, and you will be ready for all that is offered for capturing.

MY SUCCESS STORY

Amanda Jones now works as a medical assistant in a very busy private practice medical office, supporting several doctors. Because of her attention to detail, skill in dealing with patients, and excellent organizational skills, she is being provided with further training and development so she can also work the front office, including medical billing and general office management.

Amanda explains the key to her success at such an early stage in her career: "I think the one most important skill I learned and practiced in school was how to take accurate and detailed notes. I quickly learned—through a lot of practice—how much more I learned when I wrote down the information my instructor was teaching. I think just the physical act of writing the notes in my notebook helped me to better understand and remember the mountain of information that we were being taught.

"Now in my daily work activities, my excellent note-taking abilities mean my medical charting is accurate and complete, messages to doctors are not forgotten, and conversations I have with patients are accurately and completely described in my notes. I know that this is one big reason the physicians are training me for additional duties and, so I am told, higher pay!"

Amanda's efforts to apply effective study techniques as a student have paid off for her in a way she probably never imagined while she was in college. Now as a professional, she is a highly valued member of the medical staff, in large part because of her skills in accurately capturing important information.

After Class: Organization and Clarification

Keeping your notes organized will help you refer back to specific information in them quickly and easily when you're studying, which will reinforce your learning.

To keep your notes organized, create a separate binder, folder, or notebook for each course. Use a fresh page for each class session. At the top of each page, write the date of the class session, as well as the primary topics covered.

After class, while the material discussed is still fresh in your memory, do a quick and easy recheck of your notes. Make sure any words you abbreviated are clear and understandable. Use the spaces you left in the margin and between sections to clarify any major points or to add details that you could not write down quickly enough during class. To make key information in your notes easy to find, consider going over them with a highlighter and marking what you want to remember, just like you would with a textbook. If needed, ask the instructor for clarification of an unclear point or check with other students in the class to make sure your interpretation of it is the same.

A Note on Taking Notes While Reading

Taking notes when reading is similar to taking notes in class, whether you are reading a book, article, or essay. Here are a few tips to keep in mind when taking reading notes:

☐ Instead of the date of the class session or title of the lecture, write the title, author, chapter, section, and page numbers of the reading material at the top of the page.

☐ As with taking notes in class, don't try to capture everything. Focus on what is important, and take notes on that.

☐ Be sure that you are explaining concepts in your own words, not in the author's words, to make sure you are understanding the material and not just copying what you see written.

Practicing the Cornell Note-Taking System

In this section, you learned how to organize your notes during a lecture with the Cornell Note-Taking System. Giving your notes structure will make the process of listening and recording important information a lot easier, making you more successful at capturing essential material.

However, in order to improve in your note-taking abilities, you must practice and challenge yourself to work on grasping spoken information every day. To assist you with this process and help you to adapt to the Cornell Note-Taking System, your instructor will deliver a short lecture. The proper Cornell format has already been completed for you on the facing page. During the lecture you will be responsible for filling in the missing elements in all three sections. Good luck and remember to implement the five steps of the Cornell Note-Taking System as you listen to the lecture: record, reduce, recite, reflect, and review.

Once the lecture has concluded, and you have finished filling in your summary, respond to the following questions to evaluate your note-taking process:

1. How long did the lecture last?
   _____

2. Was it easier for you to record the information on the board? Why or why not?
   _____
   _____
   _____

3. What could you improve on to be more successful in taking notes during class?
   _____
   _____
   _____
   _____

☐ Leave room on the page (between points and, if you're using the Cornell System, in the Cues column on the left) for other notes you might add later when you read related information, or to add information that is discussed in class.

Cues	Notes
What: (Reduce ideas into cues/key words and questions that you might see on a test about the material.)	*What:* (Record information from the lecture using shorthand, abbreviations, phrases, and blank spaces.)
• • • • • • • • • • • • • • •	• • • • • • • • • • • • • • • • •

Summary

What: (Summarize the main ideas after the lecture is over.)

_____

_____

_____

_____

In this module, we have looked at the vast amount of information available to you and have discussed that if you want to capture that information so that you can use it in the future, you have to be an active participant in the process, whether listening or reading, in a conversation or in a classroom.

We have learned there are specific strategies for tasks like reading a textbook and taking notes that you can learn and practice. During your academic experience, you will have a chance to establish foundational habits that affect the way you acquire information and whether you are able to retain and use it later in life. These habits are no small issue for your consideration at this early stage in your academic life. What will you decide to do about them?

DISCUSSION QUESTIONS

1. What is the best way for you to capture important information?
2. What are study techniques that have worked well for you?
3. What is the single greatest barrier for you for studying?
4. What can you do to overcome the barriers you see for effectively capturing important information?

KEY TERMS

active listening: Listening in a way that involves you in the communication process, including interacting with the speaker verbally and/or nonverbally. Being an active listener helps you capture spoken information. (p. 3)

active reading: Reading in a way that causes you to engage with the written material, including taking notes and asking yourself questions as you read. (p. 13)

cues: Memory triggers used to help you remember important points from a lecture or book. (p. 24)

nonverbal communication: Ways of communicating without words, including body language, expressions, tone, and inflection. (p. 8)

recitation: The act of reinforcing learning by speaking the material out loud to yourself. (p. 15)

SQ3R Method: A method for reading a textbook that involves five steps: survey, question, read, recite, and review. (p. 13)

References on Reading

"Reading a Textbook," UWMC Freshman Seminar, University of Wisconsin Marathon County, www.uwmc.uwc.edu/freshman_seminar/read.htm

"Reading, Note Taking, and Study Skills," Office of Learning Resources, Middlebury College Center for Teaching, Learning, and Research, www. middlebury.edu/academics/resources/ctlr/olr/study

"Reading Your Textbooks Effectively and Efficiently," Academic Skills Center, Dartmouth College, www.dartmouth.edu/~acskills/success/reading.html

"The SQ3R Reading Method," Joe Landsberger, *Study Guides and Strategies*, www.studygs.net/texred2.htm

"Survey, Question, Read, Recite, Review (SQ3R)," Nora E. McMillan and Carol A. Keller, Strategies for Success, San Antonio College History Department, Alamo Colleges, www.accd.edu/sac/history/keller/ACCDitg/SSSQ3R.htm

"Time Management—Study Skills," Michigan Tech Counseling Services, Michigan Technological University, www.counseling.mtu.edu/time_ management.html

References on Investing in Stocks and Mutual Funds

"Fast Answers—Key Topics," U.S. Securities and Exchange Commission, www.sec.gov/answers.shtml

"Foolsaurus," The Motley Fool, http://wiki.fool.com/Foolsaurus

"How to Read Stock Tables," New York Stock Exchange, www.nyse.com/pdfs/NYSE_posterA_Mech.pdf

"Mutual Fund Prospectus, Tips for Reading One," U.S. Securities and Exchange Commission, www.sec.gov/answers/mfprospectustips.htm

"Stocks Basics: How to Read A Stock Table/Quote," Investopedia, http://www .investopedia.com/university/stocks/stocks6.asp

"Watch 'Turnover' to Avoid Paying Extra Taxes," U.S. Securities and Exchange Commission, www.sec.gov/rss/ask_investor_ed/turnover_rate.htm

References on Note-Taking

"Cornell Method PDF Generator," Ryan Stewart, Cornell-Notes.com, www.eleven21.com/notetaker/

"Cornell Note-taking Graph Paper PDF Generator," Kevin MacLeod, Incompetech Creative Industries, http://incompetech.com/graphpaper/cornellgraph/

"The Cornell Note-Taking Method," Russell Conwell Educational Services Center, Temple University, www.temple.edu/rcc/NoteTaking/cornellnotetakingmethod.htm

"Geek to Live: Take study-worthy lecture notes," Gina Trapani, Lifehacker, http://lifehacker.com/202418/geek-to-live—take-study+worthy-lecture-notes

"Note-Taking in Lecture Classes," UWMC Freshman Seminar, University of Wisconsin Marathon County, www.uwmc.uwc.edu/freshman_seminar/notetak.htm

Studying for Quizzes and Exams

LEARNING OUTCOMES

In this module, you will:

1 Approach studying in a way that will improve your success as a student.

2 Learn how planning can help you prepare for tests and exams.

3 Understand how memory works and how this knowledge can help you learn.

4 Practice several memory-enhancing tools and techniques.

5 Examine the different types of tests and test questions, and strategies for each.

6 Discover ways to maximize your score on any test and in any class.

Tests can make some people panic, while others prepare.

- What are the first three words you think when you hear "There's going to be a test"?
- Do you panic, prepare, or do a combination of both?

Preparing for and taking tests in college can be *far* more challenging than it was in high school. In your college classes, more material is covered more quickly, you must memorize more information, and often you must analyze the material you've learned and be prepared to apply it to real-world situations.

Unlike high school, where you usually saw your teachers every day, now you might only see your instructor once or twice a week. Also, you are now an adult with adult responsibilities, which may include a job, being a parent, or both. These responsibilities can compete for your study and test-preparation time.

The stakes are higher in college, too. If you fail a course, you have to take it—and pay for it—again. And research has shown that on average, for every 1.0 increase in grade point average, annual earnings increase by about 9 percent. This makes sense considering another study, which revealed that 70 percent of hiring managers say they screen job applicants based on their college GPA.[1]

So how can you earn good grades in this challenging college environment? In this module, we'll identify methods and strategies that will help you study better and remember material at test time and beyond. You will learn how attitude, beliefs, and actions relate to test results. You will also learn techniques you can use while taking a quiz or an exam that can help you perform your best.

Figure 1 If the tests are harder, you'll need to study harder for them. *Do you have the tools you need?*

I. The Right Approach to Studying and Planning

What drives our actions? What makes us do things the way we do them?

Our actions are often driven by our attitudes, which generally flow from what we believe. An *attitude* is a mind-set, or a way of thinking about something. You may not be able to see someone's attitude, but you can usually see the actions that result from it.

Let's look at two students to see how different attitudes and beliefs can lead to different actions as they prepare for an exam and respond to their exam grades. Takeisha and Michael are in the same math class and are about to take their first exam.

The day of the math test, Takeisha arrives in class a few minutes early, in time to eat an apple while reviewing her notes one last time. She slept well last night, and though she's feeling nervous, she still feels very positive about her preparation for the exam.

Michael dashes in to class late. He worked double shifts the last two days, hasn't looked at the math material in a week, is tired, and feels so anxious that he can hardly focus on the words of the test. Michael is afraid that he will fail in school—starting with this test—because he cannot handle all his responsibilities.

Who do you think will get a good grade on this exam? Who do you think will do poorly?

If you guessed that Takeisha did well, and Michael did poorly, you guessed right. Here's another question: Who gets the credit for Takeisha doing well? Who takes the blame for Michael doing poorly?

LO 1 Taking Responsibility: Your Locus of Control

Michael could have blamed his poor performance on the instructor and his job and believed that Takeisha was just lucky to get a good grade. He might have said, "This instructor doesn't know how to teach, and that test was too tricky. She wants us to fail," or "I think my boss also wants me to fail because he keeps me so late at work," or "Takeisha was just lucky that the instructor asked questions that were easy for her." Have you ever heard classmates say things like that after doing poorly on a test? Have you ever said anything like that yourself?

Statements like that reflect what psychologists call an *external* **locus of control**, where "locus" (pronounced low-cuss) means "place." In other words, if Michael believes those statements, he believes that he is not in control of his fate, but instead that his fate is controlled by external, or outside, forces, like his instructor and boss.

> **locus of control:** *Perceived place of control over your situation, either external (outside you) or internal (inside you).*

However, Michael did *not* blame his teacher or his boss. Instead, Michael took responsibility for his poor performance. He has an *internal locus of control* regarding his schoolwork, which means he believes that he is in control of his destiny. In this case, he understands that his bad grade was mostly his fault. When he got his low grade back from the instructor, he told himself, "Although math is not my hardest subject, I could have spent more time studying when I had the time. I'll put the next exam date on my calendar right now so I can start planning for it."

Recognizing his own behaviors as the source of his poor grade is the first step to raising his exam grades. Next, Michael must determine what he needs to do differently to improve his exam performance. Most importantly, he must summon the will to do it.

As you begin your college education, you should ask yourself, *"Do I have an internal or external locus of control concerning my school work?"*

Takeisha also feels strongly that she is in control of her school life. Because she did poorly in math in high school, she initially felt stressed about having to take math in college and was afraid she would fail the course. However, instead of saying, "Math and I never got along. I might as well give up on school now," she resolved to do whatever it took to succeed. After all, she reasoned, the course was required for her major, so it must be needed for her future career. Is Takeisha's locus of control external or internal?

Keeping her eyes on the career she is pursuing, Takeisha made sure to attend every class, even when she wasn't feeling well. She sat in the front of the class, where she could best see and hear the instructor. When her instructor asked for volunteers to work problems on the board, she overcame her reluctance and raised her hand. Although she got stuck the first time at the board, the instructor coached her through the problem and relieved her discomfort. She felt proud

when she finished that problem and made up her mind to ask more questions and volunteer more often.

When Takeisha realized she needed extra help outside class, she asked her instructor about resources. As she couldn't meet with the school's free tutor due to her daughter's school schedule, a library assistant showed her how to use a computer program on the library's computers for extra practice. After each class meeting, she spent a few minutes reviewing her notes and then started working on the next assignment. At least once a week she met with one or two of her math classmates (her "study buddies") in person or on the phone to work their homework problems together. She made sure she understood what the homework assignments were and handed in all of the homework exercises on time. As a result of all this concentrated effort, Takeisha was able to celebrate that good grade on her first exam with her favorite treat—a trip to the ice cream shop with her little girl.

Though they approached their first math test very differently, Takeisha and Michael both value their education. Like you, they want to do well in school and have a good career. Both have concerns and worries about school and their performance in school, as all students do. However, their positive outlook, their willingness to take responsibility for their success, and their disciplined determination will enable them to succeed. Their ability to identify and confront their fears, establish what they need to do, and then draw upon and develop their strengths will ensure their success.

LO 2 Totally Prepared: Using Anticipation to Help You Succeed

What do successful students do to be totally prepared for tests and quizzes? They anticipate!

Think about Takeisha's pre-test activities. They indicate a quality that will serve her well as a student: **forward thinking.** She anticipated problems, thought of ways to overcome them, and took appropriate action to be well prepared for her exam.

forward thinking: An approach that involves anticipating problems, thinking of ways to overcome them, and taking appropriate action to be well prepared for an upcoming challenge, such as an exam.

In sports, top athletes anticipate all the time. Defensive football players anticipate the next play the opposing quarterback will call, a golfer anticipates the effects of the wind, and batters anticipate what the next pitch will be. Their predictions won't always be right, but the act of anticipating helps them be more prepared for whatever happens.

Top students anticipate, too. For example, Takeisha also anticipated questions that would be on her next test. Not all of her predictions were exactly right, but the act of anticipating before and during class and while reading her textbook kept her focused on the material. Staying focused made her better prepared for the actual test. What can you do to anticipate test questions?

Figure 3
Planning ahead is the very best thing you can do to succeed in your education.

Anticipating Before Class

First, you can *preview* the course text before the first class. This means reading the table of contents and then flipping through the pages to get an overall idea of what the course is about. A preview can also uncover what study aids the book has to offer, such as a *glossary* that defines specialized words or phrases used in the course's subject area. If a separate, shorter *study guide* accompanies your textbook, preview it also to see if it contains chapter summaries, outlines, or practice tests.

Anticipating in the First Class

Forward thinking continues in class where you receive your course **syllabus.** This document specifies what you'll be studying in the course, what your homework assignments are, and the dates when you will take exams and tests. You should get a syllabus for each class on the first day of the course. Keep this important document in the pocket of your notebook for the course or, better yet, punch holes in it and put it in the front of your three-ring binder for the

syllabus: *A document that specifies what you'll be studying in a course, what your homework assignments will be, and the dates when you will take exams and tests.*

course. As soon as you get the syllabus, put all of the exam and quiz dates in your calendar in red or some other bright color. You can then work backward and block off time to study in the days and weeks before each test.

The first class is also a good time to anticipate that you will want to find a study partner (or two). If you know someone in the class who you think would be a good study partner, ask if he or she would like to study with you throughout the class. If you don't know anybody in the class, introduce yourself, and let people know you're looking for someone to study with. When you find some-body, be sure to write down her or his name, e-mail address, and phone number!

Study Partner Contact Information

Name _____

E-mail address _____

Phone number _____

Anticipating When Reading the Text

Instructors usually test students on their understanding of the main ideas and concepts and their ability to recall important terms and facts presented in the textbook or by the instructor. Here are some ways that can help you find the main ideas and key concepts in the assigned chapters of the text:

ON THE JOB

Evaluations and Advancement

Some students think that they won't need to use study and test-taking skills after they graduate from college, so they don't put much effort into strengthening them. Jasmine said, "I got by in high school without being organized or trying to anticipate what would be on a test. Once I graduate, I'll never need to study for a test again, so I don't need to learn these test-preparation skills."

What do you think? If you agree with a statement below, make a checkmark in front of it.

- Jasmine is right. The use of study and test-taking skills is limited to school.

- Jasmine is naïve about what today's careers require. There is always more knowledge to be gained.

- The planning, forward thinking, and self-discipline developed to effectively study for tests will serve students just as well in the world of work as they do in college.

For career-minded people, the second and third statements can describe today's professional work environment. Many people must pass one or more tests to obtain a position. For example, massage therapy graduates must pass an exam in order to become licensed massage therapists. Some companies require prospective employees to pass keyboarding or other skills tests. Have you or has someone you know had to take a pre-employment test?

After people are hired, they must keep learning to stay current or to advance in their field. That's why employers often send employees to training sessions

- Look for chapter titles, section headings, and any material that is emphasized in larger, bolder, or different-colored type. The **bolded** or *italicized* words or phrases are usually key words or concepts that you may need to define or explain on a test.
- Read the introductory and concluding paragraphs of each chapter and the first and last sentence of each paragraph, where main ideas are often placed.
- Study any numbered or bulleted lists of suggestions (like this one), since you may find the material in these lists on tests.

Anticipating during Class

Reading the assigned material *before* class helps you *during* class. You can anticipate what your instructor will talk about, which will help keep your mind from wandering. Also, you can ask any questions that came to mind as you read the text. Bring your textbook to class, since the instructor may point out important ideas or facts from the text.

If the instructor emphasizes material in class, it will probably be on a test. In their lectures, instructors sometimes add supporting ideas, key terms, and other information that is not in the text. Take notes on this material as well. As you pay attention in class, listen for vocal hints such as when the instructor says certain words or phrases more loudly or repeats them. When you hear, "This is important" or "This will be on the test," take the hint, write it down, star or underline it in your notes, and remember it. Also, watch for visual clues, like gestures that underscore an idea.

Write down in your notes what the instructor writes on the board or shows on a projector, and keep any handouts the instructor provides so you can review them later. You can safely predict that you will see some of those words again on a test. What else can you do to predict test questions?

(another name for classes), where an instructor teaches them or a facilitator guides their learning. Marketing representatives are taught about their company's new products. Members of a new team may learn how to be more effective meeting participants. What other training examples can you think of?

In many fields, once you have a job, earning certifications or licenses will allow you to get a promotion or earn more money, and in most cases, you have to take a test to get the certification or license.

Even if you don't have to take a certification or licensing test, you will be "tested" after your training sessions or self-study when you must perform new tasks using the information you have learned. If your performance is good, you will "pass." Who is more likely to be promoted or get a raise—the person who just barely passes or the employee with solid study and test-taking skills who excels at the new task?

Who's in Control?

Answering the following questions will help you determine whether you have an internal or an external locus of control concerning your test preparation.

1. Think back to a time when you did poorly on a test. What do you think caused your poor performance on that test?

   a. The instructor gave a really hard/long/tricky test.

   b. I didn't do enough soon enough to prepare for the test.

   c. My family/friends/job kept me from studying for the test.

2. Next, recall a time when you performed well on a test. To what do you attribute that success?

   a. I got lucky.

   b. I prepared well for the test.

   c. I think the instructor added my points wrong.

3. Consider a time in school when you realized that you needed help with an assignment. How did you ensure that you received the necessary assistance to complete the project?

   a. I just guessed.

   b. I called some of my classmates for help.

   c. I didn't; no one offered to help me.

4. Remember a time when you took a class you did not enjoy or considered to be your weaker subject. What was your attitude like when you attended that class?

   a. At least I showed up.

   b. I hate this class, but I will do what is necessary to pass.

   c. It's not my fault I'm bad at this subject, so I'll probably fail.

What do your responses reveal about your locus of control?

If you answered "a" to the majority of these questions, your locus of control is inconsistent, which means that in certain situations you believe you are in control of your actions, but in other instances you defer to an external locus of control, believing that the outcome is controlled by luck or fate.

If you answered "c" to the majority of these questions, your locus of control is external, which indicates that you believe you don't control your actions, but rather your fate is controlled by outside forces.

If you answered "b" to the majority of these questions, your locus of control is internal, which is the mark of successful students because it reveals that you take personal responsibility for your actions.

What are three strategies you can implement in your test preparation that demonstrate an internal locus of control:

(*Example:* I can practice forward thinking to anticipate problems and think of ways of overcome them.)

1. _____

2. _____

3. _____

In this section, identify one area of a winner's locus of control you want to improve:

1. _____

How will progressing in this area positively affect your ability to be a successful test taker?

_____

_____

_____

Ultimately, the first step to taking internal control is to commit to a positive change. Fill in the blank with at least one new action you will take, starting today, to be a successful student:

"Today I will _____ ."

Remember, this commitment to a positive change can only be accomplished by taking personal responsibility for your actions—demonstrating an internal locus of control.

How can taking personal responsibility for a failure improve your ability to be successful?

_____

_____

_____

As a class, identify five areas of school that students tend to make excuses for or blame others for if they are unsuccessful:

(Example: Procrastinating on assignments)

1. _____

2. _____

3. _____

4. _____

5. _____

Then, as a class, brainstorm five strategies of how to take personal responsibility in each of the areas you and your classmates identified:

(Example: Create a homework schedule, and list the days and times for completing homework in each class, then write the schedule in a daily planner.)

1. _____

2. _____

3. _____

4. _____

5. _____

Anticipating Distractions

Forward thinkers also anticipate interruptions and other distractions while they are studying, and organize their study environment so they can avoid those distractions and maintain their focus. Some students turn off their phones or let their calls go to voice mail during study time, leave the children at day care an extra half hour, or turn on a fan next to their study area at home to block out household noises. What are your distractions and solutions?

Acting the Part of a Successful Student

Worry can be a major distracter. Worrying about getting a bad grade, not having enough money to complete school, or other personal problems can rob students of the concentration needed to study. Perhaps in the past, you did not do as well as you wanted to in school or in certain subjects. Rather than worrying or trying to ignore it, here's something positive you can try: *Act the part of a successful student.*

Think of the first time you picked up a cell phone. Did you stare at it and then put it down and walk away? More likely, you started pushing buttons, even though you didn't know exactly what you were doing. You were acting the part of a cell phone user, and pretty soon, you weren't acting anymore—you knew what you were doing!

Starting now, begin acting the part of a successful student who:

☐ Has a positive attitude
☐ Has an internal locus of control
☐ Takes ownership of problems
☐ Is disciplined
☐ Anticipates what is needed to succeed

What one action can you take today or what different behavior can you do today to play the part of a successful student? Perhaps you will write a things-to-do list for tomorrow or buy a three-ring binder and begin to organize your class materials. Maybe you will overcome your shyness enough to ask a classmate to study with you after class, or ask your instructor a question during class. What will you do first?

Where Successful Students Place Their Locus of Control

Successful students have an internal locus of control concerning their studies. They recognize that the better prepared they are for a test, the better they will do. They believe that learning the material for a test will help them in their careers, and they know they will do well in their courses if they work hard at it. They are forward thinkers who anticipate test questions as well as obstacles to their success. They confront their fears and take action to overcome those obstacles.

Successful students therefore discipline themselves to arrive on time for every class. In class, they pay attention and participate respectfully. Outside class, they do their homework and assignments on time to learn the material and do well on tests. When they make mistakes, they learn from them and change their behaviors so they will do better on the next test. When a roadblock appears on the path to success, they don't give up but instead stay focused on their goal and persist until they remove or get around that obstacle.

Figure 4 Having an internal locus of control doesn't mean you have to work and study alone.

II. Strengthening Memory for Test-Taking Success

GET READY

When you meet someone for the first time, how good are you at remembering the person's name?

- Can you share any tricks you use to help you remember?

Let's do a simple exercise that will show how memory ordinarily works. Take a piece of paper and write the month, day, and year of your birth in numbers, your street address, the name of your first boyfriend or girlfriend, and your mother's first name. Easy, right? Now write down the number of words in the last sentence of the previous section in this module. (No peeking!) Too hard? Okay, instead, write the number of objectives listed for this module and then write all of the **bolded** and *italicized* words from the previous section of this module that you just went over. Still not easy?

Why were you immediately able to recall the first set of numbers and words but not the rest? Your birth date and address were easy because you say and write those important numbers frequently, and recalling the names was effortless because they have emotional connections for you. Conversely, the *number* of words or objectives is unimportant and unworthy of memorizing. Although you

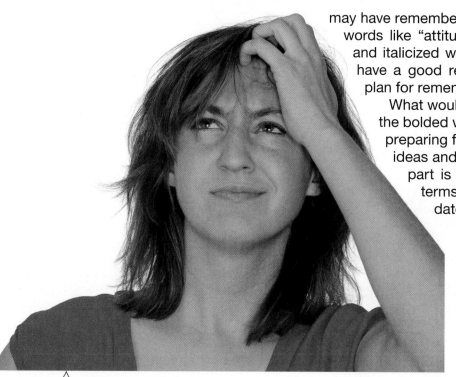

may have remembered some of the familiar italicized words like "attitude," there are too many bolded and italicized words to recall easily—unless you have a good reason to remember them and a plan for remembering them.

What would be a good reason to remember the bolded words in this module? One part of preparing for tests is grasping the important ideas and concepts of the course. Another part is remembering the specifics—key terms and their definitions, the names, dates, facts, and figures.

Testing gives instructors feedback on whether their students have acquired a working knowledge of the course material. During testing, your ability to recall both major ideas and specific information, and to demonstrate your ability to apply that material, shows your instructors that you have that working knowledge. To better understand what it takes to remember what you need to remember, let's first look at three kinds of memory.

Figure 5 Not all information is worth memorizing, so your brain filters out what it thinks is unimportant.

LO 3 How Memory Works

When you drive to the airport, you have three options: If you're flying and will be gone for a day or more, you can park your car in a long-term parking lot. These lots are often vast, open spaces filled with cars. If you're only going to be there for an hour or so—for instance, you're meeting someone at the baggage claim and will help take their luggage to the car—you can leave your car in a smaller short-term parking lot. If you're dropping someone off or picking someone up, you'll just stop for a few minutes at the loading/unloading zone and then be on your way.

Believe it or not, memory is a little like taking a car to the airport. Psychologists explain that the images and sounds that constantly flash into our consciousness through our senses go into our *immediate* or *sensory memory,* and, like cars at the loading zone, most leave our brains just as quickly as they arrived.

An image or information that you focus on in order to remember it a bit longer goes into *short-term memory.* For example, when you turn a book's page to continue reading, you must remember the words at the bottom of the first page for a few seconds, after which those words are forgotten.

Like short-term parking garages, the space in short-term memory is limited. One limitation is the ability to recall only five to nine numbers or items—unless that information is transferred into *long-term memory* where an unlimited number of memories can be kept for extended periods of time.

Like choosing where to park, people must choose how to learn. In addition, they must take action to remember. Otherwise, they will fall victim to the drastic memory loss that is expressed in the *curve of forgetting.*

Have you ever forgotten the name of the new co-worker you met yesterday or learned a word and its definition at the beginning of a class but were unable to recall it an hour later for a quiz? Memory experiments first done over a century ago by Hermann Ebbinghaus, a German philosopher, indicated that, only an hour after being exposed to information, people forget about half, with more information swiftly slipping away as time goes by—if nothing is done to reinforce that learning (Figure 6).

The First Step to Remembering—Learning

Here are suggestions to help you with the first step in memorization—learning the material you need to remember.

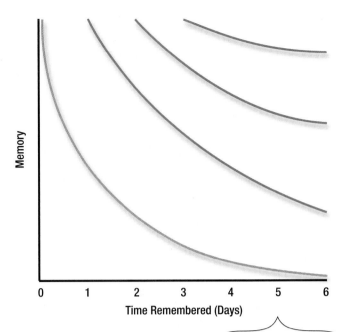

X-axis: **Time Remembered (Days)** — 0 1 2 3 4 5 6
Y-axis: **Memory**

Figure 6
Ebbinghaus' dramatic Forgetting Curve. With each repetition of the memory, the curve gets shallower and more of the memory remains.

1. *Concentrate.* Have you ever read a paragraph when your mind was really on something else? After finishing the paragraph, have you stopped and thought, "What did I just read?" If the material doesn't transition from your short-term to your long-term memory, you'll have nothing *to* remember. To better focus when you're reading your textbook or listening in class, prepare yourself physically and mentally. Instead of slouching in your chair, sit at attention, up straight, leaning forward slightly, in the athlete's "get set" position. Convince yourself the material is important. If necessary, pretend at first, and urge yourself, "This is important. Concentrate!" If your attention wanders, give your body a little shake or blink your eyes, and refocus.

2. *Comprehend it.* People can memorize a series of nonsense words for a short time, but remembering for the long term is far easier if you understand what you're reading. When you don't understand that sentence or paragraph, reread it. Look up the meaning of any unfamiliar words. Read the next sentences to determine if they help explain the confusing part. If it's still unclear, write a question mark by it, and ask your instructor about it. When you have a question during class, ask your instructor for clarification. You'll probably be doing a favor to classmates who have the same question in mind.

3. *Make it personal.* Think about what the material means in general and its significance to your life or your future career. Making those personal connections between you and what you need to memorize will make the material more memorable. For example, John, who is studying marketing, wonders how his art history classes will fit into his daily work routine. He then begins to imagine that he's reviewing different designs for print advertisements for a product he is marketing, and thinks about how his knowledge of art, perspective, and color might help him choose a powerful ad.

Finding Memorization Methods That Are Right for You

Once you've decided what is important to remember and are clear about what it means, choose one or more memorization methods to get the material into your long-term memory. How do you know which methods to choose?

CONSIDER YOUR LEARNING AND THINKING STYLES Some athletes have a body build suited to excel at football while others are built more for swimming.

Although most people have a combination of learning styles, some people learn and remember best what they've seen **(visual learners),** others what they've heard **(auditory learners),** and still others what they've done **(kinesthetic learners).**

visual learners: People who learn and remember best what they've seen.

auditory learners: People who learn and remember best what they've heard.

kinesthetic learners: People who learn and remember best what they've done.

People who are primarily visual learners learn better if they can see the material, such as when reading a text, watching a video, or looking at what the instructor has written on the board or on a PowerPoint slide. Taking notes, making lists, and adding color to what they've written help them learn and remember. Auditory learners may learn better if they read their textbook material out loud, listen to an instructor's lecture, and talk about the material with classmates. They can record what they read onto a digital music player, and then play the recording over and over to intensify their learning. Kinesthetic learners learn best if some kind of physical action is involved, such as working with models, practicing tasks in a lab class, pacing while reading, or writing notes.

In addition to learning styles, scientists have found differences in how a person learns and processes material according to whether the left or right hemisphere of the brain is more dominant or influential.

People who are **left-brain dominant** tend to be organized and analytical and can easily recognize patterns and categories. They may want to outline the material from a chapter or lecture, putting the information into related groups.

left-brain dominant: Influenced largely by the left hemisphere of the brain; people who are left-brain dominant tend to be organized and analytical and can easily recognize patterns and categories.

Right-brain dominant people are more intuitive and spontaneous. They like to use their imaginations to memorize, and prefer seeing drawings and pictures and making *mind maps,* which are drawings with key words circled and connected by line to show relationships among ideas.

right-brain dominant: Influenced largely by the right hemisphere of the brain; people who are right-brain dominant tend to be more intuitive and spontaneous. They like to use their imaginations to memorize and prefer seeing drawings and pictures and making mind maps.

Middle-brain thinkers have characteristics of both. Some of the memorization methods you'll read about involve making mental pictures, something that visual learners and right-brain thinkers may prefer. Try several methods to see which ones work best for you.

THE POWER OF MIND MAPS **Mind maps** can be used instead of outlines to plan an essay, a speech, or an answer to an essay question. Mind maps that you make of a text chapter or a lecture can function as a memory aid because you can literally see connections between ideas. Figure 7 shows a sample mind map concerning the material on learning and thinking styles from this module.

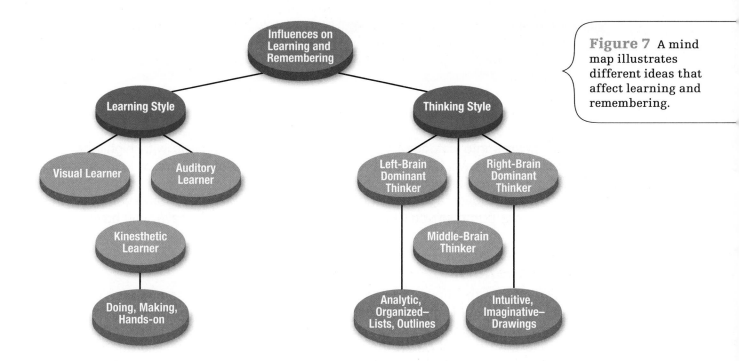

Figure 7 A mind map illustrates different ideas that affect learning and remembering.

mind map: Drawings with key words circled and connected by line to show relationships among ideas.

LO 4 Memorization Tools and Techniques

No matter what your learning style, there are many tools and techniques you can use to help you memorize material that you need to learn.

Flashcards

Flashcards are valuable memorization tools because they engage all three learning styles and can appeal to different types of thinkers. You may have used flashcards to memorize words and their definitions by writing the word on one side of an index card and its definition on the other. To test if you know the definition, you look at the word and try to define it without flipping over the card. Then you check the back side to see if your definition was correct. You can also write questions on one side of a card and the answers on the other side.

flashcards: Note cards used to help the user learn or memorize information. A typical flashcard may have a word on one side and its definition on the other, or a question on one side with the answer on the other.

While ready-made flashcards can be purchased for some courses, it's better to make your own. The act of writing involves your body and your mind, which helps you learn and remember. As you write the words (a kinesthetic activity), you see them develop on the page (visual).

After you write a card, read it aloud. Reading silently is good, but reading your cards out loud is better. This powerful act of **recitation** brings all three learning styles into play. Recitation is visual because you see the material as you read the cards, kinesthetic because of the body actions required for you to speak, and auditory because you hear yourself speaking. When reciting, you can have some fun by singing the words or speaking with an accent. Such imaginative activities appeal especially to right-brain thinkers. Left-brain thinkers may organize their flashcards into categories. Adding color to the flashcards with highlighters or colored pens will help visual learners. Which kind of thinkers or learners might choose to add drawings to their flashcards?

Another advantage of flashcards is their portability. You can keep them in a pocket or purse so you'll be ready for a quick review whenever you have a bit of spare time.

Mnemonics

Mnemonics (pronounced nee-mahn-icks) are strategies to increase your ability to remember material, such as lists of items. Mnemonic devices include acronyms, initialisms, sentences, rhymes, songs, and visual associations to make the material catch the mind's eye. As you read these strategies, think about ones you have used before. What learning or thinking styles does each appeal to?

☐ *Acronyms* are made by using the first letter of each word to make another word. For example, BOYFANS is a made-up word used to remember the coordinating conjunctions **b**ut, **o**r, **y**et, **f**or, **a**nd, **n**or, **s**o. The **B** stands for **b**ut, the **O** stands for **o**r, and so on. Can you name the current POTUS? (See the hint in the Key Terms list at the end of this module.)

☐ *Initialisms* are a kind of acronym in which the letters are read individually, such as FBI for **F**ederal **B**ureau of **I**nvestigation. Many text messages, such as OMW for **o**n **m**y **w**ay, include initialisms as well as abbreviations. What initialisms have you used or seen in text messages? Did you always know what they meant?

☐ *Mnemonic sentences,* such as "**P**lease **e**xcuse **m**y **d**ear **A**unt **S**ally," help math students remember the order in which to perform mathematical operations to solve a problem. The first letter of each word stands for a step—**p**arentheses, **e**xponents, **m**ultiplication, **d**ivision, **a**ddition, **s**ubtraction—with the first step being **p**arentheses and the last step being **s**ubtraction.

☐ *Rhymes* and *songs* make information easier to recall. The colors of the poisonous coral snake are identified in the rhyme, "Red on yellow, deadly fellow." Remembering "righty tighty, lefty loosey" will help you turn a screwdriver the correct way to tighten or loosen the screw. Rhymes put to music that are sung repeatedly tend to stay in long-term memory. Perhaps you learned the alphabet by singing the letters to the tune of "Twinkle, Twinkle, Little Star."

Chunking

Chunking is another device to help remember words and numbers. Most people can hold in their short-term memories only five to nine items. Have you noticed that your nine-digit Social Security number and your ten-digit phone number are both separated by hyphens into three shorter groups of numbers? That

MY SUCCESS STORY

Student Jessie Harrell, after earning her first A+ on an English quiz, was asked how she did it. Jessie, who plans to be a pharmacy technician, said, "Basically, it was the flashcards. I go over them a lot. My boyfriend quizzes me. And I wrote my own sentences and went over them with him." Jessie prepared herself for success by using a variety of approaches to learning and remembering:

- First, she wrote the cards (kinesthetic).
- Then she reviewed them with her boyfriend, reading the material aloud (visual, auditory, and kinesthetic) and saying it again when he quizzed her (repetition).
- Next, she put the information she was memorizing into practice by writing her own sentences (right-brain creativity) and then dissecting those sentences (left-brain analysis).

Jessie's commitment to frequent practice and review paid off for her, and it can for you too.

grouping makes those numbers easier to memorize. To remember long lists of items, you can group some of them by categories or patterns that are meaningful to you—something left-brain dominant thinkers may especially enjoy. Imagine you must go to the grocery store for milk, onions, ground beef, cereal, bread, orange juice, tomatoes, bananas, lettuce, tea, and ketchup. You could chunk those items into groups by breakfast items (milk, cereal, orange juice, bananas, tea) and hamburger items (ground beef, bread, tomatoes, lettuce, onions, and ketchup). Using the chunking method, you would then only have to remember two things—breakfast and hamburgers.

The method of loci (pronounced low' sigh) is an ancient but effective memorization technique that uses visual association. *Loci* is the plural form of *locus* and means *places.* To recall a list of items, visualize each one in a separate place or location. For example, to remember the grocery list, you could imagine yourself sitting in a car. On the dashboard to your left is a loaf of bread. In the center of the dashboard above the radio is a head of lettuce. Dangling from the rearview mirror is a bunch of bananas. If you need to remember items in a certain order, choose loci such as landmarks on a familiar route or path. Place the first item on the first landmark that you always see, the second item on the next landmark you encounter, and so on.

Without rereading the previous paragraph, can you recall which item on the grocery list was dangling from the car's rearview mirror? Write that item here: _____. The more visually exciting or unusual associations you can make, the more likely you are to remember the items. Which kind of thinker, left-brain or right-brain dominant, would particularly like this method of remembering?

Post-Memorization Practice Techniques

After you've learned the material and employed the memorization methods that work best for you, how can you tell if you really know all of the material and have

Figure 8 You may not need a list for the grocery if you have it memorized, and you can shop more efficiently if you break it up in chunks.

Practicing Memorization Techniques

In this activity, you get to experiment with some of the memorization techniques you read about in this section, first by yourself and then with a classmate.

1. On a separate sheet of paper, make a list of at least seven words or phrases, such as the titles of seven of your favorite movies or TV shows or seven recording artists or actors. You'll give this list to your classmate partner, who will give you his or her list.

2. Next, select two different mnemonic devices to remember all seven items on the list you received from your partner. Maybe you can make up a mnemonic word or phrase. You might try chunking or the method of loci. How about making up a rhyme, song, or rap using the seven terms? If you've having trouble getting started, ask your partner or other classmates what they are doing. Write on a separate sheet of paper the names of the two methods you chose and your implementation of each method. Practice each method at least three times. Then return the list to your partner.

3. Think of a concept to teach to your classmate partner. Select a topic of interest to you, preferably something you're learning in one of your other courses. Jot down a few notes about that concept. Then you

it stored in your long-term memory for test time? Here are three ways to make sure you're at the top of your memorization game.

1. *Test yourself.* To determine what material you know and what you don't know yet, give yourself a practice test. Some textbooks or study guides have practice tests in them or in companion sites online. You can use flashcards you've made or that come with your textbook. Your instructor may give you a review sheet with topics or questions. You can also make up your own problems or questions. If you work with classmates in a study group, each of you can make up questions for the group to answer.

   Whichever testing methods you use, be sure to confirm the correct answers by checking the textbook or your lecture notes. Then concentrate on improving your understanding or recollection of the concepts or terms involved in any questions you missed.

   Self-testing provides additional practice that will help you more quickly retrieve the information from your memory when you take the actual test. In fact, research has shown that taking a test helps you learn material more effectively than other study methods, because testing helps you realize what you don't know—which helps draw your attention to it, which helps you learn it. The act of having to recall information for a test forces your brain to organize it and make connections related to it, which can help you in the future.[2]

2. *Teach it.* Have you ever taught a child how to tie a shoelace or work a math problem? Being able to explain something to someone else proves that you know it well. Select a concept that was difficult for you, and then try to explain it to a study buddy from another class or to a friend who is unfamiliar with the concept. Their feedback will help you recognize any gaps in your knowledge of the concept.

Try this online at mcgrawhillconnect.com

and your classmate partner will decide which of you will be the teacher first and which the student. Check to make sure your partner doesn't already know your concept; if so, select another concept. Then the "teacher" teaches the "student" about his or her concept. The teacher then asks for feedback from the student. Then trade places and select another concept to practice-teach and get feedback.

Did teaching a concept help you discover what you did and didn't know about the concept? What will you remember about your teaching experiment? _____
_____

4. Now, retrieve the list of seven items you gave your partner earlier, and ask your partner to name the seven items. Note how many items your partner can recall. Then it's your turn to try to name all seven items on your partner's list.

How many items were you able to recall? _____ Which of the two mnemonic devices that you tried worked better for you? _____ If you didn't remember all seven items, what you might do differently to recall all of those items? _____

3. *Overlearn it.* To retain the material you've learned, take advantage of small 5- to 10-minute blocks of time in your daily schedule to review your notes or flashcards, write the steps to a procedure, or recite a list of key terms. Keep practicing until you're sure you know the material. Then practice some more. Even long-term memories can become faint. As scientists recently confirmed,[3] reviewing frequently helps keep material in your memory and will improve your ability to access the information.

It takes concentration, time, and effort to move information into short-term and then long-term memory. Successful students recognize that different memorization methods appeal to different types of thinkers, and certain methods are better suited to certain learning styles. Find out what your dominant learning and thinking styles are, and experiment with different memory techniques to discover what works best for you. Then use one or more of the memorization methods that help make the material meaningful to you, so it will be more memorable.

Because it's so easy to forget, be sure to frequently review and recite the material you're learning. Some ideas to try might be: review immediately after class by writing down one to three main things you learned in class; begin transferring some notes from class onto flashcards while you're waiting for your next class to begin or when you're eating lunch; later in the day, finish transferring your class notes to flashcard form; do a quick review of your flashcards before going to bed; and do another quick review of your flashcards when you're eating breakfast the next day.

Even after you're confident you know the material, continue practicing to make it easy to recall at test time and beyond.

Figure 9 Review as often as you can, because repetition will help you remember.

III. Be Prepared for Any Kind of Test

Two people study equally hard before a class exam and believe they have an equal understanding of the material being tested. One student earns an A-. The other earns a C+.

● What are some ways that can happen?

To paraphrase Elizabeth Barrett Browning's famous poem, "How can I test thee? Let me count the ways." This section will help increase your test-taking knowledge about different types of tests and questions, and what to do before, during, and after a test.

Tests provide feedback on how well students comprehend, remember, and can apply course material to meet course objectives. Since content, objectives, and class periods vary, tests contain different types of questions, come in different lengths, and can be given under different circumstances.

For example, the instructor for one course may (for good reason) limit your time to 20 minutes to complete a 20-question test during class, while the instructor for another course with different objectives will allow a week to answer several essay questions outside class. A short quiz takes only part of a class period to complete. Exams take longer to complete, but the number and kinds of questions asked vary by instructor and course. Types of tests you may experience include demonstration or competency tests, oral exams, open-book exams, or case studies about something happening in the field of study. You may have in-class exams, take-home tests, or online tests that you complete via computer.

LO 5 Types of Test Questions

We've already talked about using forward thinking to predict the content of test questions. You can also predict the *types* of questions the instructor will ask, because different types of questions call for different kinds of study and memorization methods.

☐ True/false, multiple-choice, and matching questions require **recognition** of the correct answer. An example of recognition is spotting a familiar face in a crowd of strangers.

☐ Short answer, fill-in-the-blanks, and essay questions demand **recall,** which is remembering the name that goes with that familiar face.

recognition: *Being able to identify a correct answer upon seeing it, such as spotting a familiar face in a crowd of strangers, or knowing the right answer from among several multiple-choice answers.*

recall: *Being able to remember information on demand, such as remembering a name that goes with a familiar face.*

Recalling a word, definition, date, or list of items is more challenging, which is why you use memorization techniques to get them into your long-term memory and why you should practice frequently to keep them accessible, so you can recall them on command.

To predict question types, talk to students who've had the course before, or simply ask your instructor. If your instructor gives quizzes, you may see the same types of questions on your longer tests.

Here are some techniques you can use when answering specific types of questions. Which techniques are new to you?

Multiple-Choice

When reading a multiple-choice question, try this technique. Cover up the possible answers with one hand. Read the first part of the question, called the *stem*, and try to supply the answer before reading the choices. Then look to see which of the possible answer choices best matches your answer. If you didn't find your answer, play the odds! You have a 25 percent chance of getting it right if there are four choices or a 20 percent chance if there are five choices. First, rule out any humorous answer. Then rule out any other answer that doesn't seem right, such as one that uses terms you don't remember reading in the course materials or hearing in lectures.

On a multiple-choice test, be careful with negative questions, such those that begin with the phrase, "None of the following are true *except* . . ." When you read through the choices, put a "T" next to all true statements, and an "F" next to all false statements. If you get three "F" answers and only one "T" answer, you'll know which answer is correct. If you have more than one "T" answer, then you've at least eliminated some of the choices and narrowed down your options.

True/False

As you carefully read a true/false question, look for key words or phrases, and remember that for a statement to be true, all parts of it must be true. Go with your first response and don't change your answer unless you've had a sudden flash of insight. When you have absolutely no clue, choose true if you think your instructor writes more true than false statements.

Short-Answer

Short-answer questions usually can be answered with a phrase or a sentence or two. Here's a sample question for you to answer: How do *auditory learners best learn?* Answer: _____. If you wrote "By hearing," you chose a short but correct phrase. A different technique some students use is to turn the question into a statement to begin a sentence and then supply the requested answer. They would write, *"Auditory learners*

Copyright © 2013 McGraw-Hill Higher Education

Figure 10
You're probably very familiar with the multiple-choice test.

best learn by hearing." Copying some of the words from the question will keep you from accidentally misreading the question, help you begin answering, and perhaps kick-start your memory.

Essay Questions

Similarly, thoroughly reading and understanding an essay question will help you maximize the point value of your answer. Look for *key words* that identify how the instructor wants you to respond, and plan your answer accordingly. Here's a sample question:

Define visual learner and auditory learner, and illustrate how each learns best.

What two key words do you see? _____ and _____. The key word *define* asks for a definition, while the key word *illustrate* means you should give examples. It may help you to rewrite the question in your own words to make sure you understand it. For this question, you might write, "What is the definition of visual learner and of auditory learner? Give examples of what each learner prefers to do to learn." As with the short-answer question, beginning your response with part of the question—yours or the instructor's—will help keep you on track.

Once you have identified the key words and put the essay question in your own words, take a few minutes to write a short, informal outline or mind map to organize your thoughts and remember what you want to write. You can do this on the back of the test or on a separate piece of paper.

Other key words that are used in essay questions include *justify, relate, prove, compare, review, interpret,* and *evaluate.* When creating a test, your instructor will choose these key words carefully, so be sure you pay attention to these key words and factor them into your essay.

Some students dread essay and short-answer questions and want to skip over them, but successful students give an answer, even if they're not sure they're right. Why? While you won't impress your instructor with nonsense, your instructor may give you *partial* credit if you can show some knowledge of the material. If the question is worth 10 points, anything you write about the subject may get you a couple of points, which is better than no points.

LO 6 Maximize Your Test Score

Regardless of the kind of test, or the type of questions on it, there are a number of things you can do to maximize your score on any test.

Know How the Instructor Is Keeping Score

Perhaps the most critical point to maximizing your test score is knowing the number of points each question and each test is worth. The more points you accumulate on a test, the better your test grade. And the better your test grades, the greater your confidence that you know the material needed for your career.

Each test should indicate how many points each question is worth; if not, ask your instructor. Many tests have a total of 100 points available. How are those 100 points divided? If a test has 50 true/false questions, each question is usually worth 2 points since 100 divided by 50 equals 2. If a test has 20 same-type questions, each question is worth 5 points since 100 divided by 20 equals 5. An exception would be when an instructor wants to reduce

guessing at answers, and more points are lost for an incorrect answer than for an answer left blank.

For example, if you answer 1 of the 20 questions wrong, you lose 5 points, but you lose only 3 points if you leave the question blank. Also, essay questions are generally worth more points than true/false, multiple-choice, or matching questions since they usually require higher-level thinking skills such as application and analysis.

MONEY SMART$

Insurance Basics

Have you ever bought the extended warranty on a product? If so, you've purchased a kind of insurance. Buyers purchase insurance in order to gain some control over the cost of recovering when bad things occur. For those that purchase an extended warranty, the buyer is willing to pay an insurance premium up front in exchange for the certainty of being able to repair the item for little or no cost later on should it stop functioning before the warranty period expires.

For most types of insurance, you influence the amount of your premium by choosing what events will be covered and the maximum amount the company will pay. You may lower the amount of your premium by agreeing to pay a certain amount called a deductible before the company begins to pay a claim.

A few types of insurance are mandatory; the others are optional.

- *Auto insurance* is required by most states to ensure payment of damages you may cause as a driver.
- If you borrow money to buy a house, you may need to buy *mortgage insurance* to protect your lender in case you stop making your mortgage payments.
- *Homeowner's* or *renter's insurance* covers your home and its contents in case of theft, fire, or water or wind damage. It can also protect you from liability if someone gets hurt while on your property.
- If you have dependents (people who depend on your income), *life insurance* benefits help provide for them in your place as well as pay your funeral expenses.

How many quizzes and tests will be given in a course and how much is each worth? Check your syllabus and ask your instructor. Quizzes—those listed on your syllabus and any unannounced pop quizzes—are usually given more frequently and have less point value toward your final grade than longer tests or exams. For example, during a 12-week course, you may be graded on a research paper, five quizzes, and a final exam. The five quizzes may be worth a total of 20 percent of the final grade, the final exam by itself worth 40 percent, and the research paper 40 percent, to reach a total of 100 percent for all of the graded activities. Some instructors give a grade calculation sheet you can use to record your grades to track your progress; if not, make your own.

If the unthinkable happens and you must miss class during a quiz or test day, contact your instructor immediately. Reread the policies section of your course syllabus that covers information about makeup work. Some instructors require documentation of your verifiable emergency and then provide a makeup opportunity for certain graded activities. Other instructors do not allow students to do makeup work but do drop a low score or offer extra credit work to the class. Doing extra credit work whenever it is offered is wise because it not only acts as insurance against emergencies, it also increases your understanding of the course material.

When the Clock Starts Ticking

Knowing how the instructor is keeping score is important and is something you can do before you sit down for the text. But what about once the test begins, and the clock is ticking?

Below are a few recommendations to help you maximize your points on the most common type of test—closed-book tests that you take during class.

Before you begin answering, write your name on the test or answer sheet. If you've memorized something but you're not quite sure you'll remember it— perhaps a list of key terms, dates, or formulas—do a **data dump** right away on

- *Long-term care insurance* pays part or all of the cost of nursing home or similar care if you cannot care for yourself.

Insurance is an important benefit to research when changing jobs or choosing a new job. Many companies offer reduced-rate health, disability, and life insurance to their employees, and some also offer dental and eye-care insurance.

Should something happen, such as an auto accident, for which you have insurance coverage, you must file a claim with your insurance company. The company will then determine if and how much it will pay. You may contest its decisions if you think more should be paid. If you are ill, consider having someone such as a family member take over the tiring job of reading and keeping track of the bills and records, and phoning and corresponding with the insurance company and your care providers.

Insurance can be complicated and confusing. It is worth your time to do your homework before purchasing insurance to make sure you get the insurance that's right for you.

the back of the test sheet. Get it out of your mind and onto paper so you can relax about remembering it.

Next, scan the whole test and decide on an order for answering the questions. If the test contains more than one type of question, consider doing the true/false, multiple-choice, and matching first because they require recognition more than recall. Another reason to answer those questions first is that your instructor may help you by placing in those questions some of the key terms and references that you'll need to answer fill-in-the-blank questions, short-answer, or essay questions. Finally, notice which of these questions is worth more points so if you are running short of time, you can answer the ones with the greatest number of points first.

Can you ask your instructor a question during a test? Yes, if you need clarification of test instructions, such as whether the words on a matching list can be used more than once, or for the definition of an unfamiliar word, as long as it isn't one of the key words that you should know. Remember—your instructors want to see you succeed!

TAKE ACTION

Pop Quiz!

This activity is a *pop quiz!* Remember to use the question-reading and answering techniques you just learned in this module to maximize your points, such as covering the answers in a multiple-choice question and trying to supply the answer—but don't flip back to find the answers. You will have 10 minutes to complete the quiz by yourself. When you're finished, you and your classmate partner will compare answers, discuss the techniques that apply to the different questions, and make any needed changes. Then with your instructor's help, you'll score your final answers.

Directions: For multiple-choice questions, circle the letter of the best answer. For true/false questions, circle T for true or F for false. Fill in any blanks. Use the space provided for your answers to short-answer questions.

1. **(8 points)** A person who prefers listening to an instructor's lecture and hearing classmates talk during a study group session rather than reading a textbook is said to be:

   a. A kinesthetic learner
   b. Middle-brain dominant
   c. A tactile responder
   d. An auditory learner
   e. Useless as a study group member because everyone must talk as well as listen

2. **(8 points)** Two influences on an individual's learning and remembering are:

   a. Acronyms and initialisms
   b. Learning style and thinking style
   c. Mnemonics and plate tectonics
   d. Sensory memory and short-term memory
   e. All of the above

3. **(8 points)** *T or F* An auditory learner prefers to learn by listening to an instructor's lecture and by reading a textbook.

4. **(8 points)** *T or F* The method of loci is a way to determine if a person is a right-brain or left-brain dominant thinker.

Checking Your Work

Before you turn in your test, unless your instructor takes off more points for incorrect than blank answers, make sure you have answered *all* of the questions, including any bonus or extra credit items that can help make up for a memory lapse. Instructors feel frustrated when students lose points unnecessarily because they overlooked an easy question here or there. To ensure you've answered everything, check to make sure you *saw* all of the questions. Here's a simple checking method that takes only a minute or two and is especially helpful if the test contains a mixture of question types:

Move your finger on the test page from question #1 to question #2 to question #3

Mc Graw Hill **connect** (plus+)

Try this online at mcgrawhillconnect.com

5. **(12 points)** Fill in the blanks in the sentence: True/false, multiple-choice, and matching require _____ of the correct answer while short-answer and essay questions demand _____ of the correct answer.

6. **(12 points)** Fill in the blanks in the sentence: _____ learners learn best by doing something such as making a model or writing notes while _____ learners grasp material better if they hear it, as when an instructor lectures, or they read text aloud.

7. **(14 points)** Name one mnemonic device described in this module. Then give an example of it:

_____

_____

8. **(14 points)** What does the curve of forgetting tell us?

_____

_____

9. **(16 points)** Describe at least three things that a forward-thinking student anticipates in order to be well prepared for a test.

_____

_____

_____

_____

_____

while counting mentally "question one, question two, question three," and so on. Slowly counting the questions and keeping track of the count can help you see any question that you might have accidentally skipped.

TO ERR IS HUMAN; TO CATCH AN ERROR IS DIVINE Have you ever changed your original correct answer to a wrong answer? It's not a good idea to change an answer unless you have a really good reason to change it, such as originally misreading the question. For example, a student quickly read the following true/false question, "It is not important to practice often to remember new information," didn't notice the word "not," and so gave the wrong answer of "true." Here's a way to keep from losing points due to misreading. After you've finished entering all your answers, cover up your answers and slowly reread the test questions. Focus to keep from jumping ahead to check the answer, read the entire question, and mentally supply the answer. Then look to see whether what you wrote matches your mental answer. Rereading takes a few minutes, but which is more important—rushing out the door to get away from the test or picking up points that can improve your score?

If you do change an answer on a machine-scored test that requires you to use a #2 pencil, use a good eraser to erase your original answer completely. If any traces of your original answer remain, the machine may see it and mark your new, correct answer as incorrect. Don't lose your hard-earned points to incomplete erasing!

A last bit of testing advice: Ignore how long other students take to complete the test. A student who finishes quickly may have been unprepared and unable to answer many of the questions. Take as much time as you need within the allotted test time. The student who finishes last may actually be first in points.

Post-Test Activities to Improve Future Test Scores

Whew! You've finished the test. Now what? Some students want only to get their score. They simply look at the grade, turn the paper upside down, and ignore the instructor's comments. But a graded test can not only tell you your score, but also help you understand what you got right (so you can keep doing what works) and what you got wrong (so you can improve weak areas).

Check your text and notes immediately after the test, especially to find the answers to puzzling questions. When a graded test is returned, read any comments or suggestions the instructor has written. Teachers give valuable feedback on tests that is meant to help students. Also, keep in mind that questions on tests throughout the course may be recycled for future or final exams—so don't think you can forget about a difficult concept just because you've already been tested on it! Politely ask for clarification on any questions or concepts that continue to puzzle you. If you are still struggling with something, look into the tutoring resources at your school.

Finally, double-check the math to confirm that the total number of points you earned on the test is correct.

Test-Taking Skills Recap

In summary, if you want to meet the challenge of test-taking, and succeed as a forward-thinking student, you should work to develop the following test-taking skills:

☐ Learn the different types of tests and test questions.

☐ Find out whether the test will be written or oral; in-class, take-home, or online; and open- or closed-book.

☐ Anticipate the kinds of test questions your instructor will ask.

☐ The night before and the day of a test, prepare yourself mentally and physically so you can keep a positive focus.

☐ When you get the test in class, remain calm, read over the test, make your reasoned answers, and then review carefully to make sure you have answered all of the questions, including any extra credit items.

☐ Afterward, reflect on what study and test-taking activities helped you do well and consider what you need to do differently to improve.

SUMMARY

In the first section of this module, which focused on taking responsibility for your studying success, you examined the elements of a successful student's positive, disciplined approach to studying for tests; you determined that successful students take ownership of problems, persist to overcome obstacles, and anticipate what is needed to succeed; and you identified some of your study strengths and challenges.

In the second section, which focused on memory and memorization, you read about the kinds of memory and the dangerous curve of forgetting; you uncovered what successful students do to remember, such as considering thinking and learning styles and making mind maps and flashcards; and

you learned about and practiced several memory-enhancing techniques, including making up a mnemonic device.

In the third section, which focused on different types of tests and quizzes, and how to approach them, you read about types of tests and test questions and what to do before a test to be fully prepared and reduce anxiety, and learned ways to maximize your test score, including making sure you answer all of the questions. You also became more aware of what to do and not to do after a test to continue to improve, such as asking for clarification of puzzling questions, and you practiced specific question reading and answering tactics involving finding and understanding key words.

DISCUSSION QUESTIONS

1. Select one of the memorization techniques you read about and practiced, and explain which learning or thinking styles it is best suited for.

2. Describe something other than a memorization technique that you have done to prepare for a test that has worked well for you.

3. What advice would you give a student who is anxious about test-taking?

auditory learners: People who learn and remember best what they've *heard.* (p. 14)

data dump: Getting all the information out of your head and onto a piece of paper, such as the back of the test sheet, before beginning a test. (p. 25)

forward thinking: An approach that involves anticipating problems, thinking of ways to overcome them, and taking appropriate action to be well prepared for an upcoming challenge, such as an exam. (p. 5)

flashcards: Note cards used to help the user learn or memorize information. A typical flashcard may have a word on one side and its definition on the other, or a question on one side with the answer on the other. (p. 15)

kinesthetic learners: People who learn and remember best what they've *done.* (p. 14)

left-brain dominant: Influenced largely by the left hemisphere of the brain; people who are left-brain dominant tend to be organized and analytical and can easily recognize patterns and categories. (p. 14)

locus of control: Perceived place of control over your situation, either external (outside you) or internal (inside you). (p. 3)

mind map: Drawings with key words circled and connected by line to show relationships among ideas. (p. 14)

recall: Being able to remember information on demand, such as remembering a name that goes with a familiar face. (p. 21)

recitation: Reading aloud to reinforce learning. This practice engages all three learning styles—visual because you see the material as you read the cards, kinesthetic because of the body actions required for you to speak, and auditory because you hear yourself speaking. (p. 15)

recognition: Being able to identify a correct answer upon seeing it, such as spotting a familiar face in a crowd of strangers, or knowing the right answer from among several multiple-choice answers. (p. 21)

right-brain dominant: Influenced largely by the right hemisphere of the brain; people who are right-brain dominant tend to be more intuitive and spontaneous. They like to use their imaginations to memorize and prefer seeing drawings and pictures and making mind maps. (p. 14)

syllabus: A document that specifies what you'll be studying in a course, what your homework assignments will be, and the dates when you will take exams and tests. (p. 5)

visual learners: People who learn and remember best what they've *seen.* (p. 14)

Answer to question in "Mnemonics" section: POTUS (pronounced poh' tuss) is the acronym for *President of the United States.*

REFERENCES AND CREDITS

Footnotes

1. "Infographic: How does college GPA affect earnings?", Course Hero (blog), April 27, 2011. www.coursehero.com/blog/2011/04/27/infographic-how-does-college-gpa-affect-earnings/.

2. Belluck, Pam. (2011). "Test-taking cements knowledge better than studying, researchers say," The New York Times, January 20. www.nytimes.com/2011/01/21/science/21memory.html.

3. Everding, Gerry. (2008). "Practicing information retrieval is key to memory retention, study finds," Washington University in St. Louis, February 15. http://news-info.wustl.edu/tips/page/normal/11091.html

Figure and Photo Credits

Chapter opening photo: Chris Ryan/Getty Images

Figure 1: Rubberball/Getty Images

Figure 2: Tetra Images/Getty Images

Figure 3: © 2009 Jupiterimages Corporation

Studying on the Job: © Siri Stafford, Gettyimages

Figure 4: © Fancy/Alamy

Figure 5: allOver photography/Alamy

My Success Story: Digital Vision/Getty Images

Figure 8: Fuse/Getty Images

Figure 9: Aaron Roeth Photography

Figure 10: Corbis Premium RF/Alamy

Figure 11: Corbis Premium RF/Alamy

Money Smarts: © Sam Toren/Alamy

Figure 12: Photodisc/Getty Images

Writing with Clarity

LEARNING OUTCOMES

In this module, you will:

1 Learn the importance of knowing the purpose of your document before you begin writing.

2 Understand how to tailor the style and tone of your writing to your audience.

3 Discover a new process you can use when presented with a writing assignment.

4 Develop habits that can make you a more effective writer.

5 Learn about the kind of writing you will find in college and how to avoid plagiarism.

6 Explore the different types of writing you will find in your career, and learn some basic skills for writing business documents.

Communicating today is done largely through texting, short e-mails, or other similar messages.

- Do you prefer to call, text, IM, or e-mail your friends and family?
- Do you think clear writing is more or less important than it was 10 years ago?

> *"The beautiful part of writing is that you do not have to get it right the first time—unlike, say, brain surgery."*
>
> —**ROBERT CORMIER (1925–2000),** *American author, columnist, and newspaper reporter*

Many employers today say that writing is one of the most essential skills they seek when recruiting new employees. They say that writing is often more important than the skills employees learn in their program of study in college. Effective writing is also necessary for job retention and promotion within many organizations.

If you have done your best to avoid writing, reading the previous paragraph may have made you worried about writing you'll have to do in your future career. However, while writing may make you nervous today, this module is designed to help you become a stronger, more confident writer, ready to tackle the writing challenges you will face both as a college student and in your career.

I. Writing for a Reason and a Reader

Why do we write? To communicate ideas. To persuade someone. To express emotions. To explain that we understand. There are so many reasons we may write, and these reasons impact the many forms that our written communications can take.

Of course, writing is only one part of the communication process. The work of a written document is not done until it is read. For writing to truly succeed, it must impact its reader the way the writer intended. In this section, we will look at how to identify a purpose for your writing, and how to write for a specific audience.

LO 1 Purpose: Why Are You Writing?

Ask many college students why they are writing, and they'll groan, "Because it was assigned." Writing has a reputation as a torturous task—and if you feel the only reason you're writing is because a writing project was assigned to you, writing only feels more torturous.

Yet everything that you write—whether a report for your job, a text message to a friend, a letter to the editor of your local paper, or a paper for class—has a specific purpose. If you clearly define that purpose before you begin writing, you can write to meet that objective, which will make what you write more effective—and make the writing process less painful.

Determining an Objective for Your Writing

No matter the document, before you sit down to write, take a few minutes to consider the **purpose** of your task. For example, if you have been asked to write a report for class, review the assignment. Is the purpose to demonstrate understanding of the material? Are you being asked to present and support an opinion on something you have read or discussed in class?

purpose: The reason you are writing a document.

Write down the objective for the assignment in a separate document, being as specific as possible. Asking additional questions about your purpose can help you be more specific. For example, if the objective is to show understanding, what are you trying to show that you understand? How might you show that you understand the material?

Keep in mind that, even if the assignment requires that your paper be five pages long, the purpose of the assignment is not to write a five-page paper. Instructors choose page lengths for their assignments because they know from experience approximately how long a paper must be to sufficiently address the assignment. Writing just to fill a certain number of pages is not a clear purpose for writing.

While every document has a purpose specific to its situation, the following general categories can help you identify the purpose of what you are writing.

INFORM Many college assignments are "informing" documents, where you must provide information or explanation about a topic to show that you understand it. In business, documents such as status reports, research reports, and e-mail updates are used to share knowledge and information about a project or about ongoing research with others.

PERSUADE "Persuading" documents are used in selling and marketing. Proposals, sales brochures, and marketing copy for a website or product package all use persuasive language to convince someone of the value or benefit of a product, service, idea, politician, cause, or strategy. Usually one goal of these kinds of documents is to encourage someone to make a specific decision, such as to buy, donate, or vote.

ENTERTAIN We all know documents whose purpose is to entertain. These include novels, comic books, movie scripts, blogs, magazine articles, and so on. More specific purposes for documents that entertain may be to make the reader laugh, cry, or think.

SHARE Often the purpose of a document is to express feelings. This may be an e-mail to a co-worker sharing your frustration with a work situation, or an entry in your journal about something disappointing. More positively, a sharing document could be a love letter where you declare your feelings to the one you love.

Many documents have multiple purposes. For example, a magazine article can be used to inform and entertain, while a proposal could be written to inform and persuade. When identifying an objective for your writing, consider secondary purposes as well as the primary one.

What Are You Trying To Say? Meeting Your Writing Objectives

It's a good habit to explain your objective at the beginning of your document. This tells the reader what to expect, and why they're about to read what they're about to read. This information can help them decide if they are the right audience for the document, and also help guide how they read it. It also raises their expectations of you as a writer—they are now reading to see if you will do what you said you would do.

One way to measure the effectiveness of a document you are working on is to share it with someone else. When you share the document, explain your objectives in writing it, and ask your friend to read with those in mind. Whether or not your reader feels you have been successful, you can ask more specific questions about the document's effectiveness.

The more specific your objectives are, the better your questions can be, which can lead to more specific suggestions from your reader. Having a friend say, "It's good" may feel nice, but it won't make your document stronger, and in the long term, it won't help you become a more effective writer. Ask specific questions and get specific suggestions.

Stating your purpose clearly can also help you stay focused as you are writing. If you are struggling, and feel lost or unsure about where to go next, look back at your purpose. Are you addressing this purpose? If not, how did you get off track? What more do you need to do to help meet your purpose? Knowing your purpose can help you ask the kinds of questions that can get you back on track.

It may seem like a simple, obvious question, but "What am I trying to say?" can be a powerful tool for any writer. If you're staring at a blank page, and that question doesn't help, ask it out loud, and talk out your answer. Even better, have a friend ask, and explain your answer to your friend. Often, this can be just the trick to help get you unstuck.

Figure 2
Get someone else to read over your ideas early and often to make sure you're on the right track.

LO 2 Audience: Who Are You Writing For?

Knowing the purpose of your document is one key component of effective writing. Another is understanding who you are writing for: your **audience**.

audience: *The person or people who will read your document.*

If you are speaking without an audience, people will say you're just talking to yourself. Similarly, if you do not write for an audience, you're just writing for yourself. In some cases, such as a journal or diary, this may be appropriate. But most documents you write will be written for a specific audience. The more you know about your audience, the more effectively you will be able to achieve your document's purpose.

Understanding Your Audience

Let's say you are writing a report on a project at work. If your audience includes your co-workers, who have been working on the project with you for months, you do not need to provide background information about the project. You know that your readers already know that information. Thus, you can make the document brief and to the point, without giving the project's history or explaining its purpose or ongoing challenges.

On the other hand, if you are writing a report on that same project, but your audience is your boss, or someone in the company who has not been working closely on the project, then you do want to provide background information. You want to let them know things like the project's purpose, when work began, and the successes and challenges that you have experienced thus far.

If you gave the short update document to the second audience, they would be lost. They wouldn't have enough information for the document to be useful to them. If you gave the detailed report to the first audience, you would be wasting their time, because they would already know most of what you were writing. As you can see, it is helpful to consider your audience and what they know before you begin to write.

WHAT DOES YOUR AUDIENCE KNOW? In the example above, you knew the people you were writing for. What happens if you don't know your audience personally? If you know that your audience is made up of trained professionals, you can use technical language that they would know. If you know that your document will be read by a more general audience, you should avoid technical terms that might confuse them, and also write in shorter sentences and break your instructions down into smaller steps.

When thinking about your audience, here are a few other things to consider:

☐ Their level of familiarity with you (the author)

☐ Their amount of knowledge or experience with the information or circumstances

☐ The way the document will be distributed (e.g., online, posted on a wall, sent in the mail)

☐ Culture (formal or informal; could be professional culture or national culture)

☐ Job duties (making decisions, following instructions, etc.)

After considering your audience's knowledge, consider their expectations. Are they expecting a long report or a quick update? Do they expect it will use technical language or be written in layperson's terms? Do they expect to be able to make a decision when they are done reading?

Every document you create is an opportunity to speak to a specific audience. Just as with purpose, the more specific you can be in outlining what your audience knows, and what you know about your audience, the more effective your writing will be.

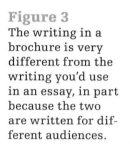

Figure 3
The writing in a brochure is very different from the writing you'd use in an essay, in part because the two are written for different audiences.

Choosing the Right Style for Your Purpose and Audience

Once you have defined your purpose and audience, you can make many decisions about how to write your document: length, format, style, and more. Writing style includes sentence length, word choice, and the general tone of the language you use. Let's examine three ways to approach writing tone.

FORMAL WRITING The formality of your document usually depends on both the setting in which it will be read and your relationship to the audience. Academic papers, legal briefs, and medical documents are examples of formal settings for writing. These call for a **formal tone** of voice in your documents.

You may also write in a formal tone if you do not know your audience very well, or you want to show respect.

Formal writing is appropriate when writing to your instructors as well. Professors often get student e-mails that begin, "Hey," if they begin with a greeting at all. "Hey" may be appropriate when e-mailing close friends, but when addressing your instructors, use

MY SUCCESS STORY

After completing high school in a large city in New York State, Cassandra Bolden began a journey that included a lot of firsts. She applied for admission to college and was accepted at Wilberforce University in Xenia, Ohio. That made her the first in her family to go to college. Traveling to Ohio to begin school was another big first. It was the first time she had left New York.

Cassandra's first year at Wilberforce also included many difficult firsts, as she struggled academically in a challenging new environment. Then came a devastating first—she flunked out of school.

She went back home and tried to find work, but this was a struggle, too. "I worked 70-hour weeks at McDonald's to pay off my debt from my first year in college (it took a year), then I applied for readmission." Despite flunking out, she wanted back in. "I was accepted, but I was placed on academic probation. First, I had to prove to the officials at Wilberforce that I was academically worthy of being allowed to continue toward my degree there."

The next few years went a little better. She still struggled, but she passed all her courses. However, her attempts to find employment, especially summer work, were not successful. When she spoke with the career-services office, she began to understand why she was having so much difficulty. "The college placement counselor kept telling me that prospective employers were consistently commenting that I used 'too much slang,'" Cassandra explained. These potential employers couldn't understand her non-standard English in both oral and written communications.

This was a wake-up call for Cassandra. She realized that she had a serious language problem, both orally and in writing. She understood that in order to succeed in college and later in the workplace, she would have to master what was in many ways a new language to her: *Standard English*.

Determined to meet the challenge, Cassandra designed her own program for success, on top of her regular courses. She read voraciously, devouring magazines, newspapers, books, and brochures. "I studied how the newscasters on The Weather Channel and national television news programs spoke English," she said, "and I watched myself pronounce words in the mirror."

When she went back home, some family members gave her a hard time about how she was beginning to speak. But the more she worked at it, the more she found success, both in the classroom and in interviews with potential employers, who wanted to be sure that she could communicate professionally in a work environment.

Cassandra was rewarded many times over for her considerable efforts. After receiving her bachelor's degree from Wilberforce, she went on to earn a master's degree, and then a doctorate in education. Today, Dr. Cassandra Bolden is an education professional specializing in program and curriculum development.

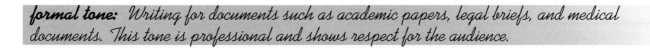

formal tone: Writing for documents such as academic papers, legal briefs, and medical documents. This tone is professional and shows respect for the audience.

more formal language to show respect for their position. Beginning your e-mail with "Dear Professor" or "Ms. Johnson" starts a message off on the right foot.

INFORMAL WRITING This kind of writing is close to ordinary speech and may include jargon and slang. This is the sort of writing you might use in personal notes, text, or some e-mail messages and in business documents only where you know your audience very well.

Keep in mind that, while language using an **informal tone** might make your listener feel more comfortable in a conversation, informal language in a business or academic document may come across as lazy, inappropriate, or disrespectful.

> *informal tone:* *Writing that is close to ordinary speech and may include jargon and slang. Used in personal notes, text, or some e-mail messages, and in business documents only when you know your audience very well.*

MEDIUM-TONE WRITING This language falls between formal and informal writing. It is not too casual and not too scholarly. Most writing for college classes and most business writing will use a **medium tone**. You will also find this kind of language in many magazine and newspaper articles, popular books, and some textbooks.

> *medium tone:* *Language that falls between formal- and informal-tone writing; not too casual and not too scholarly. Most writing for college classes, most business writing, many magazine and newspaper articles, popular books, and some textbooks will use a medium tone.*

Medium-tone writing covers a broad spectrum, with some examples falling closer to formal writing and some closer to informal writing. Again, considering your purpose and audience will help you determine the right level of formality for these kinds of documents.

"Standard" English—Writing for Different Audiences

Is there such a thing as "standard" English? If you grew up in Louisiana and have been to Kansas, or you've visited both New Mexico and New Hampshire, or have been to all of those places, as well as London, England, or Sydney,

> ## TAKE ACTION

Audience and Purpose Assessment—The Last Thing You Read

One way to learn how purpose and audience can affect the writing of a document is to look at a document through these two lenses.

To practice on your own time, you could select from a range of documents: an article in the newspaper, an e-mail from an instructor, or an editorial in your favorite magazine. However, for this activity, your instructor has preselected a document for you to analyze, for purpose and audience.

As you read, remember to make marginal notes where you can identify elements of purpose and the intended audience. Once you complete the reading, respond to the following questions about the document:

- What is the purpose of the document? How do you know? (Indicate portions of the text that help to support your identification of the purpose.)
- What makes the document effective or ineffective at achieving this purpose?
- Who is the audience for the document? How do you know this? (Indicate portions of the text that help to support your identification of the audience.)

Figure 4 You use different speaking styles when giving a presentation versus talking with your friends; writing works the same way.

- What do you know about this audience?
- What can you learn from how the writer addressed purpose and audience?

After you have answered these questions about the document, partner with another student in class. Take turns sharing your responses to each question. Identify the questions that you two responded to differently, and then discuss how each of you came up with your answer. Once you finish your discussion, respond to the following questions:

- How did your identification of the purpose of the document vary from your partner's?
- What portions of the text influenced your partner's answers?
- How did your identification of the audience vary from your partner's?
- What portions of the text influenced your partner's answers?

After sharing your responses, were you and your partner able to agree on the purpose and the intended audience? Why or why not?

Australia, you might argue that there is no "standard" English. The English language sounds different depending on where it is spoken, with accents, dialects, and vocabulary varying from one area (and sometimes even one part of town) to the next.

English is a dynamic, flexible language. It changes from place to place and evolves with the times, constantly incorporating new words and phrases from countries and cultures all around the world. For business and educational purposes, however, there is a more formal way to speak and write the language. This is known as **Standard English**.

Standard English: The universally accepted, more formal way to speak and write English; used in business and educational settings.

Speaking and writing in Standard English may feel awkward, uncomfortable, or even fake at times, but most people in most careers find that their eventual success is related to their ability to use Standard English. This need to use Standard English does not mean that the way you talk and write among family and friends—let's call that your "home" language—is wrong or that you need to abandon it.

In fact, one of the great things about English is that it welcomes so many different versions of itself. However, when people from different regions, cultures, countries, or professions need to communicate with each other, they need a common ground. Standard English is that common ground. That is the true value of being comfortable with Standard English—no matter your background, it lets you communicate with someone from a completely different background. In other words, your "home" language isn't Substandard English—it's a variation on the standard version of the language.

A VARIETY OF VOCABULARY If you've ever gotten completely lost while trying to follow a conversation with people who were supposedly speaking your language, you've probably encountered nonstandard English and a specialized vocabulary.

Figure 5 Every subject has its own special vocabulary, or jargon, and part of any education is learning those new words.

You might not think that a group of American soldiers talking about war strategy and tactics would speak a different language than you. For that matter, you might not think that pharmacists, lawyers, civil engineers, insurance agents, football players, or even teenagers—all theoretically speaking English—are speaking a different language. People in those groups often communicate using technical terms, acronyms, scientific terms, or sayings peculiar to their region, profession, neighborhood, or even their circle of friends. To outsiders, it may seem like they are speaking a strange and incomprehensible language.

However, when people in these kinds of specialized groups talk with people outside their group, they still use Standard English to get their message across. That's why Standard English is so valuable. It lets people who are "speaking different languages" communicate and connect with each other. The sooner you master Standard English, the more opportunities you will have to communicate and connect with others.

II. The Writing Process

GET READY

What is the longest paper you've ever written?

- Do you remember the process you used to get the job done on time?
- Looking back on that assignment, were you proud of your work?

Why do so many people fear writing? Writing's not easy, but there are many things that are not easy that don't scare people the way writing does.

One reason people get intimidated by writing is because they think of it as Writing, with a capital W. They think you must have grand inspiration to write or that you must be visited by the elusive writing muse. Perhaps even worse, people get scared of writing because they are afraid of staring at a blank page and not having anything to say.

LO 3 Writing as a Process (Not a Performance)

Many of us picture a writer waking up, pouring a cup of coffee, putting a blank piece of paper in the typewriter, and banging out a novel. This is an inspiring scene, but it rarely, if ever, happens that way—even for the most successful writers. Unfortunately, that myth persists, and it leads to procrastination, and writer's block.

In reality, writing is not a performance, as described above, but rather a **process**, with manageable, repeatable steps that any writer of any skill level can take. You will find that the more you write, and the more comfortable you get with the steps in the process, the better and more confident you will become as a writer.

process: Repeatable steps used to complete a task, such as writing a document.

Writing Redefined: The Steps in the Writing Process

The five steps in the writing process are *pre-writing, research and investigation, outlining, drafting,* and *revising and editing.* Each of the five steps in this

process is essential to writing, but none requires you to stare at a blank screen with no clear direction. These steps break the writing process into small, manageable pieces that help you build a strong document bit by bit. You can use these steps no matter what kind of document you are writing, no matter what the topic. These steps can also help you beat writer's block and avoid procrastination.

PRE-WRITING In the first section, we discussed purpose and audience, which are the cornerstones to **pre-writing**, the first step in the writing process.

Before you do any research or writing, get out a new sheet of paper or open a new document on your computer, and answer the questions about purpose and audience that we discussed earlier. Then, write down how you plan to achieve the purpose and what you think your audience will be looking for.

Figure 6 Good writing rarely happens in a first draft; the goal is to write something—anything—and then refine it.

This pre-writing document will not only help you get a handle on those two critical anchors for your writing, but they will also help you get additional ideas out of your head and onto the page. One reason the blank page can be so intimidating is that it doesn't provide any prompts for your writing. The "blank page" of your pre-writing document comes with specific questions about purpose and audience, which serve as built-in prompts to help you get started and build up some momentum.

pre-writing: *The first step in the writing process. Includes determining the document's audience and purpose.*

RESEARCH AND INVESTIGATION The next step in the writing process is research and investigation. You can prepare for this step in the pre-writing phase by identifying specific questions that you hope to answer in your research. Add these questions to your pre-writing document, and keep that document with you as you begin the research phase of your writing.

Your research and investigation should focus on getting answers to the questions you asked in your pre-writing document, and finding evidence to back up the argument you want to make. In this way, your pre-writing document serves as a road map for this next step. Though it can be hard to predict what your research will uncover, it's still helpful to start with an idea of where you think you're going. The more clearly you define your research path, the sooner you will know if you've wandered too far off it.

Focused research can be exciting and can help you learn many new things about your topic. Yet if research is not focused, it can also be a thief that steals hours and hours of valuable time. By spelling out what you are trying to do with your document, you can be more precise when you set out to do research, whether that means going to your librarian with a specific question or searching specific terms using Google.

In your research, you may hit a dead end and realize you can't find enough information to support your original idea. Or your investigation may lead to information related to your original topic that you think is more interesting and that you'd like to pursue instead. Such occurrences are normal. After all, if you knew exactly what you were going to find before you started your research, you probably wouldn't be writing the paper.

As you gather new information in the research process, keep track of where you find your information so you can properly cite references and avoid plagiarism (this topic is more fully covered in the next section). Also, make notes to yourself about why you think the information will be useful, such as the subtopic or question that it addresses. These notes will help you in the next step, outlining.

OUTLINING Once you have completed your research, you're ready to create an outline. The outline establishes the basic structure for your document.

To start, gather your pre-writing document and your research documents. First, review your pre-writing document. This will remind you of your document's goals and purpose.

Figure 7
Researching information about your subject will help you develop new ideas to write about.

Next, review the research you have gathered. While you were researching, you made notes on the information you gathered about what subtopics or questions the information addressed. If you took your notes on note cards, lay the notes out on a table and arrange them by topic. If you took your notes electronically, or in a single notebook, you might want to jot down a short phrase or cue about each piece of research on a note card and use the same process. Another approach is to write your cues on sticky notes and stick them on a wall.

The goal of this activity is to let you see the entire project in one view, rather than in a series of pages or documents. This can help you arrange related information together, and you can start to put the subtopics into an order that makes sense for the purpose of your document. As you look at all of your research in one place, do any new ideas or themes come to mind? If so, make note of these, either in your pre-writing document or in a new document.

Once you have arranged this information into a sequence, you have the foundation for an outline. Start a new document, and transfer the information from the note cards or sticky notes into this document. As you write your outline, don't write in sentences or paragraphs—write phrases and bullet points. In outlining, incomplete sentences aren't just allowed, they're helpful. Remember, the goal

Figure 8
Drafting doesn't
mean creating your
final document, so
you're allowed to
be messy.

of outlining is to help the document take shape. You're not trying to write your paper yet. Developing your ideas this way, in bullet points and quick phrases rather than complete sentences, can be liberating.

As you write your outline, you may realize that you need more information to support your argument or answer the question you are trying to address. At this point, it is okay to go back to the library to do more research. It is better to do more research now, while your document is still taking shape.

DRAFTING Once you have an outline you like, founded in your research and guided by your prewriting document, you are ready to begin drafting. Drafting is the stage most similar to what people think of when they think about "writing." The difference is, if you have followed the steps in the process, you won't be staring at a blank screen. You'll be starting with an outline that you can turn into a draft.

Now is the time to turn those incomplete thoughts into sentences and paragraphs. Drafting is where ideas become arguments and explanations. For many people, this is the most challenging part of the writing process, but the stronger your work in the first three phases, the easier this stage will be.

Keep in mind that your first draft is not your final draft. You're not turning in your first draft, so don't labor over every sentence. It doesn't need to be perfect. If you aren't sure how you want to say something, make a note to yourself of what you're trying to say, and come back to it later. This is a rough draft, and you will improve it in the revising and editing phase. The goal now is to get a first draft onto the page so you have something to work with.

Once you have finished your first draft, take a step back. Give yourself time to think about something else. Go for a walk, have a meal, or do something fun to give yourself a little bit of distance from the first draft before you begin revising and editing it.

REVISING AND EDITING Once you've given yourself some time away from your first draft, you're ready to revise and edit it. If possible, print a copy, so you can read it on paper and not on the computer screen.

Before you pull out a red pen to start marking up your work, read without a pen first. This will give you a general sense of the document and its strengths and weaknesses.

As you read through your draft, focus on the big issues first. Does what you've written match the document purpose you identified? Are the voice, tone, and information presented appropriate for your target audience? If not, consider what changes need to be made, and make those adjustments.

Once you've addressed the big issues, look back at your outline. How well does the first draft match up with your outline? Where are the differences? If your outline and your draft don't match up, figure out why. Does the sequence work? Is one section too long or another too short? Are you missing pieces of your argument? Address these concerns next. Do not start fixing words and punctuation line by line yet. Not only are the structural issues more important to the overall success of the document than any specific sentence or paragraph, but if you start at the small level, trying to fix words, sentences, and punctuation, you may find yourself spending a lot of time editing things that later will be cut.

The editing stage is also a good time to get input and feedback from friends. If you look at your own work long enough, particularly on a computer screen, you can often overlook obvious mistakes, because your brain reads what you meant to write—and not what you actually wrote. That's why it's a good idea to get "fresh eyes" on a document before submitting it.

Ask a friend with strong Standard English skills to read the document for you. Someone who brings "fresh eyes" to your writing can not only catch mistakes, but also offer a different viewpoint that can help you strengthen your document. When sharing your document with others, ask them specific questions about it, so you can get specific information that will help you make the document stronger. When you get feedback, whether it is from a friend or your instructor, pay attention to their edits. Their suggestions can help you become a better writer.

You will probably go through several drafts before the document is ready to submit. With each draft, start with the major issues, and work your way through to the details.

Figure 9 You can have someone read your work any time, but it's very important to have it checked before you turn it in.

LO 4 Developing Good Writing Habits

Writing is a skill that can be refined and developed over time. But this won't happen by accident. To become a better writer, you need to develop writing habits that will enable you to produce better work. No matter how strong your writing is now, good writing habits can help you to get better and be more comfortable with writing.

Avoiding the Last Minute: Giving Yourself Enough Time

One of the reasons so many people fear writing is that they put it off until the last minute, when the pressure of an impending deadline makes writing stressful. Of course, if you're always stressed when you're writing, it's no wonder you avoid it—which leads to even more stress!

The five-step writing process outlined above is a good way to help you avoid the stress of last-minute writing. When your instructor gives an assignment, usually there is only one date involved: the date the paper is due. But if that's the only deadline you write in your planner, that's likely the only one you'll respond to. A better approach is to give yourself a deadline for each of the five steps. Your editing deadline will be the same as the due date. For the other four deadlines, give yourself enough time to complete each stage.

The first time you use this process, you will have to make an educated guess as to how long each step will take you. As you use this process multiple times, make note of how long the steps take. Then, when you get a new assignment, you can do a better job of estimating how much time you need to give yourself for each stage, and plan accordingly.

The five stages outlined above leave a lot of room for interpretation. Ultimately, if your process is to work for you, it needs to be customized to what you like and what you don't. Maybe you like doing your research at the library first thing in the morning, when it's quiet. Maybe you like using sticky notes on the wall to make your outline and get excited about getting a new packet of sticky notes in fun colors for each new project.

The more you learn what works for you and do it, the less likely you will be to avoid writing. Think about everything from the best times of day for each of these steps, to the best physical locations in which to do them. Do you like working at

MONEY SMART$

Are You an Entrepreneur?

If you have always thought that you would like to work for yourself, or own your own business, then you may be an entrepreneur. Entrepreneurs turn ideas into businesses, buy and run businesses, or make a business out of providing a service.

No matter what entrepreneurial path you might pursue, good writing skills will help you be more successful. One of the first steps in starting any new business is to write a business plan. This is a significant document that describes in detail all of the various aspects of your new business, including the product or service you plan to sell, how you plan to sell it, how you plan to finance the business, and much more.

For more detail on the steps to writing a business plan, visit the U.S. Small Business Administration's website at www.sba.gov/smallbusinessplanner/plan/writeabusinessplan/index.html.

In addition to writing a business plan, most entrepreneurs must also write proposals and marketing materials to enable their business to run successfully. The strength of these documents can determine how well people understand the value of the business and help them decide whether to buy your product or service, or invest in your company. In short, good writing skills are highly valuable when owning and operating a successful enterprise. If you don't have them, you can always hire someone to

home? In the library? At a coffee shop? Do you like listening to certain music, or do you work better with earplugs in your ears? Get to know what works for you, and soon the process will start to feel natural and automatic. Then you will be able to truly focus on producing great work.

Avoiding Writer's Block

As we've discussed, one of the reasons people suffer from writer's block is sitting down in front of a blank page. If you follow the steps in the writing process, the only blank page you will sit in front of is your pre-writing document, and that blank page gets filled quickly once you start answering questions about purpose and audience.

do your writing for you; however, that can be a very expensive option!

Being an entrepreneur means taking a risk. Starting new businesses, or taking over an existing business, means that you may not have the safety of a traditional corporate structure or the consistency of a regular paycheck. But, because they are the owners of the company, entrepreneurs also often enjoy a greater reward in exchange for this risk.

Have you considered being an entrepreneur? What parts seem exciting to you? What parts are scary? How might your experience in college prepare you to be an entrepreneur?

Quick Practice on the Writing Process

The best way to get comfortable with the steps in the writing process is to practice them.

Your instructor will give you a topic for a practice paper. While you don't have time to go to the library and research, with a bit of creativity, you can practice the five steps in the process in class, in only a few minutes.

Once you have the topic, take a few minutes to complete each of the following steps.

1. Pre-writing

a. Identify the purpose and audience of the assignment _____

_____

b. Jot down whatever information you know, or need to know about these _____

_____

c. Write down any other information that will help you write the paper _____

_____

2. Research and Investigation

a. You're not going to conduct research right now, but take a few minutes to identify topics that you would research if you were in the library or online _____

_____

b. Then brainstorm as many subtopics as possible _____

_____

3. Outline

a. Take the subtopics you came up with, and make a basic structure for your paper on the sample outline on the next page.

4. Drafting

a. Pick two sections from the middle of your outline, and draft two paragraphs, just to practice turning a piece of your outline into paragraphs.

5. Revising and Editing

a. Share the section that you drafted with a classmate.

b. Your classmate will respond to the following questions with specific feedback.

   i. Does the order that the information is presented in, in the paragraphs, make sense? Why or why not?

   ii. Do the two paragraphs present a logical argument? Why or why not?

   iii. What are the writer's strengths in these two paragraphs?

   iv. What are some suggestions for improvement in these two paragraphs?

c. Then, make a few quick improvements to the two-paragraph draft.

Introduction:

   1.

      a.

      b.

   2.

Paragraph 1:

   1.

      a.

      b.

   2.

      a.

      b.

Paragraph 2:

   1.

      a.

      b.

   2.

      a.

      b.

Paragraph 3:

   1.

      a.

      b.

      c.

   2.

      a.

      b.

Conclusion:

   1.

      a.

      b.

      This was a rapid-fire approach to the writing process, but it should give you an idea of what happens in each of the steps. How did it feel to complete this process? How do you think this process will benefit your writing on a real assignment?

Another reason people often get stuck is perfectionism. They feel a sentence has to be perfect, and they write it again and again, unable to move past it. If you feel stuck on a sentence, either make a note to yourself about what you're trying to say, and come back to it later, or simply stop working on the sentence. Go work on another part of the document, or get up and go for a walk. Often, getting your body moving will help get the ideas in your head moving, and after a quick walk, you will feel unstuck.

III. Writing for College and Career

No matter which career path you choose, you will have many opportunities to write and to apply what we have discussed in this module. In this section, we'll look at how to approach some of the major types of documents you will encounter as a student and in your career.

LO 5 College Writing

College is an ideal time to develop your writing skills. When you submit your work, you can get feedback from your instructors, who have a lot of experience helping students become better writers. The harder you work on improving your writing while in college, the greater advantage you will have when asked to write important documents in your career.

Research Papers

The most common document that you will be asked to write as a student is a research paper. In a typical research paper, your purpose is to take a close look at a specific topic and demonstrate your understanding, interpretation, or evaluation of it or to present an argument about it.

When you write a research paper, you present more than just what you know personally. You build upon the research and investigation of experts. To be able to present what you have learned from these experts, you must survey a field of knowledge to gather the best, most current information on the topic that you can find.[1]

How to Avoid Plagiarism

When you write a research paper, you are exploring for ideas, information, and answers. You may explore in books, magazines, academic journals, newspapers, the Internet, or first-hand interviews or observations. You may also include your own ideas and concepts, which may come from your research, or ideas you have come up with on your own.

By definition, when you are conducting research, you are building on the ideas of others. Just as you would want credit for any ideas you came up with on your own, it is important to give others credit for their original ideas when you build upon them. Though that concept seems simple, **plagiarism** is a major problem in the academic world.

Plagiarism is literary theft: the act of stealing or passing off the ideas or words of another person as your own without giving credit or recognition to that person. Just like regular theft, plagiarism is unethical and illegal. And just like regular theft, literary theft has victims, too—people who worked hard to conduct their own research, only to have someone else steal it in an effort to take a shortcut.

plagiarism: Presenting the ideas or words of others as your own without giving proper credit or recognition.

WHY STUDENTS PLAGIARIZE If plagiarism is theft, why do students do it? Are all students who plagiarize hardened literary criminals? Do these students just not know the law of the literary land?

Some acts of plagiarism by students are indeed acts of ignorance, where students use someone else's work while genuinely not knowing the rules related to crediting their sources. Sometimes students are just careless, quoting someone else's work but forgetting to note the source in their paper.

Unfortunately, those instances are rare compared to instances of students who plagiarize and hope to get away with it. It's a sad story that happens all too often. It's often even sadder, because these students usually get caught, and the consequences can be severe. Depending on the instructor, college, and severity of the crime, the punishment may be failure on the paper, failure in the course, or even dismissal from the college.

Of course, plagiarism isn't limited to students. News stories appear regularly about professors, graduate students, researchers, and journalists who have been caught plagiarizing, and suffer public shame and disgrace. It's a good bet those people didn't learn their lessons about how to avoid plagiarism. Fortunately for you, you can learn this valuable lesson now, while you're still in college.

STRATEGIES FOR CREDITING YOUR SOURCES All of this talk about plagiarism can sound intimidating and scary. "I just want to write a research paper for

Figure 11
Plagiarism is a type of cheating, just like copying someone's answers on a test.

class!" you may be thinking. But avoiding plagiarism is easy. You simply need to accurately cite, note, or document in your written work what information you got from other sources and where you found it.

Keeping Good Records When Writing You can steer clear of plagiarism problems the moment you start doing research by keeping track of your sources. Whether using a book, magazine, or other source, keep track of anything you've read in that source that you have used, will use, or think you might use.

Decide before you start researching how you will track your resources and the information you take from them. No matter which method you choose, be consistent, and get as much information as you can for each and every source that you use.

Quoting, Paraphrasing, Summarizing: How to Present the Words of Others When you are ready to refer to the information you have found in your research, there are multiple ways to present what you have learned. No matter which you choose, each requires that you give credit to the originator of the information.

Option 1: Quoting When you **quote** a source directly, you are using their exact words, which you show by using quotation marks. Whenever you use a direct quote like this, you must identify who wrote or spoke what you are quoting.

quote: Using a source's exact words, shown by using quotation marks.

Example: "Confession," says Pennebaker, "whether by writing or talking, can neutralize many of the problems of inhibition." (1)

Option 2: Paraphrasing When you **paraphrase,** you take someone else's idea, and put it into your own words. However, even though you are using your own words, the idea still belongs to the original author, and you must give the author credit.

paraphrase: To take someone else's idea, and put it into your own words.

Example: Pennebaker says that writing or talking about thoughts and feelings can decrease the problems that arise when people hold things in. (1)

Option 3: Summarizing If you **summarize** information, you are explaining a general idea without giving specific details. You might use this to give a brief explanation about a long passage, article, or book that you used in your research. It is critical to give credit to the original author, even for just a general summary.

summarize: To explain a general idea, without giving specific details; often used to give a brief explanation about a long passage, article, or book used in research.

Example: Dr. Pennebaker's book, *Opening Up: The Healing Power of Expressing Emotions*, investigates people who have experienced traumatic events, but have not shared those experiences with anyone else by talking or writing about them. (1)

Choosing a Citation Style At the end of each of the examples above, there was a number "1" in parentheses. That number, which can appear at the end of a direct quote, or at the end of a paraphrased or summarized passage—or even in the middle of a sentence—is how you show that you are referencing a source. When you see a number like that, it means that there is a note, either at the bottom of the page (called a footnote) or at the end of the chapter or book (called an endnote) where you can find information about the source.

When you find the footnote or endnote, it may look something like this:

(1) Pennebaker, James W., Ph.D. *Opening Up: The Healing Power of Expressing Emotions.* The Guilford Press, New York, 1997, p. 2.

Sometimes citation numbers appear in smaller type that sits higher than the rest of the text. This is called superscript[2], and the small number 2 at the end of the word "superscript" earlier in this sentence shows how it looks.

There are many different types of citation styles, so ask your instructors which they prefer. Each style has rules for referencing different types of sources. Know the differences before you begin your research, so you can gather all the information you will need for your citations. No matter which citation style you use, be consistent throughout your document.

If you are unsure how to cite something, or whether you need to, ask for help. Your instructor or the college librarian should be able to answer most of your questions.

Essay Tests

An essay test is like a research paper—except you must do all your research before you write the first word of the essay and you aren't expected to use formal citations.

The goal of most essay tests is not find out if you know the facts—multiple-choice and other short-answer tests are more effective for that. Rather, instructors give essay tests to make sure you understand those facts and can explain their context, importance, or the ideas behind them.

Some instructors will let you bring research materials or textbooks with you for essay tests, while others don't. Find out what you can have with you during the essay test *well before* the test day so you can be fully prepared.

Figure 12
Computer sources need to be cited too! If someone else wrote it, whatever the medium, you must cite the author.

LO 6 Career Writing

Throughout your career, you will write many documents in many formats. Yet employer surveys indicate that as many as one-third of today's employees write poorly. One way to interpret those survey results is to worry that writing will be a struggle for you. A more positive way to read them is that developing your writing skills can help you stand out in your career.

Memos, Reports, and Other Professional Documents

No matter your career field, writing professional documents will likely be part of your job description. Whether updating co-workers on a project in a memo or report, trying to make a change in your company with a proposal, or trying to make a sale with a marketing brochure, good writing can help you succeed in the workplace.

The basic principles already discussed apply to career writing just as they do to other kinds of writing. Understanding the purpose and audience of your document is critical, and approaching writing as a process and not a performance will help make you a more efficient writer. And just as with college writing, when you find yourself conducting research for professional writing, you must credit your sources.

Let's look quickly at some of the documents you may need to write in your career.

MEMOS AND REPORTS Memos and reports are used to provide information to your boss, co-workers, or customers. Memos might include notes about what will be discussed at a future meeting, a brief update on a project's status, or a recap of the notes from a recent meeting. The audience for your memos will determine how formal or informal your writing tone should be.

Figure 13
Even though most offices run primarily on computers, there will still be a surprising amount of writing and paper!

Reports are used in many situations, but have a similar purpose: sharing information. Depending on your career field, you might encounter sales reports, incident reports, financial reports, or patient reports. Reports are often more formal than memos and also more likely to include charts, graphs, and statistics.

No matter the kind of memo or report you are writing, use simple, clear language that makes the document easy to read and understand.

PROPOSALS Proposals are persuasive documents that propose an idea or solution. The audience for proposals can be your boss, your co-workers, a potential client, or another organization, such as your city council. Proposals are often written in a more formal tone to show respect.

When writing proposals, put yourself in your audience's shoes. What are their needs and concerns? What information will persuade them to adopt your idea or solution? The more effectively you can address your audience's needs and preferences, the more likely your proposal will persuade them.

SALES AND MARKETING MATERIALS We read sales and marketing documents everyday—on billboards and bus stops, on the Internet, in magazine and newspaper advertisements, and in printed brochures found almost anywhere. Like proposals, sales and marketing materials are meant to be persuasive documents. They try to persuade the reader to buy a product or service. As with all the documents we have discussed, understanding your audience when writing sales and marketing materials is critical—perhaps as critical as understanding the product or service you are selling or marketing.

Electronic Correspondence

E-mail is the most frequently used form of communication in the world, and a significant amount of business correspondence is now done electronically, by e-mail, text messaging, instant messaging, and blogging and through social media channels like Twitter, Facebook, and LinkedIn.

Because most of us receive a huge volume of electronic correspondence every day, many people use this kind of communication without much thought. But thanks to how quickly electronic messages are delivered, and how easy they can be forwarded to anyone, it's important to pay attention to how you communicate electronically in a professional setting.

MAKING E-MAIL MORE EFFECTIVE As with all writing, it's important to remember the purpose and audience of your e-mail and to write accordingly. While the purpose and audience may change from one e-mail to the next, the nature of the e-mail format means that many readers will skim what you've written and that it may be forwarded to a secondary audience. With that in mind, here are some ways to make your e-mails more effective.

Figure 14 Not everyone can write an effective e-mail message.

Put Your Subject Line to Work If you want people to read your e-mail, use the subject line to give a brief summary of what they can expect from it. Be as specific as possible. For example, if you need a certain document, rather than a subject that says, "Need File," write, "Need notes from marketing meeting."

Many e-mail programs allow you to sort or search e-mails in your inbox by words in the subject line, so the more specific you make your e-mail subjects, the easier it may be for both you and your readers to find e-mails.

Create Guideposts: Headers, Lists, and Bullets Many e-mails are skimmed rather than read in full. While it would be nice if everyone carefully read every e-mail you sent, assume they won't and instead make it easy for your reader to quickly get the important information.

These formatting techniques can make it easier for readers to notice key information:

☐ *Headers.* Break your e-mail into sections, and give a header, or headline, to each, to preview what's coming, and help readers find what they need. Make headers as informative as possible.

☐ **Bold**, *italics*, and CAPITALS. These draw your reader's attention by making certain words stand out. Be careful which words you format this way—not everything deserves bold type. Also, if you write more than a few words in all capitals, it's like shouting at someone over the Internet.

☐ *Lists and bullets.* If presenting a series of questions or points, consider writing them as a numbered or bulleted list (like this one). This makes it easier for readers to get your main points than if the information is lumped together in one paragraph.

Also, spaces between paragraphs can make long e-mails less overwhelming. Spaces are relaxing to the eyes, while a screen full of text can be stressful.

ON THE JOB

Writing for Presentations

More and more, workers are expected to be able to make effective presentations—to co-workers, clients, and potential customers; for training workshops, conferences, and conventions; and more. Strong presentation skills are valuable for any worker.

Many factors impact presentations, including speaking skills and the ability to design and develop clear, concise visual aids. Numerous resources are available on both of those topics, and we encourage you to research them. However, this module is about writing, so we will focus on how strong writing skills can strengthen your presentations.

The steps in the writing process—pre-writing, research and investigation, outlining, drafting, and revising and editing—all apply when writing for presentations. Yet presentations are different because your written document is not the only way you communicate with your audience. In a presentation, what

you have written supports what you say out loud to make sure the audience gets your message.

Using PowerPoint in Your Presentations Many business presentations today use Microsoft Power-Point to show information on a screen that supports the words of the speaker. If you know how to use it well, PowerPoint can be a helpful tool that gives structure to your presentation and reinforces your ideas by showing memorable images and key phrases. However, if you don't know how to use it well, PowerPoint can also put an audience to sleep.

Some presenters deliver the same exact presentation three different ways at the same time: They put all of their information on the PowerPoint slides, they give the audience a printout of the PowerPoint slides, and then they go through the slides one by one, reading them to the audience. Repeating or reinforcing your point is helpful—but when you say the same thing on

Keep It Short and to the Point In e-mail, shorter is better. Short sentences and short paragraphs are more likely to be read and understood than long ones.

Thus, after you write an e-mail, read it again to see if you can say things more simply. To keep your e-mail focused, limit each e-mail to a single topic. If you need to address multiple topics with the same person, write a separate e-mail for each topic rather than lump several topics together in one e-mail. Separating your e-mail topics makes it easier to answer e-mails, and easier to follow a conversation that may run through multiple forwards and replies.

the screen, on paper, and out loud, you tell your audience that they don't need to pay attention to either what you're saying or what's on the screen, or both.

At the other end of the spectrum are presenters whose slides include only one or two words, and who don't give listeners much information at all.

Remember, the software is named PowerPoint for a reason—the idea is to highlight and support your points, not simply deliver your spoken words in another format. Keep the text on your slides brief, but long enough to make sense. Add pictures and graphics that explain an idea better than words alone can. Most importantly, think about how you can use the words and images on-screen to work with the words you are saying to deliver an experience for your audience that a simple speech or document cannot.

E-mail Etiquette Just as you should use good manners for face-to-face interactions with others, you should use good manners when sending e-mail. This is known as e-mail etiquette. Here are a few tips to help you maintain good e-mail manners:

☐ *Greetings.* Start your e-mail with a greeting. It should match the familiarity you have with your audience, and the respect you wish to show. If you know the person well, "Hello, Pat," may be appropriate. To show respect, you might write, "Dear Pat," "Dear Dr. Smith," or simply, "Dr. Smith."

☐ *Chain letters.* Sending jokes or chain letters to friends is fine, but it is inappropriate to forward them to co-workers or business contacts.

TAKE ACTION

An E-mail to a Supervisor or to an Instructor

It's time to put the concepts you just read regarding e-mail into practice by drafting an e-mail to your boss. You can draft an e-mail to your real boss about a real situation, or you can draft an e-mail to a boss that you hope to have in a future career, about a situation that you expect that you will face in your job.

Before you draft this e-mail, identify the skills that you have learned in this module, which you can put into practice:

1. _____
2. _____
3. _____

Identify the specific components of e-mail etiquette will you use:

1. _____
2. _____
3. _____

Once you have selected your addressee and have identified the skills and components you will implement in your e-mail, compose your e-mail within the provided table:

SEND	To:
	Subject:

☐ *Forward, Reply, and Reply All.* Before you forward a message, add a new recipient to a reply, or hit "Reply All," think for a moment. Are you about to share private or confidential information without the original sender's approval? Are you going to clutter a bunch of inboxes with an e-mail that not everyone on the recipient list needs to read? Paying attention to your recipient list, and being respectful and thoughtful about what you forward, is one of the most important aspects of good e-mail etiquette.

Try this online at mcgrawhillconnect.com

After you have drafted this practice e-mail, partner with a classmate. Your classmate will read your draft e-mail and respond with the following feedback:

1. Did the student include the identified e-mail etiquette? If no, what was omitted?

_____

_____

_____

2. What additional components of e-mail etiquette could the student include to improve the overall message and tone of the e-mail?

_____

_____

_____

3. Identify specific areas of etiquette success in the e-mail.

_____

_____

_____

4. Overall, what is your general response to the e-mail based on the communication skills you have learned in this module?

_____

_____

_____

- ☐ *Mass mailing.* If you must send an e-mail to a long list of people, send the e-mail to yourself, and place your recipients in the BCC: field. This keeps recipients' e-mail addresses private and keeps your e-mail header short, which can help avoid excess text in forwards and replies.
- ☐ *Humor.* Face-to-face communication includes body language, facial expressions, and vocal intonation to help get your message across. Without those, your message might be misunderstood, so be careful when trying to use humor in e-mail, as it can easily be misinterpreted by your recipient.
- ☐ *Message threads.* The "thread" of your e-mail message shows the ongoing conversation happening in the series of e-mails that you are replying to. Many business e-mails include several replies and forwards. Be sure to include the full thread of your e-mail, to ensure that your reader has enough information to follow the entire conversation.
- ☐ *Sign off.* After the body of your e-mail, before the signature, sign off, or close, your e-mail. Many people write, "Sincerely," then their name. Other common sign-off phrases are, "Thank you," "Thanks," "Best," or something more personal or specific to the content of the e-mail. Some people just put their name. As with your greeting, be sure your tone and word choice show appropriate respect to your audience.
- ☐ *Signature.* At the bottom of every e-mail message, include your name, title and company name if appropriate, and your contact information: address, phone numbers, and e-mail address. This block of information is known as your e-mail signature.
- ☐ *Spelling and grammar.* Use your e-mail program's spell-check and grammar-check features, then proofread your message to make sure you've said what you want to say.

INSTANT MESSAGING Instant messaging allows people across the world or just across the hall from each other to have ongoing, immediate, written conversations.

This form of communication is generally less formal than e-mail because, as the name implies, speed is often more important than formality when sending instant messages. However, even though checking grammar and spelling may not be critical when sending instant messages, it is still critical to remember electronic etiquette and manners. Be respectful and professional, and answer all questions as completely as you can.

TEXT MESSAGING Text messaging is even more informal than instant messaging, but is still a part of modern business communication. If you're running late to a meeting, you might send a text to let them know when to expect you. If you need to communicate with someone who you know is away from her computer, such as at a conference, but is likely to have her phone in her pocket, a text message may be the best way to reach that person without disturbing everyone else in the room.

When writing text messages, shorter is always better (and easier). The etiquette rules discussed for instant messaging apply here as well, but with text messages, there is another aspect to proper etiquette—when and where you read and send texts. If you are in a conversation with someone else, or in the middle of a meeting, it is rude to interrupt someone (or even interrupt yourself) to pull out your phone and read or send a text message. If you think the message you have received may be urgent, be polite, wait for an appropriate pause in the conversation, and say something like, "Excuse me, but I have been expecting this text. Would you mind if I read it?"

SUMMARY

While some people are more talented writers than others, anyone can learn the basics of good writing and can become a stronger, more confident writer with practice. Learning these fundamentals—including the importance of purpose and audience, the steps in the writing process, how to cite your sources when presenting research, and guidelines for proper etiquette in electronic communication—will serve you well as a college student and in your career. Take advantage of the opportunity you have as a college student to practice and get feedback on your writing.

DISCUSSION QUESTIONS

1. Before reading this module, had you ever taken time to consider the purpose and audience of a document you were writing? If so, how did that impact the effectiveness of your document? If not, how do you think using this technique might help your writing in the future?

2. Do you have a writing process already, or do you just sit down at the keyboard and start writing? If you have a process, what is effective about it? If you don't, what benefits do you think you could gain, or what problems do you think you could avoid, by applying the writing process discussed in section II?

3. What types of documents do you think you will need to write in your chosen career field? What do you know about these kinds of documents? What can you do to become more familiar with them, and better prepared to write them when you begin your career?

KEY TERMS

audience: The person or people who will read your document. (p. 5)

formal tone: Writing for documents such as academic papers, legal briefs, and medical documents. This tone is professional and shows respect for the audience. (p. 6)

informal tone: Writing that is close to ordinary speech and may include jargon and slang. Used in personal notes, text, or some e-mail messages, and in business documents only when you know your audience very well. (p. 8)

medium tone: Language that falls between formal- and informal-tone writing; not too casual and not too scholarly. Most writing for college classes, most business writing, many magazine and newspaper articles, popular books, and some textbooks will use a medium tone. (p. 8)

paraphrase: To take someone else's idea, and put it into your own words. (p. 22)

plagiarism: Presenting the ideas or words of others as your own without giving proper credit or recognition. (p. 21)

pre-writing: The first step in the writing process. Includes determining the document's audience and purpose. (p. 12)

process: Repeatable steps used to complete a task, such as writing a document. (p. 11)

purpose: The reason you are writing a document. (p. 3)

quote: Using a source's exact words, shown by using quotation marks. (p. 22)

Standard English: The universally accepted, more formal way to speak and write English; used in business and educational settings. (p. 10)

summarize: To explain a general idea, without giving specific details; often used to give a brief explanation about a long passage, article, or book used in research. (p. 22)

References for Writing

"Circular 1: Copyright Basics." (2008). United States Copyright Office, Library of Congress, Washington, D.C. www.copyright.gov.

Maimon, E., Peritz, J., and Yancy, K. (2007). *The new McGraw-Hill handbook.* Burr Ridge, IL: McGraw-Hill Higher Education.

Roen, D., Glau, G., and Maid, B. (2007). *The McGraw-Hill guide: Writing for college, writing for life.* Burr Ridge, IL: McGraw-Hill Higher Education.

Footnotes

1. "What is a Research Paper?" Empire State College State University of New York. www.esc.edu/esconline/across_esc/writerscomplex.nsf/3cc42a422514347a8525671d0049f395/ddbc866bc537f67e85256a460066ab2d?OpenDocument, accessed June 6, 2010.

Figure and Photo Credits

Chapter opening photo: Image Source/JupiterImages

Figure 1: PNC/Getty Images

Figure 2: Design Pics/Kristy-Anne Glubish

Figure 3: (top) © The McGraw-Hill Companies, Inc./Jill Braaten, photographer; (bottom) Frederick Bass/Getty Images

My Success Story: Corbis/PunchStock

Figure 4: Duncan Smith/Getty Images

Figure 5: Tom Grill/Corbis

Figure 6: © Photodisc Collection/Getty Images

Figure 7: Image Source/Getty Images

Figure 8: Image Source / JupiterImages

Figure 9: Hill Street Studios/Getty Images

Figure 10: Inti St. Clair/Getty Images

Money Smarts: ©Sam Toren/Alamy

Figure 11: © Randy Faris/Corbis

Figure 12: Design Pics / Don Hammond

Figure 13: PhotoDisc/Getty Images

Figure 14: Epoxydude/Getty Images

Figure 15: Image Source/Getty Images

Writing on the Job: © Siri Stafford, Gettyimages

Managing **Time**

LEARNING OUTCOMES

In this module, you will:

1 Understand how linking tasks with time turns plans into results.

2 Learn how routines can improve effectiveness.

3 Explore ways to plan for and manage change.

4 Identify and practice specific scheduling skills.

5 Understand the benefits of staying focused and how to maintain focus.

6 Develop strategies for avoiding procrastination.

Do you text your friends and use social media like Facebook, Twitter, or Tumblr? If yes:

- How much time do you think you spend each day on texting and social media?
- How many minutes a month do you typically talk on your cell phone?

> *If you want to make good use of your time, you've got to know what's most important and then give it all you've got.*
>
> **—LEE IACOCCA, FORMER PRESIDENT AND CEO,** *Chrysler Corporation*

Time is a crucial, limited resource. Every minute of every day can be used productively to help you reach your goals in life, or it can be used (some might say wasted) on something else. Making smart decisions about how to use that crucial resource—how to make the most of a specific amount of time—is known as **time management.**

time management: *The skills and habits used to structure tasks and make efficient use of time.*

Of course, time management isn't actually management of time. You can't manage, control, or change the number of minutes in an hour, hours in a day, or days in a week. But you can manage yourself in relation to the time you have, and learn to use time effectively and efficiently.

Making effective use of time challenges even the most successful people. Mastering the discipline and skills necessary to manage time well takes practice and a commitment to learning which time management habits work for you and which do not.

In order to make sure that their time is managed effectively, successful people:

- ☐ *Plan and prioritize* tasks
- ☐ *Link tasks with time*
- ☐ *Establish productive routines*
- ☐ *Manage change*
- ☐ *Balance* work and personal life
- ☐ *Stay focused* on their goals

In this module, we will explore different strategies behind effective time management skills. These skills apply to your academic, professional, and personal life.

As with any newly learned skill, time management takes time, patience, and practice to master. Consider the time you spend working on your time management skills an investment of that crucial resource toward your future success.

I. Making the Connection between Time and Task

Imagine you have just been assigned a paper in your history class. The paper must address a topic dealing with World War II, it is due in six weeks, and it will count for 25 percent of your final grade.

Now what? If you think, "Six weeks! That's plenty of time. I'll worry about it later. I need to focus on my other classes right now," you wouldn't be alone. Six weeks seems like a long time. But if you've had that thought before, you've probably also had this thought, usually about five weeks later:

"That history paper is due in a week?! I wish I'd started working on it five weeks ago."

The goal of this section is to help you avoid those kinds of situations. You'll learn how to connect abstract ideas—like goals, tasks, and plans—with the concrete reality of time to produce successful results.

LO 1 The Difference between Plans and Results

Let's go back to that history paper. Let's say you don't procrastinate for five weeks (we'll discuss procrastination later), but sit down to think about the assignment the day you get it, and write out a plan for completing it. Your plan looks something like this:

1. Review assignment to make sure I understand it clearly
2. Choose topic (may require review of notes, or research at library)
3. Get topic approved by instructor
4. Brainstorm ideas for the paper
5. Conduct research
6. Write outline
7. Create first draft
8. Edit final paper

Figure 1 Time can fly by, so take note—and action— as soon as you can.

First of all, congratulations! Taking the time to write out a basic plan is a good first step—especially on the day the paper is assigned. You're thinking through what must be done to complete the project, putting it on paper so you can see all of the steps ahead of you, and doing it with as much lead time as possible.

As important as this first step is, preventing that panicky feeling of "That history paper is due in a week?!" and instead turning it into a successful history paper, requires four key action items on your part:

1. Get specific
2. Anchor tasks with time
3. Prioritize
4. Take action on time

Let's take a closer look at each.

Get Specific

Developing a plan can help create a clear picture of what we want to accomplish. But a key to turning a plan into a successful result is making sure the plan is **specific** enough. Now, some people might write, "Write history paper" on their to-do list and leave it at that. You're one step ahead of them: You understand that writing a paper is actually a process, or a series of steps, and you've written out eight steps in that process. But are those eight steps specific enough?

specific: *Detailed. When determining tasks, it is important to define each item with as much detail as possible, so you can accurately estimate the time needed to complete it.*

Let's take a closer look at just one of them—*Step 5: Conduct research.* When you wrote down the plan, that may have seemed specific enough. But how much information does "conduct research" really give you about the actual work that must be done, and how much time it will really take?

For example, do you know what kind of research you will need to do? Will you need to look at microfilm of old newspapers, or will you look through books? Will you do this at the college library or the city library, or will you do it online? And, most important for our purposes in thinking about time management, how much time should you allow to conduct research?

The more specific you can get with your answers to those questions—the more you can take a general idea and turn it into a specific, concrete, realistic action—the better prepared you will be to tackle the next step: anchoring tasks with time.

Anchor Tasks with Time

One major reason things don't work out as we plan is because we often do a poor job **estimating** how long things take. For example, let's think some more about Step 5 in our history-paper plan: Conduct research. You decide to do your research at the college library and want to look at microfilm of newspapers from the three months leading up to the bombing of Pearl Harbor.

Figure 2 Making a detailed plan will help you manage your time later.

Before we start anchoring the task to time, though, we need to get even more specific. Are you going to read *The New York Times* each day for three months leading up to December 7, 1941? Maybe just the Sunday papers? Are you going to read the news section and the opinion pages, or just one or the other? Or would you prefer to read your local paper, to see what people in your area were thinking? No matter your choice, you need to get a sense of how long the task will take.

You might start by guessing how long it would take you to read the opinion pages for just one Sunday from *The New York Times* from late 1941 and take notes on any articles that might support your research. If you estimate that it will take you 30 minutes, then your next step is to estimate how many articles you will need to read to complete your research. If you think it will be 12 articles, multiply your time per article by 12, and you see that you need at least six hours to complete your research. Then, see how accurate that guess is by going to the library and looking up at least one article to learn if 30 minutes is a realistic estimate for the time it will take to read and take notes on one article.

Of course, before you even get there, you've now encountered something you might not have factored into your estimate: the time it takes to get from home (or wherever you're heading to the library from) to a seat in the library in front of the microfilm you need.

Even when estimating that time, you need to get more specific (again), and think about all the little things that go into getting from one place to the next: packing your backpack; walking, riding your bike, waiting for and taking the bus, or driving your car (and parking); getting to the circulation desk, requesting the newspapers from the dates you need from the librarian, and waiting for the librarian to get the microfilm for you; and finding a microfilm reader and sitting down to review the articles.

Do all those tasks change your time estimate?

Your estimate is your starting point. Once you test, you can then adjust that estimate until it is more accurate and realistic. Making these kinds of estimates—even if they're inaccurate—can help you think about all of the little things we often forget when we make broad lists like the one above. This habit can help you do a better job managing your time over the full time period you've been given for the task.

Figure 3
Knowing how long it takes you to find, collect, read, and take notes on the materials you want can keep you from overcommitting your time.

There is another way to calculate your time budget for a project like this: Decide in advance how long you will give yourself for a certain task. So, for example, you may decide that you will spend no more than five hours conducting research. Then, when you sit down to conduct research, you will check the clock, and stop at five hours.

Setting constraints like this can be good. Doing so creates some of the pressure and generates some of the focus and adrenaline that helps us meet deadlines when we've put things off longer than we should, yet without actually putting things off to the last minute. It is also a way to put a cap on how long things actually take, so you can fit other important things into your schedule.

However, setting constraints still requires making time estimates. You might say you will stop your research at five hours. But is that realistic? If that number is based simply on the fact that you only want to work on it for five hours, not on any estimate of how long it will take to do what you need, you may get to five hours and realize you haven't given yourself nearly enough time to complete the task.

Setting time constraints for tasks is most effective for tasks you have done before, when you can use previous experiences to make educated estimates of how long things take you and then set your constraints accordingly. Otherwise, you run a strong risk of not giving yourself enough time to do everything you need to do to give the project your best effort.

Prioritize

In our history-paper example, which step is most important? As with most things, it depends. Which is more important to your instructor—the quality and amount of your research, or the quality of your writing? Maybe picking your topic is most important. After all, if you are excited about your topic, how much easier will it be to do the research and write the paper than if you're not excited about it?

Making lists of tasks needed to finish a project is easy. Making that list complete by getting specific and breaking those tasks down into smaller steps is harder, but just as important for getting an accurate sense of what you actually need to do. Estimating the time each step will take is essential to knowing how to budget your time. But no time budget is complete without **prioritizing.**

prioritizing: *Determining which things are most and least important to you.*

You might think that for a project like this, with those eight steps laid out, you don't need to prioritize. The list is in the right order, and you know what needs to come first. But setting priorities isn't just about the order in which you do things, it's also about the time and effort you give to things. In other words, your top priority should get the most of your time and attention.

Unfortunately, we often take that list and start working through it in order, from the top, without deciding how much time to devote to those early steps. As a result, sometimes we do a great job on those early steps, only to realize later (usually too late) that those early steps weren't as important as the later steps and that we haven't left ourselves enough time to give those later steps the time and attention they deserve.

That's why prioritizing has to be about more than just putting tasks in the right sequence. Obviously, you can't get your topic approved by your instructor until you choose a topic, so choosing a topic has to come early in the sequence. But prioritizing and sequencing are not the same thing. Prioritizing is realizing that the quality of your research will have the most impact on the success of the paper, and budgeting the most time for it to ensure you do it right—even though conducting research may be Step 5 in the process.

Figure 4 One good way to prioritize is to work backward. For example, when can your friend proofread your paper? Use that date to create your schedule.

How can you determine which tasks should be your priorities? Since your instructor will be grading the paper, it would be a good idea to ask him where he places the most value. Prioritizing tasks like this takes not only thought, but time. But investing time in prioritizing before you begin a project can save you from "That history paper is due in a week?!" heartache as the deadline looms.

PRIORITIZING ACROSS PROJECTS Prioritizing your tasks within a project, like we just did above, is important. But none of us has only one project on our plates. That's why it helps to develop a master priority list, where you combine all of your projects so you can see everything that you have to do in one place. Here again, you will need to make difficult decisions, but the thinking you have done should help you prioritize tasks from one project over another.

This master priority list will help you keep on top of all of your projects, and you should check it every day to make sure you don't miss anything. A master priority list can also help you make the day-to-day choices about how to spend your time—choices that make the difference between good time management and feeling overwhelmed and out of control.

Remember, prioritizing is not only about putting things in order. It is about deciding how and when to spend your time and attention, and what tasks and projects are more important to you than others. As a busy college student, setting your priorities also means saying "no" to certain things. You can't do everything! You must decide what is most important to you, so you can say "yes" to those things and do them well, and "no" to things that can distract you from what matters the most.

Take Action on Time

Everything we've discussed so far—getting specific, anchoring tasks with time, and prioritizing—is critical to developing an effective, realistic plan. These steps make your plan more concrete and can help you realize when you're being too optimistic about how long things will take or how much time you have in your days and weeks.

However, the key to success as a student and professional is turning those plans into results. That involves taking action on the steps you've outlined in your plan and doing so on time.

One of the many benefits of these first three steps—getting specific, anchoring tasks with time, and prioritizing—is that they help you create intermediate

ON THE JOB

Planning and Tracking Your Time

No matter where you work, whether it's a small business, corporate office, hospital, or even a factory, and no matter what your job title, effective time management skills can help you do your job better.

Successful workers must make the most of the limited time they have during their work days to meet their work goals and achieve their desired outcomes. Of course, managing your time effectively will not only help you in your career, but it will also benefit the company or organization that you work for. That's why many employers offer training programs or encourage employees to participate in outside workshops and seminars to help improve time management skills.

However, many employers focus on your productivity—how much work you are able to complete in a given period of time—as much as the quality of your work, and put the responsibility on you to figure out how to be most productive. This is when your time management skills will be tested.

In order to use effective time management skills at work, you must determine the needs and expectations for your particular workplace. Do you need to track your own time or report your activity to a supervisor throughout the workday? Are you in charge of the activity or progress of a group of workers, or are you only responsible for your own productivity?

You will also want to determine what time management tools are available to you. Does your workplace require you to use a certain time management method, or do you have the flexibility to bring in your own time management tool? For instance, many companies require that their employees use a Microsoft Outlook calendar so that managers and supervisors can view their team's activities and know when people are available for work-related meetings and events.

One thing that can help you meet the demands of your work environment and manage your time effectively is to find someone who has worked at your job for some time and succeeded in managing her time well. Often, someone who has been in your

Figure 5
Breaking up a big project into smaller tasks can make it less overwhelming.

deadlines. For example, when you examine your history project like we have, you realize that only the final paper is due in six weeks and that you need to set targets and deadlines between now and then to do your best work on the steps in between.

shoes before you can provide some valuable tips for making the best use of your time. Don't be afraid to ask for help!

Finally, no matter your job or work environment, it's important to take time out of your day or week to manage your time. This may mean taking 10 minutes first thing in the morning to review your to-do list for the day or taking 30 minutes on Friday afternoon to review your calendar for the upcoming week. These small investments of time can make a big difference in helping you keep on top of your work responsibilities. Effective time management takes time, so be sure to allot sufficient time for it.

These in-between deadlines can help you budget your time and measure whether you are on, ahead of, or behind schedule. But the cold, hard truth is this: If you want to turn good plans into good results, you have to do the work when you say you're going to do the work.

Now, sometimes things take longer than you expect, and that's fine—a good plan can be adjusted. But the key to managing yourself in relation to time is spending your time on action.

Planning this way is valuable because it helps you break the work down into smaller, less-intimidating steps, which encourage you to get started. If you find yourself putting off a task, re-evaluate it. Can you make is smaller? More specific? Can you picture when you will do it? Where you will do it? How and with whom? Making the task crystal clear in your mind can often help you get started, and getting started on the work itself is the real key to producing successful results in time.

TAKE ACTION

Determining Your Priorities

In this activity, you will create a priority listing of your major daily and weekly activities and responsibilities in the areas of *Home, School, Work,* and *Social Life.*

Step 1. In each of the following sections, list the five most important things you can think of that you do on a daily or weekly basis for each category. Next to each item, mark whether it is something you do daily or weekly.

Home: _____

_____

_____

_____

_____

School: _____

_____

_____

_____

_____

Work: _____

_____

II. Managing Change by Developing New Routines

Regarding your own personal daily schedule, what have you found to be different now that you are in college compared to before you enrolled?

- Do you like your new schedule?
- If there is something you'd like to change about it, what is it?

Whenever people talk about change, they agree on one thing: It's inevitable. The only thing that stays the same is change. Yet despite agreeing on this truth, we still struggle with changes in our lives. New situations at home, at work,

McGraw Hill connect plus+

Try this online at mcgrawhillconnect.com

_____

_____

_____

Social Life: _____

_____

_____

_____

Step 2.   Now take the items that you have listed and organize them into priority order. Write the number 1 next to the most important item, 2 next to the second-most important, and so on.

REFLECTION POINTS

Look back over your priority listing, and think about how you approach all of these items each day and each week. Then discuss the following questions with your group or the rest of the class:

- How closely do your priority lists reflect the order in which you actually do things on a given day or week?
- How difficult was it to assign a ranking to your lists? What made it difficult?
- How will prioritizing these lists impact your decisions in the next week? In the next month?
- If you were to make one list that included all four of the above smaller lists, what would be the top five items, in priority order?
- How has school affected your list of priorities?

at school . . . these can derail even our most thorough plans and throw us off course as we work toward our goals.

When we think about change, we often think about traumatic things: a death in the family, losing a job, the end of a relationship. But even positive change, such as going to college, can be challenging.

What makes change difficult? Often, it's that things we have gotten used to are things we can no longer keep doing after the change. We have to learn new skills, new ways to relate to new people, and new ways to manage our time. If we were comfortable with the old way, the new way can be very unsettling.

One of the reasons we grow comfortable with our old ways is routine.

LO 2 The Stabilizing Influence of Routine

Do you brush your teeth? (Hopefully, the answer is yes!) If so, do you do it at random times during the day or random days during the week? If you're like most people, you probably have a set time each day when you brush your teeth, such as just after your shower in the morning and right before you go to bed. Doing this simple task at the same times every day helps make sure that you do it. You probably don't even have to think much about brushing your teeth anymore because it is built into the rhythm of your day. Brushing your teeth has become a **routine.**

routine: *A habit or a ritual that you perform regularly and consistently, usually at the same time each day or same day each week.*

A routine is a habit or a ritual, something you do regularly and consistently. Not all routines are everyday rituals. If you have dinner with your parents the first Sunday of every month, that's also a routine. Routines can provide great comfort and stability to our lives. They help us know what's coming, making things less chaotic and more predictable.

Routines also prevent us from having to remake difficult choices again and again. In other words, routines put part of our brain on autopilot and let us relax.

Figure 6 Many people have a morning routine, and that routine may help wake them up more than coffee might.

This is why change can be so painful. The more comfortable we are with our routines, the longer we've been doing them, and the more we like them, the harder it is to let go of the familiar and comfortable and accept the new that comes with change.

Routines by Chance versus Routines by Choice

We fall into some routines and make intentional decisions about others. Some of the routines that we fall into by chance are productive. Others can be counter-productive. For instance, without giving it much thought, some students come home from class, plop down on the couch, open a bag of potato chips, and start watching TV. This routine may be relaxing and comfortable, but it won't help you reach your academic goals.

A routine by choice, however, is one that you think about in advance and make a decision to adopt. For example, what if you went straight to the library to study for two hours instead of heading home after your last class, where you might be tempted by the couch, chips, and TV?

At first, this might be difficult. It might feel like punishment, rather than a routine. You might get to the library and find that you have a hard time focusing and that you're not really in the right frame of mind to study, particularly if you have trained your body and brain to go into relaxation mode right after class.

However, a routine can help retrain your body and brain to embrace better, more productive habits. Plus, just as your current routines didn't become routines overnight, new routines that you choose to adopt will take time to become habits.

Evaluating Your Existing Routines

Some routines by chance can support your goals, the way brushing your teeth after you shower and before bed support your goal of good dental health. But more often, it's the routines by choice that most support our goals, such as studying or exercise routines.

Good or bad, by chance or by choice, routines become like roadside milestones, marking the way as we go through the journey of our day. Take a moment to think about your typical day. Start first thing in the morning and mentally go through your day, all the way through until you go to bed. What routines are already a part of your typical day?

Now think for a few minutes about a typical week. Are there certain routines you don't perform every day, but do perform every week? Start by thinking about a normal Monday, and go through the end of the weekend. Sometimes our routines are so automatic and ingrained in our lives that we forget we even do them.

In the chart in Figure 7, take a moment to write down at least three of your daily routines and two of your weekly routines. Then in the next column, write down whether this is a routine by chance or a routine by choice. In the final column, write whether this routine supports your goals or does not support your goals, and briefly explain why. You may be surprised about what you'll learn about yourself from reflecting upon your routines.

Respond to Change by Choosing and Developing New Routines

For most students, going to college represents a giant change in their lives. There are new responsibilities, new schedules, new things to do—homework, studying, going to class, and more. No matter what you were doing before you became a college student, things are different now. Some of your most comfortable routines have probably been disrupted, if not completely discarded.

Daily Routines	Chance/Choice?	Supports My Goals? Which One?
Example: Read the newspaper every morning	Choice	Yes, supports my goal of staying informed about current events.

Weekly Routines	Chance/Choice?	Supports My Goals? Why?

Earlier we mentioned that, with a routine, you make a decision in advance, which means you don't have to keep making the decision every day. Whether this decision is about how you spend your time, where you spend your time, or whom you spend your time with, making decisions about the routines you want in your life is a key time management strategy.

Of course, once you make that decision, you must choose to honor it every day—after all, you can't say that going to the library to study after class is a routine if you don't actually do it every day. But good routines, ones that support your goals and help you manage your time, start with a choice.

LO 3 Taking Charge of Change

As valuable and comfortable as routines can be, most don't last forever. Situations in your life change, and routines must be let go or adapted to fit new circumstances. In fact, you can already predict one situation that will change for you, hopefully in the next few years: You will graduate and no longer be a college student. When that happens, your academic routines will no longer apply to your life.

You may have smaller interruptions to your routines as well, such as the end of the term or an upcoming vacation. These changes may seem insignificant. But have you ever found yourself in a good routine before a small change and then struggled to get back into that routine afterward?

Planning for Change

As we mentioned earlier, you can't avoid **change.** In many cases, you can't predict change either. Yet in cases of change, large or small, you can plan for change, to make sure that, even if things change around you, you can still stick to your plan and continue to progress toward your goals.

change: *A new situation or circumstance that forces you to alter your behavior.*

How can you plan for change? First, you can do your best to anticipate it. Thinking in advance about potential changes you may experience, and the obstacles they may place on your way to your goals, may help lessen the shock that sometimes occurs when a change first takes place. Having a plan of action to adapt your routine to overcome the obstacles that the change brings can decrease feelings of stress if the change does in fact happen, and can help you stay focused on your goal.

Figure 8 Traffic can impact your entire day's schedule.

What type of changes could you experience? Think about changes you have experienced already, in your personal, professional, and academic life. Are similar changes likely to happen in the future?

Don't think only of negative changes; consider positive changes as well. Will you get a new job? Get promoted? Move to a new city? Start a new relationship? Get married? Have children? These can all be wonderful changes, but they also can disrupt your routines and make it difficult to manage your time. The more you can think through changes that might affect your life, the better decisions you can make about how you will adjust and manage your time and your routines once those changes come.

Anchoring a New Routine to an Old One

One way that you can adjust to changes in your life is to anchor a new routine to an existing one. For example, imagine that you have come down with a sinus infection, and your doctor has prescribed an antibiotic to treat it. You must take the antibiotic once a day, every day, for 10 days. However, you don't normally take pills, and you are worried about forgetting. How can you remember to take your pill each day?

Well, what else do you do every day, at a consistent time? You could pick something like eating breakfast or brushing your teeth—something that's already a habit that you don't have to think about—and use this routine as your anchor. Then you can attach this new activity—taking your medicine—to this anchor. So, when you sit down to eat breakfast, you remind yourself to take your pill, until that too becomes a habit.

Anchoring can be effective for other tasks as well. The key is to identify a habit that is already in place that can be used as the anchor, and a new routine

MY SUCCESS STORY

Julian and Roger were good friends. They took almost all the same classes and had similar interests outside class, too. But when it came to schoolwork, that's where the similarities ended.

Roger lived life by routine. Every Monday after his last class, he went right to the library. He sat at the same spot every week and, as soon as he sat down, reviewed all his assignments for the week. He broke new assignments down into steps, to determine the specific tasks needed to complete each one. Then he estimated how much time he needed for each step and matched those steps with the study times he had blocked out on his calendar—the same time blocks every week.

After about 45 minutes, he had the rest of his week mapped out: assignments and deadlines, study blocks for doing schoolwork, times for exercise, times for his part-time job, even when he would sleep. The predictable structure let him focus on doing his best work, because he didn't have to worry about when he was going to work, where he was going to work, or even if he'd have time to work out.

When Julian got out of class Monday afternoon, he thought, "Whew! I'm done for the day," and had no plan. Most weeks, he'd grab a snack and talk to friends at the coffee shop, killing time until he realized he had to run to his part-time job. Each day when class was done, the world seemed full of options. If it was warm, he might go for a run; if it was rainy, he might go to the coffee shop. When deadlines loomed, he'd go to the library—and usually realize he should've started working sooner. This freedom and spontaneity made every day interesting, but Julian's grades suffered from his disorganization and lack of structure.

Most days, while Julian felt frazzled and stressed, Roger looked calm and relaxed. One Monday, Julian asked Roger how he seemed so together and organized. Roger asked Julian what his calendar looked like. "I don't have a calendar," Julian confessed. "I just remember when my classes and work are and go." Roger asked about his study routine. "Well," Julian said. "I study when I need to study—when something's due, I guess."

Roger said, "If you want to be stressed, that's the way to do it. Routines help me keep on top of my work. I don't get stressed, because I don't have to make lots of decisions every day. I know what to do and when to do it, so I can get my work done, and relax on the weekends."

Julian liked flexibility, but didn't like struggling with school, so he asked if he could learn from Roger's routine. "Of course!" Roger said. "It's no secret. The key is making the choice now to find a routine, and keep improving it until it works for you." Julian was excited—and after their last class, they went straight to the library.

that you want to adopt that you can attach to it. For instance, if you wanted to create a new routine that involves going to a quiet space to read your textbook for an hour each day, which of your current routines would serve as a good anchor?

When you use existing routines as anchors for new routines, you can make change easier and support your goals and plans.

LO 4 Scheduling Your Time

We've discussed several time management strategies so far in this chapter. One we haven't focused on yet is scheduling, which is the way we anchor our plans, priorities, and routines in time.

Scheduling your time—writing down on a calendar what you will do when—seems like the simplest time management strategy. And while it is an obvious strategy, it is not as simple as it looks. In fact, if you have a calendar, but don't work on planning, prioritizing, and routines, that calendar can quickly become more of a wish list than a productive guide for using your time.

However, you have thought about and worked on these critical strategies, which means that you are now prepared to develop a schedule that works for you.

Making Your Schedule Work

Most of us have certain non-negotiables in our weekly calendar. As a student, the time periods when you have class fall into this category. But what about the rest of the hours in your day and week? This is where scheduling can really help manage your time.

The tool you use to keep your calendar is up to you. Some people prefer paper calendars and have specific kinds they like, with certain layouts for the days, weeks, and months. Others prefer to keep their calendar on their computer, online, or on their phone. Countless software programs and websites are available for

Figure 9
However you keep track of your time, if you're comfortable with it, you'll be consistent about it.

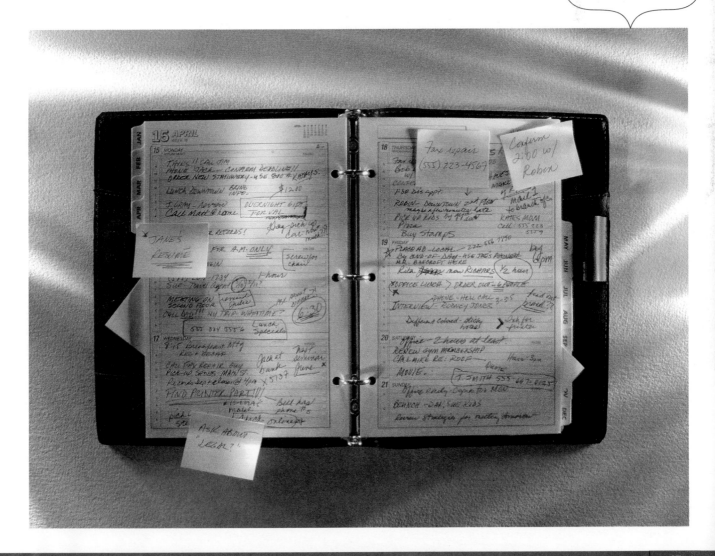

managing your calendar. There is no right way to keep a calendar—only ways that work for you and ways that do not. The way to learn what works for you is to keep trying different approaches until you find something that you keep using and that helps you feel in control of your time.

When you sit down to prepare your calendar, start with a basic week. This basic week may be different from one school term to the next, but start with one that you know will be the same for a while.

First, put all of your nonnegotiables into your calendar—classes, work hours, and so on. Next, think about the logistics of those items. Do you need travel time to get to class? If so, put that in your calendar as well. Doing so helps you allow for travel time and avoid the trap of running late because you were overly optimistic.

TAKE ACTION

Evaluating and Choosing Routines to Support Your Academic Goals

Identify your most important academic goal—what really matters most to you in school.

Academic Goal: _____

_____

Now consider the various routines you have throughout the week—favorite TV shows, outings with friends, family time, study time. After examining your weekly routines, identify one that supports you in achieving your academic goal.

Example: Weekly study group on Wednesday

_____

Then identify one or more routines that do not support you in accomplishing your goal.

Example: Surfing Facebook for hours every day; waiting till the night before to study for a test

_____

_____

In order to set yourself up for success, you may need to better manage or eliminate any potential obstacles or poor habits, such as the routines listed above that could stifle your ability to reach your academic goal.

Think about the most difficult aspects of stopping this routine. Be honest with yourself. The more aware you are, the more you can take control. Identify what will be the most difficult parts of stopping this routine.

_____

_____

_____

Next, think about your priorities. Where do they fit on your calendar? Do you have routines associated with these priorities? Add these as well. In addition, be sure to include things like studying and exercise.

Now that you can see your week laid out visually, how do you feel about it? Is this the kind of schedule that will help you accomplish your plans and reach your goals? Or is it something that feels overwhelming? Remember, you are in control of your schedule. If you don't like what you see, what choices can you make to make it better?

Your schedule should not limit what you do, but should help you see where you are currently spending your time; anticipate and prepare for your responsibilities; and make informed, realistic choices about changes you wish to make.

To assist you in creating strategies to overcome any of the difficulties you listed, partner with a class-mate. Share with your classmate the routine you selected to stop and the challenges you will experience in ending this routine. Together with your classmate, brainstorm three strategies to help you success-fully stop this routine.

1. _____

2. _____

3. _____

To aid in ending this unsupportive routine, it will help you to create a new one to replace it. In order to successfully develop a new routine, you will need to be realistic. For example, if you are ending a rou-tine of hanging out with your friends late Sunday evening, you will need to supplement it with a new one that is productive, but will not leave you feeling resentful. Now spend five minutes brainstorming new "replacement" routines with your partner. After your discussion, write down the three best routines the two of you developed.

1. _____

2. _____

3. _____

Then with your partner, spend five minutes brainstorming three strategies you can use to help you incorporate and maintain this routine.

1. _____

2. _____

3. _____

Remember to consider what will encourage and motivate you to achieve your academic goal.

III. The Power of Focus

GET READY

Some students find studying alone to be one of the most challenging aspects of college.

- What are a few things you do to focus on homework and studying when there are so many other things you could be or need to be doing?

The most historic matches in the history of the Wimbledon tennis tournament have been played at Centre Court at the All England Lawn Tennis Club, before thousands of fans and television audiences in the millions.

Until 2010, that is.

In the first round that year, American John Isner and Nicolas Mahut of France played a match on out-of-the way Court 18, a small stadium where the seats number in the hundreds. It began as a normal match, with Isner taking the first set, then Mahut bouncing back to win the second and third. Isner rallied to win the fourth, forcing a fifth set.

Then it got interesting. There is no fifth-set tiebreaker in Wimbledon's rules, so when Isner and Mahut were tied at six games apiece at the end of the fifth set, they had to keep going until someone had a two-game lead.

So they kept going. And going. And going. The match, which started on a Tuesday, had to be extended into Wednesday because of darkness. Now on Wednesday, they were running out of daylight again. With the score tied 59-59 in the fifth set, after 10 hours of play, more than 7 hours in the fifth set alone, the match was called because of darkness a second time.

Finally, on Thursday, the third day, after playing each other for more than 11 total hours, Isner won the fifth set of the longest tennis match in history, 70–68.

Clearly, this match required an incredible amount of physical skill and stamina from both players. But it also required an amazing mental toughness.

After the match, Mahut was asked about the pressure he felt being one point down and having to serve to stay in the match—which happened to him 65 times. Did the pressure get to him? "I was not thinking about this," Mahut said. "I was just thinking about winning the game I was playing, just the point I was playing, again and again."[1]

Isner, the winner, had an approach that was equally simple. "Hitting a serve and trying to hit a forehand winner is the only thing I was doing," he said.[2]

Though the match may not have been on Centre Court, both players were playing in tennis' most famous tournament, and by the third day, their match had drawn the attention of people from around the world. On Thursday, tiny Court 18 was packed with news photographers, reporters, television cameras, and fans craning just to get a look.

Figure 10
Focusing on what is in front of you can help you maintain focus over a longer-term goal.

Yet point after point, despite everything going on around them, Isner and Mahut did something both simple and critical to their ability to stay in the match as long as they did: They maintained their **focus.**

focus: *The state of giving your full attention to a task.*

LO 5 The Benefits of Staying Focused

It's unlikely that you will ever find yourself in an 11-hour tennis match. Yet learning how to stay focused for the challenges that you face is a time management strategy that is critical to achieving your goals.

In fact, all of the time management strategies we have discussed in this module require focused attention to be executed well. For example, you may have developed an outstanding plan for achieving academic success this term, prioritizing your assignments, scheduling your study sessions, and developing a great routine of going to the library to study. But when you are there in the chair in the library, and the clock is ticking on your two-hour study session, it's focus that determines whether that session is productive or not. It's focus that will determine whether you learn what you need to learn and are prepared for your test or not.

If you are focused—meaning your mind is engaged in the material, you maintain your attention on what you're studying, and you execute the steps in your study plan one at a time—you will manage those two hours well, and they will help you be prepared.

If you do not focus—meaning you let your mind wander, you take a phone call, you respond to a few texts, you check your e-mail, and you talk to a friend who stops by to say hello—then a major chunk of those two hours will be spent on something other than studying, and you won't be prepared.

There is a time and a place for all of those other things: daydreaming, phone calls, and so on. But if you've planned a study session, that session is for studying, and it takes focus and commitment to ensure that you use that time wisely and productively, as you planned.

Planning is important. But it's focus that turns plans into achievement.

Finding a Balance

If you found that example of unfocused studying familiar, don't feel bad. It's a common occurrence, which makes sense. Text messages, checking e-mail, talking to friends . . . these are all fun. Sometimes focusing on schoolwork can be hard, and we want a break, so we are tempted to wander off into other activities.

This temptation is a reminder that we cannot focus on work all the time. Our brains and bodies need downtime, otherwise we get run down and burned out. Finding a balance in how we spend our time helps us get more work done *and* enjoy life more, because if we know that there is time in our schedule for play, it makes it easier to focus when it's time to work. When we don't give ourselves balance and everything runs together, maintaining focus becomes harder and harder.

Figure 11 No one can be "on task" 100 percent of the time, so take breaks when you start losing focus.

You may not be able to strike a balance every day. At certain times of year, certain things take up more of your focus, such as family during the holidays, and school during final exams. The more you can anticipate when there might be a shift in balance, the better you can prepare yourself and manage your time, so when it's time to focus on family, you can do so, knowing that you have taken care of your schoolwork—and vice versa.

Strategies for Staying Focused

Sometimes staying focused is easy. Have you ever gotten completely immersed in something—a project around the house, something on television, a great conversation with a friend—and when you look up, you can't believe how much time has passed? In these situations, your attention is highly focused on what you are doing, without even trying. Whatever you're doing is interesting to you, and it engages your brain fully and completely.

Of course, other times, when the task is not quite as interesting, focusing is difficult, and we are easily distracted and interrupted. At these times, we need strategies to help us stay focused, so we can make productive use of our time.

FOCUS ON YOUR END GOAL Within an individual work session, the strategies and tactics you considered in the previous section can help you maintain your focus for a short period of time. But what about maintaining focus over a long period of time—the kind of sustained focus that is needed to achieve your long-term goals?

One of the most powerful ways to help you focus over the long run is to keep your end goals in mind. These goals will help motivate you to work harder, stay committed to your plan, and block out distractions. These goals can also help you measure and evaluate your time management choices, at the short-term level and long-term level.

For example, think about your goals as a college student. Are your work in class, your extracurricular activities, and your learning outside of the classroom all serving as stepping-stones to your dreams? Is the way you spend your time each day supporting your larger efforts in those areas?

There will no doubt be days when you really don't feel like studying or even going to class. There will be days when sitting on the couch, watching television, sleeping late, or hanging out with friends sounds much more enjoyable and tempting. It takes discipline in these situations to do the thing that will support your long-term goals.

Sometimes a physical reminder can help us stay focused on those end goals. The reminder might be a picture of something you want to achieve posted near your workspace at home. It could be an inspiring quote on your computer desktop, or a wristband that serves as a small, daily reminder of what you are trying to achieve. What kind of reminder might help you focus on your end goal?

DEFEATING DISTRACTION—STOPPING THE TIME THIEVES How much does **distraction** cost us? Imagine you're at the library, reading a textbook and taking notes in preparation for class. You are really focused and really feel like you are grasping the material. Suddenly, you hear the sound that lets you know you have a text message.

distraction: An interruption to your focus or attention.

You take your phone out of your backpack, just to see who the message is from. It's from your good friend, who is just asking you a quick question about your plans for tomorrow night. You text back your answer, then ask a question back. You wait a few seconds for a reply, then read your friend's reply. You send another quick reply back, then put the phone in your pocket.

The entire text exchange may have only taken a minute or two. But when you go back to your textbook, you can't remember where you were. You rescan your notes and the page you were reading, but none of it looks familiar now. When you figure out where you think you were, you start reading again, but it feels fuzzy. You feel like you need to backtrack and review the page before, to reconnect with what you were reading. That focus you had, which made you feel you were making great progress and confident about your understanding of the material, is now gone. How long will it take you to get it back?

According to productivity expert Julie Morgenstern, "Aside from the actual time lost to the interruptions, there is additional recovery time which negatively impacts productivity. Once interrupted, it takes 20–25 minutes to regain the level of focus we had attained prior to the disruption. In addition, close to 50% of the time, we never even get back to our original task. So a 5 minute interruption really costs you 30 minutes of time off task . . . and a strong possibility you'll never get it done at all."[3]

If you only had an hour for that study session, and after 20 minutes you spent 2 minutes on that text-message exchange, there's a good chance that, by the time you return to the level of focus you were at before you got the text, you'll only have 10–15 minutes left before you have to interrupt yourself again. In other words, you will have surrendered almost half of your allotted study time to that simple little text message.

Is that a cost you're willing to pay?

Figure 12
Even minor distractions—or people around you—can derail you.

STAYING FOCUSED IN A CONNECTED WORLD We live in a wired, connected world. Years ago, if you were working in the library, it was just you, the books, and other people working around you. Today, you can be "working" in the library, but be sending text messages to friends, engaging in an instant-messaging conversation (or four), checking e-mail, posting notes to your Facebook account, checking sports scores . . . the list is almost endless. And while it may look to an observer like you're working, you can spend hours like this without actually getting anything done.

Today more than ever, focus is a choice. The technology that surrounds us is always calling us, but we can choose to answer when it is convenient for us and in a way that supports our focus. What does this look like?

Think back to the story about the text message. You can't control when your friends send you a text. You can control whether you leave your phone on when you are in the library. By choosing to turn off your phone, you are also choosing to focus on your work.

If you are someone who is used to having a lot of windows open on your desktop and always being connected, it may not be easy to disconnect, even if it's only for a few hours at a time. You may feel phantom vibrations in your pocket, even when your phone is turned off. Staying focused in the face of all the technology in our lives takes not only the decision to focus, but also the commitment to keep at it. If you're not sure how it would feel to disconnect, give it a try and see what kind of impact it has on your focus and productivity.

DECLARE YOUR FOCUS TO THE WORLD Even if you unplug from distracting technology, you cannot completely eliminate distractions and interruptions. How will you handle them? Better yet, how can you prevent them?

Again, one step is to make choices that support your focus. If you choose to do your homework in a busy place on campus where you know many of your friends might walk by, you're almost asking to be interrupted. If you choose to work somewhere out of the way, without a lot of foot traffic, you are making the choice to focus.

You may also benefit from telling others that you are in a "focus zone." If you are worried about being interrupted by family members or roommates, but want to work at home, you might want to tell them, "I'm going to study for the next two hours. Please don't interrupt me, so I can stay focused and productive." Often, people are afraid to say something like this, because they fear they will be thought rude. Yet your friends and family will probably appreciate your honesty and respect your commitment to school.

This strategy can work well in an office setting, too. If you work in an area with many other people, you can put a note on your cubicle or workstation that says something like, "Focused work in progress, please do not disturb." Obviously, not everyone will pay attention to your request, but by making these kinds of requests, you are declaring your seriousness about focusing, and giving other people the opportunity to support you.

Whether turning off your phone or letting others know you are trying to focus, you must take responsibility for focusing. If you blame others or the technology, you will never truly control your focus.

GETTING BACK ON TRACK Even if you follow all of these strategies, you will sometimes lose focus. Something will distract and interrupt you. When this

Figure 13 A large set of headphones can both cover distracting sounds and show people you're "in the zone."

MONEY SMART$

Self-Employment and Small-Business Planning

Making the most of their time on a daily, weekly, and monthly basis helps professionals work efficiently. Often, financial success is a direct result of the ability to use time effectively. For small-business owners and self-employed professionals, managing time is even more important, because in a smaller workplace, inefficient use of time has an even greater impact.

Using the methods and strategies in this module will help if you start planning for your own small business. You may need to use strategies in planning your time throughout your day, week, and month so that you are fulfilling all your business responsibilities in an efficient manner.

If you are self-employed, or a small-business owner, it's critical to prepare yourself for changes that may occur in your business. What changes would create minor—or major—obstacles for you? How can you best prepare for the worst-case scenario? Keep in mind that owning a small business often comes with unexpected obstacles and challenges, and when you are your own boss, you are responsible when a crisis emerges.

Resources for Small-Business Planning Many resources, services, and support systems are available to help small-business owners with aspects of their business that large corporations have entire departments to handle.

happens, don't get down on yourself. Decide to focus once again, and do the things you did to focus originally.

It is tempting, and easy, to get lost in the distraction and to let it completely derail you from where you were going. What will you do when you get distracted? If you haven't given this question any thought, you're more likely to stay distracted and be frustrated that you have managed your time poorly.

To avoid this, think now about how you can get back on track after a disruption. For example, if you are reading a textbook and get distracted for some period of time, when returning to your reading you can rescan the introduction of the chapter as well as the subsequent section headers leading up to where you left off. That way when you begin reading again, your frame of reference is sufficiently prepared to enable you to better understand the new material. Your focus is restored in short order. Now if you have a plan for how to regain your focus, then you can activate that plan when a distraction happens and quickly get back on the path to productivity.

LO 6 Don't Procrastinate—Think Now, Not Tomorrow!

Procrastination is a state in which you continuously delay the performance or execution of a task. Procrastination can be caused by a lack of focus, and it can also cause a loss of focus. When procrastinating, you may get distracted by another activity instead of the one you need to be doing, which may lead to losing your motivation to complete a task.

Figure 14 If you procrastinate too much, you can end up pulling a lot of all-nighters.

procrastination: A state in which you continuously delay the performance or execution of a task.

For instance, the Internal Revenue Service and Small Business Administration offer helpful tools and support for small-business owners. From providing sufficient information on planning, starting, managing, building, and possibly closing small businesses, they also provide tools and documents that small-business owners may need for every aspect of their business. These resources and tools are available online and also at physical locations in your community.

Web Resources

- Internal Revenue Service: www.irs.gov/businesses/index.html
- Small Business Administration: www.sba.gov/services/financialassistance/index.html

Discovering Your Personal Focusing Secrets

PART I: NOT FOCUSED

Think about the last time you sat down to work on a school assignment, *but struggled to stay focused* and at the end felt like you didn't get very much done. What can you remember about that experience? Complete the following questions.

- Where were you working? Think about the general location (library, home, coffee shop, etc.) as well as the specific place in that location (study carrel, kitchen table, comfy chair, etc.) Did this setting support your focus or support distraction? How?

  _____

  _____

- When were you working? Was this a time of day when you felt sharp and energized, or slow and sluggish?

  _____

  _____

- Did you take breaks? How often? What did you do on these breaks? Did you set a time limit for these breaks? Did you stick to that time limit, or did the breaks run long?

  _____

  _____

- Who were you working with? Were you alone or with others? If you were with others, how did you interact with each other?

  _____

  _____

- What else was happening in your work environment? Was there music in the background? Was there a television on? Were people walking by? What impact did these things have on your focus?

  _____

  _____

- What else were you doing besides your schoolwork? Did you answer the phone? Did you check e-mail? Did you surf the Internet? Did you check Facebook?

  _____

  _____

- How did you fuel your body? Did you have a coffee? A soda? A bottle of water? Snacks? Were you hungry? Were you feeling full and sleepy?

  _____

  _____

PART II: VERY FOCUSED

Now repeat the exercise above, except this time think about a time when you were *extremely focused—when you had a super-productive work session* and felt great about what you had accomplished at the end. Ask yourself those same questions about this great work session, and write down your answers.

- Where were you working? Think about the general location (library, home, coffee shop, etc.) as well as the specific place in that location (study carrel, kitchen table, comfy chair, etc.) Did this setting support your focus or support distraction? How?

  _____

  _____

- When were you working? Was this a time of day when you felt sharp and energized, or slow and sluggish?

  _____

  _____

- Did you take breaks? How often? What did you do on these breaks? Did you set a time limit for these breaks? Did you stick to that time limit, or did the breaks run long?

  _____

  _____

- Who were you working with? Were you alone or with others? If you were with others, how did you interact with each other?

  _____

  _____

- What else was happening in your work environment? Was there music in the background? Was there a television on? Were people walking by? What impact did these things have on your focus?

  _____

  _____

- What else were you doing besides your schoolwork? Did you answer the phone? Did you check e-mail? Did you surf the Internet? Did you check Facebook?

  _____

  _____

- How did you fuel your body? Did you have a coffee? A soda? A bottle of water? Snacks? Were you hungry? Were you feeling full and sleepy?

  _____

  _____

What do you notice about the differences between your two sets of answers? The closer you examine your productive and unproductive work sessions, the more clues you will uncover about the situations and circumstances that help you focus and those that keep you from focusing.

(continued)

When you catch yourself procrastinating, take a step back to examine what is happening. Ask yourself:

☐ What type of task am I putting off right now? Do I often put off tasks like this?

☐ When did I start procrastinating? At the beginning, middle, or end of the task?

☐ Was there a specific reason that I lost my focus? Was the task boring or difficult, or something else?

☐ Am I motivated to do this task that I am procrastinating? Why or why not?

To remain focused on your tasks, it is important to identify the reasons why you are procrastinating and then take the actions necessary to steer yourself away from them. For instance, if you find yourself always procrastinating from finishing homework assignments for a specific class, you may actually be losing your motivation to do well in that class. Can you regain your motivation? Should you talk with the instructor about whether the class is right for you? There are active steps you can take to deal with the root cause of your procrastination.

Once you have targeted the reasons you are procrastinating, you may find that you need a boost to your motivation to do the work. What motivating factors will

TAKE ACTION (concluded)

With a partner, share your nonfocused experience and then record the similarities in your responses.

_____

_____

_____

_____

_____

_____

With these nonfocused similarities in mind, discuss with your classmate why you may have shared some of the same answers.

Then with a partner, share your focused experience and then record the similarities in your responses.

_____

_____

_____

_____

help you stay focused on the task until it is complete? Reviewing where the task fits into your larger time management strategy, such as how it fits into a plan or to-do list, can help you remember the importance of finishing the task. Using these tools can also help you connect the task to your larger goals, which will help remind you what completing the task can lead to.

Here are a few additional tips to help you avoid procrastination:

☐ Maintain and establish a routine to actively review and maintain your to-do list.

☐ Keep your to-do list accessible so you can update it easily.

☐ If you feel overwhelmed, take a step back, and try to see the task as a challenge.

☐ Make sure that your goal involves timely deadlines.

Procrastination at its core is about putting something off until tomorrow that you should be doing today. However, you probably already have something else you need to do tomorrow. If you decide a task needs to be done today, commit to a "now, not tomorrow" mind-set. Keeping this in mind will also help you plan ahead. What other tasks do you need to accomplish tomorrow? How can completing a task now help you complete your other tasks tomorrow?

After sharing both of your nonfocused and focused experiences, you and your partner will create what you two envision to be the best focused learning environment in order to be successful in school. Consider the location, time of day, distractions, and time frame. Is the library the best-suited location? In the morning the best time of day? Leaving your cell phone at home, so you will not be interrupted? Studying for an hour?

Describe this ideal focused environment below.

_____

_____

_____

_____

_____

_____

Now that you have a strong awareness of what will keep you motivated and on track, you will need to put these focused experiences into practice by implementing the learning environment you created into your study routine.

SUMMARY

Throughout this module, you have learned methods for planning, prioritizing, and managing time effectively. We reviewed the importance of anchoring tasks with time, and being specific and realistic with your plans, to ensure that you actually have enough time to do all the things you set out to do.

We also examined the many benefits to be gained from developing effective routines, and looked at how staying focused can help you use your time effectively. Your life—as a student and professional—is certain to include many challenges and obstacles, some you can predict and some you can't. Learning to manage your time effectively now, as a college student, will help you be better prepared for whatever challenges come your way.

DISCUSSION QUESTIONS

1. What time management methods work best in the college setting?

2. How can planning ahead in college impact your success?

3. How can you best incorporate planning tools into your academic time management methods?

4. What planning tools do you feel work for you and your current lifestyle?

KEY TERMS

change: A new situation or circumstance that forces you to alter your behavior. (p. 14)

distraction: An interruption to your focus or attention. (p. 22)

estimating: The process of predicting how long something will take so that you can budget your time. Good time managers update and revise their estimates to make them more accurate. (p. 4)

focus: The state of giving your full attention to a task. (p. 21)

prioritizing: Determining which things are most and least important to you. (p. 6)

procrastination: A state in which you continuously delay the performance or execution of a task. (p. 25)

routine: A habit or a ritual that you perform regularly and consistently, usually at the same time each day or same day each week. (p. 12)

specific: Detailed. When determining tasks, it is important to define each item with as much detail as possible, so you can accurately estimate the time needed to complete it. (p. 4)

time management: The skills and habits used to structure tasks and make efficient use of time. (p. 2)

Footnotes

1. "Isner, Mahut Postmatch Interview," ESPN.com, June 24, 2010. http://espn.go.com/video/clip?id=5323273.

2. "World-Class Concentration—Examining the Uber-Focus of Isner and Mahut," *Tennis View*, Fall 2010. www.tennisviewmag.com/concentration.html.

3. Morgenstern, J. (2009). "The Cost of Interruptions . . . and 5 Ways to Cope," Julie Morgenstern Enterprises (blog), November 22. www.juliemorgenstern.com/blog/?pID=7.

Figure and Photo Credits

Managing **Money**

LEARNING OUTCOMES

In this module, you will:

1 Develop a broader perspective on the financial value of an education.

2 Explore the connection between responsible money management and college success.

3 Analyze your personal spending habits to better understand your personal money management strengths and weaknesses.

4 Develop an action plan to manage your personal finances while you attend college.

5 Prepare yourself to make the tough financial decisions that will help you reach your financial goals.

You've been handling money for most of your life; think about how you learned to manage it.

- Share a lesson about money and how you learned it.
- What's the most important topic about money that you think high school students should be taught?

Walk into any bookstore, and you'll find entire shelves dedicated to books on personal financial management. These books explain personal budgeting, credit, home buying, investing, insurance, benefits, retirement planning, and more. Unfortunately, too many students figure they don't have enough money to manage to bother with those kinds of books.

Yet even as a college student, you will find personal financial management is critical to your success. At the very least, you need to manage your finances well enough to stay enrolled in school long enough to finish your program and graduate. Most people think that every college student who can handle the academic load can make it to graduation, but financial hardship is a real challenge for many students, and it often derails both college hopes and career dreams.

This hardship can be very difficult to anticipate. Tuition, mortgage or rent, food, gas, and utilities can be planned for and managed. But what about when your car breaks down? When your computer dies? Or when a simple toothache turns into an $800 dentist bill? How do you manage to pay all the bills at home, pay school expenses, *and* set aside enough money for emergencies and unforeseeable expenses?

Unlike a general course on personal financial management, this module focuses on the day-to-day financial decisions that confront the typical adult college student, who:

- ☐ Works at least part-time while attending college
- ☐ May have to support, or help support, a family
- ☐ Receives little or no help from parents for tuition or related college expenses
- ☐ Is attending college to realize a dream for a more fulfilling and better paying career

Do any or all of these describe you?

Figure 1 Good money habits mean preparing for emergencies.

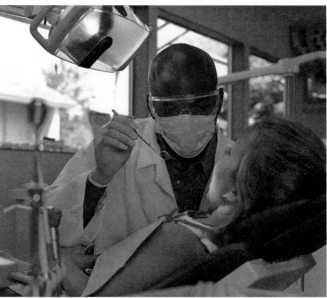

I. Understanding the Big Picture: The Financial Value of an Education

Everyone can benefit by taking a course on personal financial management. Like the books mentioned earlier, these courses teach the financial fundamentals for successful personal money management. But most will not help you answer the one critical question that directly relates to your own long-term personal financial success. It's a question so important, we're going to set it off to highlight it:

What is the true value and long-term financial impact of complting your education?

LO 1 The Value of Finishing: Developing Your Financial Perspective

When you clearly understand the value of finishing college, you can put the day-to-day financial challenges you face while in school into context. Or to put it another way, have you ever considered what it would cost you in the long term if you don't finish school?

How well you manage your personal financial situation *while* you attend school may have a direct impact on whether you *graduate* from school. Money—or more to the point, a lack of money—can be a big factor in determining whether you are able to stay enrolled all the way through to graduation. However, with the proper tools, and the ability to critically analyze and manage the financial decisions you can control, you can *maintain the freedom to stay in college* all the way until graduation day.

Figure 2 Take a step back from the details to see the big picture.

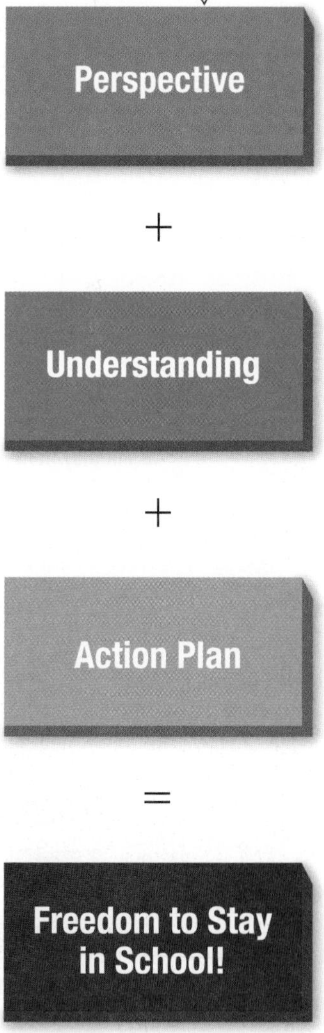

Perspective

+

Understanding

+

Action Plan

=

Freedom to Stay in School!

One Million Dollars

Study after study demonstrates that graduating from college dramatically improves average income and lifetime earnings potential. When you enrolled in school, you may have seen some of these statistics, as well as salary averages for the fields of study you were considering. If so, it's worth reviewing that information again. The research says that, for every level of education completed, average earnings increase. That doesn't mean everyone's pay automatically goes up because they earned a degree, although that is true in some professions. It does mean that, in the long term, earning a diploma (or multiple diplomas!) will likely mean many more dollars in your pocket. Consider this quote from the U.S. Census Bureau:

> In 2005, a college graduate could expect to earn about $25,000 more than someone with only a high school degree.[1]

That is a *one-year* salary difference. Multiply that dollar amount by the number of years you plan to work, and the numbers become truly significant. Now we're talking million-dollar differences between those who complete a college education and those who don't:

> The estimated lifetime earnings of professional degree-holders are $4.4 million. This compares with $3.4 million for those with PhDs, $2.5 million for master's degree-holders, **$2.1 million for those with bachelor's degrees, $1.2 million for high school graduates and $1.0 million for high school dropouts.**[2]

It bears repeating: Those with a bachelor degree will earn on average $2.1 million versus only $1.2 million in earnings for those who graduate only high school. In other words, earning a college degree is as valuable as winning the lottery! Seen from this **perspective**, the relatively short time you devote to getting an education looks like a relatively small investment that can pay valuable dividends for the rest of your career, including your retirement.

perspective \pər-'spek-tiv\: *The ability to accurately judge a situation or idea and its relative importance.*

Even if you are not enrolled in a bachelor's program right now, the differences between those who have completed some (diploma or associate's degree) college versus those who haven't are still very high. But if you are not pursuing a bachelor's degree, you might find yourself thinking about it more and more as you progress through and complete your current program. Fortunately, there is no age or time limit for reaping the benefits an education can bring. Many students find that they really enjoy school and continue to pursue higher degrees for many years. By moving forward one diploma or one degree at a time, you will be able to enjoy and benefit from each new milestone as you achieve it.

The Cost of Opportunity

How much does something cost? In most cases, the answer is very simple: The *cost* is whatever is paid by the buyer. In some cases, the price is flexible, so the cost of the item will vary depending upon the buyer's negotiating skills. When it comes to pursuing a college education, cost involves more than just tuition. Books, lab fees, supplies, transportation, childcare, and more all add to the cost of earning a diploma or degree.

Opportunity cost is another kind of cost—it's the value of *not* doing or buying something, and instead choosing something else. At first, this can be a strange concept. How can there be a cost for not doing something? Consider this example:

Figure 3 Impact of education on employment rate and earnings.

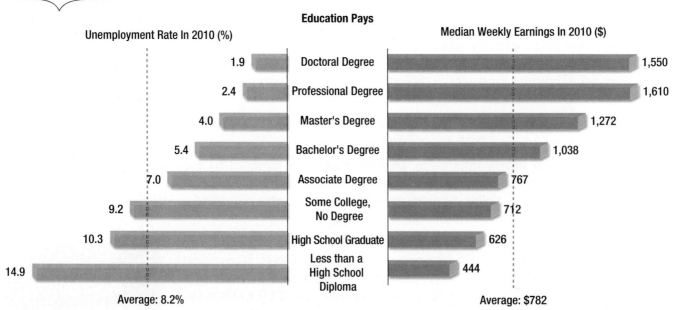

Education Pays

Unemployment Rate In 2010 (%)		Median Weekly Earnings In 2010 ($)
1.9	Doctoral Degree	1,550
2.4	Professional Degree	1,610
4.0	Master's Degree	1,272
5.4	Bachelor's Degree	1,038
7.0	Associate Degree	767
9.2	Some College, No Degree	712
10.3	High School Graduate	626
14.9	Less than a High School Diploma	444
Average: 8.2%		Average: $782

opportunity cost *The value of not doing or buying something and instead choosing something else.*

Joe is attending a traditional university full-time and his schedule won't allow him to work while going to school. His parents are paying his tuition and book costs. If Joe were *not* going to college, he could earn $25,000 per year working in his parent's restaurant. Over four years, Joe's opportunity cost to attend college is 4 × $25,000, or a total of $100,000.

In this example, Joe's time has value. He decided that putting his time and energy into his education would have greater value than the $100,000 he could have earned working in the restaurant. Joe understands that his first-year salary potential when he graduates college in four years is $60,000. It will only take him a few years of work after college to make up for the "cost" of not earning money while in school. Joe clearly understands that if he worked in the restaurant, he might not earn that much money per year for a long time, if ever.

In Joe's case, the $100,000 opportunity cost to attend college involves very *real* dollars. All he had to do was choose to work in the restaurant, and in four years, he would have earned $100,000. But Joe decided that, to lead the lifestyle he desires and be able to support and raise the family he plans to have some day, he needs to make more money than his restaurant salary.

What would Joe's opportunity cost be if he chose to work in his parent's restaurant instead of attending school? In other words, what is Joe's opportunity cost of not going to school? We'll assume that cost-of-living salary increases and job promotions would be relatively equal for both choices. In simple terms, over 20 years, Joe's *opportunity cost* for not pursuing a college education is as follows:

1. Joe goes to school for four years and then earns $60,000 per year after graduating:
   16 years of working × $60,000 per year = $960,000

2. Joe chooses to work in the restaurant for 20 years:
   20 years × $25,000 per year = $500,000

3. Joe's opportunity cost to *not* pursue an education:
   $960,000 − $500,000 = $460,000

Figure 4 Joe is "losing" money in the short-term to gain it back and more in the long-term.

How much does opportunity cost impact your situation and decisions regarding school? Since you are already in school, you may be sacrificing additional income that you could be earning at this time. Whether you thought about it as an opportunity cost or not, you have already weighed the value of the potential lost income you could be earning and decided that college is still worth it. Congratulations—you have made a very wise decision! For most people, getting an education is one of the most valuable investments they make in their lifetime.

Earlier, we asked the question, "What is the true value and long-term financial impact of completing your education?" Answering that question requires considering not only how much you can expect to earn if you get your diploma, but also how much you can expect to earn if you *don't* finish college. Calculating how much an education can mean in real dollars over the number of years you plan to work can provide a powerful incentive to do whatever it takes to continue in school when a financial (or other) emergency occurs.

Finding a solution for any financial problem you may encounter means having the right attitude and approach, but also being proactive in getting to know the experienced financial advisors in your school's business office. Do not hesitate to let them know when an emergency occurs, but also get to know them when everything is okay. If you reach out to them early in your school experience, you will find that you'll become a financial team, working together to find solutions that will make your life easier and your financial situation more manageable.

Your Personal Definition of Wealth

The dollar value of an education is well documented and easy to understand. But what does the dollar value mean to you? Everyone interprets success differently, and the value of an education is linked to more than just money. One example is the long-term satisfaction that working in a challenging and rewarding career field will bring.

With this in mind, how would you complete the following sentence?

I will be wealthy when . . ..

The way you finish the sentence will help you think about your definition and attitude toward personal wealth. Here's one example:

"I will be wealthy when I'm not living paycheck to paycheck and am capable of purchasing a home of my own."

MONEY SMART$

Employee Benefits—Saving for Retirement

Enrolling in college is an investment in your future. Compared to the length of your career, your time spent in school is relatively short, but this short-term effort can produce long-term gain.

Planning for retirement is just the opposite: The long-term actions you take over your working years will determine the quality and quantity of your retirement. Have you thought about at what age you'd like to retire? How long you might live beyond retirement age? What kind of retirement lifestyle you want to lead? How much all that will cost, and where the money will come from? These are just a few of the questions that must be considered when planning for retirement. And unlike planning for your education, the earlier you begin planning and saving for retirement, the easier it will be to reach your financial goals.

How do you save for retirement? For most people, the best way is through an employer-sponsored retirement benefit plan. Here are just a few of the various retirement savings programs currently available:

401(k) Plans Many small- to large-sized, for-profit companies offer their employees a 401(k) retirement savings plan. Employees who participate in these programs enjoy several advantages, including employer matching and the ability to save money using pre-tax dollars, which lowers your current income and employment taxes.

While private, for-profit companies can participate in 401(k) programs, 403(b) programs are the equivalent retirement plan offered by schools, religious, charitable, and some other tax-exempt organizations.[3]

Defined Benefit Pension Plans These retirement plans were common in the past, with few private organizations now offering them. However, they

If you haven't already, take a minute to give the sentence some thought, and come up with your own answer. Be sure your answers are grounded in "expected" reality. Yes, you may win the lottery someday, but for this exercise let's only include those financial pursuits that you have some measure of control over, such as your career goals and progression.

I will be wealthy when . . .

_____
_____
_____

Examine your answer. Your personal definition of wealth is shaped by your *values, goals, and self-image.* Not only do these three areas influence how you perceive wealth, but they also shape your educational, career, and lifestyle choices. Let's see how this works.

Reflect on your answer and now consider what it will take to achieve each priority you identified to its fullest. You will find that most, if not all of your financial priorities will require some combination of long-term effort, including education, work, and

Figure 5 Home ownership is a common dream, but what's yours?

are still common in government and military jobs. The important advantage of these plans is that "defined benefit" means you know how much you will receive each month in retirement based upon a simple table that includes salary level and number of years worked for the company.[4]

IRA Small employers often offer simple IRA (individual retirement account) savings plans. A simple IRA lets you invest a portion of your pretax income on a tax-deferred basis. Likewise, your employer may elect to make a matching contribution to your account as well.

The simplified employee pension, or SEP, IRA is ideal if you are self-employed. Like the 401(k) and simple IRA, your money is invested using pretax dollars, with income tax paid on the money once you take withdrawals in retirement.[5]

Social Security As long as you work, you pay into Social Security through automatic payroll deductions.

You can receive monthly payments as early as age 62 or wait a few years to receive increased payments. Few people can live comfortably in retirement on Social Security income alone, so most people use the savings plans listed above to provide additional money.

Career Path Income

First answer the questions below based upon your own knowledge of your career field. Then, seek additional information, which can be found through research. Use the services and resources available through your campus career services office. If you need additional information, check the library and information available via the Internet. The following example shows what a completed analysis will look like.

EXAMPLE ANALYSIS

Program name: Automotive Technology
Your education level upon graduation: Diploma
Potential education level for this field: Associate degree, with further degree levels in business

Entry-level job titles for this field:

1. Auto Mechanic   Pay Rate: $15.00 per hour
2. Auto Parts Store Manager   Pay Rate: $38,000 to $60,000 per year

Mid-level job titles for this field:

1. Certified Auto Mechanic   Pay Rate: $24.00 per hour
2. Saab Auto Technician   Pay Rate: $50,000 to $80,000 per year

Upper-level job titles for this field:

1. Owner—Repair and/or Body Shop   Pay Rate: $90,000 to unlimited
2. Dealership Service Manager   Pay Rate: Not listed

Number of years at entry-level salary × Average annual salary   = 4 × $30,000 per year
Four years of entry-level salary   = $120,000
Number of years at mid-level salary × Average annual salary   = 8 × $60,000 per year
Eight years of mid-level salary   = $480,000
Number of years at upper-level salary × Average annual salary   = 8 × $90,000 per year
Eight years at upper-level salary   = $720,000

Add the entry totals from three levels:
$120,000 + $480,000 + $720,000 = ***$1,320,000 salary potential over 20 years!***

Now complete the analysis for your career field.

Your program name _____

Your education level upon graduation from this program _____

Potential education level for this field _____

1. List two entry-level job titles for this field. These positions require little or no prior experience. Any prior experience requirements can often be met by general work experience in a nonrelated field. Include pay rates for each job if available.

   a. _____   Pay rate _____
   b. _____   Pay rate _____

2. List two mid-level job titles for this field. These are positions that typically require two to five years experience and may or may not be at the supervisor/manager level. Include pay rates for each job if they are available.

   a. _____ Pay rate _____

   b. _____ Pay rate _____

3. List two upper-level job titles for this field. These positions typically require seven to ten years of prior experience and are very competitive or require some form of investment (such as an entrepreneur starting a new business). Not everyone who desires a position at this level will achieve it. Include pay rates for each job if they are available.

   a. _____ Pay rate _____

   b. _____ Pay rate _____

4. Add up the salaries for the years spent at the various levels, selecting your one most desired or favored position and salary at each level in your calculations.

For number of years at each salary level, use your judgment, as well as the guidelines used in the example for a 20-year career: 4 years at entry-level, 8 years at mid-level, and, if appropriate, 8 years at upper-level. For those careers that don't lend themselves to upper-level positions, use 16 years at mid-level salary for this analysis.

Number of years at entry-level salary × average annual salary (ex: 4 × $39,000) _____

Total entry-level salary = _____

Number of years at mid-level salary × Average annual salary _____

Total mid-level salary = _____

Number of years at upper-level salary × Average annual salary _____

Total upper-level salary = _____

Add entry totals from three levels.

Total salary for 20-year career[6] = _____

How did you do? Are you surprised at your 20-year number? Keep in mind, the purpose of this exercise is *not* to tell you exactly how much money you can expect to make in the 20 years after you graduate. No one can do that. Rather, the purpose is to give you a heightened appreciation for the value and importance of your current endeavor. Armed with this information, the auto technology student in the example above can choose to view his schooling as preparing him to earn $15 per hour upon graduation—or he can view his schooling as preparing him to earn over $1.3 million. Which do you think is more motivating? Which perspective do you now choose?

smart saving/investing. To demonstrate this principle, let's look at one typical career path for a college graduate.

1. **Student attends college and graduates, leading to an entry-level position.** Position enables graduate to support himself and begin to establish a financial foundation and security.

⬇

2. Student **works hard and is promoted** to higher paying job.

⬇

3. Student decides to **seek higher-level management position** (at much higher pay) or to be his own boss and decides **additional schooling is required** to achieve this.

⬇

4. Student **returns to college,** but maintains employment while in school.

⬇

5. Student **graduates from college** (again!) and eventually receives the promotion he seeks or strikes out on his own to start his own business.

⬇

6. **Student now has experience, expertise, and the necessary education** to achieve all of his financial priorities, although he has already realized several of them along the way.

What will it take for you to achieve your financial priorities?

Figure 6
Graduating is the best thing you can do for your financial future.

Big-Picture Career Path Income Opportunities

What is the potential financial value of one particular career path? Most vocations begin with entry-level positions, then progress to advanced or supervisory positions, and then, for some, to upper-management or ownership positions. For many workers, the true earning power of their career path doesn't occur until they have obtained considerable experience. From the entry-level worker's perspective, it may be hard to envision themselves in those roles, especially if the path to those positions is not direct.

For example, a graduate of a medical assistant diploma program may find it difficult to see herself in the future being in charge of the nursing staff of a large hospital. But that's what can happen. Here's how: She first earns her diploma and works in a doctor's office for five years gaining valuable experience, and then decides to go back to school to earn a degree in nursing. After graduating (again!) from nursing school, she lands a job in a hospital. It's not long before the hospital administrators recognize her leadership abilities and then the promotions begin—first to heading the staff of her unit, then a few years later to the top position. Her amazing journey could not have been possible without completing that first step—earning her diploma in medical assisting.

YOUR PATH TO ACHIEVE FINANCIAL SUCCESS
As illustrated in this section's activity, reaching long-term financial goals usually requires completing

a series of smaller steps along the way. Skip one of the steps, and it becomes very difficult, if not impossible, to achieve that goal. Your decision to include college in your long-term planning is to be congratulated! Clearly, you understand the important role it plays in achieving success and personal wealth, no matter how you define it.

As you face the challenges of your daily commitments and obligations, try to remember this high-level perspective on the value of an education. Stepping back and looking at the value this college experience can add to your life in the long term can make the day-to-day commitments a little easier and a little more manageable in the short term. You will find more strength to manage your hectic daily schedule of commuting, classes, work, family, and studying when you feel strong in your long-term purpose and goals.

Someday, when you look back on your life's major milestones, there's a good chance you'll feel that the years you spent in college were some of the best years of your life. You'll appreciate the increased earning power, for sure, but the friends you made, the instructors you had the privilege to learn from, and your own high-energy efforts will have combined to make an unforgettable and fulfilling experience. You will probably feel some of this appreciation and nostalgia at graduation, and for most people, the good memories only get better with time.

II. Personal Expenses and Spending

GET READY

How often you receive money can change how you budget.

- When you work a full-time job, how would you prefer to be paid: once per month, once every two weeks, or every day (such as a job that pays tips)? Why?

As the definition of the word **manager** implies, those who manage have the *responsibility* to control or direct some sort of resource, whether supervising employees, or making decisions regarding the running of a household or business. Given that definition, are you a manager? You may not currently be working, or if you are, you may not be employed as manager, but that doesn't mean you aren't a manager. Do you have income or other sources of money that you must decide whether to spend, save, or lend? Do you sometimes borrow money or use credit? If the answer is yes, then you're a manager. Now the question is, are you a *good* manager? If so, could you be an even better manager?

man·ag·er A person who controls and manipulates resources and expenditures, as of a household.

Why is it important to be a good money manager? It's not uncommon for impulse buying, overuse of credit, and other unnecessary spending to lead to financial hardship for college students. Over time, seemingly insignificant spending decisions can lead to a shortage of money when it comes time to pay rent and utilities, purchase books for the next term, or make ever-increasing minimum monthly credit card payments.

Figure 7 If you decide where your money comes from and goes to, you're already a manager.

LO 2 Be a Good Financial Manager: Understand Your Current Financial Situation

Excessive **discretionary spending** is the spending that causes the most financial hardship for college students. Discretionary money is what you spend beyond your basic living expenses each month. For example, let's say Jose earns $1,800 per month. His rent, groceries, and utilities add up to $1,100. This leaves him with $700 of discretionary money to spend or save each month. Of course, discretionary spending can easily exceed the amount you have left after the bills are paid. If Jose decides to buy a new plasma TV (placing the entire amount on a new credit card he got during a promotion at school), his discretionary spending for that month equals the $700 he normally spends, plus the cost of the TV.

discretionary spending *Money you spend beyond your basic living expenses each month.*

What's the financial impact of Jose purchasing the TV? Because of the higher balance on his credit card, his minimum monthly payment on the card goes up, lowering his monthly discretionary spending amount. Now what happens when Jose needs to make another large purchase on his credit card? What if, for example, his car needs a major repair and he doesn't have any savings to cover the expense? His minimum payment goes up again, and his discretionary dollars go down even further. It won't take too many months of this kind of spending for Jose to get into real financial trouble. Even worse, if he makes a late credit card payment, he'll pay a high late fee and may dramatically increase his interest rate.

Figure 8 You get to decide what to spend your discretionary money on, but choose wisely.

Since Jose is a college student, he soon may not have enough money to buy books or pay tuition. Jose may decide he needs to drop out of school, so he can work more and pay off his credit card debts.

Making good choices with everyday financial decisions can mean the difference between being able to support yourself through college and having to drop out due to financial hardship. *Believe it or not, being a good manager of your discretionary spending is one of the most important tasks you have as a college student.*

What discretionary spending decisions do students commonly make? Some are listed in Figure 9 on the next page.

Being a good manager requires you to take action. It requires decisive decision-making. But before you do either, you must have a very good understanding of the current situation and have a clear idea of what areas need improvement. It means you need to understand your spending and savings habits. And it means understanding how those habits may or may not be helping you toward your goal of graduating from college. It means looking for ways to improve your everyday financial decision-making.

Your money management decisions play a big role in your ability to control your current and future financial health. This can mean real dollars to you. By controlling spending, you will have more to save and more to cushion you when unexpected expenses come up. Having a plan or a method for your spending decisions and sticking to it, saving money on a regular basis, and actually planning for unexpected expenses will all help you maintain the power of choice, including the choice to stay in school and graduate!

Figure 9 Some common discretionary spending decisions.

Discretionary Spending

- Eating and drinking out in restaurants, bars, and clubs
- Music, video games, and other entertainment
- Mobile phone charges
- Premium coffee drinks
- Credit card purchases that will not be entirely paid off with the next billing statement
- Late payments on credit cards ($29 fee or higher, plus interest-rate hikes)
- Playing the lottery
- Gambling—online or otherwise
- Use of payday loans
- Using ATMs that charge fees
- Purchasing a new car, flat-screen television, or other big-ticket item

Can you think of others?

LO 3 Smart Spending, Smart Choices

Day in and day out, from the time we wake up in the morning to the time we fall asleep at night, Americans are bombarded with the marketing efforts of those who have something to sell. Whether we like to admit it or not, these marketing and advertising campaigns do work.

Imagine this scenario: You see and hear ads for the latest mobile phone in magazines, on television, in the newspaper, on billboards, and on the radio. Plus, your friends have that phone and love it. When you walk past the phone store at the mall, you're primed to buy. *You want that phone.*

Figure 10 What if you were offered this phone for "free"?

Hidden Costs

So you walk into the store, and the sales representative is friendly and knowledgeable. (Of course, he's not your friend—he's trained to be friendly to encourage you to buy his phone). The rep confirms everything you've seen and heard, and makes you an offer you can't refuse. You walk out of the store with a shiny new phone, $250 less in your pocket, and a two-year commitment to pay $49 per month—plus taxes—for service (meaning it's actually closer to $60 per month). Add it up, and over the life of the contract, you will pay at least $1,690. If you had thought about it that way, would you have been so eager to make that purchase? Advertising and sales efforts guide what we purchase, when we purchase it, and how much we're willing to pay.

Impact Advertising

Do advertisers know how much you have to spend? Do they care? No, they don't. Do they care that you have bills to pay, a family to support, and a long list of other financial obligations each month? No, they don't. But they do like that you have a family, because that means they can advertise toys to your kids. Think

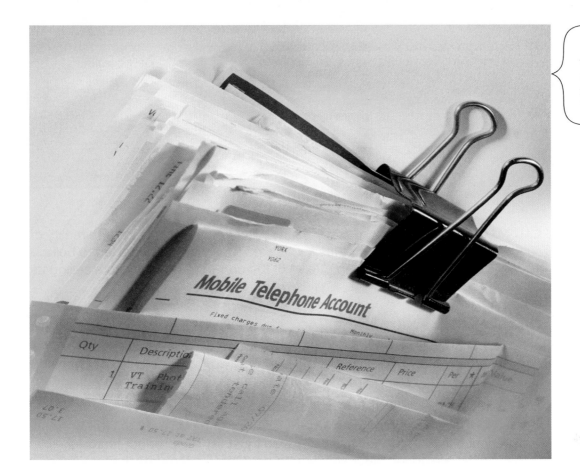

Figure 11 Be wary of purchasing ongoing contracts; make sure your "deal" makes sense.

for a moment about the cell phone you just bought. A good-quality cordless home phone costs less than $100. Computer technology enables virtually free calling to almost anywhere in the world. But the mobile phone industry has found a way to extract an additional $1,500 from millions of people for the privilege of going mobile in style. How did they do this? By creating perceived need through relentless—and very effective—advertising.

You may justifiably feel that carrying a mobile phone is now a necessity, and if you have to have one for work, or family communications, or just because you're never home to receive a regular phone call, then you might as well have a nice one. But $1,690 nice? Not long ago, nobody paid $1,690 for a cell phone—they didn't exist! How did we all function without one?

The point of this story is about choices. Many people would contend that a mobile phone is now one of the necessities of life. Even so, the differences in cost between a premier phone and plan and a more modest phone and limited plan are significant. To buy or not to buy is not the only question—often, the question is how much to buy.

Relentless advertising of a product that already appeals to you diminishes your ability to think rationally and without emotion about the purchasing decision. In effect, *advertising diminishes your freedom to choose wisely.* How does it do that? By telling only part of the story—the part the marketer wants you to hear—and not telling you about the rest of the story. In other words, they sell the glamour and excitement, but not the complete picture that represents the entire experience (consequences) of purchasing and living with (using) the product. Figure 12 demonstrates this concept in more detail.

Figure 12
Purchasing a cell
phone may involve
more than you
think.

Cell Phone Purchase Outcomes		
Advertising Claim	**Product Reality**	**Consequences**
"Nationwide coverage"	Your reception is often poor	Dropped calls, miscommunication
Cell phone has great features	Many features aren't used	Money down the drain
Cell phone has great features	Features are hard to find	More frustration
Cell phone is a great buy	Required contract is not	Long-term financial commitment
Phone company has great service	Long lines, long hold times	Wasted time, wasted money
Long battery life	Not exactly	Constant charging
Cell phone is reliable	You drop your phone one time	Time to buy a new phone

REAL VALUE As is true with so many things we purchase, the long-term reality of living with and using a product is less satisfying than what we were led to believe through the sales and advertising efforts of the company and the store selling us the product.

Wise Choices: Examining Your Own Spending

Recognizing and acknowledging that the purpose of selling and advertising is to provide you with the side of the story that encourages you to buy is critical to making smart buying decisions. To help you make the best buying decision *for you*, ask yourself the following questions before making a significant purchase:

1. ***What are the reasons for making this purchase?*** What benefits will you experience if you own this product? Don't just list the product features—that's what the advertiser wants you to do. Only list features that are important to you, that you will use, and that will truly benefit you. If the cell phone you are considering has a built-in camera, that camera is only a benefit if you will actually use it and benefit from it.

2. ***What are the reasons against making this purchase?*** Your answer should include the financial impact of this purchase. What about opportunity cost? What else could you do with the money if you didn't buy this product? You might identify other reasons against making the purchase by using a compare/contrast analysis, measuring the product you're considering with another of the same type (this may raise the "How much should I buy?" question). For example, the phone you're looking at only comes in one color, but another comes in six different colors. And don't forget about your time. How much time will you spend with this product? What else could you do with that time that might be more fun/productive/worthwhile? If the product requires a lot of time just to learn how to use it properly, that would count as a negative.

3. ***What don't I know about this product that is important to know before making this purchase?*** In our cell phone example, it would be wise to make sure the phone and service you're considering has great reception in the places where you'll use the phone the most. It would also be important to know the penalty or cost for breaking the contract early. Depending upon the product, the list of things you don't know—but need to—could be long. Remember, you can't rely on product salespeople to give complete answers to these questions. After all, it's their job to convince you to make a purchase, and stop talking once that has occurred. Try to answer as many of these questions as possible before you go to the store, and make sure they are all answered satisfactorily before you make a purchase decision.

MY SUCCESS STORY

When Kyra Sanford decided to attend school at night to earn an associate's degree, she thought she had planned for everything. She received approval from her supervisor to leave the office once a week no later than 5 P.M. to get to school on time. She had a well-defined course plan that put her on a path to graduating in a little less than two years, and she had successfully navigated the financial aid paperwork to ensure that her tuition would be taken care of for her first year in school.

One thing Kyra had not planned for were the high costs of textbooks. She was shocked when she spent $125 on her first course alone. Her college courses were five weeks long, and she was scheduled to take one at a time for the duration of her program. Being on a limited income, Kyra quickly realized that she was going to have to make some adjustments to her personal spending habits if she was going to be able to afford these new expenses associated with school.

"After that first trip to the bookstore, I went home and took a hard look at my monthly spending habits, because I knew that I didn't have that much extra money every five weeks after paying my rent and other bills. I wanted to create a plan that would let me buy the required books without having to use my credit card," Kyra explained.

"I didn't know about budgets or financial planning, but I did know enough to write down every place I spent money, and how much," Kyra continued. "That included rent, utilities, grocery stores, restaurants, going out on weekends, shopping for clothes—everything I could think of. I was surprised how much money I spent on things that were not absolute necessities. It was the first time I truly looked at my discretionary spending (I didn't know what that term meant at the time). I was encouraged by what I found. I calculated that I could shave almost $100 off my personal monthly spending just by doing a little less shopping, eating out less often, and being more careful with my spending on the weekends. I knew I could do it, and as it turns out, I was able to purchase my textbooks for each course after that first one without using my credit card."

Kyra's success in adjusting and managing her personal spending so she could pursue her dream of earning a college degree is a great demonstration of one kind of change that students often need to make in their personal lives to create college success. Whether it's making adjustments to allow extra time for reading and studying, or adjusting work and child care schedules, every student has a unique story. If you are anything like Kyra, you can and will find ways to make the necessary adjustments in your life to stay on track toward graduation.

These three steps—which cause you to step away from an emotional decision and rationally consider important factors—will strengthen your decision-making process. Sometimes the process will affirm your desire to make the purchase, but other times, a negative may jump off the page and tell you that making the purchase is not a good decision. Walking away from a potential purchase can be satisfying when you know that *you*, not a barrage of one-sided advertisements tugging at your emotions, control the decision.

Money Decisions

Think for a moment about the decisions you make every day about your money. In this activity, make a list of the various decisions you made regarding spending, saving, and borrowing money for a recent 30-day period. Each section has room to list 4 to 12 items. Stop at the last number, even if you have more items you could write down. Do your best to remember as much as you can—the activity still works even if you can't remember every item!

Month and year the following money decisions occurred:_____

DISCRETIONARY AND UNEXPECTED SPENDING

Consider your spending for items you *chose to buy, as well as unexpected or emergency spending,* such as a car repair, unexpected medical bill, or a cash loan to a friend in need.

List items you paid for with cash, check, or debit card. If you paid with a credit card on which you carry a balance each month, list that item in the next section (borrowing decisions). Include any spending of any amount, from a coffeehouse latte to concert tickets, to dinner out. *Do not include regular, essential expenditures, such as rent or mortgage payments, utility payments, gas for your car, clothing for your child, or basic groceries.*

1. _____ $ _____

2. _____ $ _____

3. _____ $ _____

4. _____ $ _____

5. _____ $ _____

6. _____ $ _____

7. _____ $ _____

8. _____ $ _____

9. _____ $ _____

10. _____ $ _____

11. _____ $ _____

12. _____ $ _____

BORROWING DECISIONS

Include items you paid for using credit (do not include debit cards or credit cards in which you pay the entire balance each month) as well as any new loans or other borrowing that occurred during the 30-day period.

1. _____ $_____

2. _____ $_____

3. _____ $_____

4. _____ $_____

5. _____ $_____

SAVINGS DECISIONS

Include deposits into a savings account, 401(k), or other investment account; or even a piggy bank you keep at home for rainy-day needs.

1. _____ $_____

2. _____ $_____

3. _____ $_____

4. _____ $_____

How did you do? Were you able to think of 10 or more items for which you spent money during your 30-day period? How about any new borrowing or savings? This exercise demonstrates that, regardless of your income level, you make many decisions regarding your finances over a month's time. As you can see, even small decisions to spend or save money can add up over time.

Here's a simple example: If you spend $3.00 on a fancy coffee drink each weekday at work, that little indulgence adds up to $750 per year. If instead you deposited that coffee money into a personal savings account that earned on average 4 percent interest, after five years your account would be worth over $4,000. Later on in this module, we'll explore the decision-making processes for spending, saving, and borrowing, and how you might apply some of those concepts to the management of your own discretionary spending.

III. Developing a Personal Budget

School expenses can add up to a big financial commitment.

- Have you changed how you spend money since you entered school?
- Share a budgeting suggestion you'd give to a new student.

How do you track your money each month? Do you spend what you have until you don't have any more—until your ATM gives you an "insufficient funds" response when you try to withdraw $40—and then anxiously wait until your next paycheck arrives? Or do you carefully plan your spending, regularly check the balance in your bank account, reconcile your checkbook, look ahead to make sure you have enough money to pay bills, save for future purchases, and prepare for "rainy day" expenses? If you do the latter, then you are actively engaged in managing your personal budget.

LO 4 Actively Managing Your Personal Finances

A **budget plan** is a financial tool that enables you to plan for income, spending, and saving over a set period of time, usually a month. The main purpose of a personal budget plan is to give you a clear understanding and guide for your monthly saving and discretionary spending. It is the foundation for good personal financial management.

budget plan: A financial tool that enables you to plan for income, spending, and saving over a set period of time, usually a month.

A typical budget plan includes the following (see also Figure 14):

- ☐ Monthly income from work and other sources of financial support.
- ☐ Monthly savings. This is the amount you plan to deposit into one or more savings accounts. This could include a work-related retirement plan.
- ☐ Monthly expenses. Expenses fall into two general categories:
  - ○ *Fixed:* Items that stay the same each month. This would include rent, car payment, loan payment, etc.
  - ○ *Variable:* Items that change, or vary, each month. These could include utility bills, gas for your car, credit card payments, books for school, etc. Discretionary spending, discussed in the previous section, also falls into this category. Restaurants, vacations, entertainment, etc., are discretionary spending that you have the power to control.

The Key to Budgeting: Looking Ahead

The key to effective budget planning and management is simple: Write down how much you plan to earn, spend, and save each month, appropriately categorizing each item. Then during the month, track your progress, and try to limit your actual spending to the dollar amounts assigned to each category (the budget limitations) in your plan.

Figure 14
A typical monthly budget looks something like this.

Monthly Budget	Monthly Amount	Actual
Income		
Household take-home pay (you and spouse)		
Other income and/or sources of financial support		
Total Monthly Income		
Savings		
Work plan [401(k) or other]		
Personal savings account		
Investment savings		
Total Monthly Savings		
Home Expenses		
Rent or mortgage payment		
Property taxes (annual amount divided by 12)		
Car payment		
Car insurance (6-month premium divided by 6)		
Health insurance		
Home or renter's insurance		
Other insurance		
Gas and electric		
Telephone (landline)		
Telephone (mobile)		
Television/cable/satellite		
Internet		
Other		
Total Home Expenses		
School Expenses		
Tuition/student loan payments (while attending college)		
Books (average amount per term divided by number of months in term)		
Lab and uniform fees		
School supplies and related expenses		
Total School Expenses		
Personal Expenses and Discretionary Spending		
Groceries		
Gas for car		
Other transportation (bus, train)		
Child care		
Credit card payments		
Clothing		
Personal care		
Medical and health care		
Food and drink—restaurants		
Entertainment		
Other purchases (e.g. new cell phone)		
Other		
Gifts and charity		
Total Personal and Discretionary Spending		

When developing your budget, *your planned spending cannot exceed your planned income.* One exception to this rule would be the planned addition of debt through a loan, but only when and if you also include a plan for how you will repay the loan. For college students, this includes taking student loans to pay for tuition, with the understanding that upon graduation, you will need to earn a higher income that will support both your monthly living expenses and monthly loan payments.

At the end of each month, check to see how well you managed your spending. You will have one of the following situations:

1. Income = Spending	You have planned well and are "on budget."
2. Income < Spending	You have overspent (or underearned) and have likely added to your level of debt.
3. Income > Spending	You have money left over and can either spend it on something fun or add it to your savings.

Each month you repeat this process, adjusting your dollar amounts for each category with the goal of ending each month with income equal to spending, your savings account increasing, and any debt (e.g., credit card, car loan) accounts decreasing.

The Challenge: Stick to the Plan

Once the plan is in place, managing your budget requires you to carefully consider each purchase or borrowing decision you make. Is there room in your budget for the expenditure? Will the decision strengthen your financial position or weaken it? You will need to make adjustments in your discretionary spending if your income is less than you planned for or your expenses run higher than expected. Managing your budget means becoming a more educated and savvy consumer.

Sticking to a budget can be a big challenge. For successful businesses, creating and managing yearly and monthly budgets is a required activity. In fact, businesses hire purchasing professionals for the sole task of researching, negotiating, and making buying decisions. But in your "personal business," it's just you. Fortunately, the vast amount of information available online gives you a tremendous amount of leverage when it comes to budget planning and making buying and borrowing decisions. In addition to the price comparisons you can do on sites like Amazon.com, several free personal budgeting and financial management tools are available on the Web. Here are a few worth investigating:

☐ Mint: www.mint.com
☐ Just Budget: http://justbudget.com
☐ Kiplinger: www.kiplinger.com/tools/budget

Figure 15 You get to decide what your spending priorities are, but don't overlook necessary expenditures like a professional wardrobe.

LO 5 Planning for Unexpected or Significant Expenses

Financial challenges can come to us in ways over which we have little or no control. They can occur if you're "right-sized" from a job (laid off), or when an unexpected illness causes high medical bills that go beyond what insurance will pay. Even a spike in gasoline or food prices can noticeably affect your monthly budget.

For most students, the cost of college qualifies as a significant new expense. Unless you have received a scholarship for tuition and living expenses, your employer provides 100 percent tuition assistance (if so, keep that job!), or your family is fully paying for your education, the fact is that for you, as well as most college students in the United States, going to school has a significant financial impact that must be properly managed if you want to be successful in completing your education.

However, planning ahead can help you anticipate and meet these financial challenges. When you enrolled in college, you likely met with a financial aid counselor. Hopefully you came away with a solid plan to pay for school, as well as a good picture of what your financial obligations would be once you graduate. Of course, in the whirlwind of enrolling, registering for classes, buying books, and everything else that goes with starting college, certain aspects of your college financial plan may still feel unclear, especially when you consider how the additional costs may fit into your existing budget.

That's why, even as a college student, planning for significant and unexpected expenses is just as important as creating and managing a monthly budget. If you have a credit card, you may think you can just use it in an emergency. But the risk of relying on your credit card to get you through financial emergencies is that it doesn't take too many financial hits to put you in deep debt, with minimum

ON THE JOB

Budgets at Work

Successful businesses create and follow a strategic plan and then make adjustments as time goes by. Planning for future income and spending is part of this process and an important management task. The heart of this plan is the yearly budget, which plays a big role in determining whether the business will be healthy and prosperous. The typical budget process involves developing plans and projections for several distinct parts of the business, some of which include planning for (or forecasting) sales revenue, or money coming in to the business; planning for business operations and overhead expenses; planning for capital investments (for example, purchasing new equipment) for the purpose of growing the business; and planning cash flow to ensure that money is available during the year to pay for expenses when they arise.

Revenues can come from many different sources, but the largest is usually sales of the business's product or service. Expenses include anything a business plans to spend money on in the coming year, such as the cost of making the product the business sells, employee salaries, rent, marketing costs, and other related expenses. The cash flow forecast is a month-

Principal Budget Components

Revenue Projection	Expenses
Sales projections	Material and production costs
Other revenue sources	Employee expense
	Marketing expense
	Overhead (rent, utilities, etc.)
	Capital improvements

Cash Flow

Planned monthly money flow into and out of the business over the coming year

by-month projection of the projected revenues minus the projected expenses.

Following a budget plan is important for a healthy business. If expenses go beyond what has been

monthly payments that exceed your ability to pay. Typical out-of-pocket college expenses—which may not seem unexpected or significant by themselves—add to this pressure. For example, most people don't include buying books in their monthly budget, because they don't buy books every month. But if you don't have a plan to pay for your books each term, this expense alone will stress your debt level as well as your budget plan.

It's understandable that these types of significant and unexpected financial challenges can threaten a student's ability to pay college bills and related expenses while in school. To protect your financial stability while in college and beyond, you should create a plan that anticipates and addresses these potential and significant expenses. Your plan can then be

planned for, especially for long periods of time, the business may experience serious financial difficulty and may even fail. On the other hand, when sales are strong and expenses are under control, profits will increase and the leaders of the business will have the opportunity to make decisions about whether to reinvest those profits back into the business to help it grow larger, pay off debt the business may have, distribute the money to employees as bonuses, or perhaps all three!

Businesses adjust their budgets throughout the year. If in the middle of the year the business experiences a large, unforeseen expense, spending in other areas may have to be cut back in order to make up the difference. Employee hiring, as well as layoffs, are a direct result of continuous monitoring and managing of the business's budget plan.

Near the end of the year, businesses begin planning for the next year's budget, as well as evaluating their performance on the current year's budget plan. Employee bonuses may be paid based on whether or not the business met its budget goals. These bonuses usually vary depending on how well the business performed beyond the minimum budget plan. And so, the budget cycle starts again, providing the business

with a road map to follow, and a target destination in mind, so it knows when it has reached and possibly exceeded its goals.

Develop an Action Plan for New and Unexpected Expenses

STEP 1: IDENTIFY POTENTIALLY BIG EXPENDITURES

Create a list of items that you think could require *significant financial resources* at some point in the following 12 months. Include in your list items you may wish to purchase, such as a new car, furniture, television, etc. Include possible or likely expense items, such as tuition and books, medical or dental expenses, car or home repair, or upcoming family expenses. Finally, list significant expenses that you don't expect to have, but that *could* happen.

Example

Possible Desired Purchases	Amount
1. New flat screen TV	$1,000
2. New couch	$1,200
3. Vacation	$2,000

Possible or Likely Expenses	Amount
1. Replace tires on car	$600
2. Books for school	$500
3. Dental work	$500
4. Summer trip to family reunion	$1,200
5. Travel to friend's wedding and gift	$400

Unexpected Expenses	Amount
1. Significant car repair (high miles)	$2,000
2. Dental work more than anticipated	$1,500
3. Illness (high-deductible health insurance)	$2,500
4. Family emergency	$1,000

Possible Desired Purchases	Amount
1. _____	$ _____
2. _____	$ _____
3. _____	$ _____
4. _____	$ _____
5. _____	$ _____

Possible or Likely Expenses | **Amount**

1. _____ $_____
2. _____ $_____
3. _____ $_____
4. _____ $_____
5. _____ $_____

Unexpected Expenses | **Amount**

1. _____ $_____
2. _____ $_____
3. _____ $_____
4. _____ $_____
5. _____ $_____

Total of all possible significant expenses for the next 12 months: $_____

STEP 2: IDENTIFY FINANCIAL RESOURCES

List ideas for how you will pay for the things that you listed in the previous section. Since you are forecasting *possible* expenses, you do not need to plan to pay for all of them. However, you should create a plan that assumes a certain percentage of the expenses will actually happen.

List Sources of Funding

1. Current savings account balance: $_____

2. Regular monthly savings rate × 12: $_____

3. Other savings or investments amount: $_____

4. Extra income from work—list details: $_____

(This amount could include an expected bonus or overtime pay.)

5. Credit (current available credit): $_____

6. Expected new loans (e.g., student loan): $_____

7. Other potential financial resources (e.g., family): $_____

(continued)

TAKE ACTION *(concluded)*

STEP 3: CREATE AN ACTION PLAN

Compare the amount of your possible expenditures with the total amount listed in your funding sources. How do they line up? If your funding resources exceed your possible expenditures, then you are in a strong position for the following year. If your possible expenditures exceed your current funding sources, then it's time to think about what you can do to be ready when the unexpected does happen. Use the following cues to create your own plan.

Budget items: What can you do to reduce your regular or everyday spending in order to be able to put more money into a savings account? List at least three things you can do as well as the amount you could save from each.

_____

_____

_____

Income Sources: List at least two ideas for how you can bring home more money in the following year through work-related activities. List amount of additional earnings.

_____

_____

_____

incorporated into your monthly budget. For example, if you estimate that you will need to spend $1,000 next year on out-of-pocket college expenses, then you would be wise to adjust your monthly budget to save $84 per month ($1,000 divided by 12) to cover those costs, instead of just adding those costs to your credit card balance.

For everyone, including the person who lives by the balance shown on his ATM receipt, a budget plan is an effective way to better manage and control personal finances. However, your budget is only part of overall planning and management that is critical to financial stability and success. As a good financial manager, you also need to develop a plan for the unexpected expenses that *everyone* experiences, so that when the unexpected does happen, you will know how to handle it.

Try this online at mcgrawhillconnect.com

Loan Sources: This is not preferred, but in some cases may be necessary. List one or two possible sources of money you can borrow. Take into account your credit rating or history and current credit situation. List credit limit or expected loan amount.

_____

_____

Family or Other Sources: If you have other resources for *emergency* funds through family or friends, list them here. List possible amounts.

_____

_____

_____

_____

Congratulations! You have now proactively created a plan to defend yourself against potential financial hurdles for the coming year. It's a good idea to review and update this plan as the year progresses. You may find that adjustments to your everyday spending enable you to save enough money to purchase one of the luxury items on your list without using credit, or help you avoid incurring debt. In addition, you now have a list of actions you can take in the next 12 months to protect your financial position and maintain the power of choice to complete your education and pursue your dreams.

SUMMARY

College students have a seemingly endless list of new and unique responsibilities and commitments that go along with the decision to enroll in school. One of the bigger commitments is the commitment to meet the required financial obligations of college.

This module provides a perspective on the long-term value that earning a college diploma brings. Having a clear picture of what you are investing in (that is, a college education) can help later on when you need to make tough financial decisions. Most students have never calculated the value of the career path their education is leading them toward and are surprised at the incredible earnings opportunity that completing their education can provide.

Many financial challenges students face can be avoided simply through better management and control over spending. You analyzed your spending, savings, and borrowing habits to gain a greater understanding of your financial strengths and weaknesses and are now prepared to create a plan for spending, savings, and borrowing during your time at school.

Your college financial action plan includes two components. The first is to proactively consider potentially large and unexpected expenses that could derail your ability to stay enrolled. This helps you make a plan to manage these events before they happen. The second component is to develop a monthly budget plan. Through planning and diligent management of your financial resources, your chances for college success will improve tremendously, enabling you to reap the long-term rewards that a college education can bring.

DISCUSSION QUESTIONS

1. Recall a big purchase you made in the past that you paid for using cash. It could be your car, a vacation, or any item that you desired, but had to save for over a long time in order to be able to make the purchase. Once you achieved your savings goal and made the purchase, was it worth all the effort to plan, and not spend your money on other "impulse" buys, in order to have enough money to make the big purchase? How did it feel watching your savings grow toward your goal? Did you find that the more you saved toward your goal, the more motivated you became to achieve it?

2. Think of a large "unexpected expense" you've had in the past. How did you manage to pay for it? How did the expense affect the rest of your finances? What could you have done, both before and after the unexpected expense occurred, to diminish its impact on your finances?

KEY TERMS

budget plan: A financial tool that enables you to plan for income, spending, and saving over a set period of time, usually a month. (p. 20)

discretionary spending: Money you spend beyond your basic living expenses each month. (p. 12)

manager A person who controls and manipulates resources and expenditures, as of a household. (p. 11)

opportunity cost: The value of not doing or buying something and instead choosing something else. (p. 4)

perspective: The ability to accurately judge a situation or idea and its relative importance. (p. 4)

REFERENCES AND CREDITS

Footnotes

1. www.census.gov/pubainfo/www/broadcast/photos/census_bureau/004313.html#school
2. Ibid.
3. www.irs.ustreas.gov/retirement/article/0,,id=172430,00.html
4. www.usd.edu/elderlaw/archives/pension_plans.htm
5. www.irs.gov/retirement
6. This is a very rough estimate of the value of a career. We don't include many of the typical perks that go along with many jobs, including the value of health care benefits, retirement savings plan benefits, life and disability insurance, and annual cost-of-living increases that are commonly offered by many employers.
7. www.dictionary.com

Websites

http://justbudget.com

www.fool.com/Retirement/Retirement02.htm

www.kiplinger.com/tools/budget

www.mint.com

Figure and Photo Credits

Chapter opening photo: Stockbyte/Getty Images

Figure 1 (left): Frances Twitty/Getty Images; (right): © Brand X Pictures/PunchStock

Figure 3: Bureau of Labor Statistics, Current Population Survey.

Figure 4: © moodboard/Corbis

Figure 5: John Lund/Drew Kelly/Blend Images LLC

Figure 6: Mike Kemp/Getty Images

Money Smarts: ©Sam Toren/Alamy

Figure 7: Ariel Skelley/Blend Images/Getty Images

Figure 8: Fuse/Getty Images

Figure 10: Lourens Smak/Alamy

Figure 11: Brand X Pictures

My Success Story: Image Source/Getty Images

Figure 14: Digital Vision/Getty Images

Figure 15: Big Cheese Photo/SuperStock

Figure 16: © 2009 Jupiterimages Corporation

Money on the Job: ©Siri Stafford, Gettyimages

Figure 17: Rubberball/Getty Images

Focusing on **Health**

LEARNING OUTCOMES

In this module, you will:

1 Understand the importance of proper nutrition and incorporate nutritional guidelines into your life.

2 Learn the benefits of good sleep and adopt good sleep habits.

3 Examine the value of exercise, and learn how to include regular exercise in your lifestyle.

4 Understand the impact of mental and emotional health on your success.

5 Learn how to develop positive attitudes.

6 Explore the sources and symptoms of stress.

7 Discover strategies for coping with and reducing stress and for practicing integrated health.

Food, sleep, exercise. Which of these three is most important to you for keeping a high energy level?

● Which is the first thing you skip when you're stressed?

> *"The chief condition on which, life, health and vigor depend on, is action. It is by action that an organism develops its faculties, increases its energy, and attains the fulfillment if its destiny."*

**—PIERRE-JOSEPH PROUDHON
(1809–1865),** *French philosopher*

Have you ever felt tense, anxious, uneasy, overwhelmed, or apprehensive? Have you felt your muscles tighten up, your heart beat faster, or your breathing pattern change when faced with major life changes or even with a small but unexpected change? Have you noticed that during and after periods of extended worry that you feel tired and drained, prone to headaches and muscle aches, and generally more likely to get sick?

If you answered yes to any of these questions, then you're familiar with *stress*. And you're not alone. Stress is common among college students and just about anybody trying to balance the challenges and responsibilities of modern life.

In this module, you'll learn how to deal with stress on a physical, mental, and emotional level. As you learn to recognize what causes stress and how we react to it, you will also learn different stress-control techniques to help you maintain a healthy body, mind, and emotional self.

We'll examine how attitudes, perceptions, and behaviors are related and how they affect your response to others and to situations you experience.

You'll also learn how your body and mind are integrated and how finding balance and harmony can help you function in a healthy and productive manner.

Figure 1 Creating a healthy, balanced life for yourself is key to your success.

We'll start by taking a look at how eating, sleeping, and exercising well can all reduce stress, give you more energy, and make you more productive and effective, and we'll learn ways to incorporate these healthy habits into busy lives like yours.

I. Physical Health

Do you have the energy you need to succeed? Before you answer that, think about how you have felt over the last few days. Have you jumped out of bed in the morning, ready for the day ahead? Have you been alert and focused in every class? Have you had enough brainpower to tackle your homework assignments quickly after class and to invest quality time studying each day?

Or have you groaned when your alarm went off, and hit snooze as many times as you thought you could get away with? Have you struggled to pay attention in some classes, found your mind wandering, or even dozed off in the middle of a lecture? Do you find that homework takes much longer and your study time feels much less productive than you thought it would, and that when you come home, you feel like you only have enough brainpower to sit on the couch and watch television?

If you found yourself agreeing more with the second set of questions than the first, you're in good company: Many college students feel that way more often than they'd like.

What you and most every college student could use is more energy to tackle all the things you have to do. But ironically, because of their busy schedules, students often sacrifice the things that are most likely to give them that energy: eating well, sleeping enough, and exercising often. In this section, we'll look at how to get what you need from food, how to get enough sleep to keep you healthy and rested, and how to fit exercise into your hectic life.

LO 1 Getting What You Need from Food

If you've ever felt full and sleepy after a big Thanksgiving meal, then you know the effect that food can have on you. But post-Thanksgiving food "coma" is just one way that food can impact your body. The foods you choose, and when and how you eat them, can give you energy, help you sleep, make you strong, and keep you fit—or they can do the opposite.

As a college student, you're busy. It's easy to say, "I'll try to eat better after I graduate, when I have more time." That's why lots of college students eat meals from fast-food restaurants and from vending machines. But the time to start making good eating choices is now. If you get into good eating habits now, it will be much easier to adapt those good habits to life after college than if you eat whatever's in front of you now, and try to make a big change later.

In fact, big changes are hard and scare people from even trying. So rather than try to make a big change, we're going to look at small changes you can make that will make a big difference. Each small change begins with small choices. First up: what to eat.

Small Choices: What You Eat

When people think about eating better, they often think they're going to have to give up everything that they like and start eating a bunch of food they don't like. But eating healthy doesn't mean suffering. It does mean being informed

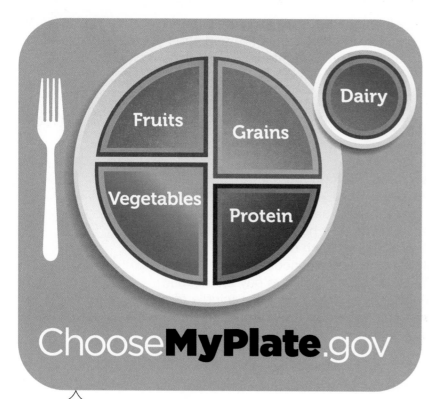

about what you put into your body. Once you've learned how different foods affect you, you can make smart choices when it's time to eat.

MyPlate (shown in Figure 2) was developed by the U.S. Department of Health and Human Services and the U.S. Department of Agriculture to help you visualize a balanced diet and make healthy choices about what you eat. The sections of the plate (and the accompanying cup) each represent one of the five food groups, and give you a visual idea of the proportions in which these food groups should fill up your plate to ensure you are eating a nutritionally balanced diet.

Every body is different, so the nutrients and calories you need to sustain a healthy diet and good health will be based on your age, gender, and activity level. However, eating in balance from all five of the major food groups and keeping fats, sugars, and salt to a minimum is smart for everybody. Figure 3 shows the recommended amounts in cups and ounces of the different food groups for someone eating 2,600 calories a day, which is the recommended average for a specific person's age, height, weight, and activity level. (For a more detailed explanation of MyPlate and the Dietary Guideline, visit www.choosemyplate.gov/.)

Armed with this information, you will be more prepared to read nutrition labels. Most food in the grocery store has a **Nutrition Facts** label (fruits and vegetables will not). This will give you information about recommended serving sizes, and what a serving includes in terms of calories, fat, fiber, protein, sugar, cholesterol, vitamins, and more.

Figure 2 MyPlate from the U.S. Department of Health and Human Services helps you easily visualize a balanced diet.

MyPlate: *A nutritional model developed by the U.S. Department of Health and Human Services and the U.S. Department of Agriculture to help you visualize a balanced diet and make healthy choices about what you eat.*

Nutrition Facts: *A label on packaged food that provides information about recommended serving sizes, and what a serving includes in terms of calories, fat, fiber, protein, sugar, cholesterol, vitamins, and more.*

Nutritional Guidelines: Mixing It Up

Below are some general suggestions that can help you eat a better, more balanced diet:

☐ *Eat a wide variety of foods.* By eating a lot of different foods, you will be more likely to get the essential nutrients you need.

☐ *Eat more vegetables.* Vegetables are a valuable source of fiber and many essential vitamins. Fiber (also found in fruits and certain grains) helps you digest your food.

ChooseMyPlate.gov

OMB Number 0584-0535

| Home | About Us | News & Media | Site Help | Contact Us |

Search website

[   ] [Go]

Subjects

- The Basics
  - *Food Groups*
  - *Tips & Resources*
  - *Print Materials*
  - *Interactive Tools*
- Specific Audiences
  - *General Population*
  - *Pregnant & Breastfeeding*
  - *Preschoolers*
  - *Kids*
  - *Weight Loss*
- Multimedia
- For Professionals
- Partnering Program
- Related Links
- Questions?

You are here: Home / Daily Food Plan

Daily Food Plan

Eat these amounts from each food group daily. This plan is a **2600** calorie food pattern. These amounts should maintain your current weight, which is above the healthy range for your height. It is based on average needs for someone like you. (A **31** year old **female**, **5** feet **8** inches tall, **200** pounds, physically active **30 to 60 minutes** minutes a day.) Your calorie needs may be more or less than the average, so check your weight regularly. To prevent weight gain, you may need to adjust the amount you are eating.

▶ **Grains**[1]	9 ounces	tips
▶ **Vegetables**[2]	3.5 cups	tips
▶ **Fruits**	2 cups	tips
▶ **Dairy**	3 cups	tips
▶ **Protein Foods**	6.5 ounces	tips

Click the food groups above to learn more.

[1] Make Half Your Grains Whole

Aim for at least 4.5 ounces of whole grains a day.

[2] Vary Your Veggies

Aim for this much every week:

Dark Green Vegetables = 2.5 cups weekly
Orange Vegetables = 7 cups weekly
Dry Beans & Peas = 2.5 cups weekly
Starchy Vegetables = 7 cups weekly
Other Vegetables = 5.5 cups weekly

Oils & Empty Calories

Aim for 8 teaspoons of oils a day.

Limit your empty calories (extra fats & sugars) to 360 Calories.

Last Modified: September 15, 2011 06:23 PM

View, Print & Learn More:

- ▶ Click here to view and print a PDF version of **your results.**

- ▶ Click here to view and print a PDF of a helpful **Meal Tracking Worksheet.**

- ▶ For a more detailed assessment of your diet quality and physical activity go to the **The Tracker.**

- ▶ You can view/print the **My Daily Food Plan Results** and the **Food Tracking Worksheets** for any or all of the 12 calorie levels.

- ▶ You will need the free Adobe Acrobat Reader plug-in to view and print the above PDF files.

Figure 3
ChooseMyPlate.gov provides recommended daily amounts of various categories of food.

☐ *Eat more fruits.* Fruits are a source of sugar, fiber, and Vitamin C. Vitamin C is believed to aid in fighting colds and helps strengthen skin tissue.

☐ *Eat more (whole) grains.* Grain products, including rice and products made from cereal grains, such as breads, baked goods, cereal, pasta, and macaroni, produce significant amounts of carbohydrates. Grains, like fruits and vegetables, tend to be low in fat and cholesterol. When choosing grains, look for whole grains, such as whole wheat bread, which are better sources of fiber and other nutrients than refined grains, such as white bread.

- □ *Drink more water.* Water is a nutrient and comprises approximately 60 percent of your body mass. It is essential for transporting nutrients to your body cells, excreting waste products, and regulating your body temperature.
- □ *Reduce fat and oils.* While oils and fats do make things taste good, unfortunately, they contain very few nutrients. Limit your fat intake and choose fat-free or low-fat dairy products and lean meats and poultry.
- □ *Reduce processed sugar.* Sucrose (common table sugar or cane sugar) provides energy, but your body will burn through it quickly and you'll feel tired or sleepy as a result. Jelly, jam, candy, and pastries are all foods high in sugar. The Nutrition Facts label will list, in descending order by weight, the ingredients in the food. If you see sucrose (table sugar), dextrose (glucose), lactose (milk sugar), fructose (fruit sugar), maltose (malt sugar), or syrup as the first ingredient, it means there is more sugar in the product than anything else.

A Little Planning Goes a Long Way

Now that you know a little more about what you should eat, let's take a look at how you eat. Eating well, like other life activities, requires some scheduling and planning. If your daily schedule is full or if you don't get hungry regularly, then a little planning can really help. Review your daily schedule, think about times you have breaks and times you usually get hungry, and specifically plan times to eat. Try to schedule times when you think you will be able to have a meal without rushing or being stressed. Try to spread out your meal times throughout the day and evening. Also, avoid eating right before going to bed, which can cause indigestion and interfere with your sleep.

Planning ahead will also help you snack healthy. Keeping healthy snacks with you can help you stay fueled between meals and prevent you from hitting the vending machine when you get hungry. Choose snacks like nuts, granola, and peanut butter crackers that provide energy and are satisfying.

Your health and energy level—which affect your ability to perform and succeed—depend on the small choices you make about how you fuel your body. The secret to maintaining your energy throughout the day, and a healthy body throughout your life, is to plan ahead.

Figure 4 If you do have to eat on the go, many vendors provide healthier alternatives to candy bars.

LO 2 Getting Enough Sleep

If you want to have the energy you need to succeed, in addition to balanced nutrition, your body needs sleep. When you sleep, you reduce fatigue and allow your body to recover and revitalize. Although sometimes you may feel you need to sleep less to get more work done, eventually you will feel drowsy and be forced to sleep.

How much sleep do you need? Everyone is different, but most adults need between 7 and 9 hours of sleep a night.

To see if you're getting enough sleep, try recording how much you sleep, when you sleep, and how you feel during the day. This can help you make smart choices about when you might need more sleep and might help you get to bed just a little earlier.

While the amount of time you sleep is important, the quality of your sleep matters too. If you get in bed early, but lie awake tossing and turning or keep waking up in the middle of the night, your sleep won't be restful, and you'll be dragging the next day.

Here are a few suggestions to help you get a good night's sleep:

☐ *Have a sleep routine.* Your body needs to get into a regulated pattern, an established biological rhythm, to properly rest and recover. If you stay up cramming the night before a test (and load up on caffeine to stay awake), you throw off that rhythm. Go to sleep and wake up at the same times every day—even if you don't have to go to class or work. Keeping the same sleep schedule each night will help you stabilize your body and regulate your internal clock, which is the key to good, consistent sleep.

☐ *Wind down.* As your sleep time approaches, slow down. Avoid high-energy activities, like studying or exercise, in the few hours before bed. Avoid caffeine and any prescribed medications that are stimulants. Wrap up your activities from the day, and make notes to yourself about what you need to do tomorrow, so you don't lie awake reliving your day or worrying about what you have to remember for tomorrow. Slowing down and closing out the day tells your body and your mind to relax, which will help you sleep better.

☐ *Keep it quiet.* Noise, whether a loud radio or television, a loud neighbor, or other activities in your house, can be highly distracting and interfere with rest and relaxation. If you can't control outside noise and you haven't adapted to it, consider using earplugs or a white-noise machine.

☐ *Reserve your bed for sleep.* Your bed acts as a cue for sleep. If you don't fall asleep after 10 to 15 minutes, get out of bed and do something else, preferably outside of the bedroom. If you stay in bed and don't sleep, you may start to associate the bed with not sleeping. (This is also why you should avoid studying in bed.) After 10 to 15 minutes, return to bed and try again.

☐ *Use relaxation techniques.* Use stress-management techniques like breathing exercises, progressive muscle relaxation, meditation, and visual imagery to refocus your attention and calm your body and mind.

☐ *Get regular exercise.* Getting exercise during the day will help you feel tired at night. But if you exercise right before you go to sleep,

Figure 5
It's important to get enough sleep so that you don't miss anything when you should be awake.

MY SUCCESS STORY

When she started college, Michelle wanted to take advantage of every opportunity. She joined several student groups, went to see lots of interesting speakers, participated in exciting service projects, and spent many late nights studying at the coffee shop with her new friends—although many of those "study" sessions involved more hanging out than getting work done.

At first, Michelle was having the college experience she hoped she would have. But then mid-terms hit, and with less and less time to fit everything in, she started sleeping less and less and fitting meals in when she could. Soon, she got so sick she couldn't go to class—coughing, sneezing, fever, the works. When she went to the student health center to get some help getting better, she got some unexpected questions instead.

"How much are you sleeping each night?" the nurse asked.

"Well, I usually go to bed pretty late, and I have to be up early for my first class. Maybe five or six hours," Michelle replied.

"How about meals?" the nurse asked. "Are you sitting down for breakfast, lunch, and dinner, or are you eating on the run?"

"Eating on the run," Michelle said sheepishly.

"Are you getting any exercise?"

"Does walking to class count?" Michelle asked.

"it's better than nothing," the nurse said. "But you're showing all the signs of someone who's trying to do too much and not taking care of herself. That's why you got sick. This time of year, lots of people get sick, and they assume it's unavoidable, that some kind of bug is going around. It may be true that something's going around, but when you get run down like you are—not sleeping enough, eating on the run, not getting much exercise—you suppress your immune system, so you can't fight off whatever is going around like you normally would. If you really want to get the most out of college, you need to make sure you take care of yourself first. Let's talk about some things you can do to make sure I don't see you in here again any time soon."

The nurse worked with Michelle to look at her sleep habits and to recommend some ways she could get more, and more restful, sleep. They talked about eating and identified ways that, even on the run, Michelle could eat a more healthful diet. And they also talked about some ways Michelle could get in some exercise too, in the small windows in her day. Michelle also decided she would cut back on some of her activities. She realized she simply couldn't do everything.

When she left the student health center that day, she still had a cough and was still congested, but she was feeling much better. She now had a plan to take care of herself and to put her health first, so she could really get the most out of her college experience.

your brain and muscles will be stimulated, which may keep you awake, so exercise earlier in the day.

☐ *Nap carefully.* For some people, a quick nap can be refreshing. For many, naps interfere with their sleep routine. If you are a napper, and it works for you, great. But if you are not usually a napper, but feel like you need to nap because of the new demands on you, be careful. Try out naps of different lengths, at different times, to find what works for you. If napping interferes with solid sleep at night, discontinue immediately.

LO 3 Getting What You Need from Exercise

Regular exercise is one of the main defenses against stress. Stress makes you weaker both mentally and emotionally, and your body becomes weaker and more vulnerable to illness and disease. Exercise, along with proper nutrition and sleep, can counteract your reactions to stress by strengthening your immune system and various organs in your body and giving you more energy. When you exercise regularly, you also make a positive affirmation about yourself. You take control—not the stress.

Understand that many things can be considered exercise. If you're not a runner or a weight lifter, that's just fine—the key is to find something you like to do that is active, will work your muscles, and will raise your heart rate. This could be

Figure 6
Moderate exercise can make you more energetic overall.

Figure 7
Exercise has some surprising benefits.

Health Benefits of Regular Physical Activity

Some of the health benefits of regular physical activity as outlined by the Department of Health and Human Services and the U.S. Department of Agriculture:

- Increases physical fitness
- Helps build and maintain healthy bones, muscles, and joints
- Builds endurance and muscular strength
- Helps manage weight
- Lowers risk factors for cardiovascular disease, colon cancer, and type 2 diabetes
- Helps control blood pressure
- Promotes psychological well-being and self-esteem
- Reduces feelings of depression and anxiety

dancing, walking, playing basketball, or even vigorous housecleaning! No matter your body type or health condition, exercise is valuable to everyone.

Getting the Exercise You Need Regularly

Often, the major obstacle to getting the exercise you need is finding the time. Just like finding the time to shop for groceries and eat right during the day, it's worth taking the time to plan exercise into your schedule.

The Past Two Days: What Did You Eat?

If you're serious about wanting to have more energy, stay fit, and feel good more often, then it's important to take an honest look at what you feed your body. The more you know about the nutritional value of what you eat, the better food choices you can make each day.

Instructions: The best way to understand your eating habits is to track them. Complete the quick self-report below, writing down what you ate and drank for the past two days.

To make things easier, if you are completing this exercise in the morning, then "Day 1" is what you ate yesterday. "Day 2" is the day before yesterday. If you are completing this activity in the afternoon or evening (after lunch or later), then "Day 1" is today, and "Day 2" is yesterday. Think carefully and try to record everything you ate!

In the first column, write down what you ate. In the columns to the right, provide an *estimate* of how many servings it was. One food item may fall into multiple columns. For example, if you eat a turkey

DAY 1

Food Item / Food Groups	Grains Bread Cereal Pasta Rice	Fruits	Vegetables	Milk Yogurt Cheese	Meat Fish Poultry Dry Beans Eggs Nuts	Fats Oils Sweets
Total (oz/cup)						
Recommended Servings	6 oz/day	2½ cups/day	2 cups/day	3 cups/day	5½ oz/day	Sparingly
Difference						

While planned exercise each day is the most optimal, it's not always the most practical. Yet you can still find time to exercise by making lots of small choices to be active. One easy option is regular walking. Even 30 minutes each day is beneficial—and those 30 minutes don't all have to come in one shot. If you can get up a few minutes early and walk 10 minutes before you leave the house, walk another 10 minutes at lunch, and 10 minutes more when you get home, it will make a difference. At the end of the day, it is the total amount that counts.

sandwich with lettuce and tomato for lunch, you would put the bread in the grains column, the lettuce and tomato in the vegetables column, and the turkey in the meat column.

At the end of each day, compare what you ate with the U.S. Department of Health and Human Services and U.S. Department of Agriculture's recommended servings for each group, and write down the difference in the bottom row.

Obviously, not every two days in your life will look just like the two days you just recorded, but those two days should give you a pretty good idea of what a typical eating day might look like.

This knowledge can frame the decisions you make the next time you sit down to eat, and help you eat a balanced diet that will give you the energy you need. As you go about making the small choices about what to eat multiple times each day, think about whether you are getting enough of the essential foods to stay strong. In short, how can you improve your future eating habits?

DAY 2

Food Item \ Food Groups	Grains Bread Cereal Pasta Rice	Fruits	Vegetables	Milk Yogurt Cheese	Meat Fish Poultry Dry Beans Eggs Nuts	Fats Oils Sweets
Total (oz/cup)						
Recommended Servings	6 oz/day	2½ cups/day	2 cups/day	3 cups/day	5½ oz/day	Sparingly
Difference						

II. Emotional and Mental Health

Name something you really like to do. Something that you look forward to or excel at.
Name something you dread. Something that you are either not very good at, or just don't like doing.

- Which is harder for you to do? Why?

In the last section, we discovered the importance of improving your physical health and some practical steps you can take to become healthier. In this section, we will take a closer look at emotional and mental health and give you some tools to be mentally and emotionally focused on success. You will understand the interrelationship between attitudes, perceptions, and behavior and be able to develop a positive attitude.

How successful you become depends on you. Learning to understand yourself and approach life with a positive attitude is one of the most significant steps you can take toward your own growth and a healthier, more productive, and more rewarding lifestyle.

Figure 8 Serious mental health issues should be taken directly to a professional, and there are many who work on a sliding scale.

LO 4 The Importance of Mental Health

In this section, we're going to focus on attitudes. These are key to emotional health and are also something we have control over.

However, mental health, in most cases, is not something we can control in the same way. Mental health problems can affect people regardless of age, gender, race, ethnicity, or socioeconomic status. The diagnosis and treatment of these problems are best dealt with by trained health professionals.

Moderate to severe signs of depression, schizophrenia, eating disorders such as anorexia or bulimia, panic or stress disorders such as PTSD (post-traumatic stress disorder), and substance abuse are just a few examples of issues that should be referred to a mental health professional for proper clinical intervention.

You can certainly do a lot to help as a family member, friend, or co-worker, and you can get a lot of support from these important people in your life if you are suffering from a mental health problem. However, if you are concerned for yourself or someone you care about, it is always best to seek out professionals with the appropriate education, training, supervision, and experience to diagnose and treat any mental health concerns.

Your campus health service or community resource center are excellent resources. There, you can consult with a counselor, or they can help you contact a private practitioner. Help is available. Do not be afraid to ask!

The Power of Emotional Health

Your **emotions** or feelings come in many forms and can be expressed in many ways. The term emotion is derived from the Latin word *moveo,* which means "to move." This is also the origin of the word *motivation,* which is understood as an internal process that directs your actions to some goal or targeted outcome. As you can see, emotion and motivation are related.

emotions: Feelings. Derived from the Latin word moveo, which means "to move." Emotions come in many forms and can be expressed in many ways.

Emotions are initially the physical response your brain has to some internal mental process, memory, or external change in the environment. Your brain recognizes the change, responds, and triggers your emotions. Emotions are subjective feelings that you have come to learn and perceive, such as fear, anger, love, joy, or happiness. These feelings then become displayed in your facial expressions, physical posture, body movement, and in the words you choose to convey them.

Being emotionally healthy means that you can function every day with clarity and intent. It gives you the ability to incorporate what you have learned from others, from society, from culture, and from the world around you into your life. Any change to and development in how you emotionally experience life begins by examining your attitudes.

LO 5 Positive and Negative Attitudes

What is an attitude? An **attitude** is a tendency to act toward yourself and others in a positive or negative manner as a reflection of your thoughts and beliefs. In this way, attitudes can be good predictors—that is, your attitude is a good indicator of how you will think, feel, and act when faced with a certain situation in the future.

attitude: A tendency to act toward yourself and others in a positive or negative manner as a reflection of your thoughts and beliefs.

Positive attitudes are positive feelings and beliefs that influence how we act toward someone or something, including ourselves. For example, if you feel good about someone, you will tend to have positive beliefs about that person and consequently act positively toward them. The same is true of yourself. Think about someone whom you respect, trust, and appreciate. How does this attitude about that person impact how you might react to her? Will you give her the benefit of the doubt, or will you be quick to judge if she makes a mistake?

Negative attitudes operate the same way. If you are unhappy with yourself (*a feeling*) and you believe yourself to be incompetent or inferior (*a belief*), then you will tend to act in a way that is self-demeaning (*an action*). While many things factor into success and failure, having a negative attitude, especially toward yourself, is almost a perfect recipe for being unsuccessful.

Attitude Development and Change

Where do your attitudes come from? How do you learn them? How did they develop? The root of many of our attitudes is personal experience. If you had an experience that left an impression on you, that impression is stored in your memory with the accompanying thoughts and emotions.

MONEY SMART$

Employee Benefits

Once you graduate and gain full-time employment in your chosen field, most employers will offer an "Employee Benefit Package" in addition to your salary. Being aware of and understanding the benefits offered to you can be a big part of your decision to choose one work environment over another. In some cases, employee benefits make up a significant percentage of an employee's total compensation.

Employers have the right to change or terminate any benefit plan or establish other plans. Employers also have the right to increase, decrease, or eliminate the amount of the company's contribution to any employee benefit plan. Here are some basics on employee benefits.

Vacation and Sick Pay Most companies offer some sort of vacation and sick pay benefit. Full-time employees usually get a certain number of days off for each year worked. One typical plan that is offered is two weeks per year of vacation pay (80 hours), and one week per year of sick pay (40 hours).

Vacation and sick pay benefits typically accrue over time, so don't expect to be able to take your annual two-week vacation in your fourth month of employment!

Saving for Retirement Your new employer may offer a benefit plan that will enable you prepare financially for retirement. There are many different kinds of plans, with varying qualifications and requirements, so it will be very important for you to read in detail about your plan once you qualify (some plans require one year on the job before the employee is eligible for the plan). Some types of employer-sponsored plans include:

- Defined benefit pension plans
- 401(k) and 403(b) plans
- Simplified employee pension (SEP) plans

Other sources of attitudes are your family and your encounters with others in school. Through these encounters you become exposed to different viewpoints, opinions, and attitudes. Some will be similar to your own, while others will seem different or unacceptable. This is particularly true during childhood. As you develop and mature, your family members, teachers, and even your peers have a strong influence on your attitudes. Teenagers and adults alike are subject to the powerful impact of peer pressure to conform to the values, standards, and attitudes of the group. In addition, the media has a strong influence on attitudes.

Yet changing your attitudes can be done, if you are open to it. If you believe it is too much or it's impossible, then you will fall victim to your own beliefs (your own negative attitude) and will likely prove yourself right. But with a positive attitude about yourself and about change, you will see that developing and changing your attitudes is something you *can* control. Here are some tips to help:

- ☐ *Be open-minded.* Be open to cultural, ethnic, racial, and social diversity. Interact with others, learn from them, and note how your new experiences impact your attitudes and expectations. Regardless of the past or what others have told you, give people a chance.
- ☐ *Be honest.* Be honest with yourself. College is not the time to judge yourself about your attitudes and beliefs. You are at a new stage in your life. Take an honest inventory of what you believe, your emotions, and your behaviors. Ask yourself "How do I relate to others?" Begin to make the decision to change what does not feel right to you.
- ☐ *Be optimistic.* Optimism—focusing on the positive and not the negative in a situation and in your life—will enhance your life. Pessimism—focusing on the negative—will only help you find things to criticize and add more stress to your life. If you feel down and frustrated, think about why you went to college

Health Benefits Your new employer may offer a health insurance package for you and your family. Most employers do not offer this benefit for free; however, the monthly cost is usually a small fraction of what it would cost to purchase the insurance on your own. The health benefit may or may not include dental and vision coverage. Another common benefit offered with health plans is a basic life insurance policy. If available, these additional benefits usually come at a small additional cost. Paying for health benefits is easy. Your employer will simply deduct your cost of the benefit from your regular paycheck.

There are numerous other benefits that employers can provide, depending upon the company and the job. Some employers offer tuition assistance if you choose to enroll in school while working. Some employers have a workout facility on-site at the company location so you can exercise before or after work. Still others may offer the employee the option to work from home for part of the time, including providing the

computer equipment and Internet access to be able to communicate with your co-workers.

Your new employer will be more than happy to discuss in detail the benefits offered to employees, so don't hesitate to ask about them. The best time to have this conversation is after you have been offered the position, but before you accept it.

Attitude Survey Exercise

In Part I of this activity, complete the following survey. Identify your attitudes toward each of the subjects listed by completing the sentence. In Part II, you will outline steps for how you might convert your negative attitudes toward certain subjects into positive ones.

PART I

Attitude Survey
Instructions: Complete the following sentences. There are no right or wrong answers. Your responses indicate only your attitudes.
My attitude toward . . .
my family is
being in college is
drug use is
death is
marriage is
pregnancy is
test taking is
people is
sports is
my childhood memories is
most men is
most women is
most children is
my co-workers is
different races is
poverty is
homelessness is
unemployment is
politics is
music is
dancing is
studying is
public speaking is
other religions is
divorce is
different cultures is

sleep is	
math is	
divorce is	
my boss is	
exercise is	
financial aid is	
road rage is	
stress is	
myself is	

PART II

For those subjects above toward which you have a negative attitude, describe some action steps you can take to develop a new, positive attitude. Also, identify how having a positive attitude toward this subject could be of benefit to you.

Subject 1:

Steps I can take: _____

_____

_____

Benefits to me for a positive attitude on this subject: _____

_____

_____

Subject 2:

Steps I can take: _____

Benefits to me for a positive attitude on this subject: _____

_____

_____

Subject 3:

Steps I can take: _____

_____

_____

Benefits to me for a positive attitude on this subject: _____

_____

_____

in the first place, and focus on your future. If something looks bad, ask yourself, "What's good?"

☐ *Be passionate.* Whatever you do, whether school, career, or family life, be passionate about it. Commit yourself to it, and make the decision to complete your undertaking, regardless of the obstacles. In other words, follow through with conviction. Approach each day with a purpose that is health- and life-affirming.

☐ *Be kind.* Most people think about being kind to others, but it's important to be kind to yourself too. Let go of any need to be self-critical. Be kind and compassionate to yourself as you might to someone else. Use positive thinking to reassure yourself that you have what it takes to succeed. Believe it!

While attitudes are emotional, one of the most significant benefits of establishing positive attitudes is physical—you'll have more energy. When you are engaged in something you like doing, you have more energy and enthusiasm. You will get much more accomplished in school or at your job, and you might actually have some fun doing it.

Your mental health is also affected by positive attitudes. If you are presented with a task and you approach it positively, you are more likely to complete it. When you are working with others, your positive attitude can motivate them to pursue and achieve their goals, too. A positive attitude can provide you with feelings of satisfaction, achievement, and growth.

Strategies for Maintaining Positive Attitudes

To succeed in college, the workplace, and in your personal life, you must believe in yourself and what you are capable of. The shift to a more positive mind-set will significantly impact your approach to your life as a student, an employee, and a member of society.

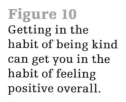

Figure 10
Getting in the habit of being kind can get you in the habit of feeling positive overall.

The key is to learn how to develop and maintain positive attitudes, even when times are tough. In the academic environment, one way is to focus on success. Remind yourself of what you have already accomplished, what goals you have already achieved, and what things about yourself you are most proud of. Give yourself credit for the work you've done, while acknowledging that work may still need to be done.

It can also help to remind yourself that you're doing the best you can with the skills, tools, and information you have, and you have lots more to learn. As you continue to learn, you'll build on past experiences and knowledge and keep getting better. Keep in mind that who you are and how you feel today is not permanent. It is a snapshot of a moment in time. Having a positive attitude toward yourself and school will help you remember that today's frustrations are temporary and help you shift any self-defeating attitudes into positive outcomes.

A positive attitude makes just as much impact in the workplace. An employee's performance is commonly evaluated on a number of criteria, one of which is attitude. For example, is your attitude positive? Is it helpful in assisting co-workers in their development? Does it contribute to teamwork and cooperation? Does your attitude lend itself to positive customer or consumer satisfaction?

Most people know what they do well and what they need to change and improve. To strengthen and maintain a positive attitude, invest in your own self-development and motivate yourself to reach your potential. If some day you own your own business, you will need to work hard and will face many challenges. A positive attitude will translate into a passion for your work and a personal commitment to succeed. In your personal life, surround yourself with people who tend to have positive feelings toward others. Spend time with people who differ from yourself, but share positive attitudes. Approach them in the context of openness and shared respect. The more we extend ourselves, the greater the possibility of positively changing and maintaining our attitudes.

III. Stress and Major Life Event Management

GET READY

You are learning to deal with stress all the time. Think about something you did today (drove your car, went to work, asked a question in class, etc.)

- Talk about the very first time you remember doing that.
- Were you nervous? Did it get easier?

The first two sections of this module have focused on physical, emotional, and mental health. And, throughout the discussion, we've talked repeatedly about *stress* as something that can be a challenge to your physical, emotional, and mental well-being.

But what exactly is stress? What causes it? How does it impact your overall health and wellness? And what can you do about it? *Should* you do something about it? In this section, we'll take a close look at stress and its effects, but most importantly, we'll learn how to manage stress so that you can succeed in college and life.

LO 6 Stress

The term **stress** has many definitions. There are many opinions about its sources and just as many theories on how to cope with it. Some of these theories focus on the biological causes of stress. Others focus on internal causes and solutions—that is, our own thoughts and emotions—while others point more to external influences in our environment.

No matter the reason behind it, stress can be defined as a complex personal reaction that occurs when you must respond to a situation that you perceive or experience as demanding or challenging. Any situation that causes stress is defined as a **stressor**. **Stress management** is how you handle the stress in your life.

stress: *A complex personal reaction that occurs when you must respond to a situation that you perceive or experience as demanding or challenging.*

stressor: *Any situation that causes stress.*

stress management: *How you handle the stress in your life.*

How Stress Works

Stress is an effect—a physical and emotional reaction to an external or internal source. When you experience a situation that you perceive as challenging or threatening, your brain responds and emits a signal that evokes an emotion, such as fear. This emotion triggers changes in your body: Your heart rate speeds up to pump more blood through your body and send it to your brain. Your breathing becomes faster and shallower. Your skin perspires more, and your palms may begin to feel clammy and sweaty. You may experience nausea or "butterflies" in your stomach. Your body is now alert, awaiting a decision about what to do next.

This sequence of physical reactions is a survival mechanism. It prepares you to adapt to or cope with the threatening or stressful situation. If you are faced with an immediate danger, your body is now ready with a "fight-or-flight" response.

In many situations, after the urgency of the stress has passed, your body will automatically return to a more relaxed state. For example, if you are walking down the street and suddenly hear the loud bark of a dog that you haven't seen, you will experience all of the stress reactions described above. Once you realize that the dog is behind a fence and on a chain and that there is no immediate danger, you will calm down and keep walking.

Most of the stress you experience doesn't call for a fight-or-flight response. For example, while the stress you feel about finals week is very real, it's also very different from the stress you feel from the barking dog.

Calming down from this kind of stress—in other words, managing the stress—is not automatic. You must take steps to use strategies and skills that send the message that the stress, demand, or challenge is not life threatening and can be managed.

Figure 11 Stress can make you feel physically and mentally run down.

Figure 12 Your body can't tell the difference between school stress and fear.

Your ability to adapt or cope through the use of stress-reducing strategies will allow you to take control and return your body to a more relaxed state. That's why understanding what stress is, and being able to identify the signs and symptoms of stress, is essential to managing stress effectively.

Physical and Mental Responses to Stress

When you are born, your body is preset for optimal levels of performance required for you to remain healthy. If you experience any change or disruption in body temperature, nutrition or fluid intake, sleep patterns, or activity level, your body will automatically seek to restore itself to its normal state.

However, when you are stressed or under strain for long periods, your body starts to experience a severe imbalance and will struggle to make things right. As your body works extra hard to combat the stress, you can become mentally and emotionally out of balance and physically susceptible to sickness and disease. That's why it's important to understand and take care of your body's primary needs and learn how to manage stress. When you take care of your body's needs—when you eat right, sleep well, and exercise—you will be better able to handle stress you experience. And, when you learn to manage stress, you can make sure that stressful situations and experiences don't throw your health out of balance.

Being able to recognize the common symptoms and effects of stress when they appear will alert you that you are experiencing a certain level of stress. Early detection helps you act before your stress level becomes unmanageable. See Table 1 on the next page for some common symptoms that result from stress.

Reactions that involve restless activity and muscle tension are often immediate and direct. Relaxation techniques and breathing exercises work well with these symptoms. Digestive symptoms include a loss of appetite, stomach butterflies, nausea, and stomach discomfort, including uncomfortable feelings of pain or pressure. These usually occur immediately and may require nutritional and active physical care. Dietary adjustments, such as proper nutrition, and avoidance of alcohol, caffeine, and nicotine during periods of stress may be helpful, as may exercise, like walking, swimming, or biking.

Table 1 General Stress Symptoms

The following are symptoms that you may experience when you are under stress. How many of these have you felt before?

Cardiorespiratory

- Heart feels like it is pounding
- Breathing is short and shallow
- Hand shakes or trembles

Restless Activity and Muscle Tension

- Muscles feel tight
- Feel the urge to pace
- Feel tension in shoulders and/or neck
- Feel tension in back
- Feel restless

Digestive

- Loss of appetite
- Butterflies in stomach
- Stomach feels uncomfortable

Indirect

- Feel fatigued and exhausted
- Headache
- Backache

Mental

- Worry too much about how difficult things are
- Worry too much about not knowing where I stand
- Worry too much about not having what it takes
- Worry too much about demands and pressures
- Take things too seriously
- Burdened by thoughts and worries

Emotional

- Feel discouraged
- Feel too irritated or annoyed
- Feel too much contempt
- Feel too much disgust
- Feel too shy
- Feel too fearful
- Feel depressed
- Feel anxious

Figure 13
Eating well, sleeping, exercising, and making reasonable plans can help you relax overall.

Indirect symptoms include feelings of fatigue and exhaustion, general physical heaviness, tension headaches, and backaches. These symptoms often present themselves as delayed signs of stress and may appear continually when you are experiencing ongoing stress. To relieve these symptoms, adequate rest and sleep, massage, and progressive muscle relaxation may prove beneficial.

Mental stress symptoms are reflective of negative thought patterns, self-defeating statements (e.g., "I don't have what it takes"), and unrealistic expectations (e.g., "I have to do things perfectly.") Often these thinking patterns reflect a need to be perfect, fear of failure, and/or fear of disapproval. To address these symptoms, you can change your negative thoughts and perceptions about yourself to positive ones and evaluate your self-expectations to determine how realistic they are.

Emotional symptoms often reflect feelings of frustration, fear of personal rejection, and an ongoing, persistent fear. Dealing with these symptoms involves expressing your feelings and increasing your awareness of feelings of powerlessness or lack of control.

LO 7 Coping with Everyday Stress

In your everyday life, you will face personal and professional challenges, some big, some small. You will react to physical, emotional, and psychological demands from family, relationships, work, school, finances, personal loss, and life events. You have probably come to accept these demands as part of being an adult, yet how you respond to them can make the difference between a healthy lifestyle and one troubled with poor health.

How can you adapt to stress? First, understand that you can't eliminate it. Stress is a part of life. Things won't go as you planned. Events will change and disrupt your comfortable routine. You will experience difficult circumstances beyond your control. Co-workers or fellow students will do something frustrating, maybe even something you have to fix.

Stress can be as big as losing your job or as small as getting stuck in traffic that makes you late for class. Unless you learn how to deal with the tension that comes from these situations, minor irritations can become major sources of stress, and major situations can become totally overwhelming.

Learning how to respond to stress requires using daily coping strategies and plenty of practice. The first step is to be patient with yourself. The next step is to think about how you have responded to stress in the past and to evaluate how effective your approach was. Based on your past experience, what can you do differently the next time you encounter a stressful situation?

Here's an example: The person next to you in class is disruptive, and you can't concentrate on the instructor. What would you do? Would you speak to the student, move to another area of the classroom, or speak to the instructor? Sitting there and putting up with it may seem like the easiest solution at the time, but how might that add to your stress level?

Time, or the lack of it, can also be a major cause of stress. If you struggle to get to school or work on time, do you need to make some adjustments to your schedule? Are you giving yourself enough time to do everything you need to beforehand? If you feel stressed about time, it may be a sign that you need to make a change—to both reduce your stress and become more effective.

Managing Stress While in College

A lot of college stress comes from minor situations—everyday annoyances and frustrations. Minor as they may be, these situations still tense your body and occupy your thoughts. Some people try to deal with the stress by smoking, drinking alcohol, or taking drugs. All of those stress-relief approaches have serious side effects and in the end will destroy your body, not strengthen it.

When faced with smaller everyday stresses, consider these approaches instead:

☐ *Take a break.* At any moment, something at school or work might make you irritable, impatient, or anxious. If so, take a break. Step back, breathe deeply, and pause. Step away from the situation and perhaps do something else, until you feel yourself calming down.

☐ *Work step by step.* When you have a lot to do, break the tasks into small steps. Taking it all on at once will make you feel overwhelmed and exhausted. It is better to perform well on small goals and make continual progress than to try to do too much and constantly feel incomplete and unfinished.

☐ *Get help.* At school and work, there are people who can help. Other students and your instructors are usually quite willing to lend a hand. After all, if someone asked you for help, wouldn't you help them? Explore your school's resources. Where can you find the help you need? When is it available? How do you obtain or request it?

☐ *Avoid procrastination.* Getting things done reduces stress, but putting things off increases it. Create a weekly to-do list and, most importantly, get started. Waiting until later does not make the project or situation easier, but it can make it overwhelming and extremely stressful.

Of course, there will be times when life or school throws you a curve, and the stresses are bigger. When this happens, consider these stress-management strategies:

☐ *Evaluate the situation.* Try to understand the situation, how you are feeling about it, and why. If you see it negatively, then that is probably how you are going to feel. On the other hand, if you see the situation as a challenge with a potential for a positive result, that is most likely how you will handle it.

☐ *Learn to compromise.* There are many things in life—including other people—that we cannot control. Be flexible and accept that nothing and no one is perfect. Accept also that sometimes you might not be able to immediately deal with the source of your stress. Nonetheless, continue to look for solutions.

☐ *Communicate.* Be open and willing to express how you feel. When confronted by the unexpected, we tend to feel defensive or deny that a particularly stressful event has occurred. Expressing yourself can release negative feelings, but holding on to negative feelings will make you feel worse. Your body will feel tense and your mind will be filled with worry. Let go of the negative, and visualize a positive outcome.

Figure 14 Try to create a relaxation plan to use when you're stressed.

Specific Stress-Management Techniques

In addition to the general stress-management strategies discussed above, several techniques have proven useful in reducing stress and dealing with some of its causes. With practice, these techniques can prove beneficial not only during your college years but throughout your entire life.

PROGRESSIVE MUSCLE RELAXATION (PMR) When you are stressed, your muscles naturally tighten up as your body prepares for fight-or-flight. Progressive muscle relaxation (PMR) is used to relax the muscles, lower blood pressure and pulse and heart rates, and slow down rapid breathing. This easy technique reduces tension by tensing and then relaxing each of your muscle groups one at a time. As you move through each group, your body will feel progressively less stressed and more relaxed. This technique takes about five minutes and can be done sitting or lying down.

Figure 15 You don't need any special training to take a deep, calming breath.

Health

ON THE JOB

Being Ready to Work

The pressure to perform well in school can be intense, and this module makes it clear that you can improve your chances of success by paying attention to your physical and emotional health. Your actions in this area can and will have an impact on your school performance, while at the same time enabling you to better manage the stress and pressure.

The same principles apply once you graduate and are working full time in your career. In the work environment, however, the stakes are much higher. Your employer will be evaluating your performance on an ongoing, possibly daily basis—your abilities to perform the skills of your profession, your ability to successfully interact with others in your work environment, and your overall ability to be responsible for the job tasks that are assigned to you.

Assuming you have the knowledge and skills for the job, practicing integrated health—taking care of your body and your emotional health and managing your stress levels—can be one of the most important factors for job success.

Woody Allen once said that, "80% of success is showing up." This famous quote has stood the test of time because of the surprisingly simple truth in its message. To be clear, for job and career success, "showing up" means more than just arriving at work each day on time.

Compare and contrast two employees who both arrive at the office on time at 8:00 A.M. Sally signs in and proceeds to her desk to turn on her computer and immediately begins reviewing her task list for the morning. She is well rested, had a great breakfast at home, and is eager to begin her day. Tom also arrives with Sally, but after signing in, he heads down to the break room and gets a cup of coffee. He is very tired this morning because he didn't get to bed until 1 A.M. the night before. While he's waiting for his coffee to brew, he takes a seat at the table and pulls out the muffin he brought with him (he didn't have time to eat breakfast at home because he slept late), and reads the front section of the newspaper. Twelve minutes later, he heads back to his desk but along the way, he stops and has a five-minute conversation

The first step is to pay attention to your breathing. Notice your breath becoming more even and regular, establishing a rhythm. Once your breath has reached a comfortable rhythm, start with your feet. Inhale and tense all the muscles of your feet and ankles. Exhale and relax both feet and ankles completely. You may feel a sense of heaviness in your feet. That is normal and a sign of relaxation. Next, inhale again and completely tense the muscles in your legs. Then exhale and relax. Continue up your body, repeating the procedure until you have gone through all the muscle groups. A typical progressive exercise might relax each of the muscle groups in the following order:

☐ Feet and ankles
☐ Calf muscles
☐ Thighs
☐ Pelvic area
☐ Abdomen
☐ Chest and back
☐ Neck and shoulders
☐ Facial muscles
☐ Arms
☐ Wrists and hands

Once you have completed the exercise, if any area still feels tense, focus on that area and tense and relax those muscles again.

with a co-worker about last night's baseball game that didn't finish until very late. At 8:20 A.M., Tom finally gets to his desk and turns on his computer. Tom *arrived* at work at 8 A.M., but he didn't *show up* until 8:20. His supervisor sees this and makes note of it. If Tom makes this a habit, he could put his job in jeopardy.

Trace Tom's work habits back to his choices in practicing a healthy lifestyle. Because his priorities are elsewhere, he is unable to get proper sleep and that has a negative impact on his job readiness and performance. To put it another way, if you were an employer paying employees to do a job, would you be happy if they were constantly using office time to recover from their busy personal lives?

POSITIVE THINKING What you feel and how you act is in part influenced by what you think, specifically what you think about and say to yourself. This *self-talk* directs your emotions and your behavior. Negative thoughts lead to negative emotions. When you tell yourself something negative about yourself over and over, you begin to believe it and identify with it, even if it's not true. Repeating negative thoughts reinforces their importance and strength and significantly

TAKE ACTION

Major Life Event

PART I

Stress can be experienced physically, mentally, and emotionally. Take a moment and reflect upon different situations or events in your life in which you feel stressed. What are the sources of the stress? How do you handle them? What helps you deal with it? To evaluate your personal reactions, first identify a situation in which you felt stressed. Then, place a check mark next to each of the symptoms that follow that best describe what you experience.

Describe stressful situation: _____

_____

_____

Symptoms that occur as a result of the stress:

Cardiorespiratory

_____ My heart feels like it is pounding.

_____ My breathing is short and shallow.

_____ My hand shakes or trembles.

Restless Activity and Muscle Tension

_____ My muscles feel tight.

_____ I feel the urge to pace.

_____ I feel tension in my shoulders and/or neck.

_____ I feel tension in my back.

_____ I feel restless.

Mental

_____ I worry too much about how difficult things are.

_____ I worry too much about not knowing where I stand.

_____ I worry too much about not having what it takes.

_____ I worry too much about demands and pressures.

_____ I take things too seriously.

_____ I am burdened by my thoughts and worries.

Digestive

_____ I lose my appetite.

_____ I feel butterflies in my stomach.

_____ My stomach feels uncomfortable.

Indirect

_____ I feel fatigued and exhausted.

_____ I have a headache.

_____ I have a backache.

Emotional

_____ I feel too discouraged.

_____ I feel too irritated or annoyed.

_____ I feel too much contempt.

_____ I feel too much disgust.

_____ I feel too shy.

_____ I feel too fearful.

_____ I feel too depressed.

_____ I feel too anxious.

contributes to intense feelings of stress. Here are some examples of negative thinking or self-talk:

- ☐ "I don't have what it takes."
- ☐ "I am not smart enough."
- ☐ "I am not good enough."
- ☐ "I am always worried about not knowing where I stand with others."

PART II

Now, describe a *major life event* that occurred in the past and describe what happened with regard to your stress level. Starting college could be considered a major life event. Others could include getting married, having a child, joining the military, moving to a new city, and so on. What happened to your stress level? If this occurs again in the future, how would you handle it or what stress-management techniques and coping strategies might you use?

Describe major life event _____

_____

_____

_____

What kind(s) of stress did you experience? _____

_____

_____

Based upon your experience and what you have learned in this module, how would you handle the situation if it were to

happen again? _____

_____

_____

_____

Negative self-talk usually involves the word "not," to deny that you have an ability, skill, talent, or other positive attribute. Recognizing negativity is the first step to changing it. Two strategies are most often used to change negative thoughts to positive ones:

☐ *Thought stopping.* This strategy simply replaces the negative thought with a positive one—in other words, it stops the negative thinking. The positive thought doesn't have to be the exact opposite of the negative one. For example, if the negative thought is, "I'm afraid I'll flunk that test," you don't need a positive thought that says, "I'm confident I'll ace that test." But you can say, "I'm glad this class is challenging me and that I still have time to study for that test." It's good to have a few thought-stopping statements ready so you can stop a negative thought quickly and not use the same one over and over.

☐ *Reframing.* This approach reframes, or re-labels, how you interpret a situation. This is similar to thought stopping, because the key is to first be aware of negative judgments you have of yourself. Watch for the words "never" or "always." For example, "I am never going to understand this material. I'm not good at this subject." Reframing that statement, you could say, "I'm struggling with this material, but I'm learning too. This may not be my best subject, but I know I can improve." With the reframed mind-set, you can improve your emotional functioning and improve performance.

TAKE TIME TO RELAX One of the most valuable things you can do for your mental, emotional, and physical health is simply taking time to relax. Your body and mind need downtime, and you have to make the choice to take it.

You don't have to go on a fancy vacation to truly relax, either. You just need to do something that will help you get away from the stress and grind of daily life, even if it's just for a little bit. Play music, go for a walk, visit with friends, go dancing, bake a cake, lay on the couch and read magazines—just make sure you do something you really enjoy. Taking time to settle down will help return your body and mind to a more peaceful and balanced state.

Practicing Integrated Health

To function in a healthy and productive way, your physical, emotional, and mental health must be integrated, meaning they must be in balance and harmony.

At any stage of development in your life, whether a toddler, a teenager, or an adult, you are an interwoven expression of your heredity, your experiences, and your own distinct personality and behaviors. How you structure your life, the decisions you make, the values you hold dear, and the attitudes that drive your actions are all influenced by these three factors.

These factors also impact your physical and emotional health and your awareness of yourself as a whole, complete, and unique individual living life with purpose and meaning. Understanding how life events can either help or hurt

Figure 16
Taking time to relax and do nothing for a while is just as important as eating and sleeping.

your overall health and well-being will help you develop, make choices, handle stress, and foster and sustain a fulfilling way of life.

By understanding the relationship between physical, mental, and emotional health, you will be able to strengthen your ability to respond to obstacles and stressful events, and see them as opportunities for learning. By recognizing what causes you stress, and how you react to it, you will be able to use different stress-management techniques as well as daily coping strategies to handle it. Nobody can eliminate stress from their lives; everybody's life has some stress in it. But you can learn how to manage the stress that is a natural part of your life, so that you can stay healthy and in control.

SUMMARY

Successfully taking care of your health and wellness means applying the things we have discussed in this module. Eating nutritionally and choosing a variety of healthy foods will help you reduce the chance of illness and supply your body with the nutrients it needs each day to produce the energy your busy life requires.

Getting enough rest and a good night's sleep will help you be more productive and alert and will improve your ability to learn. Committing yourself to regular physical activity will increase your energy and help you have a stronger body.

To live a balanced life, it's important to take care of your mental and emotional health as well as your physical health. A key component of emotional health is a positive attitude. Keep in mind that attitudes are not fixed. They can change, helping you learn and grow.

Stress is unavoidable, but you can do many things to manage and reduce it. By working to manage your stress, you contribute to your mental, emotional, and physical health.

By pursuing integrated health and paying attention to all the things we have discussed in this module, you are choosing a lifestyle that will dramatically improve your success in school, professionally, and throughout your life.

DISCUSSION QUESTIONS

1. Does being in a college environment make it easy or difficult to eat well? What specific things make it challenging to eat well as a student at your college? What things make it easy to eat well? What could your college do to make it easier for students to eat more healthy meals?

2. When was the last time you saw how someone's attitude affected his words, behavior, or decisions? Do you think that person was aware of his attitude? When was the last time your attitude affected something you said, did, or decided? Looking back on that situation, did your attitude help or hurt? What can you learn from that situation?

3. What can you do to help relieve stress for a fellow student? What sorts of things would you want other students to do that could help you manage your stress? How could you get more students to help each other deal with stress?

attitude: A tendency to act toward yourself and others in a positive or negative manner as a reflection of your thoughts and beliefs. (p. 13)

emotions: Feelings. Derived from the Latin word *moveo,* which means "to move." Emotions come in many forms and can be expressed in many ways. (p. 13)

MyPlate: A nutritional model developed by the U.S. Department of Health and Human Services and the U.S. Department of Agriculture to help you visualize a balanced diet and make healthy choices about what you eat. (p. 4)

Nutrition Facts: A label on packaged food that provides information about recommended serving sizes, and what a serving includes in terms of calories, fat, fiber, protein, sugar, cholesterol, vitamins, and more. (p. 4)

stress: A complex personal reaction that occurs when you must respond to a situation that you perceive or experience as demanding or challenging. (p. 20)

stress management: How you handle the stress in your life. (p. 20)

stressor: Any situation that causes stress. (p. 20)

REFERENCES AND CREDITS

References

Department of Health and Human Services and the U.S. Department of Agriculture. (2005). *Dietary guidelines for Americans 2005.* Retrieved February 1, 2009, www.healthierus.gov/dietaryguidelines

Department of Labor. (2005). *Employment law guide* (Publication OASP-01). Washington, DC: U.S. Government Printing Office.

Ellis, A. (1962). *Reason and emotion in psychotherapy.* New York: Lyle Stuart.

Holmes, T. H., and Rabe, R. H. (1967). The social readjustment rating scale. *Journal of Psychosomatic Research, 11*(2), 231–218.

Renner, M. J., and Mackin, R. S. (1998). A life stress instrument for classroom use. *Teaching of Psychology, 25*(1), 46–48.

Smith, J. C., and Siebert, J. R. (1984). Self-reported physical stress reactions: First- and second-order factors. *Biofeedback and Self-Regulation, 9,* 215–227.

Figure and Photo Credits

Chapter opening photo: David Buffington/Getty Images

Figure 1: Tanya Constantine/Brand X Pictures/Jupiterimages

Figure 2: U.S. Department of Agriculture. ChooseMyPlate.gov Website. Washington, DC. Current Graphics. http://www.choosemyplate.gov/global_nav/media_resources.html. Accessed October 26, 2011.

Figure 3: U.S. Department of Agriculture. ChooseMyPlate.gov Website. Washington, DC. Daily Food Plan.

http://www.choosemyplate.gov/myplate/results.html?name=undefined&age=31&gender=female&weight=200&heightfeet=5&heightinch=8&activity=low&originalweight=200&validweight=1&validheight=1&weightN=126&heightfeetN=5&heightinchN=8&option=9. Accessed October 26, 2011.

Figure 4: © The McGraw-Hill Companies, Inc./John Thoeming, photographer

Figure 5: © Mike Kemp/Getty Images

My Success Story: Image Source/Getty Images

Figure 6: Blend Images/Getty Images

Figure 7: Department of Health and Human Services and the U.S. Department of Agriculture.

Figure 8: © Andrea Morini/Getty Images

Figure 9: © image100/PunchStock

Money Smarts: ©Sam Toren/Alamy

Figure 10: © Digital Vision/Getty Images

Figure 11: Ingram Publishing/SuperStock

Figure 12: Jose Luis Pelaez, Inc/Getty Images

Table 1: Adapted from Smith & Siebert (1984).

Figure 13: Royalty-Free/CORBIS

Figure 14: © John Lund/Drew Kelly/Sam Diephuis/Blend Images LLC

Figure 15: © Royalty-Free/Corbis

Health on the Job: ©Siri Stafford, Gettyimages

Figure 16: Matthias Tunger/Getty Images

Building a **Career** Foundation

LEARNING OUTCOMES

In this module, you will:

1 Learn how your habits affect your pursuit of career success.

2 Examine how behaviors impact your effectiveness in different situations.

3 Discover the attitudes employers look for in a new hire, and the importance of practicing them while you are in college.

4 Understand how getting involved on campus can help prepare you for your career.

5 Explore opportunities to get involved in your chosen career field while still attending college.

6 Build a résumé to be ready for work opportunities that may present themselves while you attend college.

Words can be very powerful. The right words can change your life when they lead to actions.

- What are some powerful phrases? They can be mottos, advertisements, or movie quotes.
- What is it about those phrases that feels powerful to you?

Building a career foundation begins early. Believe it or not, you've been preparing for your career your whole life. Learning how to make new friends, play fairly, and interact respectfully with others are all skills you had to learn to get along with other children, and those same skills contribute to success in your adult life—especially your work life. Remember learning how to get ready for school, how to show up to class on time, and how to complete work assigned by your teacher? How about learning the consequences of your actions when you misbehaved and when you excelled? These important things, along with many others you learned as a child, are just as important as you launch a new career.

Employers need and want the skills you will have as a college graduate. But employers need and want more than just a set of skills. They need a person who can become an integral member of a team and be a positive influence on others in the workplace. They want someone who will make their lives easier, not harder.

Hiring a new employee is a big, expensive decision. For an employer, a "good" hire exceeds expectations and a "poor" hire fails to do so. Many of those expectations are listed in the formal job description, but those expectations are usually limited to tasks, responsibilities, and duties. An employer's true expectations for a new hire usually go well beyond what's listed in the job description to include the habits, behaviors, and attitudes that person brings to the job. This module will examine how to develop those qualities to not only meet your next employer's expectations, but also exceed them.

How you plot your career path also contributes to your ultimate level of career success. The more you know and understand about your potential career, the better decisions you can make and ultimately the more control you can exert on your career path.

Your career foundation is many things, and it's never too early—or too late—to prepare to make the most of the career opportunities that lie ahead for you.

I. The Habits, Behaviors, and Attitude That Lead to Career Success

Think for a moment about enjoying a successful 20-year career working at a job you love, in an industry that you are passionate about. What would it take to make that dream a reality?

A career like that begins with an opportunity to break in to the industry with an entry-level job. If you take that job knowing that the job and the industry are a good fit, and invest your best energy and effort into it, your hard work will be rewarded with promotions and raises throughout your career until it's time to call it quits and retire. If you aren't sure about the job and the industry, you may decide to switch careers midstream, moving to a completely different industry and job, sometimes doing this several times before retiring. Or you may start your career in a job and industry without knowing whether it is a good fit, but discover that the industry suits your skills and interests, and grow into it over time, turning a *job* into a *career.*

Figure 1
Employers are interested in your diploma, but also how well you work with others.

Although you can take different paths to a happy and successful career, education and skill development can help you find greater success no matter your career or path. Of course, you know this already—that's why you're in college. Attending, and especially finishing, college will be a very important contributor to your long-term career satisfaction and success.

While some measure of your success depends on finding a job and an industry that are a good fit for your skills and interests, arguably an even greater part of your success depends on what you bring to that industry and job. Regardless of your career path, certain individual characteristics will help or hurt your chances for reaching your career goals. Do you know what these are?

LO 1 Your Habits

As defined above, a **habit** is an "automatic" pattern of behavior that someone does repeatedly. We often perform habits without thinking about them or at least without giving them very much thought. For example, when you brush your teeth, you probably don't need to think much about what you're doing. You've done it so many times, your brain can just go on autopilot.

> *habit:* *An automatic pattern of behavior in reaction to a specific situation; may be inherited or acquired through frequent repetition.*

Habits help relieve us from having to consciously control every aspect of our lives. In other words, they free us to be able to do one thing and think about another. For example, when you compose words on paper, you don't have to think about forming the individual letters. The writing habits (penmanship) you developed as a child free your mind to think mostly about the words and message you want to communicate.

However, let's say you'd like to handwrite a letter to your friend. But because your penmanship has become so poor (you mostly write now using a computer), you know that the only way your friend will be able to read your writing is if you slow your writing way down and concentrate much more on the clarity of each letter of each word. If you've ever tried it, writing with a focus on legibility *and* conveying a message at the same time is much more difficult and requires your brain to work much harder than just writing to convey your message.

Like the penmanship skill example above, habits are developed by repeating the same action or thought pattern (that is, behavioral habits) and are usually referred to as being either "good" or "bad." Bad habits include smoking, drinking too much alcohol on a regular basis, constantly being late, paying bills late every month, and so on. Good habits include exercising regularly, eating healthy and nutritious food, getting enough sleep each night, regularly brushing your teeth (and flossing!), and maintaining a regular study schedule.

> *"A habit is something you can do without thinking—which is why most of us have so many of them."*
>
> —FRANK A. CLARK

Learning New Habits

Since habits are learned through repetition, you can learn new habits—good or bad—by repeating a new behavior. The challenge to developing a new, good habit is that, for the action or behavior to become a habit, you have to consciously think about it each time you do it until the habit is formed. There are

Figure 2
Having a reliable bedtime and morning alarm can get you in the habit of waking up on time.

many theories on just how much conscious repetition it takes to form a new habit, but everyone seems to agree that the action must be repeated over and over and that it must be repeated over a period of time.

To understand just how challenging this can be, let's look at Tim. Tim is a college student who for his first six months of school walked in to every class, every day, between 5 and 9 minutes late. In his mind, he wasn't late unless he was at least 10 minutes late, so he made every effort to be in his seat before that 10-minute limit was reached. One day, one of his instructors pulled Tim aside after class to have a word with him. "Tim, you seem to be a bright young man who could go far in life. Let me tell you something: A famous man once said, '80 percent of success is showing up.' That will be all, Tim."

Tim thought about what his teacher said and after a couple of days, he realized that he wasn't really showing up to class. He was showing his instructors, his fellow students, and the school administrators who saw him walking down the halls after class had started that he had other priorities ahead of school. So Tim decided to make showing up a part of his life—a new habit.

This meant a pretty drastic change in Tim's daily routine. To make it to his first class, he needed to leave home at least 20 minutes earlier than he had been leaving to be 100 percent sure he'd be in his seat before his first class started. That meant he had to start waking up earlier, which meant he had to go to bed earlier. And those were just the changes he had to make for his first class of the day! He had to make adjustments for every other class and scheduled obligation he was chronically late for as well.

Tim struggled through this change for most of the rest of that term. When the new term started, though, he found he had to think less and less about it, because he had developed a new habit around giving himself enough time to be able to show up. Tim's instructors noticed the difference almost immediately. They no longer had to worry about giving him lower grades for tardiness. Ultimately, he became a strong student that his school's career center director felt confident in when helping to set him up for job interviews as he neared graduation.

> *"Motivation is what gets you started, habit is what keeps you going."*
>
> —JIM RYUN

Think about some of your daily routines and habits. Do they contribute to your school and career success, or are they a detriment?

Read through the list of behaviors below. Do you have good habits related to these behaviors, or bad habits?

- ☐ Being on time to appointments, class, work, and meetings with friends
- ☐ Getting enough rest, exercise, and eating healthy
- ☐ Reading a newspaper or other news source on a daily basis
- ☐ Keeping your schoolwork organized
- ☐ Dressing for success
- ☐ Spending and saving

This is just a short list, but it may get you thinking about habit changes you could make that would be beneficial. As you consider the list, be objective and be honest. If you have bad habits in any of these areas now, you will likely be at a disadvantage in the workforce. So, if you find that change is in order, the time to work on it is now, before it costs you money.

Unlike a habit, **behavior** is associated with actions and responses to individual situations. For example, how does a father react when his baby starts crying? How do your speech, dress, and actions differ when going out with friends to a club versus going to a work-related holiday party? Like habits, your behaviors in school, with family and friends, and especially at work play a large role in your ongoing success within each area.

behavior: *Manner of behaving, whether good or bad; mode of conducting one's self; conduct; deportment; carriage.*

Behaviors are so important because in these situations, like it or not, performance counts. Your behaviors tell others a great deal about your capabilities for performing the task at hand.

Behaviors in a Business Setting

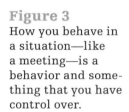

Figure 3
How you behave in a situation—like a meeting—is a behavior and something that you have control over.

Let's take a common example from a business setting. Have you ever worked with a know-it-all? These are good people whose behaviors can annoy those around them. In the workplace (and many college settings), group work is common. In these settings, everyone's contribution and input has value. That's why each person has been chosen to be a member of the group. Yet too often, a know-it-all will take over the group meeting, constantly offering their ideas and opinions and not giving others the opportunity to speak. If they do let someone

else talk, the know-it-all will often openly disagree with that person, giving them a choice between two bad options—start an argument with the know-it-all in front of the group or let the know-it-all have his way.

The know-it-all's behavior is demotivating to others in the group, and until the supervisor steps in (unless the supervisor *is* the know-it-all!), everyone's motivation could suffer and overall group performance could go down. So how can the know-it-all improve his performance in a group setting and stop annoying everyone else? A few simple behavior modifications will solve the problem.

The know-it-all needs to be coached to do two things—improve his listening skills (he's jumping to conclusions before the idea gets a full discussion by the group) and treat others more respectfully. It's rude and selfish to take over a conversation and even worse to belittle someone's thoughts in front of others. Instead of disagreeing with the co-worker's input, the know-it-all can respectfully acknowledge the input. Consider these two different ways of responding to an idea from James:

> *Before:* "That idea won't work, James. I can't believe you would even think that it would!"
> *After:* "That's an interesting idea, James. How do you think it would work?"

Another approach is to encourage more discussion about the idea, to let others draw their own conclusions about whether it's a good idea or not.

> *Or:* "That's an interesting idea, James. Let's try to figure out a way to make it work within the scope of the project at hand. What does everybody else think?"

This response acknowledges the idea and then gives James and others an opening to try to make it work. It's important to note that the know-it-all never actually knows it all—and so ideas he think might be ridiculous may be in fact good ideas.

You can see how one simple behavior—your actions and responses in a group setting—can have a big impact on the performance of the group, as well as others' impressions of you.

Improving Your Behaviors

> *"Quality means doing things right when no one is looking."*
>
> —HENRY FORD

Once you recognize your behavior, practicing an improved version is not difficult, though it does take effort. But recognition must come first. In the example above, our know-it-all may not have realized how destructive his behavior in a group setting was until someone pointed it out. After all, in his mind, he was just being honest when he was telling others how bad their ideas were. This know-it-all isn't made up—and in real life, after some brief coaching to recognize the problem, he became a much better team member whose opinion was respected by others. This is one of the basic premises of the field of behavioral psychology, that behaviors are learned. Good behavior is not for just certain people. It can be practiced, improved upon, and *learned.*

Now, consider your own behaviors in the following areas:

☐ Ethical decision making and conduct
☐ Working in a group (as in the example above)
☐ Working on your own or remotely (away from an office)

- [ ] Attention to quality and detail
- [ ] Effort and determination to complete a task
- [ ] Preparation
- [ ] Being proactive versus reactive

All of these areas apply to the work environment. How you behave within them will affect your career progression. Simply put, positive behavior in these areas will translate to greater long-term career success and possibly higher earnings.

Consider your actions within these areas, and see if there are any that you may be able to improve. Just as in business, these areas apply to your efforts in college as well, so there is no better time than now to make necessary adjustments, practice them, and build solid habits that will serve you well in any environment.

LO 3 Your Attitude

We've talked about your habits and behaviors. Now let's look at the one that impacts both of those and more: your **attitude**. Habits and behaviors are pretty specific and concrete (if your habit is being late, you can be sure your co-workers or fellow students will accurately describe you as always being late). Attitude is subtler. It reflects your state of mind—how you truly and honestly think about things. It's hard to hide your attitude, because you reflect it outwardly, through body language, facial expressions, voice inflections, and the words you choose to convey a message.

attitude: *A complex mental state involving beliefs and feelings and values and dispositions to act in certain ways; "he had the attitude that work was fun."*

Even though attitude is more subtle to read than habits and behaviors, in some respects, your attitude carries more importance and greater influence on how others feel about you than either your habits or behaviors. In a work environment, your job productivity will be evaluated largely on your behaviors and to some degree on your habits. Yet your overall value to the growth of the organization will be judged by your attitude *as perceived by your supervisor and co-workers.* And that is the challenge. It's difficult to control others' thoughts about you, especially

Figure 4 Bad behaviors and habits can hold you back, but with some guidance, they can also be changed for the better.

MY SUCCESS STORY

Success stories come in all shapes and sizes. David Barnes' story is big—he's a big man, with a big heart and big aspirations. But what sets him apart is his big job performance.

David was not your typical college student. His first career was a four-year stint in the United States Marine Corps in which he served in Kuwait during Operation Desert Storm. He then had a successful (but short) career driving 100-car freight trains across the country, which was cut short after a serious job injury.

Having to start over again, David went back to school at Platt College in Ontario, California, to learn a completely new skill, creative art, which had been a passion of his since he was a child.

While earning his degree in visual communication and learning the technical skills he needed for his career, David applied the attitude and discipline that he learned during his years in the military. On any given day at school, David was the first student to arrive in class and the last to leave—a habit he carries to this day on the job. David's attitude in school could best be described as a "sponge on steroids." He wanted to learn and practice his new trade as much as possible, as he knew the time would come when he'd have to demonstrate his new skills where it really counted—on the job.

While in school, David met Dan Byram, president of Curriculum Technology, LLC, a learning solutions company, when David was hired to complete a small design project. After graduating, Dan contacted David again , asking if he could help fix a big problem with a major project. David would have to immediately take on a leadership role with the project team.

Through a combination of technical skills he learned at Platt College, work habits that put everyone on notice that he was a serious member of the team, work behaviors that demonstrated his desire for excellence, and an attitude that inspired those who had been struggling so much before, David led the team through the project to completion and, ultimately, customer satisfaction.

"Our project was over budget, our client was not happy, and there was no end in sight until David came in and applied his skills and a solid work ethic to help us achieve a successful outcome. We knew immediately that we wanted David to be a long-term member of Curriculum Technology," said Dan. "Since then, David has become a significant leader in the company, taking on the title of director of technology solutions."

Clearly, David has utilized his training and skills learned through his college experience. It is also clear that David brings much more to the job—traits that employers look for in every new hire.

when those thoughts are placed in the context of everything else that's going on in their lives at that moment.

To complicate matters, the attitude that others perceive you to have may not be the same as you actually feel. You may walk into the office in the morning feeling like you are ready, willing, and able to take on the world; however, because it's your *habit* not to smile and acknowledge your co-workers on your way to your desk (you're focused on creating a mental to-do list on your way to work each day), they could perceive your *attitude* to be aloof or not a team player.

You're the Boss

In this activity, you will play a role that many people aspire to for their own careers.

As a successful business owner of a small but profitable company, one of your most important responsibilities is to interview and approve every new hire into the company. Your company is big enough that you have managers reporting to you who conduct the initial résumé review and first-round interviews. When one of your managers finds someone she wants to hire, she then brings that person back for a second interview with more of the staff and the rest of your managers, finishing off the day with an interview with you.

After the interviews, the managers who interviewed the candidate meet to discuss the candidate and make a yes or no hire decision. During this process, you listen carefully and usually agree with the group's decision. As the owner of the company, you have the power to make the final decision, and sometimes your decision goes against the group's desire. Everyone who is a part of the process appreciates the opportunity to voice their opinion. After all, they may have to work side by side with this new candidate for eight hours a day, five days a week!

In your experience, how a new employee works within your company culture can be just as important as his or her skill set. You know that your business requires that your employees work together and communicate together on a daily basis, and without that effective communication, productivity suffers.

In this activity, you will create a list of standard interview questions that you'd like to ask as the owner of the business. The form below is divided into three sections: the worker's *Habits*, *Behaviors*, and *Attitude*. Write three interview questions for each section, and then share and discuss them with your classmates.

Interview Questions for My Business

Habits

Question 1:

_____

_____

Question 2:

_____

_____

Question 3:

_____

_____

Behaviors

Question 1:

_____

_____

Question 2:

_____

_____

Question 3:

_____

_____

Attitude

Question 1:

_____

_____

Question 2:

_____

_____

Question 3:

_____

_____

Does taking the role of the employer who is asking the questions give you a better understanding of the qualities a hiring manager might be looking for beyond just being able to "do the job"? For each question you wrote, consider how you would answer the questions in an interview situation. Does this perspective give you a realistic idea of the impression you might give in an interview?

Based upon your own answers, what can you do, starting now, to improve those answers and give yourself the best chance of landing that job when the opportunity presents itself? List one or more ideas:

1. _____

2. _____

3. _____

4. _____

5. _____

6. _____

7. _____

Once you arrive at your desk, your supervisor's *habit* is to come to you and ask how the "big project" is progressing, and you always light up with excitement about how well it's going and how great the client is going to love it. Your supervisor walks away feeling that your attitude is great. So without even trying, you've helped to create one perception about you among your co-workers and a different one from your supervisor.

Taking Control of Your Attitude

"Attitude is a little thing that makes a big difference."

—WINSTON CHURCHILL[1]

Like habits and behaviors, you can control your attitude and use that power appropriately to convey to others how you feel, giving them a positive impression: the impression that your attitude is excellent and nothing is going to hold you back from achieving success. First, understand that you must actually have a positive attitude to convey one. If your attitude is negative (i.e., "I hate my job"), it's hard to hide that. Eventually, the truth will be known, and it's then that action is usually taken—either by you in the form of an attitude adjustment or by your employer in the form of an employment adjustment.

Figure 5 Even if you don't feel positive on a given day, if you're in the habit of behaving positively, that can carry you through.

Now, consider the signals that you send that others perceive and process into judgments about your attitude:

☐ The manner, pace, and energy with which you walk (yes, walk!). Walking briskly, with shoulders back and head held high, tells others you have places to go and people to see. A slow shuffle with your head down and shoulders slouched tells everyone the opposite.

☐ The way you greet your co-workers and supervisor. Do you look them in the eye, give a warm smile, and ask how they are? Or is being friendly an afterthought as you walk away from them before they can connect with you? The former says you care, the latter says you don't.

☐ The quality of the attention you give others when discussing work topics, individually or in meetings. Do you look them in the eye, listen to what they have to say, then respond positively? Or do you check text messages on your phone while someone is speaking to you? The former says you are focused on the important work topics being discussed, the latter says you have more important things to do.

☐ The manner in which you convey information. Is it from a positive point of view or a negative one? Successful people want to be around positive people. They shy away from negative ones.

This list could be summed up with the old expression, "Be here now." Just like the bad (and dangerous) driver who weaves all over the road while checking text messages, it's very hard to be an effective employee if you are doing or thinking something else besides the task at hand. In the example above, when you are walking down the hall to your desk in the morning is the time to greet your co-workers, set a good impression, and inject some positive energy into the office. Either write your to-do list at home or wait until you settle in to your desk to shift your focus on the day's tasks. Your attitude is like a beacon for others to follow—make yours shine brightly and others will naturally gravitate toward you.

II. Getting Involved in Your Career Field

GET READY

Everyone gets nervous about something, but sometimes nervous energy can help!

- Share an event you prepared for that made you nervous, like a big game, giving a speech, or meeting new people.
- How did you prepare and how did you feel when it was over?

You enrolled in college to gain the knowledge and skills needed for future career endeavors. Earning a diploma is obviously another big reason to enroll in college, as many employers won't hire you for your knowledge and skills unless you can show that you successfully completed your program of study.

As you work on a daily basis toward that diploma, it may seem hard to imagine, but your time at college will go by very quickly. Before you know it, you will be thrust into a new reality of searching for and landing your first job out of college. Or, if you are currently working—possibly full time while attending school—there will come a day when you will have the opportunity to put your diploma to use, either to gain a promotion or to change career fields.

Yet while you keep your eye on the finish line, it would be wise to consider what else you can do while working toward your diploma that will help you once you finish school. Perhaps you have heard something like this from one (or more) of your instructors:

"I expect you to come to school and treat this part of your day with the same focus, sense of responsibility, and productivity as will be expected of you once you are out on the job. The time to practice the skills you'll need to be successful is now—when you make a mistake in school, you have the opportunity to learn from it and practice it again. If you make the same mistakes on the job, your employer may not be so sympathetic."

The more practice you can get right now, and in the coming months and years, the better prepared you will be when the time comes to put your knowledge to work on the job.

Figure 6 Tests aren't the only measure of your success; find activities related to your career and start networking now!

What more can you do besides attending classes and studying? Even as a student, you have many opportunities to get involved in your chosen profession. Some of those opportunities will come simply as a result of being enrolled in your program. For example, if your program includes an externship, you will soon have no choice but to get *very* involved in your career field. Other opportunities may be available, but only if you seek them out and actively pursue them.

In most, if not all cases, the big difference between these activities and simply attending class is that you are the one who brings the commitment to the activity. You can either choose to get involved or not. When on your externship, your commitment, responsibility, and performance is completely up to you. For these reasons, employers often lean toward hiring those who have gone above the minimum required to get through school. They know that these applicants are more likely to have the habits, attitudes, and behaviors that will lead to success in the workplace. Let's now explore some of them and learn more about how getting involved now can pay off in a big way down the road.

LO 4 Campus Involvement

Every campus offers numerous ways to get involved in your career field early on. Begin with your **career services** department. If you haven't personally sat down with someone from that department to discuss its services, that should be at the top of your to-do list. Through your typical career services department, you'll find out about:

- ☐ *Upcoming career fairs.* Even if you are not ready to start interviewing for work, it doesn't hurt to attend these and try to get to know some of the companies that are there. In fact, it can be easier to begin a conversation with a company if you are just curious about them and would like to know more.
- ☐ *Work-study programs.* In addition to externships, some schools and programs offer a work-study option in which you can earn credit for working at an approved part-time job.

career services: *The college department focused on supporting students in their career search. Services include résumé assistance, interview prep, externship placements, and career advising.*

☐ *Résumé writing assistance.* You'll want to have a strong résumé that makes a good case for you as a job candidate. Most career services departments offer résumé-writing workshops and personal consultations to help you get your résumé in good shape.

☐ *Externship interviews and placement.* When the time comes, you'll be sent on an externship interview. This experience will usually be no different than a regular job interview. Letting the career services representative get to know you will make him better able to place you in the best externship sites for your needs.

☐ *Job interviews.* An effective career services department will work with you to set up job interviews for you prior to graduation. Again, getting to know the people who work in that department will allow that process to be more successful.

☐ *Job shadowing.* If you are really lucky, you may be able to set up a "job shadowing" visit to an employer. For a student in a criminal justice program, that could involve going out on a ride-along with a police officer, or a tour of a courthouse.

☐ *Volunteering.* Your career services department may also know about volunteer opportunities that are connected to your desired career field. For example, if you are training to be in a medical profession, there are likely hospitals or clinics in your area that welcome volunteers. Volunteering is an excellent way to spend time in the environment and with the people who you will be working with later. You can select a volunteer commitment on your terms, that is, working the number of hours and days that you like or even just doing it on an event-by-event basis, much like those who volunteer to serve turkey dinners on Thanksgiving.

Figure 7
An externship, an internship, or job shadowing can give you an inside scoop on your industry and may even lead to a job interview.

In addition to career services, your campus may also offer **student services** or student groups that provide information and networking opportunities with others in your program or career field. There are many ways to find out about the existence of these groups on campus—typically they will have a website or post information on a bulletin board on campus. These groups can be very beneficial and even fun.

student services: *A college department that supports student development and activities. May be able to connect you with activities or student groups that provide information and networking opportunities with others in your program or career field.*

Many schools have student mentoring programs that pair new students with an experienced student who is nearing graduation. The purpose of these programs is to give new students someone they can easily talk to when they have questions and who can help keep them on track while they get used to attending classes, studying, taking tests, buying books, and everything else that goes into the big effort of going to school. As a new student, you should take advantage of a program like this if one is offered.

Later on, when you are an experienced student, consider returning the favor and volunteering to be a student mentor. It will take some of your time, it will take some work, and there is a certain level of responsibility associated with the role. However, if you do this well, not only will you have the appreciation of the students you mentor, but you will also have the attention and sincere gratitude of your instructors and the school administration—and that could make a really big difference in the number and quality of job interviews you are sent on as you near graduation.

MONEY SMART$

Setting Realistic Salary Goals and Expectations

Receiving a job offer is a big moment, filled with emotion and excitement. Regardless of the amount of the offer, just getting an offer for employment validates everything you've done to that point—your training, education, and experience; the work you put into your résumé; your efforts in getting an interview (or two or three) and doing well on the interview; and your follow-up actions afterward, thanking the potential employer for his or her time and consideration.

After all of that, the offer of employment is a moment of truth. If you say yes, you're choosing a job that will impact your life as long as you hold it, and if you say no, you're choosing to pass on one opportunity for another.

What if the offer is made, but the pay rate or job conditions are less than you had hoped for or expected? How do you handle that? How do you make sure you maintain your composure and not express immediate disappointment?

When the offer is made, make sure you do two things, regardless of the amount of the offer: (1) express genuine pleasure and thanks for being given the offer, and (2) politely let the employer know you need to consider the offer for a short time (one day at the most) before accepting.

This moment will be easier if your expectations are in line with the reality of the current job market for your city and career field. If you have ever taken a course in economics, you probably remember that market conditions are a major factor in setting the price for various goods and services. The concept of supply and demand is central to the subject. In short, if a good or service is in short supply and/or high demand, under normal conditions the price for that item will go up. The reverse is also true—if the supply of an item is high and/or the demand is low, the price for the item will fall.

Salaries work in much the same way. If a potential employee has a specialized skill (one that's not very common), or the skill she possesses is in great demand, she can expect a stronger offer when

LO 5 Professional Organizations

What's your major? Chances are that, whatever it is, there is a professional/trade organization that you can join, even as a student. These groups represent your future, and they can be a great benefit to you today while you are in school. Here is a small sampling of organizations that offer student memberships or products and services for students:

Medical Assisting:	American Association of Medical Assistants www.aama-ntl.org
Accounting:	American Accounting Association http://aaahq.org
Computer technologies:	Computing Technology Industry Association www.comptia.org (certification programs)
	Network Professional Organization www.npanet.org
Business:	Business Professionals of America www.bpa.org
Criminal Justice:	Academy of Criminal Justice Sciences www.acjs.org

Most of these groups offer student memberships at a minimal annual cost, typically $40 or less. The benefits can be substantial, including subscriptions to monthly

offered a new position. In addition, your level of experience using and developing your skills can be one of the most important factors in determining an employer's salary offer. A medical assistant with five years' experience working in a doctor's office will normally have more value to a doctor than one fresh out of college. Your salary expectations can be framed in much the same manner.

For every job in every city or region, there is a range of salaries currently being paid. Do your homework to find out your job's salary range in your target city. (Salaries are also affected by cost of living, which varies by location.) Your career services department can help with this. When considering a salary range, remember the value of benefits, if offered. For some people, health benefits are more important than salary! Other benefits, including vacation, retirement, tuition assistance, and on-the-job training and development that can and will lead to promotions, greater responsibility, and more pay should all be included in your calculation.

Lastly, to give yourself a reasonable chance of having your salary needs and expectations met, apply for those jobs that will give you the greatest chance for success. And then when the offer does come, smile, take a deep breath, and give yourself a hearty congratulations for a successful job search!

Figure 8 Trade shows are a wonderful opportunity to meet people in your field.

or quarterly trade publications, admission to conferences and national association meetings, local chapter networking and events, employment bulletins, the ability to participate in the organization's governance, and more.

Besides professional organizations that are associated specifically with your career field, there are other organizations that are more general in nature that you can be involved with that could be just as helpful. Local chamber of commerce events, a Toastmasters meeting, job and career fairs, and local conventions and conferences should all be considered.

Building a Professional Profile Online

Lastly, spend some time building a professional profile on a web-based networking site. LinkedIn (www.linkedin.com) is currently the most popular site for professional social networking. You can build your profile like a résumé, including your education, experience, and activities; make connections with people you know through your professional network; and make recommendations of and get recommendations from people in your network. LinkedIn also offers numerous groups that you can join to help you learn about and discus topics related to your career field.

Of course, there are many other websites, news sites, and blogs that provide information and answers about your specific interests. Find a few that suit you and make a habit of reading them regularly. You will find that the more you read, the more knowledgeable you will become about your chosen profession. That knowledge will pay dividends as you continue to develop your foundation for career success.

With any social media or electronic communication network, it is important to remember: The Internet never forgets. Anything you post, whether a status update, comment, photo, or video, can be used against you by an employer making a hiring decision. When you post online, treat these sites with the attention and respect they deserve. As a student who is training to prepare for launching a new career, the time is now to begin developing a professional online profile that will benefit you for years to come. That means carefully considering the content that you post to any website, as well as monitoring information that is posted about you.

When Should You Get Involved? Now!

In the My Success Story feature in the first section, David Barnes didn't know it at the time, but he launched his new career while he was still in school. The first small contract job he completed made a big impression on the owner of the company. Later on, when the owner needed help again, he called David because

Figure 9
A LinkedIn profile can act as a virtual business card, résumé, and address book.

he knew David was someone he could count on to do great work and who also had an excellent work ethic (habits, behaviors, and attitude).

There are many ways you can get involved and take advantage of these opportunities for yourself while still maintaining your college studies—part-time employment, contract work, volunteering, and internships are just a few of the possibilities. And there's no time like the present. By the end of the day today, you could be involved in something new that will help you succeed in your career.

We should point out here that the *last* thing this section is recommending is to stop school to seek employment before graduating. Finishing what you start (starting now with school) is the best way to ensure both short-term and long-term career success. In fact, in David's case, he got the small contract job opportunity in the first place because he was in school, and he was given the opportunity to interview for a full-time job with the company because he finished school.

Research: Getting Involved in Your Chosen Career Field

In this activity, you will begin an in-depth exploration of your career field. Completing this activity will require access to various resources, including, but not limited to:

- Computer with Internet access
- Campus and community library
- Your campus career center
- Field trip

- Off-site visit to a workplace
- Former graduates of your school and program
- An industry-related job fair

List organizations on campus that are connected to your career field, including student organizations, career services department, on-site clinicals, and so on.

_____

_____

_____

_____

List professional organizations and trade publications that are related to or specific to your industry. Highlight (***) those that provide a focus on students and interns.

_____

_____

_____

_____

List events that are related to your industry (trade shows, conferences, conventions, professional development courses and training, certification workshops, etc.)

_____

_____

_____

_____

List websites that are related to your industry (this may repeat information from above lists). Just include the web address and a short description here.

_____

_____

_____

_____

_____

List local resources (local to your acceptable job location) related to or specific to your industry. This can include networking groups, chambers of commerce, local chapters of professional organizations, etc.

_____

_____

_____

_____

Action Plan

List a minimum of three of the resources from above and describe an action that you plan to take to get involved in each of them in some manner in the next 30 days. The following actions are some examples:

- Meet with career services advisor to find out the best local resources and actions I can take now, while I'm in school
- Attend a Chamber of Commerce mixer, networking event, or job fair
- Join a professional organization (for those that have a student or junior membership)
- Subscribe to a trade magazine
- Join an online trade group through LinkedIn or related website

Your 30-Day Action Plan:

1. _____

_____

_____

2. _____

_____

_____

3. _____

_____

_____

4. _____

_____

_____

5. _____

_____

_____

It's easier to succeed if you anticipate problems instead of simply react to them.

- Can you share a situation where you anticipated a problem and fixed it?
- How about a situation where you let a problem get too big to manage alone?

Applying the concepts discussed in the previous two sections of this module—successful attitude, habits, and behaviors, as well as learning about and getting involved in organizations related to your career field—quite possibly could result in excellent work opportunities in your chosen career field, even before you graduate.

Because of the strong position you have put yourself in just by enrolling in and attending college, and because you plan to use your education to continue or launch a successful new career, you need to create and maintain a résumé so you can be ready whenever an opportunity presents itself. The time to do this is *now*, even if you have never had a job or never had a job related in any way to your chosen career field or even if you have no plans to work at all while you attend college.

You need a résumé that you would be proud to show someone, because you never know when you might meet someone—a fellow student, an instructor, someone from the career services department, or a potential employer—who may think you would be great for a position and will need a copy of your résumé to move the conversation forward.

If you already have a résumé, it's time to take it out and review, edit, and update it to reflect your current status as a student and new things that you're involved in. It's true that if you don't have a résumé and an opportunity presents

Figure 10 Your résumé is how you introduce yourself to a possible employer, so you should put your best foot forward.

itself, you can always throw one together quickly. But doing that is asking for mistakes, and mistakes on your résumé give the reader a poor first impression of you. Writing a résumé, even one that is only one typed page, is hard work, and it takes time. It's very difficult to get it right if you're doing a rush job.

LO 6 A Great Résumé

Having a great résumé does not guarantee that you'll win an interview. But it sure doesn't hurt your chances. When you have a great résumé, your goals, experience, and education are the focus of the hiring manager. When you have a poor résumé, the hiring manager's focus is on the mistakes you made in presenting yourself, instead of your qualifications. Most times, a poor résumé assures that you won't get an interview.

What Should You Include in Your Résumé?

A great basic résumé will include the following sections:

- ☐ *Header Section.* This is your contact information. At a minimum, you need your name, address, telephone number(s), and e-mail address. This section does not have a title.
- ☐ *Objective.* Here is where you describe in a few sentences how your qualifications and current job goal are in alignment and will serve the potential employer.
- ☐ *Skills.* This section is encouraged if you have specialized skills, such as experience with industry-specific software, keyboarding, or certification in a skill or technology.
- ☐ *Work Experience.* This section includes the name, city, job title, and dates of employment of your work history. Include brief descriptions (short sentences or bullet points) of your responsibilities and accomplishments on each job. Be sure your job skills come through clearly!
- ☐ *Education and Training.* List completed education as well as coursework that is relevant to the position. Also include any licenses you hold as a result of your training. This section can be listed before the Experience section if you have little or no job history.
- ☐ Optional sections:
  - ○ *Activities and Awards.* Use this if you are active in student groups or volunteer organizations or have been recognized for outstanding achievement.
  - ○ *References.* Putting your references on your résumé is optional, but you will need them. If you list them on your résumé, list at least three and be sure the contact information on each one is up-to-date!

Common Résumé Mistakes to Avoid

The first hurdle in the hiring process is getting someone to actually read your qualifications. For many jobs, employers receive dozens, if not hundreds of résumés. This means they often don't have time to read everything on every résumé so, to decide which ones to read closely, they'll do a quick scan of each. If they have a hard time finding the important information in your résumé or they find a few mistakes right off the bat, it makes it easy for them to reject you. Your job is to make it hard for them to reject you, by taking care of the details and avoiding the most common résumé mistakes.

Here are a few things to consider and address if you want your résumé to help, not hinder, your chances of getting an interview:

☐ *Format.* The résumé sections must flow naturally for the reader. Too often, job seekers use text boxes around each section and the result is a visual mess. If your layout or format is confusing or sloppy, the reader may have trouble identifying what's important in your résumé. Instead of text boxes, use appropriate spacing and section headers.

ON THE JOB

Triggers for Being Set Aside: The Employer's Perspective

Let's take a moment to look at the résumé process from the other side—the employer side. After all, the purpose of your résumé is to get a prospective employer to consider you for the next step in the hiring process, usually an interview. Having great experience and being a good match for a position are important, but if your résumé can't convey these things, it won't stand out from all the other résumés in the stack.

Why does one qualified candidate get hired when another does not? What is the difference between getting hired and getting frustrated? In a competitive job market, the difference can be small, even though the end result is huge.

Compare the job-hunting process to a professional golf tournament. A typical tournament has 150 competitors, but only one winner who gets the trophy and the rewards that go with it. The winner not only earns money—typically around $1 million—but is also virtually guaranteed to qualify to play on the professional tour the next year as well.

What makes the difference between winning and not winning?

All 150 players in the tournament are professionals and exceedingly good at their sport. The winner may take around 270 shots. The second, third, and fourth place finishers may take 271 (fewer is better). So after four days, competing for five hours each day, the difference between winning and not winning is one shot!

It's not unusual for 150 qualified people to compete for one job opening. That's 150 résumés and cover letters sent to the hiring manager's desk, in hopes of an interview. Your résumé and cover letter must convince that hiring manager to want to spend five minutes to read what you have sent, then ask you for an interview.

The odds of landing that first interview are not as bad as they may sound, though, because many of those 150 applicants make enough mistakes in the presentation and content of their cover letter and résumé that the hiring manager almost immediately

- ☐ *Layout.* The font style and size, margins, white space, and artistic style must not get in the way of the message. Some résumé consultants advise using a unique layout to set your résumé apart from all the rest. Be very careful taking this advice, as your idea of unique just might be the employer's idea of annoying. The words are ultimately what count. Make it easy for the reader to read them.

- ☐ *Spelling, grammar errors, and typos.* Simply put, there is no excuse for these kinds of mistakes, but this is an all-too-common problem. Don't just use spell check and grammar check. Print the résumé out and read it. Give it to a friend to have a fresh set of eyes read it. Then read it yourself again before sending it to a potential employer.

- ☐ *Content.* Be honest. An employer can easily tell when the responsibilities on a previous job are being embellished and exaggerated.

- ☐ *Writing quality.* If the hiring manager can't understand your résumé or if it's hard to read, he or she won't read it. It is worth having a second or third person read and edit your résumé for its writing quality before sending it out to anyone.

- ☐ *Résumé length.* Keep yours to one page, two pages maximum. Résumés longer than that are reserved for those who have a long career history and have the need to document all of it.

- ☐ *File format.* Employers commonly request electronic versions of résumés, sent via e-mail or uploaded to a website. The employer must be able to easily open and read your résumé file. Unless the employer specifies the file format or uses a proprietary form to input information, always send your résumé using a format that will maintain its integrity regardless of the operating system or software that is viewing it. Sending your résumé as a PDF file (which can be created using Adobe Acrobat or Microsoft Word, as well as other programs) is an excellent way to ensure that the reader actually

sets them aside, leaving a much smaller pile of candidates from which to choose the three or four candidates who will be called in for the first interview.

Why do so many résumés get passed over? Candidates make basic, fundamental mistakes, triggering the hiring manager to immediately draw several conclusions—the candidate doesn't pay attention to detail, can't present a professional image in our company and to our clients, doesn't really care about this job or this company, and so on.

Do hiring managers really make all of those conclusions, just from a few typos on a cover letter? Sometimes they do. That's why you don't want to give the hiring manager any easy reasons for setting your résumé aside. When sending out résumés, remember that the strength of your résumé is more important than how many you send. Sending 10 résumés you have carefully edited and proofread will be much more effective than sending out 20 résumés you've done in a rush—and that make it easy for hiring managers to drop in the wrong pile.

sees what you see. The second choice is to send it in Microsoft Word format. Web-based résumés services can be difficult to use and are still risky as different web browsers may interpret your web page (i.e., your résumé) differently.

☐ *Sending methodology.* If you e-mail your résumé, it's still necessary to include a cover letter, either in the body of the e-mail message or as a second attachment to the message. *Do not* send your résumé in the body of the e-mail. Always attach it as a separate file.

Sample Résumés

The following résumé was submitted in the body of an e-mail responding to a job posting on Craigslist. Only the top portion is included, and the formatting has been maintained, although the names and numbers have been changed.

Sample 1

1620 555 1212
MARYANN GONZALEZ

Objective
To achieve and surpass the goals that are set by my employer and superiors, utilizing my past experience and knowledge.

Summary of Skills

☐ Bilingual-English & Spanish
☐ Extensive public relations and customer service skills;
☐ Knowledge of Microsoft software programs- Excel, Word, Quick books; Type 35 WPM.

Self Description
I am a very well taught responsible woman with many goals I would love to achieve. I love to be at great help, be as direct as possible with any answers or questions. I get the job done well and prompt. A great person to be around, I bring positivity to negativity. Smile always! I'm here to fulfill your open position and more to your expectations. Give me this opportunity please, I will exceed and succeed for the business and myself. I do whatever it

Professional Experience
UCS Painting Escondido, CA   **Jan 2010–December 2010**

Office Manager

☐ Shipping
☐ Major experience with Microsoft word/Quick Books/Excel/Outlook/etc
☐ Order forms/P.O.
☐ Holding weekly meetings
☐ High quality of multi phone lines/Collections
☐ Payroll/Daily balances
☐ Errands for Company

How many fundamental résumé errors can you spot in this résumé? Here are some hints—look for errors in grammar, spelling, format, layout, writing, and content. For example, she claims to have "Major experience with Microsoft word/ Quick Books/Excel/Outlook/etc. Given what you see here, is she exaggerating her experience and capabilities?

Sample 2 is an example of a well-done résumé. (This is not the full résumé, but an abbreviated version.) An employer can quickly scan the document and get a good sense of Sandra's experience and capabilities. There is enough detail and explanation of her job responsibilities, but not too much to overwhelm the reader.

Sample 2

Sandra Dustyevsky
1995 Main Way
Escondido, AZ 93658
cell: (744) 555-3691 — sandy0995@tw.org

Objective
To obtain a long-term position which can advantageously utilize the abilities that I have acquired through work experience and classes attended.

Employment

Tom Anderson Development, Inc.
Escondido, AZ   (760) 555-1919
☐ *Accounts Payable From: March 2005 to June 2010*
Responsibilities included: Processing incoming invoices from vendors and subcontractors for bi-monthly billing cycles, preparing loan draw requests for submittal to banks holding construction loans, bank reconciliations, payroll for approximately 60 people. Quarterly payroll taxes, processing W-2s and 1099s. I was also responsible for obtaining insurance certificates from vendors and verifying that the vendors meet all of the insurance requirements of the company.

Ridgeline Moulding
San Marcos, CA   (760) 555-9321
☐ *Administrative Assistant Outside Sales From: June 2000 to March 2004*
Responsibilities included: Compiling measurements taken on the job site by the sales representative and preparing a quotation for the prospective client, purchasing materials, coordinating deliveries and billing completed contracts. During my employment at Ridgeline, I worked closely with finish carpenters in the field to supply the necessary materials to complete their projects.

Education

☐ Palomar College San Marcos—A.S. in Accounting, June 2008
☐ R.O.P. Office Training and Lotus 1-2-3, Dun and Bradstreet seminar for Lotus 1-2-3 and Excel

---

Objective Statements

In this activity, your task is to write an objective statement that is customized for two different classified ads. Assume that you have the skills required for both jobs, and both jobs are ones you would like to be interviewed for.

Once you have completed each statement, share yours with your partner or group, taking turns playing the role of the hiring manager who is reading the other's statement for the first time. The "hiring manager" can then give his impression on whether the statement makes him want to read the rest of the résumé and call for an interview.

Job 1

Classified Ad

> **Medical Assistant** (back-office) for a busy pediatric practice. Work 4½ days (~32 hours) Monday–Friday per week. Job qualifications:
> - Enjoy interacting with children
> - Knowledge and ability to administer vaccines
> - Bilingual (English, Spanish) preferred

Your custom résumé objective:

_____

_____

_____

_____

Job 2

Classified Ad

> Busy Family Practice office looking for experienced **Medical Assistants** for full-time & part-time positions. Responsibilities include both front- and back-office duties.
>
> Ideal candidates: a self-starter and team player with a minimum of 1 year experience as a Medical Assistant.
>
> Candidates with these qualifications are invited to submit a résumé. Interviews will be scheduled the week of December 6

Your custom résumé objective:

_____

_____

_____

_____

Share

Now, share your two statements with a partner or study group. The partner should read each statement from the viewpoint of the hiring manager who has received 20 résumés *that day alone* for this one job posting. Based on this volume of résumés sitting on her desk, the hiring manager looks at your résumé for an overall impression and then reads the top statement to decide whether to even read the rest or ask for an interview.

Based upon the feedback you receive from your partner, list the things you could have done to make a stronger impression:

1. _____

2. _____

3. _____

4. _____

5. _____

Now, edit your two statements for greater impact.

Job 1

New objective:

_____

_____

_____

_____

Job 2

New objective:

_____

_____

_____

_____

Writing Effective Objectives Statements

One of the best and quickest ways to personalize your résumé for the specific job you are applying for is to edit the Objectives section of your résumé. This enables you to highlight the skills and qualities you believe are going to be important to the hiring manager who will be deciding who gets called for an interview.

It's also the easiest way to customize your résumé for different kinds of positions. For example, let's say you are currently enrolled in a computer technician program and you have an opportunity to apply for two part-time jobs while still in school. You believe your work experience and college classes you have already taken qualify you for both positions. One of the jobs is for an assistant computer technician, and the other is for computer sales.

You can easily see how it would be difficult to have one objective work for both of these positions. For example, a hiring manager in sales will not be impressed with an objective that reads:

My goal is to utilize my technical skills gained through education and experience to obtain an entry-level position in a computer repair department that offers promotion opportunities to the manager level.

He might, however, be very interested in you if you present this objective:

Combining the knowledge I have gained in my computer technician program along with my successful retail sales experience, I'd like to share my enthusiasm with others to help them make purchase decisions.

SUMMARY

This module provides a broad examination of the various hard and soft skills valued by employers and hiring managers in today's job market. Often taking the employer's point of view, "soft skills," such as an employee's habits, behaviors, and attitudes, were explored, illustrating how these attributes play a critical role in enabling a candidate to get hired, stay hired, and, most importantly, earn raises and promotions.

You can get a huge head start in your career, as well as an advantage in the hiring process, by getting involved in your career field prior to attempting to land your first job in the industry. The second module section discussed some strategies for doing this in a manner that will increase your value to potential future employers, as well as clarifying your own expectations for your potential career paths upon graduation.

None of that is important if you don't have a résumé that effectively communicates your goals, experience, and education. Slight missteps in your résumé may mean you won't even get your foot in the door for an interview. This module described the very basic requirements of a résumé for entry-level positions, as well as some strategies to ensure hiring managers are able to view your résumé regardless of their electronic viewing system.

DISCUSSION QUESTIONS

1. Of the following, which has the most impact on *job and career* success: your habits, your behaviors, or your attitude? Why?

2. Of the following, which has the most impact on *college* success: your habits, your behaviors, or your attitude? Why?

3. Besides an externship, what is the one best way to get involved in your chosen career field while still in college? Have you done this yet? If not, when will you?

4. How can the career services department at your school help you with regard to résumé writing, and getting involved in your career field prior to graduation? Have you met personally with a representative from that department to learn about the assistance it can provide as you map out a plan of action?

KEY TERMS

attitude: A complex mental state involving beliefs and feelings and values and dispositions to act in certain ways; "he had the attitude that work was fun."[2] (p. 8)

behavior: Manner of behaving, whether good or bad; mode of conducting one's self; conduct; deportment; carriage. (p. 6)

career services: The college department focused on supporting students in their career search. Services include résumé assistance, interview prep, externship placements, and career advising. (p. 14)

habit: An automatic pattern of behavior in reaction to a specific situation; may be inherited or acquired through frequent repetition. (p. 3)

student services: A college department that supports student development and activities. May be able to connect you with activities or student groups that provide information and networking opportunities with others in your program or career field. (p. 16)

REFERENCES AND CREDITS

Websites

www.websters-online-dictionary.org

www.quotegarden.com

www.myfuture.com/toolbox/createresume_all.html

www.aama-ntl.org/index.aspx

Footnotes

1. Reproduced with permission of Curtis Brown Ltd., London on behalf of The Estate of Winston Churchill. Copyright © Winston S. Churchill.

2. WordNet 3.0 Copyright © 2006 by Princeton University. All rights reserved.

Figure and Photo Credits

Chapter opening photo: Comstock Images/Getty Images

Figure 1: Yellowdog Productions/Lifesize/Getty Images

Figure 2: Ingram Publishing

Figure 3: Digital Vision/Getty Images

Figure 4: © Jon Feingersh/Blend Images LLC

Figure 5: Radius Images/Getty Images

Figure 6: © Fancy Photography/Veer

Figure 7: Walter Hodges/Getty Images

Money Smarts: ©Sam Toren/Alamy

Figure 8: George Doyle/Getty Images

Figure 9: Courtesy of LinkedIn Corporation

Figure 10: Image Source/Getty Images

Figure 11: Hill Street Studios/Getty Images

Career on the Job: ©Siri Stafford, Gettyimages